THE
WINE ROADS
OF EUROPE

Marc and Kim Millon have written and illus-
trated articles in wine and food for numerous
publications, including the *Christian Science
Monitor*, *Wine and Dine Magazine* and *Wine
Bar News*. Their first book, *The Wine and Food
of Europe*, was published in 1982.

THE
WINE ROADS
OF EUROPE

Marc and Kim Millon

A FIRESIDE BOOK
Published by Simon & Schuster, Inc.
NEW YORK

To our dear friend Edna,
who loves wine as much as we do.

Copyright © 1983, 1984 by Marc Millon and Kim Millon
All rights reserved
including the right of reproduction
in whole or in part in any form
First Fireside Edition, 1984
Published by Simon & Schuster, Inc.
Simon & Schuster Building
Rockefeller Center
1230 Avenue of the Americas
New York, New York 10020

FIRESIDE and colophon are registered trademarks of
Simon & Schuster, Inc.

This book was first published in 1983 in Great Britain
by Arrow/Hutchinson

Designed by Bob Vickers
Illustrations by Kim Millon
Maps by Rodney Paull

Manufactured in the United States of America

Printed in Great Britian by Blantyre Printing & Binding Limited

10 9 8 7 6 5 4 3 2   Pbk.

Library of Congress Cataloging in Publication Data

Million, Marc.
   The wine roads of Europe.

   "A Fireside book."
   1. Wine and wine making—Europe—Guide-books.
2. Europe—Description and travel—1971-   —Guide-books. I. Millon, Kim. II. Title.
TP559.E8M543   1984   914.04558   83-27094
ISBN 0-671-50408-8 Pbk.

CONTENTS

INTRODUCTION

Touring Europe's Wine Lands

The wine roads of Europe are literally a series of sign-posted roads through the heart of some of Europe's most beautiful, congenial, and welcoming country: her wine lands. The *Routes des Vins, Weinstrassen, Strade dei Vini* and others lead wine-loving travellers and tourists to the vineyards, beautiful wine villages and wine producers of Europe. All along the many thousands of kilometres of wine roads, producers – large and small, well-known or unknown – welcome visitors to their premises. Viticultural and wine-making processes are proudly explained, wines are offered for tasting, and purchases can be made direct. Restaurants recommended by the wine producers themselves abound throughout, in unspoiled little villages or deep in the heart of the country, and here both local wines, and the native foods that accompany them so well, are served in abundance.

The wine roads of Europe are sometimes little more than brief detours off the main road into surrounding vine-covered country; others can result in journeys that last over a period of days, even weeks, leading from one happy wine village to another. All Europe's wine roads, though, lead to and through lands that could be easily by-passed, lands which may not otherwise have been noticed. Even as famous a region as Burgundy is often passed with hardly a second glance by an army of tourists en route to the south. Let them rush to their destinations. The wine roads of Europe are definitely not roads for those in a hurry.

Visiting Wine Producers

One of the most satisfying aspects of travelling the wine roads of Europe is first viewing the land in which a well-loved or -known wine is born, then tasting the product at its source. Producers in all the great wine regions are pleased to welcome wine lovers and 'wine tourists' to their premises: indeed, in many cases, this provides the small producer with an important direct sales outlet. We have corresponded personally with the hundreds of wine producers listed in this book; we explained our project in detail and, in particular, told them that our book was intended for wine-loving amateurs travelling the wine roads of Europe. We asked them if they accepted such visitors to their premises; if an appointment was necessary; what were the preferred times of visits; whether the cellars or vineyards could be visited; if wines could be tasted and purchased; and if there was a charge. The response we received was extremely heartening, and we are sure that even the most discerning wine lover will find plenty to satisfy; equally confident, too, that the tyro with little or no previous wine knowledge will be just as welcome, and will have many opportunities to learn much about this fascinating subject.

Europe's wine regions are each unique, and the customs or procedures for visits, indeed the reception that can be expected in each, is different. In Reims and Épernay, many of the great *Maisons du Champagne* offer excellent guided tours of their vast underground chalk caves where that magnificent sparkling wine is nurtured and matured; visitors are thus able to learn at first hand all the laborious aspects of the *méthode champenoise*. In northern Portugal, too, many of the famous port lodges in Vila Nova de Gaia have the facilities to welcome casual visitors to their premises to explain (in English, Spanish, French, or German) the intricacies which go into the making and maturing of that splendid fortified wine. For the establishments involved, such guided tours serve as important public relations exercises, for much of their prosperity is dependent, to a great extent, on a continued healthy export trade; indeed, for the visitor, once such establishments have been toured, it is always a pleasure to encounter and enjoy those products on returning home again. The small wine producer located along a *route du vin* in rural France, a *strada del vino* in Italy, on the other hand, may well receive visitors for the important and not insignificant direct sales that may result. Make no mistake: we feel that visitors should never feel compelled or pressured into purchasing wine; nevertheless, one should be sensitive to the situation, and not view the entries listed as simply means to 'free tastings'.

Not Just Visiting Wine Producers

This book, though, is not just about visiting wine producers, important though that is. There are many other aspects and ways to learn about the wines, the lands, and the people. Central to the concept and formation of the wine roads of Piedmont, in north-west Italy, for example, are the five regional *Enoteche* located throughout that region's wine zones. An *Enoteca* is a sort of 'wine library', which has on permanent display an extensive and comprehensive selection of its finest wines. In Piedmont, the five regional *Enoteche* are located in historic buildings or central and beautiful situations along the various *strade del vino*; they not only display the wines, they offer them for tasting and purchase; some, too, have excellent adjoining restaurants that serve traditional local foods, to accompany the *Enoteca's* wines.

Elsewhere, as another example, the best way to learn about the wines – and people – of Austria is to visit the delightful and unique wine taverns found throughout that country's various wine regions. They are called *Heurigen*, and in rural districts such as the Wachau or Burgenland, they may consist of no more than a few tables set up in a wine producer's driveway or garden, where simple foods and fresh, home-produced wines are served in quarter-litre mugs. *Heurige* is the name both of the wine tavern, and the wine itself, which should be 'this year's', as the name signifies. In Germany, too, wine producers often serve wines and simple foods in their gardens or cellars, though an equally important – and enjoyable – way to learn about German wines is at the numerous lively wine festivals which take place throughout the eleven quality-wine regions; a broad range of wines is served in small tasting measures, and thus one is able to sample wines from adjoining vineyards, of different vintages and different quality levels.

Wine and Food – Wine Producers' Recommended Restaurants

One of the most important and pleasurable aspects of touring the wine roads of Europe is enjoying local wines in conjunction with the native tastes that go so naturally and well with them. Therefore, the Restaurant section of this book includes personal favourites which we encountered on our various research trips to Europe, serving, naturally, regional foods and wines. In addition, following the sound premise that wine producers are also lovers of good food, we asked the producers we corresponded with to both recommend local restaurants serving regional foods and wines, and also good local hotels. We then corresponded personally with each restaurant and hotel listed in the book, thus ensuring that our information is correct and up-to-date, to the best of our knowledge, at the time of writing. Since prices do fluctuate (always up), we have used a simple rating of **Inexpensive, Moderate, Expensive**, and **Very Expensive** to give a general indication of prices.

Purchasing Wine

Most who visit wine producers will wish to purchase wine, either for consumption in the region or country, or for bringing home. The latter option is not as convenient for most Americans returning to the United States as it is, say, for British visitors who can easily drive to the wine country and load up their car with as much wine as they can carry. Nor is it quite as easy from the viewpoint of US Customs, for the duty free allowance for returning residents is only one litre. Amounts above this limit are liable to both customs duty and tax. Furthermore, many states may have restrictions on the amount of alcoholic beverages which may be brought in.

It is advisable, therefore, before leaving the US, to contact your nearest local Customs Station, who will be able to advise you. There are numerous Customs Stations located throughout the country. To find your nearest, telephone your local Federal Information Operator. Additionally, you can write direct to the US Customs Service in Washington for US edition revision advice:

US Customs Service
Department of the Treasury
Washington DC 20229

In addition to dealing with US Customs, one should be aware that different regulations regarding transport of wine across borders (and even, in France, from *département* to *département*) may apply. Therefore, it is prudent to check with each country's Embassy if amounts of more than a few cases per person are involved.

Drinking & Driving – A Word of Warning

The concept of 'wine roads' is a dangerous one, for it implies both driving and drinking. It is not our intention to encourage this, despite the fact that there are so many tasting opportunities along the wine roads of Europe. *Don't drink and drive*. Not only is it dangerous, penalties in Europe are severe. Better to share the driving on a rotating basis, or to hire a teetotal local driver. Spitting, not swallowing wine, is one way to keep a clear head and licence.

Note

Where possible we have given the postal code of towns and villages. These appear as prefixes to the name of the town, e.g. **67310 Traeinheim.**

Back home . . .

As always, all good things must come to an end. But the marvellous beauty of roaming the wine roads of Europe is that once home again, a small whiff of the magic and beauty of these wonderful lands is recreated every time a bottle of wine, sampled in some dimly lit cellar, in some far-off corner of Europe, is re-encountered and uncorked.

October 1982
Topsham, Devon

—FRANCE—

ALSACE

Historic Alsace, a province in north-east France, nestles both under and
alongside the border with its friendly neighbour West Germany. Today it is a
peaceful, hardworking, and idyllic wine region. A gentle meandering wine
road, the *Route du Vin d'Alsace*, winds its way leisurely along the foothills of the
Vosges Mountains, through lush, well-tended vineyards and unspoiled
medieval wine villages. Along the way, roadside stands offer local wine,
served in characteristic tall, green-stemmed glasses, while numerous wine
producers welcome visitors to their cellars. When you consider that the region
also offers a distinctive regional cuisine which reflects its historic past, with
numerous restaurants, bars, and wine gardens in which to sample it, plus
lively folk and harvest festivals, a fascinating history, breathtaking natural
beauty spots deep in wooded mountains, and ample recreational facilities, it is
clear why Alsace is so popular with wine-loving travellers.

If Alsace today is at peace, it has not always been so. It stands cut off from

How to Get There

By Car
From Ostend take the E5 to Brussels, and
then the E40 (parts of which are under
construction) on to Luxembourg. From
Luxembourg take the A31 south to Metz,
and then the A32/A34 south-east to
Strasbourg.

From Paris take the A4 through Reims,
(stopping, perhaps, to enjoy the
Champagne country) en route to Metz.
From Metz take the A32/A34 on to
Strasbourg. A slower alternative route
from Calais or Boulogne is via Cambrai;
pick up the N43 which passes through the
Ardennes, and numerous small towns and
villages en route to Metz.

A motoring tour of Alsace can be
combined comfortably with tours of other
wine regions. From Luxembourg, the
Moselle Valley is easily visited before
continuing south to Metz. The *Deutsche
Weinstrasse* which meanders through
vineyards and wine villages of the
Rheinpfalz is a virtual continuation of the
Alsatian *Route du Vin*; it is perfectly natural
(and most pleasant), when the end of one
is reached, to continue along the next,
comparing the types of wine produced in
each. And as already mentioned, the
vineyards and cellars of Champagne can
be visited en route to Alsace from Paris.

By Plane
The main French international airport is
at Paris. Air Inter, the internal French
airline, flies from Paris to Strasbourg.
Direct flights also from London to
Strasbourg.

the rest of France by the Vosges Mountains, but divided from Germany by the Rhine River. In the last century alone, Alsace was repossessed by Germany after the Franco–Prussian war; an Allied victory in World War I brought it back to France; Hitler recaptured the region and submitted it to four brutal years of occupation and intense Germanization; after Hitler's defeat, Alsace became once more part of France.

Such a turbulent history naturally has had a profound effect on the character of the region. The Alsatian today, for a start, is probably as intensely pro-French as any of his compatriots, but the villages along the *Route du Vin* seem very similar, on the surface, at least, to those along *Weinstrassen* further north, in the Rheinpfalz, or east, in Baden-Württemberg, nestled under the brooding Schwarzwald. Houses with waving, uneven roofs and half-timbered frames seem a far cry from those found in smug French provincial villages to the south. Food, too, betrays a curious duality, for though *escargots* and *coq au vin* are favourites, great platters of *sauerkraut* garnished with sausages and smoked meats, as well as hearty rib-sticking stews served in Germanic portions (extra large, that is) are equally at home on the Alsatian table.

Alsatian wines themselves, sold in slender green-glass bottles that resemble those used in the Mosel-Saar-Ruwer, have German-sounding names like Gewürztraminer, Riesling, Sylvaner, and Klevner. Like those found across the border, Alsatian wines possess a fruity character balanced by an essential underlying acidity. Yet unlike most German wines they are bone dry and powerful – in other words, archetypal French wines.

This very uncertainty, this fusion of different cultures, makes Alsace a fascinating region to visit. For out of duality, a region all its own has emerged with its own unique folklore and customs, architecture, language, and not least of all, food and wine.

By Train
Four TEE trains per day travel between Paris and Strasbourg. The journey takes less than four hours, including one stop at Nancy. Strasbourg is also on the main London–Brussels–Basle route (ferry crossing at Ostend).

Local Public Transport
There is a main rail line between Strasbourg and Mulhouse with stops at Sélestat and Colmar. A coach trip (organized by Europabus) follows the *Route du Vin* in a single day, beginning and ending in Strasbourg, and stopping for lunch along the way. It runs about four times a month during the summer (details from the Syndicat d'Initiative, Strasbourg).

Car Rental Information
Strasbourg
  Avis: Entzheim Airport
    tel: (88) 68 82 53
    Galerie Marchande,
    place de la Gare
    tel: (88) 32 30 44
    264, route de Schirmeck
    tel: (88) 78 03 99
  Hertz: Entzheim Airport
    tel: (88) 68 83 76
    14 rue Deserte, tel: (88) 32 57 62
Colmar
  Avis: 9 rue de la Gare, tel: (89) 23 21 82
  Hertz: Colmar Airport, tel: (89) 24 11 80
    place Rapp, tel: (89) 24 11 80

The Wines of Alsace

Gewürztraminer A rich and attractive introduction to the wines of Alsace: the flowery, distinctive bouquet of Gewürztraminer is so full and ripe that one can almost discern the scent of herbs, grass, and wild flowers of the lower Vosges foothills where this attractive grape ripens. '*Gewürz*' means spice in German; the best Alsatian wines all share a certain pithy, peppery character, none more so than Gewürztraminer.

Tokay d'Alsace The most full-bodied and robust of all Alsatian wines is produced from the Tokay grape (known elsewhere as the Pinot Gris, and in Germany as Ruländer). It bears no resemblance to either the great Hungarian dessert wine of the same name, or to Tocai from north-east Italy. Most Alsatian wine is particularly well-suited to accompany food; Tokay d'Alsace is forceful enough to accompany even red meat and game dishes.

Muscat d'Alsace Though elsewhere this delicious table grape is used to make extremely sweet and fragrant dessert wines, here in Alsace, the opulent, heavy bouquet remains, yet the wine is bone-dry and crisp. Muscat d'Alsace is a favoured aperitif of the region.

Riesling d'Alsace Highly regarded as the Emperor of Alsatian wines, Riesling d'Alsace is full-bodied, forceful wine with a remarkably crisp finish, combining the fruity scent and aroma of this distinctive noble grape with an underlying acidity balanced with a fairly high alcohol content.

Sylvaner Good, everyday wine of the region which the Alsatians themselves are so fond of. Though Sylvaner may lack the depth and elegance of Riesling, it too is firm and fresh, and particularly good with the freshwater fish specialities and *charcuterie* of the region.

Klevner Another name for the often overlooked Pinot Blanc. A useful wine which is both dry and clean, and which, at best, has considerable distinction.

Pinot Noir d'Alsace The only red wine of the region: pale, fruity, pleasant on a picnic. It is, surprisingly, lighter in body and depth of flavour than the great white wines of Alsace.

Edelzwicker Wine produced from a blend of 'noble' grape varieties, that is, any of those mentioned above.

Crémant d'Alsace AOC sparkling wine, produced, generally, from a *cuvée* blended from the various Pinots, then made sparkling by the *méthode champenoise*.

Vendange Tardive Official term indicating 'late harvest' (as in German *spätlese*). Though the classic wines of Alsace are bone-dry, in exceptional years such 'late harvested' grapes produce a fine range of sweet wines. *Sélection de Grains Nobles*, for example, indicates a superlative category of wines produced from individually selected berries (the Alsatian equivalent of *Trockenbeerenauslese*).

Eaux-de-Vie d'Alsace Clear, powerful local brandies distilled from fruit such as Mirabelle plums, wild strawberries, cherries, William pears, raspberries, and also from the *marc* of 'noble' grapes.

The Wine Road of the Alsace
Route du Vin d'Alsace

From the wooded Vosges Mountains to the verdant cultivated fields of the Rhine Valley, through medieval walled towns, and slopes of firm, ripening grapes, runs the 145 km (90 mile) long *Route du Vin d'Alsace*. This well-signposted road is both easy and extremely pleasant to follow. It meanders along the foothills of the mountains, pausing every few miles in a village or wine town, and along the way scores of producers invite you to sample their product. Many have brightly-coloured roadside stands, decorated with boxes of scarlet geraniums, displaying their varied wines. Others require nothing more than a telephone call in advance, or a postcard indicating your likely time of arrival.

A tour of Alsace begins in Strasbourg, capital of the region, and home of the European Parliament. Located on the trading crossroads of Europe, Strasbourg today is a modern and important industrial and cultural centre, though its former medieval prosperity and wealth is still evident. The old quarter around the spiny sandstone Gothic cathedral retains a brooding ancient atmosphere: dark, intriguing streets lined with ornate inns and restaurants, former merchants' houses, wine and other shops (there is one, for example, which only sells varieties of *foie gras*, an Alsatian delicacy), lead to quaint footbridges which span the River Ill. The nearby Petite France quarter is equally charming, a collection of artisans' houses built around a system of quiet canals. If the activity of craftsmen is somewhat less than in its heyday, there is ample recompense in the numerous excellent restaurants located in former workshops. The *choucroute* at the Maison des Tanneurs is possibly the best in town, though there are other fine restaurants in this fascinating quarter. Strasbourg is a delight to explore, a capital city which does not overwhelm. Spend time strolling its winding streets, then (dare we say it in a wine book) relax at an outdoor café in the place Klèber and sip a cool Alsatian beer (the best in France) while observing the activity before you.

Leave Strasbourg on the N4 to Paris to reach the beginning of the *Route du Vin* at Marlenheim (there are, incidentally, a few wine towns further north near the border town of Wissembourg – they will be encountered if travelling in that direction towards the German Rheinpfalz). Begin the meandering tour of the wine road at Marlenheim and continue through Wangen, Westhoffen, Traenheim, Dangolsheim, and other villages. Though each has its own charm, it is best to simply pick your way along, stopping when the mood strikes, to wander about on foot, enjoy a glass of Edelzwicker, or gather the makings for a fabulous picnic – a slice of *tarte à l'oignon*, a slab of Munster cheese, or the smoked pork sausages and *charcuterie* for which Alsace is so famous.

Molsheim and Obernai are two larger towns on the upper section of the wine road (paradoxically called the Bas-Rhin because the river flows north into

Germany). Either would make a convenient base from which to explore the region, though many will prefer to settle in any of numerous smaller villages amidst the vineyards. Molsheim is an interesting university town set amongst orchards as well as fields of vines; it is also a convenient starting place for excursions into the Vosges Mountains. In Obernai, old buildings such as the fifteenth-century

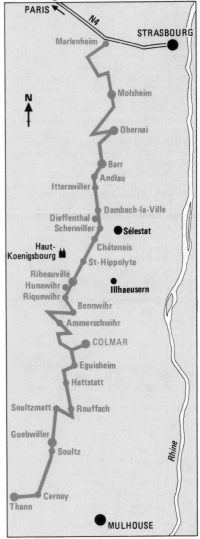

Corn Market and the Town Hall Assembly Chamber are worth exploring.

The *Route du Vin* continues south through a host of delightful towns such as Mittelbergheim, Andlau, Itterswiller, Dambach-La-Ville, and Scherwiller, the latter dominated by the ruined castles of Ortenbourg and Ramstein, high on the hills above. St Hippolyte is a picturesque medieval town below the commanding Haut-Koenigsbourg, somewhat overzealously restored by Kaiser Wilhelm II in the early part of this century to reflect *his* conception of what a medieval castle should look like. Drive up to this imposing monument, for the view from the ramparts of Haut-Koenigsbourg is superb: vineyards, like a waving sea of green, extend in a slender fertile strip along the lower foothills of the Vosges while further down, along the flatter plains of the Rhine, agricultural produce takes over until the river is reached. On a clear day, the Black Forest is visible on the distant horizon.

The finest Alsatian wine comes from the lower half of the wine road, in the *département* of Haut-Rhin. Here the mountains are slightly higher, the microclimates more sheltered and favourable. A principal town in this lower stretch, and an excellent touring centre, is Ribeauvillé. The three castles of Ribeaupierre which rise behind the town are an important landmark of the Alsatian countryside. Ribeauvillé hosts a lively wine festival on the last Saturday and Sunday of July, while the *Fête des Ménétriers*, held at the beginning of September, is a well-known event during which time the town's fountain is said to overflow with wine.

Riquewihr, just a few miles further south, is a perfectly preserved walled medieval village, one of the few which survived intact the bombings of World War II. Surrounded by some of the finest vineyards in Alsace, here also are the offices and *caves* of some of the region's most famous and well-known wine producers and shippers. Despite the fact that Riquewihr is packed with coachloads of tourists throughout the summer, the town retains a wonderful and unspoiled charm, with its half-timbered houses whose roofs are topped with shaggy storks' nests (and storks, too!), and its cobbled courtyards, intricate wrought iron signs, and the delightful reflecting fountain in the town centre.

(Though it is not on the actual wine road, any serious gourmet will wish to make a detour to Illhaeusern, home of the Auberge d'Ill, one of the great restaurants of France. Another famous temple of gastronomy is located in nearby Ammerschwihr, Aux Armes de France; in fact, there is a profusion of fine places to eat and drink in this area, in all price ranges.)

Colmar is the largest town along the wine road, and an important centre of the wine trade. Here, as much as anywhere else, the fusion of French and German tradition and culture is evident; explore the medieval quarter, with its leaning painted and intricately carved houses and shops, and the area known as 'Petite Venise', where a little canal threads its way through shaded streets. While there are numerous excellent restaurants in Colmar, one of the treats not to be missed on a visit to Alsace is an outdoor breakfast in the old section of town, consisting of *Kugelhopf*, accompanied by coffee and a tot of Alsatian eau-de-vie.

The wine road continues south from Colmar, often branching off from the too-busy N83 to loop through numerous little wine villages. Make a detour (on D10 from Turckheim) to Munster, where you can buy the famous cheese direct from farms which make it. Also continue west to explore the wilder western slopes of the mountains, and to discover the beautiful lakes which are popular resorts for the French: Lac de Gérardmer, Lac de Longemer, and the smaller Lac Blanc. Further south, Soultzmatt boasts the highest vineyard in Alsace (called Zinnkoepfle), while Guebwiller leads to the beautiful Florival, valley of flowers. Thann is the final village on the wine road, and boasts a ruined castle, Gothic church, old tower locally famous for its colony of nesting storks, and rich, spicy wines.

Wine Producers

Alsace is an informal and easy-going wine region, and those who roam this pretty wine road are offered numerous opportunities to sample and to purchase wine, as well as to visit cellars. During spring and summer there are countless roadside stands where wine is offered for tasting and sale. In addition, many producers also invite tourists and wine-lovers to 'visitez les caves', either without appointment at the hours shown, or by prior arrangement (a telephone call in advance, or a postcard indicating likely time of arrival is usually sufficient; alternatively, have your hotel help with arrangements).

67310 Traenheim

Cave Vinicole de Traenheim et Environs
RN 422
tel: (88) 50 66 21
Vins d'Alsace, Crémant d'Alsace,
Eaux-de-vie d'Alsace
Mon–Fri 8–12h; 14–17h
Appointment necessary only for groups.
Max 60 pers.
Small charge for tasting.

67120 Molsheim

Neumeyer, Lucien et Fils
19, rue du Général-de-Gaulle
tel: (88) 38 12 45
Vins d'Alsace, Crémant d'Alsace
daily 8–12h; 13–19h except Sun afternoon
Appointment necessary for groups of
more than 10.
Max 50 pers.
English spoken.
Small charge for tasting.

67210 Obernai

Seilly, J Paul
18, rue du Général-Gouraud
tel: (88) 95 55 80
Vins d'Alsace, *vin du pistolet d'obernai*
daily (visit lasts ½ hour)
Appointment necessary for groups of over
50.
Small charge for tasting.

67140 Barr

Domaine Klipfel
6, avenue de la Gare
tel: (88) 08 94 85
Vins d'Alsace
daily 10–12h; 14–18h
Appointment necessary only for large
groups.
Max 250 pers.
Tastings and meals in the caves can be
arranged for groups larger than 25.

Willm, S A
32, rue du Dr Sultzer
tel: (88) 08 19 11
Vins d'Alsace
daily 10–15h
Appointment preferable.
Max 40 pers.
English spoken.

67140 Mittelbergheim

Boeckel, Emile
2, rue de la Montagne
Route du Vin
tel: (88) 08 91 02
Vins d'Alsace, Crémant d'Alsace,
Eaux-de-vie d'Alsace
Mon–Fri 9–12h; 14–17h
Sat 9–12h
Appointment necessary only for groups.
Max 50 pers.
English spoken.
Small charge for tasting.

67140 Andlau

Gresser, André
2, rue de l'École
tel: (88) 08 95 88
Vins d'Alsace
daily 8–12h; 13–19h
Appointment necessary only for groups.
Max 50 pers.
A little English spoken.

67650 Dambach-la-Ville

Gisselbrecht, Willy et Fils
tel: (88) 92 41 02
Vins d'Alsace, Crémant d'Alsace,
Eaux-de-vie d'Alsace
Mon–Fri 8–12h; 14–17h
Appointment necessary only for groups.
Max 60 pers.
English spoken.

68750 Bergheim

Eschenauer, Louis
91, rue des Vignerons
tel: (89) 73 63 02
Vins d'Alsace, Eaux-de-vie d'Alsace
Mon–Fri 8–12h; 13h30–17h
Max 50 pers.
English spoken.
Small charge for tasting.

Gustave Lorentz S A
35, Grand-Rue
tel: (89) 73 63 08
Vins d'Alsace
Mon–Sat lunchtime.
English spoken.

Jérôme Lorentz & Fils
1, rue des Vignerons
tel: (89) 73 63 05
Vins d'Alsace
Mon–Sat lunchtime
English spoken.

68150 Hunawihr

Cave Coopérative Vinicole
de Hunawihr
tel: (89) 73 61 67
Vins d'Alsace
Mon–Fri 15–17h
Appointment necessary.
Max 35 pers.
English spoken.
Small charge for tasting.

Ermel, David et Fils
5, route de Ribeauvillé
Vins d'Alsace
tel: (89) 73 61 71
Mon–Sat 8–18h
Appointment preferable.
Max 30 pers.
English spoken.

68340 Riquewihr

Dopff 'au Moulin'
2, rue J.-Preiss
tel: (89) 47 92 23
Vins d'Alsace, Crémant d'Alsace,
Eaux-de-vie d'Alsace
daily 8–12h; 14–18h for tours of the caves
and sparkling wine cellars.
Appointment necessary only at weekends
and out of season.
English spoken.
Small charge for tasting.
Restaurant-Hostellerie 'Au Moulin' in
Riquewihr

Dopff et Irion
Au Château de Riquewihr
tel: (89) 47 92 51
Vins d'Alsace, Eaux-de-vie d'Alsace
April–Oct daily 9–19h
Nov–March, and for groups over 10 by
appointment.
Max 80 pers.
English spoken.

Hugel et Fils SA
tel: (89) 47 92 15
Vins d'Alsace, Eaux-de-vie d'Alsace
Mon–Thurs 9–11h; 14–17h
Fri 9–11h
Appointment preferable.
English spoken.
Max 40 pers.
Informative slide show.

Preiss-Zimmer Jean
42, rue du Général-de-Gaulle
tel: (89) 47 92 58
Vins d'Alsace
weekdays 8–11h30; 14–18h by
appointment.
Max 100 pers.
English spoken.

68770 Ammerschwihr

Caves J B Adam Succ
5, rue de l'Aigle
tel: (89) 78 23 21
Vins d'Alsace, Crémant d'Alsace, Le
Kaefferkopf
Mon–Fri 8–12h; 14–17h
Appointment preferable.
Max 40 pers.
English spoken.

Vins d'Alsace Tempé SARL
12–14, rue de la Rivière-aux-Bains
tel: (89) 78 24 65
Vins d'Alsace, Crémant d'Alsace
Open daily.
Appointment necessary only for groups.
English spoken.

68000 Ingersheim

Cave Coopérative des Viticulteurs
d'Ingersheim
1, rue Clémenceau
tel: (89) 27 05 96
Vins d'Alsace
weekdays 7h30–12h; 13h30–17h
Appointment necessary.
English spoken.

68230 Turckheim

Schleret, Charles
1–3, route d'Ingersheim
tel: (89) 27 06 09
Vins d'Alsace
daily 9–12h; 14–19h except Sun
afternoon
Max 20 pers.

68420 Eguisheim

Beyer, Léon
2, rue de la 1ère Armée
tel: (89) 41 41 05
Vins d'Alsace
Caveau Dégustation open Aug 1–Sept 15
Cellar visits Mon–Fri by appointment.
English spoken.

68420 Husseren-les-Châteaux

Kuentz-Bas
14, route du Vin
tel: (89) 49 30 24
Vins d'Alsace, Eaux-de-vie d'Alsace
Mon–Fri 9–12h; 14–18h
Appointment preferable.
Max 25 pers.
English spoken.

68500 Orschwihr

Reinhart, Paul
7, rue du Printemps
tel: (89) 76 95 12
Vins d'Alsace
daily 8–12h; 14–18h
Max 50 pers.

Wine Festivals

2nd Sunday of March	Presentation of new wines	Eguisheim
Early May	Wine Festival	Molsheim
End of May	Wine Festival	Guebwiller
June 11th	Kugelhopf Festival	Ribeauvillé
Mid-July	Wine Festival	Barr
2nd Sunday in July	Open Caves	Dambach-la-Ville
Sunday after July 14th	Fête des Guinguettes d'Europe	Husseren-les-Châteaux
Before last weekend in July	Wine Festival	Ribeauvillé
Before last weekend in July	Riesling Festival	Riquewihr
End of July	Wine Festival	Wettolsheim
Last weekend in July	Wine Festival	Mittelbergheim
1st weekend in Aug	Wine Festival	Turckheim
1st Sunday in Aug	Fair of the Almond Trees	Mittelwihr
2nd weekend in Aug	'Mini' Wine Fair	Obernai
1st fortnight in Aug	Wine Festival	Dambach-la-Ville
1st fortnight in Aug	Regional Wine Fair	Colmar
Last Sunday in Aug	Vintage Festival	Eguisheim
1st Sunday in Sept	Fête des Ménétriers	Ribeauvillé
Beginning of Sept	Wine Festival	Wolxheim
During the vintage (October 1st to 15th)	Fête des Vendanges	Barr, Hunawihr, Itterswiller, Katzenthal, Niedermorschwihr, Obernai, Rosheim
2nd weekend in Oct	Wine Festival	Molsheim
3rd Sunday in Oct	Fête des Vendanges	Marlenheim

(For precise dates, it is essential to check with local tourist offices.)

Wine Courses

The *Institut International des Vins et Spiritueux* in Bordeaux organizes a six-day course in Alsace and Champagne which includes seminars, tastings, tours of vineyards, and conferences. Three days are spent in Alsace, based in Colmar and Obernai.

Further information from:

Institut International des Vins et Spiritueux
10, place de la Bourse
33076 Bordeaux
tel: (56) 90 91 28

Wine Museum

68240 Kientzheim

Musée du Vignoble et des Vins d'Alsace
Château de la Confrérie St-Etienne
tel: (89) 78 21 36
Open June–Sept
daily 10–12h; 14–18h

Regional Gastronomy

Escargots à l'alsacienne Snails in garlic and parsley butter.

Bäckeofe Hearty one-pot stew of several types of meat including mutton, pork, and beef, cooked together with potatoes and onions in an earthenware crock. Used to be taken to the bakers and left to slow-cook in bread ovens for several hours.

Coq au Riesling Chicken *flambéed* in brandy, then simmered in cream and Riesling d'Alsace; served with home-made egg noodles.

Choucroute Garni Alsacienne Sauerkraut cooked in white wine, and served garnished with Strasbourg sausages, smoked ham, black pudding, knuckles of pork, bacon, potatoes, and cabbage.

Foie Gras Fattened goose liver, cooked whole in special mixture of spices, and infused with black truffles. Sometimes served in *brioche* pastry.

Tarte à l'oignon Simple onion and cream tart which is excellent picnic fare.

Tourte de la Vallée de Munster Rich oven-baked puff-pastry with Munster cheese. Also good picnic fare.

Truite au bleu Extremely fresh local trout poached in winy *court bouillon* which turns the fish a striking shade of blue.

Matelote au Riesling Freshwater pike, tench, perch, trout, and river eel simmered in Riesling d'Alsace.

Kugelhopf Takes its name from the earthenware or copper mould in which this bread-like pastry is baked. Delicious for breakfast. Moulds make a nice souvenir.

Tarte aux Mirabelles Dessert flan made with yellow mirabelle plums – try with a tot of eau-de-vie de Mirabelle.

Munster cheese One of the great cheeses of France, made in farms around and above the town of Munster (can be purchased direct from village producers along the *Route du Fromage*). Served here with a shaker of caraway seeds.

Restaurants

67000 Strasbourg

Restaurant Crocodile
10, rue de l'Outre
tel: (88) 32 13 02
Elegant cuisine; sophisticated ambiance.
Closed Sun and Mon
Expensive

Restaurant Buerehiesel
4, parc de l'Orangerie
tel: (88) 61 62 24

An old Alsatian farm in the heart of the *parc de l'Orangerie* serving regional and *nouvelle cuisine*.
Closed Tue eve; Wed
Expensive

Au Gourmet Sans Chiqué
15, rue Ste-Barbe
tel: (88) 32 04 07
Centrally located, and serving regional specialities.
Closed Sun
Expensive

Maison des Tanneurs
42, rue Bain-aux-Plantes
tel: (88) 32 79 70
A fascinating old craftsmen's workshop, now an excellent restaurant directly on the Ill, serving all regional specialities and Alsatian wines.
Closed Sun and Mon; Dec 22–Jan 23; June 27–July 7
Expensive

Maison Kammerzell
16, place de la Cathédrale
tel: (88) 32 42 14
In the shadow of the Gothic cathedral, a classic Alsatian dwelling built in 1427 now houses a typical *Winstub* on the ground floor serving traditional dishes, and four restaurants on the first and second floors serving *nouvelle cuisine*.
Closed Fri
ground floor: **Moderate**; first and second floors: **Moderate** to **Expensive**

Winstub Strissel
5, place de la Grande Boucherie
tel: (88) 32 14 73
Only 200 metres from the cathedral, this atmospheric *Winstub* offers grills as well as many Alsatian specialities.
Closed Sun eve; Mon; three weeks in July; one week in Feb
Inexpensive

Aux Deux France
2, place Benjamin Zix
tel: (88) 22 15 17
Inexpensive little restaurant with outdoor tables in the heart of the Petite France quarter. Alsatian specialities and wines.

Auberge du Pont St-Martin
13–15, rue des Moulins
tel: (88) 32 45 13
Informal, traditional Alsatian restaurant on the Ill, in the quiet and quaint Petite France quarter.
Inexpensive

67140 Mittelbergheim

Winstub Gilg
1, route du Vin
tel: (88) 08 91 37
Family-run restaurant with authentic Alsatian atmosphere.
Specialities include *pièce de boeuf au Pinot Noir, pâté vigneron*.
Closed Tue eve; Wed; Jan–Feb; June 28–July 9
Moderate

67650 Dambach-la-Ville

Caveau Nartz
12, place du Marché
tel: (88) 92 41 11
Simply-prepared Alsatian specialities, served with own-produced wines.
Open daily July–Aug
Inexpensive

68150 Illhaeusern

Auberge de l'Ill
rue de Collonges
tel: (89) 71 83 23
Situated on the banks of the Ill, surrounded by lovely flowered gardens, this is one of the best restaurants in France, specializing in elegant Alsatian cuisine: *foie gras, mousseline de grenouilles, noisettes de chevreuil*.
Closed Mon eve; Tue; Feb; first week in July
Very Expensive

68340 Riquewihr

Auberge du Schoenenbourg
2, rue de la Piscine
tel: (89) 47 92 28
On the outskirts of this walled medieval village, with a garden where meals are served in good weather. Closed Wed eve; Thurs
Moderate

68770 Ammerschwihr

Hôtel-Restaurant Aux Armes de France
1, Grand Rue
tel: (89) 47 10 12
Excellent and well-known restaurant with specialities of *foie gras frais Pierre Gaertner, filet de sole aux nouilles pyramide, pièce de boeuf au Pinot rouge*. Closed Thurs; and Wed eve from Oct–June
Expensive
Also a **Moderate** hotel; closed Jan

68000 Colmar

Restaurant Schillinger
16, rue Stanislas
tel: (89) 41 43 17
Visit the cellars before dining from an
extensive menu.
Closed Sun eve; Mon
Expensive

Restaurant Au Fer Rouge
52, Grand Rue
tel: (89) 41 37 24
Nouvelle cuisine in the old part of Colmar;
wide range of Alsatian and other French
wines.
Open every day.
Moderate

La Maison des Têtes
19, rue des Têtes
tel: (89) 24 43 43
17th century Alsatian house in the old part
of Colmar serving regional specialities and
wines.
Open Tue–Sun lunchtime.
Moderate

Restaurant au Trois Poissons
15, quai de la Poissonnerie
tel: (89) 41 25 21
Fish restaurant in the Petite Venise section
specializing in *matelote, friture, and grillades*.
Closed Tue eve; Wed.
Inexpensive to Moderate

Lucienne Clergue
3, rue des Têtes
tel: (89) 23 34 72
For *Kugelhopf*, coffee, and eau-de-vie, sit at
an outdoor table in the heart of old
Colmar.
Inexpensive

68420 Eguisheim

Caveau d'Eguisheim
3, place du Château-St-Léon
tel: (89) 41 08 89
Typical Alsatian house built in 1603
opposite château where Pope Leo IX was
born. Alsatian specialities, and wines
principally from this superb commune.
Closed Wed eve; Thur; Jan 15–March 1;
last week of June.
Moderate to Expensive

68400 Les Trois-Épis

L'Auberge
tel: (89) 49 80 65
Serves local wines and regional specialities
in a typical Alsatian house. In summer,
meals served on terrace.
Open daily.
Inexpensive to Moderate

Hotels

(note: in addition to the hotels listed
below, there are numerous opportunities
to stay in **Inexpensive** private rooms in
houses and farmhouses in the heart of the
wine country. Look for signs offering
'Chambres' or 'Zimmer'.)

67000 Strasbourg

Hôtel Gutenberg
31, rue des Serruriers
tel: (88) 32 17 15
18th century building with period décor,
without restaurant.
Closed first ten days Jan.
Inexpensive

Hôtel Monopole-Métropole
16, rue Kuhn
tel: (88) 32 11 94
Alsatian décor and antique furniture.
Garage, bar, no restaurant.
Closed Christmas and New Year.
Moderate

Hôtel des Rohan
17–19, rue des Maroquin
tel: (88) 32 85 11
Situated just opposite the cathedral in a
quiet pedestrian area.
Open all year round.
Expensive

67520 Marlenheim

Hostellerie du Cerf
30, rue du Général-de-Gaulle
tel: (88) 87 73 73
An old Alsatian coaching inn with
comfortable rooms, located at the start of
the *Route du Vin*. High quality cuisine with
menu reflecting local traditions and
seasonal produce.
Closed Mon–Tue.
Expensive

67120 Obernai

Hôtel du Parc
169, rue Général-Gouraud
tel: (88) 95 50 08
Typical timbered Alsatian building yet
with every modern convenience, including

sauna, solarium, and spa. Hotel open all
year; restaurant closed Sun eve; Mon.
Moderate

67530 Ottrott

Beau Site
1, rue du Général-de-Gaulle
tel: (88) 95 80 61
21-room geranium-decked hotel with
restaurant serving regional specialities.
Hotel closed Jan. Restaurant closed Sun
eve; Mon.
Expensive

Hostellerie des Châteaux
11, rue des Châteaux
tel: (88) 95 81 54
Wonderfully situated on the edge of the
forest for walks and possible winter
cross-country skiing, with Alsatian
cooking accompanied by *rouge d'Ottrott*,
the local red wine.
Hotel closed Nov 15–Dec 15.
Restaurant closed Tue.
Expensive

67140 Andlau

Hôtel Kastelberg
tel: (88) 08 97 83
40-room hotel with restaurant 'Au Canon'
(located just down the road).
Moderate

67140 Itterswiller

Hôtel-Restaurant Arnold
route du Vin
tel: (88) 85 50 58
In the heart of the vineyards, at the foot of
the Vosges Mountains, this 28-room hotel
has great charm and atmosphere. Excellent
restaurant serves all regional specialities;
shop selling Alsatian pottery, wines,
foods, and souvenirs.
Hotel open all year
Restaurant closed Mon
Moderate

67730 Chatenois

Hostellerie de l'Aigle
87, rue Mal-Foch
tel: (88) 92 12 67
An historic 15th century inn with a very
reasonable restaurant serving regional
specialities such as *coq au Riesling, Bäckeofe*,
and *matelote*.
Hotel closed Feb
Restaurant closed Wed in low season.
Inexpensive to **Moderate**

68590 Saint-Hippolyte

Hôtel Aux Ducs de Lorraine
16, route du Vin
tel: (89) 73 00 09
Magnificent views from the comfortable
bedrooms across to the vineyards and
Vosges Mountains. The restaurant
specializes in *foie gras frais maison,
choucroute à l'alsacienne, langouste fraiche
grillé*, and fish and game in season.
Hotel closed first two weeks in Dec, and
Jan 10–March 1
Restaurant closed Mon
Moderate

68150 Ribeauvillé

Le Clos St Vincent
route de Bergheim
tel: (89) 73 67 65
Wonderful views over the vineyards.
Hotel closed Dec–Feb
Restaurant closed Tues, Wed
Expensive

Pépinière
route de Sainte-Marie-aux-Mines
tel: (89) 73 64 14
Set in the midst of the Vosges, with
comfortable rooms and charming
restaurant.
Hotel closed Jan; Feb
Restaurant closed Wed
Moderate

68340 Riquewihr

Hostellerie 'Au Moulin'
8, rue du Général-de-Gaulle
tel: (89) 47 93 13
In the centre of the town, with comfortable
bedrooms and restaurant serving Alsatian
specialities, and Dopff 'Au Moulin' wines.
Moderate

68240 Kayserberg

Hôtel-Restaurant Chambard
9, rue du Général-de-Gaulle
tel: (89) 47 10 17
Very comfortable 20-room hotel with
restaurant serving sophisticated cuisine.
Hotel open all year
Restaurant closed Sun eve; Mon
Expensive

Hôtel-Restaurant du Château
38, rue du Général-de-Gaulle
tel: (89) 78 24 33
Specialities include *truite aux armands,
tartes aux fruits*, and *mousse au kirsch*.

Hotel closed Nov 21–Dec 25 and all of Jan
Restaurant closed Thur
Inexpensive to **Moderate**

68000 Colmar

Terminus Bristol
7, place de la Gare
tel: (89) 23 59 59
Comfortable 100 room hotel in centre of
Colmar.
Open all year.
Moderate

Novotel
49, route de Strasbourg
tel: (89) 41 49 14
Conveniently located by the Colmar
airport with swimming pool, terrace, and
restaurant.
Open all year
Moderate

68230 Turckheim

Hôtel-Restaurant des Deux Clefs
3, rue du Conseil
tel: (89) 27 06 01
Ancienne hostellerie: half-timbered building
with atmospheric panelled dining room
serving all Alsatian specialities and wines.
Hotel closed Dec–Jan
Restaurant open daily
Inexpensive to **Moderate**

68600 Andolsheim

Hôtel-Restaurant du Soleil
1, rue de Colmar
tel: (89) 71 40 53
Small family hotel with restaurant
specializing in fish and game, when in
season.
Closed Tue
Moderate

68410 Les Trois-Épis

Le Grand Hôtel Mapotel
tel: (89) 49 80 65
Situated high in the mountains and
surrounded by forest, with panoramic
terraces, swimming pool, sauna, and
luxurious bedrooms. The restaurant serves
regional specialities as well as refined
classic cuisine.
Hotel closed Jan 4–Feb 11
Restaurant open daily
Expensive

68250 Rouffach

Château d'Isenbourg
tel: (89) 49 63 53
Surrounded by vineyards, overlooking
village of Rouffach, this 33-room luxury
hotel serves regional food in converted
15th century vaulted cellars. Hotel closed
Jan 10–March 15.
Restaurant open daily
Hotel **Expensive**; Restaurant **Moderate** to
Expensive

68111 Westhalten

Hôtel du Bollenberg
tel: (89) 49 62 47
Family run 45-room hotel with Restaurant
'Aux Vieux Pressoir' serving regional
specialities in an intimate atmosphere.
Cellars can be visited, and wines
purchased.
Restaurant open daily
Inexpensive to **Moderate**

Where to Get Additional Information

Comité Interprofessionnel des Vins
d'Alsace
8, place de Lattre de Tassigny
68003 Colmar
tel: (89) 41 06 21

Office de Tourisme
10, place Gutenberg
67000 Strasbourg
tel: (88) 32 57 07

Office de Tourisme
4, rue Unterlinden
68003 Colmar
tel: (89) 41 02 29

Office Départemental du Tourisme du
Bas-Rhin
47, rue du Maréchal Foch
67000 Strasbourg
tel: (88) 35 56 26

Office Départemental du Tourisme du
Haut-Rhin
68020 Colmar

68500 Jungholtz

Ferme de Thierenbach
tel: (89) 76 93 01
Located in the heart of the Vosges forest, a quiet country hotel which offers local specialities in a relaxed and tranquil atmosphere.
Hotel closed Nov 15–Jan 15
Restaurant closed Mon
Inexpensive to **Moderate**

Hôtel-Restaurant Biebler
tel: (89) 76 85 75
Inexpensive Restaurant and Hotel.
Open daily all year round

Camping

Strasbourg
La Montagne Verte tel: (88) 30 25 46
Molsheim
Camp Municipal tel: (88) 38 11 67
Obernai
Camp Municipal tel: (88) 95 61 31

Barr
Saint-Martin tel: (88) 08 00 45
Sélestat
Les Cigognes tel: (88) 92 03 98
Ribeauvillé
Pierre-de-Coubertin tel: (89) 73 66 71
Riquewihr
Camp Intercommunal tel: (89) 47 90 08
Colmar
L'Ill tel: (89) 41 15 94
Eguisheim
Camp Municipal tel: (89) 23 19 39
Kaysersberg
Camp Municipal tel: (89) 47 14 47
Cernay
Les Acacias tel: (89) 41 15 94

Additionally, there are numerous well-appointed campsites in the lake district of Gérardmer and Longemer.

Bibliography

Wines and People of Alsace, by T. A. Layton, Cassell 1970

BORDEAUX

Bordeaux is the world's greatest quality vineyard, famous for long-lived château-bottled claret from estates in the Médoc, St Emilion, Graves and Pomerol; for dry, fragrant white wine from Graves and Entre-Deux-Mers; and for sweet, nectar-like dessert wines from Sauternes and Barsac. It is a region of grand (and not so grand) châteaux, of elegant eighteenth-century estates, and cool, low-lying *chais* where new wine rests in new oak barrels; it is rich in tradition and prestige, for established families have made or shipped fine wine here for generations, wine enjoyed by an equally élite, equally select clientele.

Yet neither Bordeaux, the wine, the city, nor the region itself, is, in fact, élite. Its most famous estates take time off to welcome casual visitors, to show off premises and explain wine-making techniques, and to offer tastings of their precious product. Bordeaux wine itself, in addition, is more than just the flag-bearing aristocrats that fetch the highest prices; indeed Bordeaux still produces vast quantities of basic, bracing reds and honest whites that

How to Get There

By Car
The most direct route from Paris is the A10 autoroute through Orléans, Tours, and Poitiers. From Poitiers, take the N10 south through Angoulême to Bordeaux.

From the channel ports in Brittany, head for Nantes, and then take the N137 through La Rochelle, Rochefort, Saintes, and Bordeaux.

From Spain there will eventually be a continuous autoroute from the border up to Bordeaux. At present, the A63 is only open to just past Bayonne, where it joins the N10, then restarts for a small stretch before entering Bordeaux.

Trans-Gironde run two car ferry routes across the Gironde from Royan to Le Verdon, and from Blaye to Lamarque. They run from April to September, and take about thirty minutes to make the crossing. This is a good way to reach the Médoc if travelling from the north, without having first to struggle through Bordeaux itself. For further information contact:

Trans-Gironde
9, place du Parlement
33000 Bordeaux
tel: (56) 52 63 76

By Plane
The main French international airport is at Paris. Air Inter, the internal French airline, flies from Paris to Bordeaux. Air Inter flights are bookable through any Air France office, or through travel agents. Direct flights also from London to Bordeaux several times a week.

demonstrate the character of the region, yet which remain relatively inexpensive. The region is easy-going and welcoming, a generous and rich land with a *bonne table* to match its finest wines, and a varied country of old, quiet, and historic villages, and vast, surprisingly unspoiled stretches of sandy beaches which allow sun worshippers, water sports enthusiasts, nature lovers (and naturists), to hide from the rest of the world behind a protective screen of huge sand dunes (the highest in Europe), backed by the tall, dark, majestic pine forests of the Landes.

The British have always felt a particular affinity to this region, for when young Henry Plantagenet (later to become King Henry II of England) married Eleanor of Aquitaine, her lands, which the Romans some thousand years earlier called 'Aquitania', meaning 'land of waters', became an English possession. And so they stayed, for some three centuries, during which time the Englishman and his beloved claret – which is simply red Bordeaux wine – became inseparable. Even after English rule in Aquitaine came to an end in 1453, the wine trade continued to prosper (indeed, in commercial terms, the English market remained an important one, for the French monarchy, in alliance with the powerful Dukes of Burgundy, gave preference to the wines of the Côte d'Or). Even the Methuen Treaty, signed between England and Portugal in 1703, which conceded a preferential tariff on Portuguese wines imported to England, and led to a greater consumption of port, did not dissuade faithful connoisseurs from the wines of the Médoc, Graves, Sauternes, St Emilion, and elsewhere, nor cause the *Bordelais* to look elsewhere for custom. Today Bordeaux wine is loved and exported throughout the world. Yet the special relationship between the British and the *Bordelais* still remains, making this a particularly comfortable and pleasant region to visit and to explore.

By Train
There is an express train from Paris (called the 'Aquitaine') which takes less than four hours. It leaves from Paris Austerlitz weekdays.

Bordeaux is on the main Paris–Madrid line. There is no direct rail line from the Brittany ferry ports; it is necessary to change in Rennes, Redon, and Nantes. From Calais and Boulogne the easiest route is via Paris.

Local Public Transport
There is quite a good local bus network throughout the region, and it is possible to take a local train from Bordeaux to Libourne to explore St Emilion and Pomerol. The region, however, is extensive, and many of the more interesting châteaux are situated off the main routes, so it is really advisable to tour by car. The bus station in Bordeaux is at 14, rue Fondaudège.

Car Rental Information
Bordeaux
Avis: Mérignac Airport
  tel: (56) 34 38 22
  59, rue Peyronnet
  tel: (56) 92 69 38
Hertz: Mérignac Airport
  tel: (56) 34 18 87
  Bordeaux Gare,
  7/8, rue Charles Domercq
  tel: (56) 91 01 71

Michelin Maps 71, 75;
Carte Topographique 46

The Wines of Bordeaux

Bordeaux is not a single wine region but many, producing a variety of types and styles. The following is a general guideline only to the principal areas. For detailed descriptions of individual wines, consult the books recommended in the Bibliography.

Médoc The Médoc (from the Latin *medio acqua* – in the middle of water) is a triangular peninsula stretching north-west from Bordeaux to form a point where the Gironde (the estuary formed by the Garonne and Dordogne Rivers) meets the Atlantic, made up of two sub-regions: Médoc, and Haut-Médoc. The latter is that area closest to Bordeaux in which are located the finest vineyards and communes. In 1855 some sixty wines of the Médoc were classified into five levels of excellence: *premier cru, deuxième cru, troisième cru, quatrième cru,* and *cinquième cru*. Five wines today are recognized as *premiers crus* – Château Lafite-Rothschild, Château Mouton-Rothschild, Château Latour, Château Margaux, and Château Haut-Brion (the latter is actually located on the outskirts of Bordeaux itself in the region known as Graves). The red wines of the Médoc are noted for their delicacy and subtle finesse, combined, in the greatest, with an ability to improve and develop nuances in bouquet and flavour over long periods of time. The principal grape of the Médoc is Cabernet Sauvignon, small, tough-skinned, with an initially unforthcoming character which gives the wine its backbone, and which softens with age, developing a venerable elegance.

Graves A prestigious vineyard, producing both distinguished clarets, and vigorous, forceful dry white wines. Some of its greatest properties are located virtually within Bordeaux itself: Château Haut-Brion, La Mission-Haut-Brion, Château Pape Clément, and others. The region, however, extends south to Langon, and encloses the sweet wine enclaves of Barsac and Sauternes. Principal communes include Pessac, Talence, Villenave d'Ornon, Léognan, Martillac, and Cadaujac.

St Emilion Generous, full-bodied red wine produced from vineyards around this famous and picturesque medieval town. A high proportion of Merlot grapes, together with, in some instances, a deep escarpment of rich limestone sub-soil, and

elsewhere, extending beyond the town, a plateau of primarily gravelly soil result in wines that are generally fuller, more mellow in temperament, and quicker maturing than the great wines of the Médoc. St Emilion is called 'the land of a thousand châteaux'; of its numerous wine-producing estates, some 12 are entitled to the illustrious designation *premier grand cru classé* (the two most famous properties of St Emilion are Château Ausone, and Château Cheval Blanc), 72 are *grands crus classés*, and a hundred or so are *grands crus*.

Pomerol Mellow red wines of great character, delicacy, and elegance are produced from vineyards lying on a low plateau north-west of Libourne, second wine capital of Bordeaux. A richer, heavier soil, plus a high proportion of Merlot, which is much softer and faster maturing than Cabernet Sauvignon, results in rich, and readily appealing clarets that are prized throughout the world. Paradoxically, however, the great wines of Pomerol have never been classified. Nevertheless, Château Petrus is generally regarded as the region's greatest flag-bearer, while there are some forty other wines of *grand cru* class.

Sauternes and **Barsac** Luscious, extremely sweet dessert wines that are among the finest in the world, produced from Semillon grapes (primarily) which have been affected by *botrytis cinerea,* also known as *pourriture noble* ('noble rot'). Their sweetness is balanced by an alcohol content that is relatively high. In addition to Sauternes and Barsac (which are two separate AOC's), the communes of Preignac, Bommes, and Fargues also produce such fine wines which were classified in 1855. One property alone stands in a class of its own, the *grand premier cru* Château d'Yquem.

Entre-Deux-Mers Fine dry white wines produced in the picturesque, undulating country between the Garonne and Dordogne Rivers, literally *entre deux mers*. It is fruity and fresh, at its best drunk

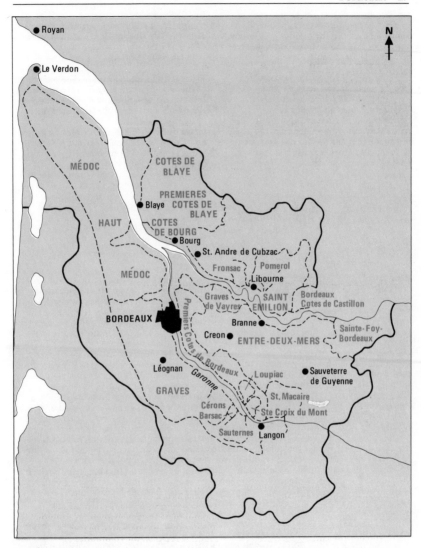

young; it is good wine to drink with the seafood and freshwater fish of the region.

Bordeaux Though the above regions produce the finest and most famous wines of Bordeaux, much excellent wine is produced in this prolific wine region and sold under the simple *appellation d'origine* Bordeaux. Bordeaux AOC, and the slightly

higher in alcohol Bordeaux Supérieur can be either red, white, or rosé. The wines can be and are produced throughout the Bordeaux region, though they still are subjected to rigorous quality control regarding permitted grape varieties, methods of cultivation, maximum yield, and minimum alcohol content. For the visitor to the region, there are literally thousands of producers, ranging from small individual farmers to immense *coopératives*; such concerns should be visited along with the famous properties; the wines that can be purchased are often remarkably good value.

Other wine regions in Bordeaux which may be encountered on wine tours:

Premières Côtes de Bordeaux Large narrow band of vineyards parallel to the river, stretching downstream from Bordeaux as far as St-Macaire, producing both quick-maturing fruity red wines as well as some dry and sweet whites.

Ste-Croix-du-Mont, Loupiac, Cadillac Minor sweet white wines produced from vineyards on the opposite bank of the Garonne from the great communes of Sauternes and Barsac.

Fronsac and Canon Fronsac Fine red wines of the Libournais, less well-known – and less expensive – than their aristocratic neighbours of Pomerol and St Emilion.

Côtes de Blaye, Premières Côtes de Blaye, and Côtes de Bourg Good solid reds and whites produced from vineyards north of Bordeaux.

The Wine Roads of Bordeaux

Bordeaux France's fourth largest city is at once the centre of the wine trade, an industrial and cultural centre, and an important and prosperous port. Though many visitors may wish to stay on the coast, or else further inland in the beautiful Aquitaine countryside, Bordeaux offers a range of accommodation to suit everyone (from five-star hotels to municipal campsites open all year round), as well as a host of superb restaurants. Even if you are not staying here, the city deserves to be explored. Visit the Grand Théâtre in the place de la Comédie to gain an impression of the rich opulence of this smug eighteenth-century metropolis; stroll down the allées de Tourny to the place de Tourny, then up along cours G Clemenceau to the place Gambetta where you can sit at an outdoor café. The nearby Musée des Beaux-Arts is well worth a visit, as is the magnificent cathedral of St-André, and the eleventh-century Romanesque church of St-Seurin. Shoppers may want to stroll through the pedestrianized rue Sainte-Catherine, while those in search of the old city will turn off to explore the Quartier-St-Pierre, a maze of tiny alleys, old houses, shops, and intimate restaurants.

Bordeaux, though a modern and busy city, is above all the capital of the wine trade. Many important and well-known shippers have their headquarters within the city itself, in old warehouses along the quai des Chartrons and de Bacalan which extend above the esplanade des Quinconces, and remind us that not long ago, and for centuries previously, Bordeaux wines were traditionally shipped by boat. The *Maison du Vin* (near the Grand Théâtre) is Bordeaux's centre for wine promotion, and offers much useful literature and maps, and also arranges visits to those properties which require appointments. Nearby also are two excellent shops offering a large selection of fine wines: *Vinothèque* (across the street from the *Maison du Vin*), and the smaller *Badie* (further along the allées de Tourny). The *Hôtel des Vins* (rue Abbé de l'Épée) not only sells a wide selection of fine wines and wine accessories, but also arranges tastings and seminars.

The approach to Bordeaux may well seem like that to any other modern city, through sprawling suburbs and vast industrial zones. But it takes little effort to find the prized vineyards. As in Vienna, some of Bordeaux's most famous lie virtually within the city itself. Château Haut-Brion, one of the *premiers crus* classified in 1855, lies, like many another city 'garden', just along the road to Pessac, a rather unexceptional suburb of Bordeaux. Indeed, the city is virtually surrounded by its vineyards: head north, and the famous estates of the Médoc are soon encountered; Graves, Sauternes, and Barsac lie to the south, while Entre-Deux-Mers, straddling the Garonne and Dordogne, is to the east; further east still are the prized vineyards which extend around the region's second wine city, Libourne, those of St Emilion, Pomerol, Fronsac, and to the north, Bourg and Blaye. This, truly, is the world's greatest quality vineyard.

Route des Châteaux – the Médoc

From the centre of Bordeaux (place de Tourny) take the rue de Fondaudège (direction of Barriére du Médoc); after crossing Président Wilson Boulevard, follow the avenue de la Libération until it becomes the Route du Médoc (follow signs for Soulac). This road eventually becomes the D1; once out of the city, find the D2E which branches right to Blanquefort (visit the celebrated shippers Barton & Guestier), Macau and, meeting the D2, Cantenac, where the *Route des Châteaux* begins.

There is an oft-repeated saying in the Médoc (and elsewhere) that the vine likes to see the water and indeed, the low, neat vineyards stretching over the slight hills in a long, almost uninterrupted band, are rarely out of sight of the now widening Gironde. It is not possible to describe more than a handful of the hundreds of properties that will be encountered. For knowledgeable and detailed descriptions, consult the books listed in the Bibliography.

In Cantenac the great profusion of châteaux begins. One of the most visible and welcoming is Château Prieuré-Lichine, owned by Alexis Lichine, the well-respected wine writer. Across the road, a stone gateway and track leads to Château d'Issan, one of the most beautiful properties in the region. The D2 wine road leads on to Margaux, passing along the way other famous properties such as Château Palmer (part owned by the British firm of Sichel), Château Rausan-Segla and, virtually within the town itself, Château Lascombes (also British owned, by the Bass-Charrington group). The prima donna of the southern Médoc, and also one of the loveliest properties of all, is the grand Empire-inspired Château Margaux, one of four *premiers crus*. Its classical facade (familiar from the wine label) looks all that a château should. While the château itself is privately owned, the nearby *chais* where the wine is made and stored can be visited. Margaux has a *Maison du Vin* in the centre of town where wine from the commune can be purchased, appointments can be made, or special requirements dealt with.

En route from Margaux to the greater wine communes to the north, lesser known villages are passed, such as Soussans, Arcins, Lamarque, Cussac and, off the D1, Listrac and, off the D5, Moulis. Though their names are perhaps less

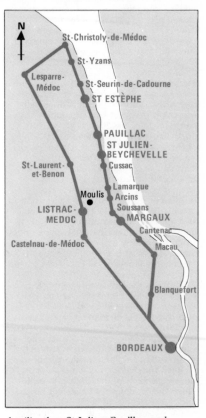

familiar than St-Julien, Pauillac, and St-Estèphe, they should not be rushed through in haste. For if their individual properties are hardly household names, nevertheless these communes all produce excellent wines; lesser properties that are often bypassed by those who seek to visit only the famous *grands crus* up the road offer a warm welcome, and their wines, which generally can be purchased, are perhaps more within the means of most of us (many of the great properties, incidentally, do not sell their wines direct, for limited quantities of these precious clarets are earmarked for valued customers in France and abroad). Lamarque has an excellent and inexpensive local restaurant where regional food can be enjoyed. The Fort Médoc, on the river's edge between Lamarque and Cussac, is worth a visit.

The *Route des Châteaux* (D2) continues to Beychevelle and St-Julien-Beychevelle, passing along the way a concentration of classed properties. One of the most famous is Château Beychevelle itself. The name, so the story goes, is a corruption of the sailors' cry as they headed up the Gironde, *'baisses les voiles'*, though whether it was necessary to strike the sails due to the treacherous currents and winds of the wide estuary, or out of respect for the vineyards is open to debate. Other well known properties in this superlative commune include Château Ducru-Beaucaillou, Château Gloria, Château Gruaud-Larose, Château Talbot (named after the region's last British commander, Sir John Talbot, who died unsuccessfully attempting to repel the French at Castillon). On either side of St-Julien lie the estates of Léoville: Château Léoville-Barton (on the right side of the road opposite the beautiful eighteenth-century Château Langoa – both properties belong to the Barton shipping family), Château Léoville-Poyferre and, closer to the vineyards of Pauillac, Château Léoville-Lascases.

Pauillac is the largest town along the *Route des Châteaux*, and still very much a working port, as evidenced by the surprisingly vast oil refinery located on its northern fringes. Yet beside this incongruous, belching monstrosity, lie some of the most famous vineyards in the world, producing long-lived, exceedingly complex and delicate red wines. Out of four *premiers crus* of the Médoc, three lie within the commune of Pauillac: Château Latour (the famous tower is just visible from the road before entering the town), Château Lafite-Rothschild, and Château Mouton-Rothschild. The latter, incidentally, was not originally classified *premier cru* in 1855, but this omission, generally regarded as erroneous, was rectified in 1973. The *chais* of Mouton are particularly impressive: rows of light, new oak *barriques* – beautifully crafted themselves, their rims bound lovingly in cane, the cask ends embossed with the regal crest of Mouton – extend majestically along the vast, low-lying building; below, in the cellars, is the Baron's private store, containing not only rare vintages of his own wines, but also extensive stocks of his rivals', while elsewhere the everyday chores of a great wine estate continue: the cleaning and repairing of barrels, the racking of the wine, the constant topping up of wine that has evaporated, the fining with egg whites, and the constant vigilance over a living, ever-changing, ever-developing product.

The great properties of the Médoc are rich in history and tradition, proud of their connections with the past, humbly aware of wine itself as a great and civilizing force. Thus, the Mouton wine museum (which can only be visited by prior appointment) celebrates the cultivation of the vine with a superb and impressive collection of paintings, tapestries, glass and other wine-associated objects and works of art.

Mouton's great rival, owned by another branch of the Rothschild family, is just up the road, Château Lafite-Rothschild, a low 'modest' building (for these parts, anyway) topped by a weather vane of five arrows, symbolizing the five Rothschild brothers who left a ghetto in Frankfurt to make their fortunes throughout the world.

The Pauillac vineyard is extremely compact, but one could stop here for days, weeks, months even, visiting the numerous and esteemed properties of this commune only. Next to Château Latour (which sits back from the road, the rows of precious Cabernet Sauvignon vines all marked with a single rose bush) is the elegant mansion of Château Pichon-Lalande; across the road lies the estate of Pichon-Baron. Both were once jointly owned by the Longueville family. Further away from the river are Châteaux Batailley and Haut-Batailley, and above the town, familiar properties such as Château Pontet-Canet, Château Mouton Baron Philippe, Château Grand-Puy-Lacoste, and Duhart-Milon, to name but a few. The local *coopérative* here is itself a château, La Rose-Pauillac, located on the road out of town towards St-Estèphe. Pauillac also has its *Maison du Vin*, where appointments to visit properties can be made in summer months.

The final great commune of the Haut-Médoc is little St-Estèphe. Separated from Pauillac by a stream, its first property of renown cannot be missed: just after Château Lafite, the D2 climbs steeply but briefly to emerge upon the outrageously whimsical Château Cos d'Estournel, a grand, nineteenth-century Frenchified oriental pagoda; across the road from it is

---

Route des Châteaux

Château Cos Labory, while numerous other *crus bourgeois* properties are encountered along the approach into the village. Just north of St-Estèphe lies Château Calon-Ségur, once a possession of the Comte de Ségur, who at the time also owned Lafite and Latour. Though he made wine at those other properties, his heart, so it is said, was at Calon, so the château name on the label is enclosed within a heart.

The Médoc is divided into the Haut-Médoc, which includes those vineyards just encountered, and encompasses most of the classified growths, and the Médoc, those lands north of St-Estèphe which produce large amounts of wine which is good, and even very good, but which does not approach the character of that from the greater communes and individual estates. Nevertheless, there are still numerous properties in the Médoc which can be visited, in villages such as St-Seurin-de-Cadourne, St-Yzans-de-Médoc (Château Loudenne, with its vast *chais*, for example, is owned by the international Gilbey concern, and gives a particularly warm welcome to visitors), and elsewhere.

Either continue north, eventually reaching the Pointe de Graves, where the Gironde enters the Atlantic, and then discover the beaches of the Médoc; or else return to Bordeaux by taking the D103 from St-Christoly-Médoc (above St-Yzans) to Lesparre-Médoc, then the faster N125 through St-Laurent, Listrac, and Castelnau, to where the D1 leads back to the capital.

The Libournais
– Fronsac, Pomerol, St Emilion

Libourne, (reached by taking the N89 east from Bordeaux) is the wine region's second capital, and an important centre of trade since at least the Middle Ages. A busy, pleasant town located at the confluence of the Dordogne and l'Isle Rivers, its picturesque quays, until the beginning of this century, were the scene of intense activity as oak *barriques* of wine were loaded onto ships to be exported throughout the world. Today, as in Bordeaux itself, the wholesale transportation of wine by ship has largely ceased; nevertheless, Libourne continues to be the important centre for the famous wines of St Emilion and Pomerol, as well as for those from Fronsac, Entre-Deux-Mers, Graves de Vayres, and for wines from further afield, too, such as those from Monbazillac and Bergerac, located in Bordeaux's beautiful hinterland, the Dordogne.

The town itself, formerly Leybornia, is named after the English governor Roger de Leyburn who built it in the thirteenth century as a bastion against the French. Designed around a central arcaded square, the town has a well-restored fifteenth-century Hôtel de Ville, and also, along the river, La Tour du Grand Port, last surviving witness of the old line of fortifications. Many wine shippers have their premises in Libourne, and the town, with its numerous hotels and restaurants, makes a pleasant base for exploration of the important vineyards which surround it. The region, however, is close enough to Bordeaux and compact enough to be visited on a day excursion from that city.

Fronsac, just over a mile west of Libourne on D670, is a sleepy little village on the banks of the Dordogne (pleasant camping along the river), and the centre of a less well-known wine district of numerous *petits châteaux* producing good to excellent wines that bear the *appellations* Côtes de Fronsac and Canon-Fronsac. Fronsac itself is old, celebrated for its hillock, formerly crowned by a château built for the Emperor Charlemagne, and from which there are magnificent views of the surrounding countryside, and the valleys of the Dordogne and l'Isle. The vineyards extend in a wedge north of the village between the two rivers, and it is most pleasant simply to meander through narrow country lanes to St-Michel-de-Fronsac, St-Aignan, and Saillans, before either cutting across to the vineyards of Pomerol, or else heading north-west to St-André-de-Cubzac, a minor centre for the production of much sound Bordeaux *rouge, blanc, rosé,* and *clairet* (the latter is somewhat heavier and fuller than *rosé*, yet lighter and paler than red wine), before returning to Libourne.

The vineyards of Pomerol are best reached from Libourne by leaving the town on the D21E towards Montagne. After the little village of Catusseau, take

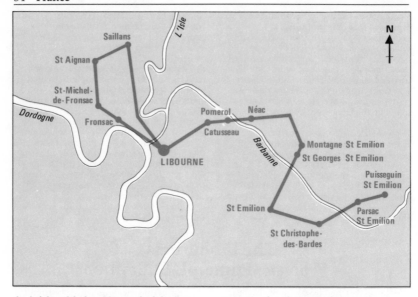

the left hand fork to Néac, which leads to
the heart of the finest vineyards. The
terrain itself is surprisingly flat, the rich
red-brown soil a contrast to the harsher,
meagre gravel of the Médoc (the character
of the wine reflects this contrast, for the
wines of Pomerol are generally richer and
more readily appealing than the hard and
austere clarets of St-Estèphe and Pauillac,
for example). Vieux Château Certan, one
of the commune's finest properties, and
the most impressive looking, is
encountered along the road to Néac. As
previously mentioned, the wines of
Pomerol have never been officially
classified (surprisingly, since the French
seem to delight in rating everything from
chickens to artichokes, and certainly
wines). Nevertheless, the next rather
unassuming property, just a few hundred
yards up the road from Vieux Château
Certan, is generally regarded as not only
the finest in the commune of Pomerol, but
a match for even the greatest wines of the
Médoc, Graves, or St Emilion: Château
Petrus.

Throughout this compact vineyard other
châteaux, their names familiar to
connoisseurs who prize this generous, rich
wine, are encountered: Château La
Fleur-Petrus, Château Petit-Village,
Château Latour Pomerol, Château
Trotanoy, and many others, whose
buildings and *chais* are rarely as imposing

or as grand as their grandiose names
suggest. Pomerol itself hardly exists; yet
the sight of the village *église* smugly
peeking over the flat, verdant fields of
vines is a delightful one.

St Emilion, on the other hand, is one of
the finest and most picturesque of all the
many medieval wine towns in France.
Perched on a steep limestone crag
overlooking the plateau of vines leading
down to the Dordogne, it is a remarkable
old fortified town of mellow ochre houses,
cobbled streets, and sunbaked tile roofs.
Park at the top of the town, outside the
ramparts by the Église Collégiale. Visits to
châteaux can be arranged in the nearby
Maison du Vin. In the lower part of the
town there is a lively little market square
selling vegetables, fat geese and chickens,
and oysters from Arcachon, as well as a
shop offering another delicious speciality,
macarons. The famous l'Église Monolithe is
also down here, a gaunt, ninth-century
church which was actually hewn out of the
solid limestone hills by Benedictine
monks. Also hollowed out of the rock is
the alleged eighth-century hermitage of St
Emilion, while the overgrown Couvent de
Cordeliers is also worth a visit. St Emilion
is steeped in tradition; every year, for
example, the *Jurade de St Emilion*, in their
scarlet medieval robes, proclaim the
harvest bans from the thirteenth-century
Tour du Roi, then lead a procession

through the winding, cobbled streets of the town.

The vineyards themselves extend both over the slopes of the hill leading up to the town – these are the Côtes St Emilion – and along the flatter plateau leading to Pomerol – these vineyards are known as Graves St Emilion, so named because of this sub-region's rockier, sparser soil which contrasts with the former's base of deep limestone. Château Ausone is the premier wine of the Côtes, and indeed, the estate's cellar, like the town church and hermitage, is actually hewn into the side of the rocky hill; its great rival from the Graves is the famous Château Cheval Blanc. Both of these wines fetch prices as high as any in Bordeaux. St Emilion proudly calls itself 'the land of a thousand châteaux', and indeed, there seem to be almost that many properties in the lands surrounding the ancient town. In addition, five nearby communes adjacent to the St Emilion vineyard have earned the right to append that famous name to their own: Montagne-St Emilion, St Georges-St Emilion, Lussac-St Emilion, Puisseguin-St Emilion, and Parsac-St Emilion. This same privilege also applies to the area known as Sables-St Emilion.

Wine Regions South of Bordeaux: Graves, Barsac and Sauternes, Entre-Deux-Mers, and Premières Côtes de Bordeaux

Though the Médoc and St Emilion might well be one's first choice for wine regions to tour, those south of Bordeaux are equally deserving. Indeed, in terms of variety, the full range of wine that the Bordeaux vineyard offers are produced from these varied slopes. From Graves come prestigious classed growth clarets, as well as vigorous white wines; the vineyards of Barsac and Sauternes produce what many consider to be the finest sweet wines in the world; from the lovely undulating vineyards of Entre-Deux-Mers come sound dry white wines, while from the Premières Côtes de Bordeaux, following the east bank of the Garonne back to Bordeaux, come everyday reds, whites, rosés, as well as sweet white wines from the enclaves of Loupiac and Ste-Croix-du-Mont. The country is a contrast to both the Médoc and the Libournais, and there are plenty of producers to visit, as well as some fine restaurants and country hotels.

Either: leave Bordeaux directly (following the Route de Toulouse to Villenave d'Ornon, and there pick up the N113 south, which leads through Graves to Barsac and Sauternes); or else, first make for the western outskirts of the city along the N650 towards Arcachon. This allows a detour to be made to Château Haut-Brion, home of a powerful, robust red wine which Samuel Pepys enjoyed in the seventeenth century ('Ho Bryen'), and whose excellence was recognized in 1855 when it was the only red wine outside the Médoc to be classified as *premier cru*. Across the road from this famous (now American-owned) estate is Château La Mission-Haut-Brion; both properties were once part of the same estate, and today the finest wines of each are comparable. Many other estates producing classified growths are found in this distinguished wine suburb, including Château La Tour-Haut-Brion, Château Laville-Haut-Brion (which produces white wines) and, further out of town, Château Pape-Clément.

From the neighbouring communes of Pessac and Talence, find the ring road around Bordeaux south to join the N113. This leads south through the outskirts of the city through Villenave-d'Ornon to le Bouscaut. Turn right onto the D111 to Léognan, another centre for the production of fine reds and whites. One property which produces both, Château Carbonnieux, is located along the D111, although presumably it was white Graves from this estate that previously used to be shipped to Muslim Turkey as 'mineral water'. Château Haut-Bailly is another classed growth of this commune, while on the far side of the village, off the N651 which leads to Saucats, lie the classed vineyards of Château Malartic-Lagravière and Château Fieuzal. From Léognan, take the D109 across to Martillac, another prestigious, if little known commune of Graves.

Return to the N113 and continue south to reach the wine regions of Barsac and Sauternes. (Before reaching the town of Barsac, however, another Bordeaux wine region is encountered, that of Cerons, one of many other surrounding areas, like Cadillac, Ste-Croix-du-Mont, Loupiac, and parts of the Premières Côtes de Bordeaux, that produce fragrant, if lighter and less distinguished, sweet white wines.)

Barsac and Sauternes are actually two separate *appellations*; but the five communes that comprise both are all governed by a distinct microclimate that produces the unique conditions necessary for the production of these rare wines. The Graves region as a whole is one of low-lying hills crossed by numerous streams; in the regions of Barsac and Sauternes, bounded by the Garonne and crossed by the smaller Ciron, early morning mists in autumn, rapidly dispelled by warm afternoon sun, cause an exceptional and desirable mould to form on the grapes. Called *botrytis cinerea* (or *pourriture noble* – noble rot), it attacks both the flesh and skin of the grape, causing it to shrivel and wither, and to turn a purplish-brown colour. This, in turn, causes the grape sugar to concentrate; moreover, acidity is reduced and the formation of glycerin is encouraged. However, as this condition only arises by the alternation of morning dampness and afternoon heat, it naturally does not occur evenly throughout the region, or even, for that matter, throughout individual vineyards. So temperamental, so unpredictable is this rare condition, that it is actually necessary to comb the vineyards several successive times, harvesting only those individual grapes that are overripe and shrivelled. In the finest vineyards, the harvest can thus continue for six or eight weeks, even longer. Moreover, if considerable amounts of rain should fall at any time during this critical period, then the remaining harvest is ruined.

The wine that is made from such grapes (and it is only the finest estates that can afford to harvest in successive *tries* – sortings) is astonishing: extremely concentrated (since a first-class vineyard is said only to produce a single glass of wine from each of its vines), luscious, rich and, unlike the famous sweet rivals of Germany, relatively high in alcohol. For it is a magnificent yet delicate balance of residual sweetness and alcoholic strength that makes the great wines of Barsac and

Sauternes so stimulating and euphoric. Moreover, the greatest vintages continue to mature and improve, gaining mellowness and distinction, for decades.

A sign-posted *Route des Grands Crus*, extending through the five communes of Barsac, Bommes, Sauternes, Fargues, and Preignac, leads through gentle and majestic countryside with numerous elegant mansions. Each commune has vineyards that were classified *grands crus* in 1855 (at the same time as the classification of the Médoc). One wine which then as now stands in a class of its own, *grand premier cru*, is the great Château d'Yquem from Sauternes. The splendid twelfth-century edifice of the Château is fitting of such royalty, for it serenely dominates the heart of the wine region from its position atop a hill overlooking the Garonne. First growth *(premiers crus)* châteaux include Coutet and Climens (Barsac), La Tour Blanche, Lafaurie-Peyraguey, Rayne-Vigneau, Rabau-Promis, and Siglas-Rabaud (Bommes), Suduiraut (Preignac), Rieussec (Fargues), and Guiraud (Sauternes). Château de Malle is a well-known second growth in Preignac, an impressive mansion with well-tended Italianate gardens that can be visited.

After touring the Sauternais, continue down to Langon (worth visiting just for the regional restaurant, Claude Darroze). Cross to the right bank of the Garonne where, standing on a rocky outcrop, is another ancient wine town, St-Macaire. The vineyards that extend behind the town bear their own *appellation*, Côtes de Bordeaux St-Macaire, and produce fragrant, gentle white wines. The most famous village in this little-known region is probably Verdelais, for it is here, in the village cemetery, that Toulouse-Lautrec is buried. Continue back to Bordeaux along the river road D10, through the picturesque hilltop wine towns of Ste-Croix-du-Mont (whose ancient wine cellars were dug out of fossilized oyster beds), and to Loupiac. The fourth-century poet Ausonius, incidentally (who is perhaps best commemorated in the region by the *premier grand cru* estate in St Emilion, Château Ausone) is reputed to have had a villa in Loupiac. Both communes produce sweet white wines that resemble their great counterparts across the river. Cadillac is another interesting fortified village, located in the

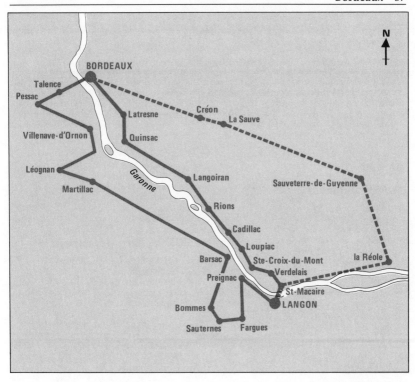

region of Premières Côtes de Bordeaux. Parts of its fourteenth-century ramparts are still intact, and it is dominated by the austere château of the Dukes of Eperon which, usefully, also houses the region's *Maison du Vin*. The narrow road winds its way back to Bordeaux through Rions, Langoiran, Quinsac, and Latresne.

An alternative and most pleasant wine tour explores the lovely country of Entre-Deux-Mers, those lands between the Garonne and Dordogne Rivers. Cross the Garonne at Langon, and head south on the N113 to La Réole, another fortified stronghold, today a busy market town with winding streets lined with old houses that lead up to the twelfth-century town hall, one of the oldest in France. From La Réole, head inland on the N670 to Sauveterre de Guyenne, and then take the N671 through the heart of this gentle rolling land. Only the slopes of the hills are planted with vineyards, for the tops are

thickly forested, while a variety of crops, including tobacco, grows in the valleys. This varied rural landscape, which has none of the imposing grandeur of the château country, produces fine, crisp dry white wine that is still relatively inexpensive.

Follow the road up towards La Sauve, and visit the magnificent ruined abbey of La Sauve-Majeure, once an important stopping place for pilgrims on the long trek to Santiago de Compostella. Créon, further north, is another fortified town worth visiting; but the real attraction of this charming, hilly region lies in turning off main roads onto meandering country lanes, stopping at modest farmhouses to purchase local wine and home-made cheese, or perhaps some locally cured sausage, then picnicking along the road or river, or stopping at a peaceful rural camping site. From here, one can always return to Bordeaux as quickly – or as slowly – as one wishes.

Wine Producers

There are hundreds of producers throughout this prolific wine region who welcome visitors, including some of the finest and most famous estates in the world, as well as small individual farmers who open their premises to the public as a means of selling their product direct. While many properties listed can be visited without an appointment, to avoid disappointment it is advisable to telephone in advance, or to have a visit arranged through one of the region's *Maisons du Vin* (they can also supply fuller lists of producers in their particular region).

Médoc

33290 Blanquefort

Barton & Guestier SA
Château de Dehez
tel: (56) 35 84 41
Mon–Fri 9–12h; 14–17h
Appointment preferable.
English spoken.

33460 Cantenac

Château Prieuré-Lichine
tel: (56) 58 36 28
Daily 9–12h30; 14–19h
English spoken.

33460 Margaux

Château Margaux
tel: (56) 58 40 28
Mon–Fri 9–12h; 14–18h
Appointment necessary.
Max 20 pers.
English spoken.

Château d'Issan
tel: (56) 58 40 72
Mon–Fri 9–12h; 14h30–18h
Appointment preferable and necessary for groups over 10.
English spoken.

Château Lascombes
tel: (56) 88 70 66
Mon–Fri 9h30–12; 14–17h
No visits during vintage.

33480 Moulis

Château Moulin à Vent
tel: (56) 58 15 79
Mon–Fri 8–12h; 14–18h
Appointment necessary only for groups.
English spoken.

33480 Listrac

Clos des Demoiselles
tel: (56) 58 25 12
Mon–Sat 8–12h; 14–19h
English spoken.

33250 St-Julien-Beychevelle

Château Langoa-Léoville Barton
tel: (56) 59 06 05
Mon–Fri 10–12h; 15–17h
Appointment necessary.
English spoken.

33250 Pauillac

Château Mouton Rothschild
tel: (56) 59 22 22
Mon–Fri 9–12h; 14–17h
Appointment necessary in July and to visit wine museum.
Closed August and last week in Dec
Max 25 pers.
English spoken.

Château Latour
tel: (56) 59 00 51
Mon–Fri 9–11h30; 14–17h30
Appointment necessary.
Max 30 pers.
English spoken in summer.

Château Lafite-Rothschild
tel: (56) 59 01 04
By appointment only

La Rose Pauillac (Cave Coopérative)
tel: (56) 59 05 43
Mon–Sat 9–12h; 14–17h
Appointment necessary only for groups.
Max 50 pers.

Château Batailley
tel: (56) 48 57 57
Mon–Fri working hours
Weekends by appointment only.
Max 50 pers.
English spoken.

33250 St-Estèphe

Château Cos d'Estournel
tel: (56) 44 11 37
June–Sept daily except Mon 12h30–18h30
Oct–May Mon–Fri 9–12h; 14–17h
Appointment necessary in winter.
English spoken.
Audio-visual.

33250 St-Seurin-de-Cadourne

Château Lestage-Simon
tel: (56) 59 31 83
Open daily.
English spoken.

Société Coopérative de Vinification
tel: (56) 59 31 28
Mon–Fri 10–11h30; 15–17h
Appointment necessary.
Max 50 pers.

33340 St-Yzans-de-Médoc

Gilbey de Loudenne
tel: (56) 41 15 23
Mon–Fri 9h30–12h; 14–17h
Appointment preferable, but not essential.
Max 50 pers.
English spoken.
There is a small museum of wine-making
and viticultural tools.

Château Sigognac
tel: (56) 41 15 04
Mon–Fri 9h30–12h; 14–17h30
Max 50 pers.
English spoken.

33340 St-Christoly

Château St-Christoly
and Château La Rose St-Bonnet
tel: (56) 41 52 95
Appointment necessary.
Max 10 pers.

St Emilion

33330 St Emilion

Château Ausone
tel: (57) 24 70 94
Mon–Sat 9–12h; 15–17h
Appointment preferable.
Max 20 pers.
English spoken.

Château Beau Sejour Bécot
tel: (57) 24 71 67

Daily 8–12h; 14–18h
Appointment preferable.
Max 30 pers.
English spoken.

Château Canon
tel: (57) 24 70 79
By appointment only.
Max 50 pers.
English spoken.

Château Cheval Blanc
tel: (57) 24 70 70
Mon–Fri 9–11h; 14–17h
Appointment necessary.
Max 10 pers.
English spoken.

Château Bellevue
tel: (57) 74 41 61
Daily 10–18h
Appointment essential.
Max 40 pers.
English spoken.

Château la Gaffeliere
tel: (57) 24 72 15
Mon–Sat 8–12h; 14–19h
Appointment preferable.
Max 10 pers.
English spoken.

Château Haut Sarpe
tel: (56) 24 70 98
Mon–Sat 8–12h; 14–18h
Appointment preferable.
Closed holidays.
Max 100 pers.
English spoken.

Château Belair
tel: (57) 24 70 94
Daily 9–12h; 15–17h
Appointment preferable.
Max 20 pers.
English spoken.

Château Troplong-Mondot
tel: (57) 24 70 72
Mon–Fri 8–19h
Appointment preferable.
Max 50 pers.
English spoken.

Pomerol

33500 Pomerol

Château Beauregard
tel: (57) 51 13 36
Mon, Wed, Fri 15–17h
Appointment essential.
Max 15 pers.
A little English spoken.

Château Petit-Village
tel: (56) 44 11 37
Open working hours Mon–Fri.
Appointment preferable.

Vieux Château Certan
tel: (57) 51 17 59
Mon–Fri 9–12h; 14–18h
Appointment preferable.
Max 40 pers.
A little English spoken.

Graves

33600 Pessac

Château Haut-Brion
Domaine Clarence Dillon SA
135, avenue Jean Jaurès
tel: (56) 98 33 73
Mon–Fri 9–11h; 14–17h
Appointment essential.
Max 8 pers.
English spoken.

Sauternes, Barsac and the right bank of the Garonne

33210 Sauternes

Château Filhot
tel: (56) 62 61 09
Daily 8h30–18h30
Except holidays.

33720 Barsac

Château Simon
tel: (56) 27 15 35
Mon–Fri 8–12h; 14–18h

Château Caillou
tel: (56) 27 16 38
Mon–Fri 9–12h; 14–18h
Appointment preferable.
Min 5/max 60 pers.
Dinner can be arranged if given
one month's notice.
English spoken.

33210 Preignac

Château de Malle
tel: (56) 63 28 67
17th-century château with Italianate
gardens.
Open Easter–mid Oct daily except Wed
15–19h
English spoken.
Charge for *dégustation*.

Cadillac, Loupiac, and Ste-Croix-du-Mont

Château Balot
Montprimblanc
tel: (56) 27 06 03
Open weekdays

Château la Bertrande
Omet
tel: (56) 27 06 57
Open daily

Domaine de Chasse Pierre
Cadillac
tel: (56) 27 12 72
Open daily

Château Vertheuil
Ste-Croix-du-Mont
tel: (56) 63 71 52
By appointment only

Château du Biac
Haut-Langoiran
Langoiran
tel: (56) 67 19 92
Open every afternoon except Sat

Château Rondillon
Clos Jean
Loupiac
tel: (56) 27 03 11
Mon–Fri 10–12h; 16–19h

Château Mazarin
Loupiac
tel: (56) 27 03 02
Appointment preferable.
Wine museum.
Meals can be arranged in *chais* for groups
of 60–70 people.
English spoken.

Maisons du Vin

The *Maison du Vin* in Bordeaux is the main centre for information and promotion of the region's wines. Maps, addresses, and much other useful literature is available, and appointments can be arranged at numerous properties. The smaller local *Maisons* serve the same purpose and in some cases offer a wide range of wines from their particular region or sub-region for sale.

Maison du Vin de Bordeaux
1, cours du XXX Juillet
33000 Bordeaux
tel: (50) 44 37 82

Maison du Vin de Margaux
place la Trémoille
33460 Margaux
tel: (56) 58 40 82
Daily 9–12h; 14–18h
Except Sun; Mon morning

Maison du Vin de Pauillac
Quai Ferchaud
33250 Pauillac
tel: (56) 59 01 91
Open June–September
Daily 8h30–12h30; 14–18h

Maison du Vin de St-Estèphe
place de l'Église
St-Estèphe
33250 Pauillac
tel: (56) 59 30 59
Daily 10–12h; 14–18h30
Audio-visual presentation

Maison du Vin de St Emilion
place Pierre Meyrat
33330 St Emilion
tel: (56) 51 72 17

Maison du Vin de Sauternes
Château des Ducs d'Epernon
33410 Cadillac
tel: (56) 62 01 38

Wine Festivals

January 18th	Fête du St Vincent	Fairs throughout the Médoc and Graves celebrating the patron saint of wine growers
May 21st	Wine Festival	Montagne-St-Emilion
end of May, beginning of June	Grand Chapître	Pomerol
1st week of June	Chapître de Printemps	Guyenne
June 14th	Fête de la Fleur	St Emilion
3rd week in June	Fête de la Fleur	Loupiac
June 19th	Fête de la Fleur	Villages throughout the Médoc and Graves
June 19th	Wine Festival	Ste-Croix-du-Mont
Sept 12th	Grand Chapître	Bordeaux
Sept 12th	Chapître	Fronsac
Sept 18th	Ban des Vendanges	Villages throughout the Médoc and Graves
Sept 19th	Ban des Vendanges	St Emilion
Nov 20th	Chapître d'Automne	Guyenne

For exact dates (since they sometimes vary from year to year) contact:

Conseil Interprofessionnel du Vin de Bordeaux
1, cours du XXX Juillet
33000 Bordeaux
tel: (56) 44 37 82

Wine Courses and Seminars

Wine courses are arranged by 'Bordeaux Wine Tours' for both the wine professional and amateur. These range from one day excursions to seven day tours, from in-depth studies of vine cultivation and vinification methods, to leisurely tours of châteaux highlighted by gourmet dinners and wine tastings. For full details contact:

'Bordeaux Wine Tours'
12, place de la Bourse
33076 Bordeaux
tel: (56) 90 91 28

The *Institut International des Vins et Spiritueux* also run week long courses with seminars, tastings, and visits to the principal châteaux in each region. For further information contact:

Institut International des Vins et Spiritueux
10, place de la Bourse
33076 Bordeaux

The *Maison du Tourisme* in Bordeaux arranges day trips to the various wine regions, and offers cassette hire in English for 'guided' tours of North Médoc, South Médoc, Sauternais, and St Emilion. For further information contact:

Maison du Tourisme
12, cours du XXX Juillet
33000 Bordeaux
tel: (56) 44 28 41

The *Hôtel des Vins* not only sells a wide variety of wine and wine accessories, it also offers wine tastings given in English (with bread and cheese); lectures (accompanied by audio-visual presentation); and seminars. For further information contact:

Hôtel des Vins
106, rue Abbé de l'Épée
33000 Bordeaux
tel: (56) 48 01 29

The University of Bordeaux has an *Institut d'Oenologie* for serious students of wine and viticulture. Contact:

L'Institut d'Oenologie
351, cours de la Libération
33405 Talence
Bordeaux
tel: (56) 80 77 91

Regional Gastronomy

Foie gras Fattened goose liver, infused with pungent truffles from Périgord.

Huîtres Oysters from the Arcachon basin, eaten raw on the half-shell, or chilled with hot, piquant sausages; delicious with white Graves or Entre-Deux-Mers.

Jambon de Bayonne From the Basque country, an air-dried ham served in razor-thin slices.

Tourin Onion soup enriched with egg yolks.

Moules à la Bassin Mussels from Arcachon, often steamed in white wine, shallots, and parsley, and eaten like soup.

Lou kencous Piquant little sausages served hot with chilled oysters.

Escargots bordelaises Plump snails stewed with chopped pork, garlic, shallots, and red wine.

Lamproie A rare delicacy: lamprey from the Gironde stewed in red wine with leeks, shallots, and wild mushrooms.

Cèpes à la bordelaise The wild *boletus* mushroom stewed in farmhouse butter, shallots, lemon juice, and parsley.

Rognons à la bordelaise Calves' kidneys cooked with red wine and mushrooms.

Daube Local casserole of beef cooked in goose fat.

Entrecôte aux sarments After the harvest, the vines are pruned in preparation for winter; this typical speciality consists of an entrecôte steak grilled over the pruned vine shoots, which impart a delicious characteristic taste to the meat.

Entrecôte à la bordelaise Entrecôte steak served with a special sauce of shallots, bone marrow, and red wine.

Alose Shad, locally prepared by wrapping the fish in a moist blanket of vine or laurel leaves, cooking it over an open fire of *sarments*, and dressing it with tarragon vinegar and oil.

L'agneau de Pauillac Baby lamb raised on the salt marshes of the Médoc.

Macarons de St Emilion Macaroons.

Restaurants

33800 Bordeaux

Dubern
42, allées de Tourny
tel: (56) 48 03 44
Elegant cuisine in Louis XV surroundings.
Closed Sat eve; Sun
Open 12–14h; 20–22h
Expensive

Restaurant Clavel
44, rue Charles-Domercq
tel: (56) 92 91 52
Sophisticated regional specialities such as
*gratin d'huîtres au foie gras, feuilleté
d'escargots Girondine, aiguillettes de canard au
miel et citron*, accompanied by an extensive
wine list.
Closed Sun eve; Mon
Expensive

Plantié
401, boulevard du Président-Wilson
tel: (56) 08 76 59
Closed Sat
Inexpensive to **Moderate**

33250 Pauillac

Le Relais du Manoir (Hôtel-Rest.)
route de la Shell
tel: (56) 59 05 47
Every weekend there is a *menu de la mer
et fruits de mer*; also other interesting
regional dishes, and excellent selection of
cheeses.
Closed Sun eve; Mon out of season
Inexpensive

33112 Saint-Laurent-de-Médoc

Hôtel-Restaurant de la Renaissance
tel: (56) 59 40 29
Bordelaise cooking and personal service.
Closed Fri eve
Inexpensive

33460 Lamarque

Relais du Médoc
Grand-Rue
tel: (56) 58 92 27
Family style restaurant with local
specialities such as *escargots bordelaise,
magret de canard, entrecôte bordelaise*.
Closed Mon
Inexpensive
Accommodation also available.

33330 St Emilion

Logis de la Cadène
place du Marché-au-Bois
tel: (57) 24 71 40
Bordelaise specialities are served in this
Inexpensive to **Moderate** restaurant
located in the heart of the medieval town,
including *lamproie à la bordelaise, grillades
aux sarments, foie gras*.
Closed Mon. Open lunchtimes only

Restaurant Chez Germaine
place Clocher
tel: (57) 24 70 88
Above the Église Monolithe, this
well-known, locally popular restaurant
serves regional dishes such as *lamproie, foie
gras, entrecôte bordelaise*, and *anguilles*.
Closed Nov 1–Jan 15; Sun eve; Mon
Open 12h15–14h; 19h30–21h
Moderate

33500 Libourne

L'Étrier
20 place Decazes
tel: (57) 51 13 59
Regional specialities accompany an
extensive list of wines from the Libournais.
Moderate
Closed Mon

33720 Barsac

Hostellerie Château de Rolland
tel: (56) 27 15 75
Inexpensive
Open daily

33210 Sauternes

Auberge 'Les Vignes'
place de l'Église
tel: (56) 63 60 06
Meats are grilled over vine shoots on an
open fire in the dining room of this
charming *auberge*.
Closed Mon
Inexpensive

33210 Preignac

Restaurant 'Du Cap'
tel: (56) 63 27 38
Comfortable regional restaurant with
terrace directly over the Garonne.
Closed Mon; October
Open 12–14h; 19h30–21h30
Moderate

33210 Langon

Restaurant Claude Darroze
95, cours du Général-Leclerc
tel: (56) 63 00 48
Well-known and popular restaurant
serving fish and game in season,
accompanied by a wide choice of wines,
particularly those of Graves and
Sauternes.
Closed Oct
Expensive

33420 St-Jean-de-Blaignac

Auberge St-Jean
tel: (56) 84 51 06
Choice of five menus ranging from simple
to gargantuan.
Closed Sun eve; Mon; Jan 1–15; Sept 15–30
Moderate to **Expensive**

Hotels

33800 Bordeaux

Frantel
5, rue Robert-Lateulade
tel: (56) 90 92 37
Just a few minutes walk from St-André
Cathedral. All 196 rooms have bathroom
and air-conditioning. 'Le Meriadec' serves
regional food; 'Le Sarment' is a grill room.
Hotel **Expensive**
Restaurants **Moderate**

Hôtel Royal Médoc
3–5, rue de Sèze
tel: (56) 81 87 51
Centrally located off the allées de Tourny,
a **Moderate** modern hotel, without
restaurant.
Open all year.

Mapotel Terminus
Gare St-Jean
tel: (56) 92 71 58
Grand facade and 90 comfortable,
well-equipped bedrooms, plus a
restaurant serving traditional and local
specialities.
Open all year.
Hotel **Expensive**
Restaurant **Moderate**

Hôtel de Normandie
7–9, cours XXX Juillet
tel: (56) 52 16 80
Centrally located, but without restaurant.
Open all year.
Inexpensive to **Moderate**

Hôtel Majestic
2, rue de Condé
tel: (56) 52 60 44
Modern, comfortable, and quiet, without
restaurant.
Open all year.
Inexpensive to **Moderate**

Hôtel Arcade
60, rue Eugène-le-Roy
tel: (56) 90 92 40
Inexpensive hotel in centre of town with
restaurant.
Open all year.
Restaurant closed Sat eve; Sun;
Open 12–14h; 19–22h

Hôtel Sofitel
Parc des Expositions (exhibition centre
north of town)
tel: (56) 50 90 14
Swimming pool, tennis courts; dinner on
the terrace in fine weather, with regional
specialities, and fresh fish. Open all year.
Expensive

33600 Pessac

La Réserve
74, avenue du Bourgailh
tel: (56) 07 13 28
In the direction of Arcachon, with tennis
courts and restaurant serving *confit de
canard*, and *grillades*.
Hotel closed Dec 20–Jan 10. Restaurant
closed Sat in winter
Expensive

33480 Listrac

Hôtel de France
tel: (56) 58 23 68
Small family hotel with **Inexpensive**
restaurant serving specialities such as
grillades aux sarments, and *confit de canard*.
Restaurant open daily 12–14h; 19h30–22h

33500 Libourne

Hôtel Loubat
32, rue Chanzy
tel: (57) 51 17 58
An **Inexpensive** to **Moderate** hotel with
restaurant serving regional specialities,
together with a good selection of wines
from Pomerol and St Emilion.
Open daily.

33330 St Emilion

Auberge de la Commanderie
rue des Cordeliers
tel: (57) 24 70 19

Well-loved by local vignerons, a comfortable hotel with restaurant serving local dishes such as *cèpes, lamproie, entrecôte à la bordelaise, confits de canard.*
Hotel closed Nov 20–Jan 1
Restaurant open daily
Inexpensive to **Moderate**

Hostellerie de Plaisance
place du Clocher
tel: (57) 24 72 32
Near the medieval church with terraces and gardens overlooking town and vineyards. Hotel with 12 individually furnished rooms and restaurant with extensive cellar of St Emilion vintages.
Expensive

33390 Blaye

Hôtel-Rest. 'La Citadelle'
tel: (56) 42 17 10
Hotel with swimming pool and restaurant serving *nouvelle cuisine* accompanied by wines from Côtes de Blaye.
Open all year
Inexpensive to **Moderate**

Camping

Bordeaux

Pessac
Camping Bellegrave
avenue du Docteur Narcam
tel: (56) 45 50 68
Merignac
Camping Cemin Long
108, rue Henri Vigneau, tel: (56) 34 07 58
Villenave d'Ornon
Camping Les Gravières, tel: (56) 87 50 68

Médoc Beaches

Soulac
Camping Les Arros, tel: (56) 59 82 75
Hourtin
Camping La Côte d'Argent
tel: (56) 41 60 25
Camping La Mariflaude, tel: (56) 41 61 97
Lacanau Océan
Airotel de l'Océan, tel: (56) 60 22 60
Carcans
Camping l'Océan, tel: (56) 60 31 16
Blanquefort (off Route des Châteaux)
Camping 'Le Peybois', tel: (56) 35 16 72

Libournais

Fronsac
Camping du Fronsadais, tel: (56) 51 31 33

Where to Get Additional Information

Syndicat d'Initiative de Bordeaux
12, cours du XXX-Juillet
33800 Bordeaux
tel: (56) 44 28 41

Syndicat d'Initiative de St Emilion et du Relais Touristique Départemental,
'Le Doyenne'
place des Créneaux
33330 St Emilion
tel: (57) 24 72 03

Conseil Interprofessionnel du Vin de Bordeaux
1, cours du XXX-Juillet
33800 Bordeaux
tel: (56) 44 37 82

Libourne
Camping Le Ruste, tel: (56) 51 01 54
St Emilion
Camping La Barbanne, tel: (57) 24 75 80

South of Bordeaux

Langon
Camp Municipal
Sadirac (Entre-Deux-Mers)
Camping 'Bel Air', tel: (56) 21 01 90

North of Bordeaux

Ambares
Camping 'Clos Chauvet', tel: (56) 06 81 08
Bourg
Camping La Citadelle, tel: (56) 68 40 06
Gauriac (near Bourg)
Camp Municipal, tel: (56) 42 06 08

Bibliography

The Wines of Bordeaux by Edmund Penning-Rowsell, Scribner 1981
Monarch Guide to the Wines of Bordeaux by Pamela Vandyke Price, Monarch Press 1978
The Wines of France by Cyril Ray, Penguin 1978
Côte de l'Atlantique Michelin Green Guide (French only)
World Atlas of Wine by Hugh Johnson, Simon & Schuster 1978

BURGUNDY

Rich, smug Burgundy: an historic, varied region with a series of wine roads
through both some of the world's most famous vineyards, as well as through
majestic and ruggedly beautiful country; numerous *caveaux de dégustation* to
refresh the thirsty; a renowned, unrivalled regional cuisine offered in grand
and humble restaurants alike; history – and prehistory – around every corner,
in every village, church, abbey, or château; a land of festivals that celebrate the
best things in life; an everchanging landscape that varies from the ordered, élite
vineyards of the Côte d'Or to the rugged, stumpy hills of Beaujolais, the flat,
verdant valley of the Saône to the majestic, unspoiled forests of the Morvan.

Conquered by Caesar in 52 BC, invaded by the Burgundians (who gave the
region its name) and then by the Franks in the sixth century, Burgundy has
always played an important and powerful role in French history. In the
fourteenth and fifteenth centuries, under the Dukes of Valois, a Burgundian
Empire extended as far as Belgium and the Netherlands. Dijon, capital of the
region, was an enlightened centre for the arts and culture. Elsewhere, at
Cluny, one of the most influential and wealthy abbeys in all of Christendom
wielded extensive power, involved in intrigue and political struggle,
flourished, and eventually declined, leaving only its bleached, Romanesque
skeleton, mute testimony of former prowess and prosperity.

Yet today Burgundy prospers still, a region with more than her fair share of
abundant resources. Wine lovers, of course, come to traverse a slender,
hallowed slope – the Côte d'Or – the names of whose villages read like the
leather-bound pages of an exclusive vintner's list: Gevrey-Chambertin,
Morey-St-Denis, Vosne-Romanée, Nuits-St-Georges, Aloxe-Corton, Pommard,
Volnay, Meursault. Yet wine is by no means Burgundy's only famous gastronomic asset. The Charolles region produces the finest breed of cattle in France,
the white Charollais. Chickens from Bresse claim an *appellation contrôlée* no less
stringent than the region's finest wines. The many rivers and lakes are para-
dise for the fisherman, yielding numerous freshwater varieties such as pike,
perch, tench, trout, and river eel, while the dense forests of the Morvan are
well-stocked with game, and also the source of pungent wild mushrooms
and valuable truffles. Such ingredients result in a magnificent local cuisine that
accompanies the region's finest – as well as its everyday – wines admirably.

Though Burgundy is rich and famous, it is a wonderful surprise to discover
that her most.famous wine villages, some no more than mere hamlets, are not
imposing in the least. Few châteaux, few grand properties shout their worth to
the world from amidst the prized vineyards. Dijon, certainly, as well as
Beaune, capital of the wine trade, with its distinctive, outlandish Hôtel-Dieu,

How to Get There

By Car
Burgundy lies along a main north–south route that runs from Paris, through Dijon and Mâcon, to Lyons and eventually to Marseilles, via the A6 and A7 autoroutes. From Paris, take the A6 autoroute, then turn off at Auxerre onto D965 for Chablis. After touring the Yonne, either continue south on the N6 (stopping to tour Avallon and Auxerre), or else carry on to Dijon via Tonnerre and Montbard, following the picturesque Canal de Bourgogne.

An alternative route, for those with time, follows the N6 south all the way from Paris, through Fontainebleau, Auxerre, and Avallon. Turn off on D70 to reach Dijon, or else continue south to Chagny, and either tour north to Beaune and Dijon, or south to Chalon-sur-Saône, Mâcon, and the Beaujolais.

From Calais and Boulogne, take the N43 to Arras and join the A1 autoroute south to Paris. From Paris, either join the A6, or the N6 routes described above. A wine tour of the Yonne (Chablis) can be conveniently combined with a wine tour of the Upper Loire (Sancerre and Pouilly), as well as with time spent relaxing in the forests of the Morvan.

By Plane
The main French international airport is at Paris. Air Inter, the French internal airline, flies from Paris to Dijon and Lyons. There are also direct flights from London to Lyons and Dijon.

By Train
Burgundy is well served by trains since it is on the main Paris–Marseilles route, as well as on routes to Italy and Switzerland. The main station for direct trains is Dijon, though many trains do stop in Mâcon as well. The TEE trains from Paris to Milan stop in Dijon, and take only two and a half hours to do the journey; the new high speed electric trains from Paris to Dijon enable a day trip to be made to Burgundy from the capital.

Local Public Transport
Dijon, Beaune, Chagny, Chalon-sur-Saône, Mâcon, and Villefranche-sur-Saône are all located along the same local rail line, with frequent trains running between them daily.

Burgundy's 2000 miles of canals also so provide a delightful way of seeing the country. *Locaboat Plaisance* run round-trip and one-way cruises from Joigny which lead to Auxerre, Tonnere, Dijon, and many other places. For further information contact:

Locaboat Plaisance
Quai du Port du Bois
89300 Joigny
tel: (86) 62 06 14

Illuminated round-trips of the Côte de Nuits and the Côte de Beaune in luxury coaches are offered from Dijon and Beaune throughout the summer months. The tour lasts two and half hours, and passes by illuminated villages, castles, and vineyards, as well as including visits to cellars with wine-tasting opportunities. The Côtes de Nuits trip leaves from Dijon town hall Mon–Sat; July 1–Aug 31 at 21h30; Sept 1–Oct 16 at 21h. The Côte de Beaune trip leaves from Beaune tourist office, Tues, Thurs, Sat; July 1–Aug 31 at 21h30; Sept 1–Sept 18 at 21h. For further information contact tourist offices in Dijon and Beaune.

Car Rental Information
Dijon
   Avis: 5, avenue Maréchal Foch
      tel: (80) 43 60 67
  Hertz: 18, bis avenue Foch
      tel: (80) 43 55 22
      Dijon airport
      tel: (80) 43 40 79
Beaune
   Avis: 135, bis Route de Dijon
      tel: (80) 22 27 00
Mâcon
   Avis: 23, avenue Edouard Herriot
      tel: (85) 38 68 75
  Hertz: 77, rue Victor Hugo
      tel: (85) 38 63 22
      Mâcon airport
      tel: (85) 38 63 22
Chalon-sur-Saône
   Avis: 49, avenue de Paris
      tel: (85) 48 85 75
  Hertz: 2a, avenue Boucicaut
      tel: (85) 43 08 88

Michelin Maps 65, 66, 69, 70, 73, 74

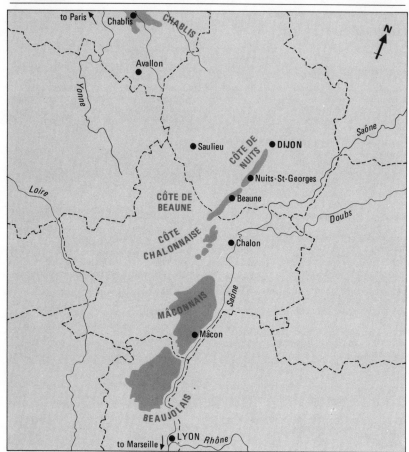

share a smug, self-satisfied sense of their own worth. Elsewhere, in busy little Chablis, in Mâcon, or in isolated villages set amidst the rugged hills of Beaujolais, one is aware of a deep-abiding, hard-working pride in craftsmanship, and centuries-old traditions still very much alive.

Burgundy is timeless. Throughout, one is aware of the past, whether strolling the narrow, winding streets of Vézelay and fortified Avallon, or listening to echoing footsteps in austere Fontenay, the perfectly restored twelfth-century abbey founded by Bernard of Clairvaux. Autun and Auxerre are former Roman towns, while the remains of prehistoric man have been found near Solutré, and in the grottoes of Arcy-sur-Cure. In ancient days, the main trade route from the north passed through Burgundy, en route to Rome. Today an army of holidaymakers, following in the footsteps of Caesar's legions, troop down the A6 and A7 to the South of France, some hardly noticing this rich but unobvious region in their eagerness. Let them pass. For us, Burgundy will always be a region to linger in, not to race through.

The Wines of Burgundy

The Burgundian vineyard is comprised of five distinct regions: Chablis, Côte d'Or, Côte Chalonnaise, the Mâconnais, and the Beaujolais. The following is a broad guideline only; for detailed assessments of vineyards and vintages, consult the books listed in the Bibliography.

General appellations Bourgogne Ordinaire, Bourgogne Grand Ordinaire, and Bourgogne are broad general *appellations* which can apply to red and white wines produced throughout the delimited Burgundian vineyard from permitted grape varieties conforming to certain strictures, including maximum yields per hectare and minimum alcohol strength. Bourgogne Passe-Tout-Grains is red wine produced from a mixture of Gamay, favoured grape of Beaujolais, and Pinot Noir, the aristocrat that produces the finest wines of the Côte d'Or. Bourgogne Aligoté, similarly, is white wine produced from the lesser Aligoté, not the noble Chardonnay. Wines produced from grapes grown on the higher, more rugged and less intensive reaches of the Côte d'Or, if approved, may be entitled to the *appellation* Bourgogne Hautes-Côtes de Beaune, or Bourgogne Hautes-Côtes de Nuits. Bourgogne Rosé and Bourgogne Clairet are the general *appellations* for the small quantities of pink wine produced in the region, while Crémant de Bourgogne is sparkling Burgundy produced by the *méthode champenoise*.

Village or commune appellations Many Burgundian wine villages or communes give their names to wines produced from grapes grown within a nearby or surrounding delimited area. Thus, it is possible to purchase a bottle of Chablis (named after the town in the Yonne), Mâcon (capital of the Mâconnais), Beaune or Nuits-St-Georges (both important wine towns in the Côte d'Or). The rationale behind such village or communal *appellations* is that each village or commune has a general but distinct and recognizable character which should be apparent in its wines. Indeed, the reliable *négociant-éleveur*, in his cellars in Beaune, Mâcon, or elsewhere, blends wines from various vineyards from within a particular commune to 'elevate' the end product to his firm's conception of the classic wine of that village or commune. Confusingly, many Burgundian villages have hyphenated the name of their most famous individual vineyard to the name of the village itself. Thus, there is a world of difference between wine from the commune of Gevrey-Chambertin, for example, and wine from Le Chambertin, one of the region's finest and most famous *grands crus*.

Premiers and Grands Crus As in most French wine regions, the greatest wines pinpoint their exact origin down to not only a specific commune, but to an individual vineyard. In Burgundy such individual vineyards are called *climats* and there are several hundred throughout the region. Exceptional vineyards have been designated *premiers crus*, while the finest are known as *grands crus*. The rules governing such designations are rather complicated, but broadly speaking, the *premiers crus* can affix their *climat* name to the village *appellation* along with the designation 'Premier Cru' (for example, Gevrey-Chambertin Clos des Véroilles Premier Cru AC). For the greatest wines – the *grands crus* – however, the vineyard name alone stands as the *appellation*, as in Le Chambertin, Musigny, Clos de Vougeot, Corton-Charlemagne, Montrachet, and others. One important additional point: whereas in Bordeaux the finest *grands crus* (the term, confusingly, is not used in the same sense in both regions – see pp. 28–30) are the product of one château only, in Burgundy, many vineyards were fragmented into numerous parcels after the French Revolution (those few which are owned or controlled by a single proprietor are known as *monopoles*); thus, both the style and the quality of even the region's finest wines can and does vary between its various proprietors.

Route des Grands Crus

The following is a broad guideline to the principal wines:

Chablis Elegant, firm, dry white wine produced from Chardonnay grape around town of Chablis. Specified *premier cru* and *grand cru* vineyards, as well as a lesser wine designated Petit Chablis. While the name 'chablis' has been abused in other wine-producing countries, it remains the epitome of a classic French white dinner wine.

Côte d'Or The 'heart' of Burgundy, and the area from where both the finest red and finest white wines come. Made up of two regions, the Côte de Nuits, extending from south of Dijon down to Corgoloin, and the Côte de Beaune, which begins north of Beaune, and extends to south of Chagny. Though both red and white wines are produced in each, the Côte de Nuits is most famous for vigorous, graceful red wines from communes such as Gevrey-Chambertin, Morey-St-Denis, Chambolle-Musigny, Vougeot, Vosne-Romanée, and Nuits-St-Georges. The Côte de Beaune produces both distinguished red wines from Aloxe-Corton, Beaune, Pommard, and Volnay, as well as magnificent and famous white wines from Meursault, Puligny-Montrachet, and Chassagne-Montrachet.

Côte Chalonnaise Red and white wines produced from vineyards growing on hills south of the Côte d'Or around communes such as Rully, Mercurey, Givry, and Montagny.

Mâconnais Southern vineyards which rise from the town of Mâcon both to the north, and to the south, producing large quantities of solid red wine from the Gamay and Pinot Noir grapes, as well as firm, fresh whites. The finest white wines of the region come from vineyards which cover the limestone slopes of Solutré and Vergisson, around intimate communes such as Pouilly-Fuissé, Pouilly-Vinzelles, Pouilly-Loché, and St-Véran.

Beaujolais The southernmost region of Burgundy, famous for light (and light-hearted) gulpable wine produced from the Gamay grape. Youngest wines are sold as *primeur* just weeks after the vintage, though longer-lived examples come from communes located on the granite hills in the north of this surprisingly large region, and are entitled to the *appellation* Beaujolais-Villages. In addition, nine communes that consistently produce wines with more character and body are entitled to their own *appellation*: Morgon, Chénas, Fleurie, St-Amour, Moulin-à-Vent, Chiroubles, Brouilly, Juliénas, and Côte de Brouilly.

Marc de Bourgogne An eau-de-vie produced from distilling the *marc* (skins and pips left over after the grapes have been pressed). This fiery, pungent caramel-coloured spirit is popular as a local drink, and is also useful in the kitchen.

Crème de Cassis A blackcurrant liqueur produced in Dijon. When mixed with Bourgogne Aligoté it becomes the region's favourite aperitif: Kir (named after a mayor of Dijon).

— *The Wine Roads of Burgundy* —
Chablis and the Yonne Valley

If travelling from the north, the first vineyards of Burgundy are encountered near Avallon, those of Chablis and the Yonne Valley. Some 90 km or so separate this tiny but prestigious 'wine island' from the rest of the region. Indeed, it seems to stand apart, away from the hullabaloo of the Côte d'Or, and the well-travelled paths between Dijon and Lyons. Little Chablis dozes in the placid lap of Le Serein – the serene – Valley, below the rolling slopes upon which lie her famous vineyards. Her wine roads extend like spokes on a wheel into these rounded and beautiful hills. A

brief tour can be made into the vineyards as follows:

From Chablis, cross the Serein River, and immediately turn left on the D91, a small road which leads to the finest vineyards immediately north-east of the town. The soil of these south-facing slopes consists of Kimmeridgian clay, rich in calcium and prehistoric fossils – so loved by the noble Chardonnay – which give the finest wines their characteristic flinty, crisp flavour and bouquet. The region's seven *grands crus* all lie side by side on this distinguished slope: Bougros, Les Preuses,

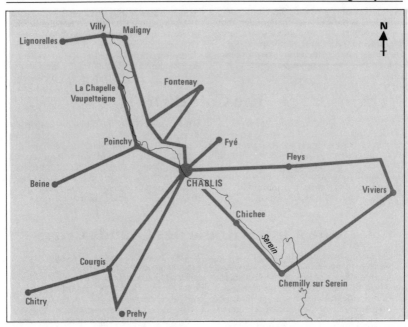

Vaudésir, Les Clos, Grenouilles, Valmur, Blanchot. Consistency (or lack of it) is a key factor throughout Burgundy, and other wine regions, too, since the finest wines are always produced where the vine has to struggle against nature. In Chablis, the great enemy has always been frost. These finest vineyards, however, protect the fragile vines either by warming the cool, damp spring air with propane heaters (a ruinously expensive operation), or else by the use of a sprinkling system that pumps water from a nearby artificial lake. By spraying the vines, ice forms on the buds and protects them from the freezing temperatures.

The D91 continues up the Serein Valley, past *premier cru* vineyards like the distinguished Fourchaume, as well as by vineyards that produce basic Chablis and the lesser Petit Chablis. At Maligny, cross the river on D35 to Villy, and continue further on to Lignorelles. These little hamlets, some with no more than a few hundred inhabitants, are the essential, unchanging wine communities of Chablis. In all, wine can be tasted and purchased directly from any number of proprietors. The premises of a small Petit Chablis producer in such outlying communities

may seem a far cry from the well-organized cellars of *négociants* in Beaune.

Return to Villy, and turn right on the D131 to La Chapelle Vaupelteigne, an ancient village with Roman ruins and a tenth-century chapel, and, further in the direction of Chablis, the important wine community of Poinchy, which clusters around its twelfth-century château. Poinchy boasts three *premiers crus*: Beauroy, Fourchaume, and Vaulorent. From Poinchy, the N65 passes through more vineyards, and the commune of Beine (recognizable by the slender spire of the church of Notre-Dame).

A pocket of fine *premiers crus* lie to the south (Mélinots, Montmains, Vaillons, and others). The D62, skirting these vineyards, passes through Courgis, and so on to the tiny wine village of Chitry. Though there is little break in the vine-covered hills, Chitry actually marks the beginning of the vineyards of the Yonne Valley. A rectangular detour can be made through St-Bris-le-Vineux, Coulanges-la-Vineuse, and Irancy. Bourgogne Irancy, a light fragrant red wine, is one of the best of the Yonne Valley. Excellent white Aligoté is also produced here, in addition to a VDQS *(vin*

delimité de qualité supèrieur) Sauvignon de
St-Bris. This reminds us, incidentally, that
these northern Burgundian vineyards are
not far from the great wine communes of
the Upper Loire, which produce pungent
and renowned Sauvignon wines at
Sancerre and Pouilly-sur-Loire.

After touring Chablis and the vineyards
of the Yonne, either continue to Dijon via
Tonnerre, or else make a detour to visit the
charming, fortified medieval villages of
Avallon and Vézelay.

The Côte d'Or

The Côte d'Or – golden slope – is but a
slender strip of gently undulating, quite
unexceptional-looking land. And yet here
are found, possibly, the finest vineyards in
the world, producing not simply rich,
full-bodied, long-lasting red wines of great
renown but also compact, profound,
highly scented – and highly expensive –
white wines. The Côte d'Or consists of two
rival sections: the Côte de Nuits, extending
virtually from the outskirts of Dijon to
communes just beyond Nuits-St-Georges,
and the Côte de Beaune, which continues
south from Aloxe-Corton through Beaune
itself – one of the premier wine towns in
the world – to below Santenay.

Côte de Nuits – Route des Grands Crus

The *Route des Grands Crus* lives up to its
name, passing by and sometimes actually
through, some of the greatest vineyards in
the world. In itself, however, we confess
that it is a trifle dull, for this single-minded
country has none of the beauty or drama of
either the Hautes Côtes de Beaune or the
rugged Beaujolais to the south. A journey
over these hallowed slopes is, nevertheless, one of the wine lovers' great
pilgrimages.

Take the N74 south out of Dijon to find
the start of the *Route des Grands Crus* at
Chenôve. Chenôve today is hardly more
than a suburb of Dijon; indeed, an
important vineyard region known as the
Côte de Dijon used to extend around the
capital, but today has been swallowed by
ever-expanding development. One relic
from that former time remains: an
enormous thirteenth-century wooden
wine press, said to be that of the Dukes of
Burgundy. After Chenôve a small road,
the D122, rises into the low, gentle range
of hills upon which lie the finest
vineyards. This leads next to the town of
Marsannay-la-Côte, which produces
Burgundy's best rosé, entitled to its own
appellation Bourgogne Rosé Marsannay.
These vineyards, like the pretty pink wine
itself, are but a prelude to those that
follow. Fixin is the first great commune on
the *Route des Grands Crus*, a picturesque
village with a quaint circular washhouse
and, in Noisot Park behind the village, a
famous statue called the Emperor's
Awakening (Napoleon was particularly
fond of the great wines of the Côte de
Nuits – he would probably be quite happy
to reawake here within arm's reach of his
beloved Chambertin). The finest vineyards
in Fixin are La Perrière, Clos du Chapître,
and Les Hervelets.

The town of Gevrey comes next; like so
many others, it has hyphenated the name
of its finest vineyard to the name of the
commune. Despite its obvious fame,
Gevrey-Chambertin remains quiet and
unassuming. Its grey stone houses sit
behind impenetrable stone walls, and it is
virtually empty at lunchtime. Though the
vineyards of Gevrey produce undoubtedly
some of the world's most prestigious
wines, there is no air of affluence or
ostentation here – just a self-satisfaction
that comes from the smug knowledge of its
own worth. And if the town square is
deserted at midday, a warm welcome and
an excellent meal are always available at
such fine restaurants as La Rôtisserie,
Le Chambertin and Clos de Bèze are
the commune's two *grands crus*;
other outstanding *climats* include
Charmes-Chambertin, Griotte-
Chambertin, Mazoyères-Chambertin,
Chapelle-Chambertin,
Latricières-Chambertin,
Mazis-Chambertin, and
Ruchottes-Chambertin.

Morey-St-Denis is as unpretentious, as
charming as its neighbour. A nunnery was
founded here in the seventh century, and
like the Cistercian monks at nearby
Vougeot, those devoted servants of God
found that the sparse, stony ground would
support little else but vines. Thus the Clos

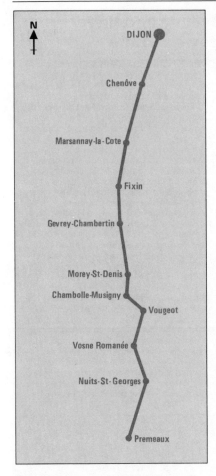

N

DIJON

Chenôve

Marsannay-la-Cote

Fixin

Gevrey-Chambertin

Morey-St-Denis

Chambolle-Musigny

Vougeot

Vosne Romanée

Nuits-St-Georges

Premeaux

descends to meet the N74 at Vougeot, a town dominated by its walled and most famous vineyard, the Clos de Vougeot. So famous, so loved are the wines made from this vast, fragmented 125-acre plot that for generations passing regiments of the French Army have been ordered to stop and salute the vines themselves (typical French *hauteur!*). The Cistercian order was founded out of disillusion with the luxury-loving secular way of life at wealthy Cluny; indeed, the Cistercians who settled here had a self-sacrificing task cultivating this miserable, shifting stony ground. Yet hard work and austerity, as always, was rewarded: the wine from the Clos de Vougeot was – and still can be – glorious! The Château du Clos de Vougeot stands within the walled vineyard, today the seat and property of the Confrérie des Chevaliers du Tastevin, a prestigious wine fraternity made up of growers, shippers, and dignitaries who hold banquets, meetings, and splendid feasts and festivals here. Visitors to this historic building see the courtyard, the great pillared hall where banquets take place, and the impressive cellars and twelfth-century wine presses.

The wine tour continues by driving up the road flanking the Clos de Vougeot. At the top it curves left (the vineyard on the right is Les Petits Musigny), to pass into the vineyards of Vosne-Romanée. This small, compact commune boasts no less than seven *grands crus*. Its greatest, Romanée-Conti, produces possibly the most expensive wine on earth. Almost as dear (and as unobtainable for most of us) are the other *grands crus* of Vosne: La Tâche, Le Richebourg, Les Grands Echézeaux, Echézeaux, Romanée-St-Vivant, and La Romanée.

Nuits-St-Georges is somewhat larger than any other town along the *Route des Grand Crus*, and it has given its name to the entire Côte. It is an important centre for many *négociants-éleveurs* who have their premises here. The name is evocative, and easily remembered, and thus much wine is sold under the basic communal *appellation*, resulting in wine of varying standards, style, and quality. Though this happens in other regions, too, the cost of fine Burgundy emphasizes the importance of finding a reliable producer or *négociant*. Disappointing bottles of wine are expensive mistakes in Burgundy. After Nuits-St-Georges, the *Route des Grands Crus* (N74) continues through Prémeaux, and past the marble quarries of Comblanchien to end at Corgoloin.

de Tart, still surrounded by its stone wall, was planted; it remains the commune's outstanding *climat*, together with Clos de la Roche, Bonnes Mares, and the tiny Clos St Denis, all producing rich, long-lasting wines.

After Morey-St-Denis, the *Route des Grands Crus* swings up the slope (still the D22) to Chambolle-Musigny, perched under a craggy outcrop of lime and marl. This commune is yet another in this extraordinarily compact profusion of famous wine towns. Its vineyards, Les Petits Musigny, Les Musigny, and the lovely-named Les Amoureuses ('women in love') are among the region's classics.

The wine road next meets the D122 and

The Côte de Beaune and the Hautes Côtes de Beaune

The Côte de Beaune begins virtually where the Côte de Nuits leaves off. A tour of this southern half of the 'golden slope' includes Beaune itself, as well as wine communes producing renowned red wines, and other famous communes specializing in the greatest whites. After following the Côte du Beaune to Santenay, a return to Beaune by way of a circular route through the Hautes Côtes gives a different perspective on the region, as well as an interlude through vineyards producing more accessible wines, such as Bourgogne Passe-Tout-Grains, Bourgogne Aligoté, and the longer-lived Hautes Côtes de Beaune.

After the *Route des Grands Crus*, the first great commune of the Côte de Beaune is Aloxe-Corton, perched on a slight, isolated hill that rises from the N74 to look down on Beaune and the vineyards to the south. The Emperor Charlemagne once owned vineyards here (he is commemorated by the great white wine Corton-Charlemagne); today, another important owner here, and throughout the Côte de Beaune, is the Hospices de Beaune, a charitable institution which, over the centuries, has had valuable plots of land donated to it. In addition to Corton-Charlemagne, the commune produces outstanding red wine, the best of which is Le Corton. The Château de Corton, with its distinctive Burgundian lacquered yellow roof, is on the outskirts of town and can be visited.

The wine road descends to Beaune itself, which must be a highlight on any wine tourist's itinerary. With its central location between the Côte de Nuits and the Côte de Beaune it is, not surprisingly, the centre of the Burgundian wine trade. The premises of some of the region's most prestigious *négociant-éleveurs* are located here and the town is riddled with underground cellars. Shops and stores, many of them in medieval, carefully restored buildings, are devoted to supplying the accoutrements of gastronomy. And the town's most visible and famous establishment, the Hôtel-Dieu, is inextricably, wonderfully linked to the wine trade. For indeed, the Hospices de Beaune holds an annual auction here during which its many prestigious wines are sold; it is one of the wine trade's most important events. Wine lovers will certainly want to take a guided tour of the Hôtel-Dieu, as well as to visit the excellent wine museum located in the Hôtel des Ducs de Bourgogne.

A wine lover's visit will also undoubtedly include a visit to one or two of this town's *négociant-éleveurs*; there are numerous whose cellars are open to the

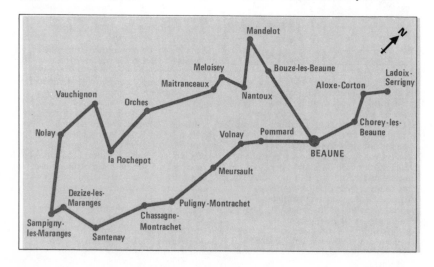

public without appointments, though for specialized attention, it is worth writing in advance or else arranging a meeting through a wine merchant at home. The classic role of the *négociant-éleveur* is to buy wine from numerous individual growers (many also own vineyards and produce their own wines), then to blend wines of the same *appellation*, and to nurture them to maturity, thus resulting in end-products that are of a more uniform character, of a consistently higher quality, and of a style particular to each house. The wines, in short, are elevated. It is a joy to watch the oenologist lever off the bung, insert his scientific-looking glass 'thief' into the new oak cask, and draw out a deep-purple, almost opaque sample of young wine. He squirts the wine into a bulbous tasting glass, swirls it critically, examines its immature bouquet, tastes, spits, then passes a satisfied judgement: *'Bon.'* The simple pronouncement is hardly that, however; indeed, should he offer you a taste of that same raw, mouth-puckering, undoubtedly rich and complex fluid, you will realize that he is judging it not on how it tastes now, but on how it will develop and mature first in cask, then in bottle, for over, perhaps, the next dozen years or more.

Leaving the cellar, we emerge to continue the tour of the Côte de Beaune. The vineyards of Beaune which actually begin not far outside the town's old walls are some of the most extensive in the region, producing red wines (primarily) that are gentler, lighter, and more round and forthcoming than the great reds of the Côte de Nuits. The best, of course, bear the names of individual *climats*; wines from the holdings of the Hospices, on the other hand, are generally sold under the name of the donor. One of the finest – and most expensive – for example, is Cuvée Nicolas Rolin, named after the man who founded the Hospices in 1443, and who began the custom of endowing it with valuable vineyards.

From Beaune, take the Route de Pommard (direction Lyons), then branch off right on the D973. The wine road now leads through Pommard and Volnay, rising somewhat as it passes through walled vineyards, and through these unspoiled and typical villages whose wine has been praised and drunk by the illustrious since at least the Middle Ages. Pommard's prosperity is apparent in such grand châteaux as the Château de la Commaraine, the old Hôtel des Ducs de Bourgogne and the Château de Pommard.

Past Volnay, the wine road branches left to Meursault. Above this large, well laid-out and prosperous town, the pitted remains of old quarries reveal a profound change in the land. For within this – virtually a separate Côte which stretches through the adjoining communes of Puligny and, on D113, Chassagne-Montrachet – a rich, complex vein of limestone and marl, so loved by the Chardonnay grape, courses powerfully. These three communes produce the greatest white Burgundies; indeed, many believe Le Montrachet itself to be the greatest white wine in the world. A famous wine festival, La Paulée, takes place annually in Meursault. Traditionally, it was a feast given for vineyard workers by the proprietors after the harvest. Today, however, it is much grander, part of Les Trois Glorieuses (celebrations which centre around the annual auction at the Hospices de Beaune), a feast for shippers, growers, and privileged guests who each bring a bottle of their finest Burgundy. Meursault's prized vineyards lie on the slopes that extend south of the town (Les Charmes, Les Perrières, and others), while Le Montrachet, straddling the twin communes that have both hyphenated its name to their own, lies proudly behind its stone wall, breached by grand stone portals that lead into it. Above Le Montrachet lies Chevalier-Montrachet while on the other side of the road is Bâtard-Montrachet.

Santenay, finally, is the last important commune of the Côte d'Or, a spa town with thermal springs, and with vineyards which produce somewhat lighter red wines similar to those found in the nearby Côte Chalonnaise. As a spa town it dates back to Roman days; today it is also a centre of recreation, with a campsite, swimming pool, numerous sports facilities, and a casino.

A return route to Beaune continues through the towns of Dezize-les-Maranges (D136) and Sampigny-les-Maranges, and climbs sharply into the Hautes Côtes. To move from the ordered, pampered vineyards of the Côte de Beaune to these surprisingly wild upper stretches is a striking contrast. Follow the road (D133 & D111) to Nolay, an important medieval town, as its impressive fourteenth-century market hall and church testify (nearby, the Taverne des Hautes Côtes serves regional specialities and local wines in an historic setting). At Vauchignon the gorge terminates at *'le bout du monde'*, which with its wild wooded cliffs, 25-foot cascade, and rugged natural grotto, seems (almost) 'the end of the world'. Return down the D111 to Bel Air, and follow the N6 right around to La Rochepot (with its fifteenth-century Gothic château set within wooded hills). The small D171 leads through remarkably unspoiled and majestic country, passing along the way numerous natural landmarks (such as the rocks at Orches), and through small isolated villages (Baubigny, Meloisey, Nantoux, Mavilly-Mandelot, and others) while at times opening out to reveal a spectacular panorama: down below, the vineyards and villages of Auxey-Duresses, Meursault, Volnay, Pommard, and finally, Beaune

itself, while beyond lie the plains of the Saône, and, on a clear day, the Jura Mountains.

The vineyards of these upper stretches produce both red and white wine, the best of which is entitled to the *appellation* Hautes Côtes de Beaune. Bourgogne Passe-Tout-Grains (the outlawed Gamay, after all, took its name from a village in these hills before retiring to splendid exile in the Beaujolais) and Aligoté are both also produced here. The circuit of the Hautes Côtes twists and winds finally to its highest point at La Balance, before descending down the Montagne de Beaune through Bouze-les-Beaune (see Restaurants), and so back to Beaune.

The Côte Chalonnaise and the Mâconnais

The transition from the vineyards of northern Burgundy to those of the south is a gradual but definite one. Below the tip of the Côte de Beaune, due south of the town of Chagny, lie the vineyards of the Côte Chalonnaise. While the vineyards of the Côte d'Or are intensively devoted to viticulture with every patch of available land jealously planted with precious vines, this southern, hilly, and overgrown region immediately feels less ordered. The vineyards are more sparse, and land is equally devoted to crops, animal grazing, or just meadows and wild, uncultivated fields of thickets and grass. Nevertheless, both red and white wines produced from these central vineyards, always important for the home market, are becoming increasingly available and finding favour abroad, particularly as the more famous wines of the Côte d'Or are, sadly, priced out of the reach of most of us. A wine road, the D981, passes near the region's four main towns, which are also the four

principal *appellations*: Rully, Mercurey, Givry, and Montagny.

The towns themselves, on first glance, are rather unexceptional, unselfconsciously busy, but they repay exploration. Givry, for example, has some lovely old town buildings, a lively marketplace, and bars and cafés full of workers wearing blue cotton work trousers and jackets, animatedly arguing, drinking, laughing. The vineyards themselves lie mainly to the west, extending around tiny villages such as Bouzeron (which produces excellent Aligoté), St Martin-sous-Montaigu, Bissey, and St Valerin. Rully and Montagny are best known for their individual white wines (the former is also the centre for the production of Crémant de Bourgogne by the *méthode champenoise*). Mercurey and Givry produce red wines which are somewhat lighter than those of the Côte de Beaune, but which approach them in character and quality.

Further south, past medieval Tournus, with its massive eleventh-century Romanesque abbey, a line of low hills rises from the flat valley of the Saône. The climate and temperament now is certainly a southern one, and rambling stone farmhouses with red-roofed tiles have their doors and windows open, while terraces are shaded by ancient and gnarled overgrown vines. This is the Mâconnais. Leave the N6 on the D56 and drive into the hills to meander through villages such as Chardonnay – a familiar name indeed –

and through others less well-known: Viré,
Igé, La Roche-la-Vineuse, and so into
Mâcon itself. Though these villages are
little known – much less so than the
famous Mâconnais wine communes to the
south – they are nevertheless important,
producing fresh, forceful white wines that
bear the simple *appellations* Mâcon or
Mâcon-Villages (or are sold simply as
'white Burgundy'). Mâcon *rouge*, produced
from both the Gamay and Pinot Noir
grapes, is strong, solid, robust red wine
without pretension.

Mâcon itself is a welcoming and relaxed
town; indeed, it comes as somewhat of a
relief after the hullabaloo of the Côte d'Or.
There are numerous restaurants that serve
hearty, traditional Burgundian fare (the
Maison du Vin itself, for example, which
also sells wine at prices more favourable
than in Beaune). The town, too, is an ideal
base from which to explore Charolles to
the west, the abbey of Cluny and the
Sacred Heart Basilica of Paray-le-Monial,
and the prehistoric valley of Solutré.
Indeed, the very limestone out of which
Cluny's abbey was built has for centuries
given the Mâconnais its finest wines. For
within the sheltered hollows formed by
the great rocky formations of Solutré and
Vergisson lie the vineyards of
Pouilly-Fuissé, St Véran and others
producing dry, fresh, fragrant white
Burgundies much loved throughout the
world.

The vineyards centre around Vergisson
(which nestles in a hollow beneath its
rearing rocks), Solutré (which because of
its rich prehistoric finds has given its name
to a paleolithic epoch, the Solutrean),
Pouilly, Fuissé, and Chaintré. From
Mâcon, take the N79 (direction of Cluny),
and turn off shortly to Prissé. The road
climbs steeply through villages that are
little more than hamlets, some of which
hardly even seem to have any shops –
though that presumably doesn't stop the
local inhabitants from eating well, judging
from the irresistible smells that assault you
at lunchtime, emanating from the open
windows of innumerable country
kitchens.

To the east of Fuissé lie lesser-known
vineyards, those of Pouilly-Vinzelles and
Pouilly-Loche, while to the south,
overlapping into the Beaujolais, lie the
vineyards of St Véran, which extend
through the communes of Chasselas (yet
another Burgundian village that has lent
its name to an important grape variety),
Leynes, St Vérand, and Chânes.

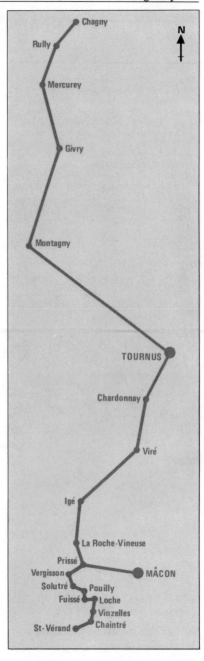

The Route du Beaujolais

South of Mâcon and the alkaline-rich hills of Pouilly-Solutré, west of the Saône river, a vast ripple of rugged, sensuously rolling hills plays its way down almost to Lyons. They say here that three rivers flow into that great gastronomic city: the Saône, Rhône, and Beaujolais. For out of these craggy, sometimes wild granite hills sprout vines that produce a veritable torrent of the world's most gulpable, most loved wine: Beaujolais. There could be no greater contrast than the manicured, precious, untouchable Pinot Noir and Chardonnay vineyards of the Côte d'Or to these rolling hills of stumpy, bushy, gnarled and free-standing Gamay plants dotted, seemingly, at random. Likewise, the precious wines of the Côte d'Or are so richly textured, indeed so expensive, that they must be sipped (almost) in awe. Beaujolais, on the other hand, straight out of the fridge, or – even worse heresy – with a lump or two of ice in the glass on a blistering summer day, is meant to be swilled back joyously, and in quantity.

A well sign-posted wine road, the *Route du Beaujolais* runs through the villages and communes in the north that produce the region's finest wines. These, unlike popular Beaujolais *primeur*, which should be consumed within weeks or months of the vintage, are wines with depth of flavour and vigour that allow them to improve with age.

From Mâcon, take the N6 south to Crêches, and then join the *Route du Beaujolais* which quickly climbs into the rugged hills, passing on its picturesque way to Villefranche-sur-Saône (centre of the Beaujolais wine trade) no less than 23 wine-tasting cellars, in addition to numerous winegrowers' *coopératives*, many of which also have *caveaux de dégustation*. The first (if you're uncontrollably thirsty, that is) is soon reached at St-Amour. Le Caveau du Cru St-Amour, which offers tastings, and sells this commune's light, grapy wine, is actually along the *Route du Beaujolais*. The lovely wine towns of Beaujolais soon follow: Juliénas, its southern, sunbaked buildings with tiled roofs guarding the stout Gamay vines, Chénas (the name comes from the ancient oak trees, *les chênes*, which used to cover these slopes), Fleurie, and Chiroubles, their gay, charming names as vivacious as the wines themselves. The Moulin-à-Vent, south of Chénas, is an armless, rounded turret set amidst the vineyards to which it gives its name (Le Caveau du Moulin-à-Vent is below the windmill at Romanèche-Thorins). Take the road from Chiroubles (D26) which leads down into Beaujeu itself, ancient capital of the region, with an aptly named *caveau*, Le Temple de Bacchus, which has a small museum displaying local crafts, and where Beaujolais-Villages can be tasted.

The *Route du Beaujolais* is reached again by returning to Chiroubles, and then continuing to Villié-Morgon (via D68), Circié, and St-Lager; or else, from Beaujeu, meander along a tourist itinerary through Quincié to Odenas. From Odenas, the *Route du Beaujolais* descends to Villefranche. An alternative circuit rises into the hills once more to Le Perréon, Vaux, and St-Julien; the Vat Room of the Compagnons du Beaujolais (one of the leading French *Confréries du Vin*) is located south of St-Julien, east of Villefranche in Lacenas.

Below Villefranche, the vineyards of Beaujolais continue. Indeed, these haphazard southern hills are the source of the great river of everyday Beaujolais (as opposed to the *crus* of the northern Beaujolais), drawn from the wood in Lyonnais bars, in Parisian cafés, and throughout the world. Various other tourist itineraries offer yet more excuses to

traverse this beautiful region, and to stop at any number of *caveaux de dégustation.*

Wine Producers

There are numerous wine producers – large and small – who offer a particularly warm Burgundian welcome to visitors. No wine tour would be complete without visiting a *négociant-éleveur* to learn about the unique and essential role that he plays in the wine trade of this region. Additionally, there are local wine *coopératives* to visit, and tasting (and purchasing) opportunities abound in the many *salles de dégustation* (roadside stands), and *caves touristiques* found throughout the wine region. Do beware, however; though casual establishments can be found throughout the French wine regions which are geared to making money from the passing tourist (as opposed to those which exist to promote a region's wines), 'le rip-off' in Burgundy generally comes somewhat dearer.

Chablis

89800 Chablis

Louis Michel et Fils
11, boulevard de Ferrières
tel: (86) 42 10 24
Daily 9–12h; 14–19h
Max 25 pers.
English spoken.
Charge for *dégustation.*

Simonnet-Febvre
route de Tonnerre
tel: (86) 42 11 73
Mon–Sat 8–18h
Appointment preferable.
English spoken.

Côte d'Or

21700 Nuits-St-Georges

Morin Père et Fils
Quai Fleury
tel: (80) 61 05 11

Daily 8–12h; 14–18h
Appointment necessary for groups.
English spoken.
Charge for *dégustation.*

21700 Vougeot

S G V V La Grande Cave
21, Côte d'Or
tel: (80) 61 11 23
Daily 8–20h
English spoken.
Appointment necessary only for large groups.

Château du Clos de Vougeot
proprieté de la Confrérie des Chevaliers du Tastevin
tel: (80) 62 86 09
Daily 9–12h; 14–18h
English spoken in summer.
Audio-visual.
Appointment necessary for large groups.
Max 40 pers.
Charge for *dégustation.*

Domaine du Château de la Tour
Daily April–Sept
English spoken.
Appointment necessary for groups.
Charge for *dégustation*.

21420 Aloxe-Corton

Pierre André
Château de Corton-André
tel: (80) 21 40 00
Daily
English spoken.

21200 Beaune

Maison Bouchard Aîné et Fils
36, rue Sainte Marguerite
tel: (80) 22 07 67
Mon–Fri 9–12h; 14–17h
Closed August.
English spoken.

Caves des Batistines
20, rue du Faubourg Madeleine
tel: (80) 22 09 05
Daily 9–19h30
English spoken.
Appointment necessary only for groups.
Max 50 pers.
Charge for *dégustation*.

Patriarche Père et Fils
7, rue du Collège
tel: (80) 22 23 20
Daily 9–11h40; 14–17h40
Max 80 pers.
Tour lasts about 40 minutes.
Charge for *dégustation*.

Maison Mallard-Gualin
La Cave du Bourgogne
28, rue Sylvestre-Chauvelot
tel: (80) 22 18 34
Daily
English spoken in summer.
Appointment necessary only for groups.
Max 50 pers.
Cold buffet available for groups if given
advance notice.

Calvet S A
6, boulevard Perpreuil
tel: (80) 22 06 32
Daily except Mon 9–11h30; 14–17h
English spoken.
Appointment necessary only for groups.
Max 100 pers.

Caves des Cordeliers
6, rue de l'Hôtel-Dieu
tel: (80) 22 14 25
Daily 9–19h

English spoken.
Appointment necessary only for groups.
Max 20 pers.

Reine Pédauque
Porte St-Nicolas
tel: (80) 22 23 11
Oct 1–May 31 Mon–Sat 9–11h30; 14–17h30;
Sun 10–11h30; 14–17h30
June 1–Sept 30 Mon–Sat 8h30–11h30;
14–18h; Sun 9–11h30; 14–18h
Max 80 pers.

21420 Savigny-les-Beaune

Château de Savigny-les-Beaune
tel: (80) 21 55 03
Daily 9–12h; 14–18h
Appointment necessary.
Charge for *dégustation*.

21190 Volnay

Le Cellier Volnaysien
Place de l'Église
tel: (80) 22 00 93
Caveau de dégustation with adjoining
restaurant.
Closed Wed

21190 Meursault

Domaine du Château de Meursault
tel: (80) 21 22 98
Daily 9h30–11h30; 14h30–18h
English spoken.
Max 50 pers.
Charge for *dégustation*.

Ropiteau Frères
13, rue du 11 Novembre
tel: (80) 21 24 73
Daily March–Oct
Appointment necessary only for groups.
Max 50 pers.
A little English spoken.

21590 Santenay

Domaines Prieur-Brunet
tel: (80) 20 60 56
Mon–Fri 9–12h; 15–19h
English spoken.
Charge for *dégustation*.

21200 Chorey-les-Beaune

Domaine Tollot et Voarick
tel: (80) 22 11 82
Daily 9–19h
Appointment necessary.
Max 100 pers.
A little English spoken.

Côte Chalonnaise and the Mâconnais

71390 Buxy

Caves des Vignerons
Bissey-sous-Cruchaud
tel: (85) 42 12 16
Daily 9–11h30; 14–17h30
Appointment necessary.
Max 50 pers.

Caveau de la Tour Rouge
Grande Rue
tel: (85) 42 15 76
Daily except Mon 10–12h30; 14h30–20h30
A little English spoken.
Max 100 pers.
Charge for *dégustation*.

71640 Mercurey

Les Vignerons du Caveau de Mercurey
tel: (85) 47 16 53
Mon–Fri by appointment only.
Max 50 pers.
A little English spoken.
Charge for *dégustation*.

71260 Lugny

Caveau St-Pierre
tel: (85) 33 22 85
Daily except Wed
Max 80 pers.
Charge for *dégustation*.

71000 Mâcon

Caveau du Baraban
Union des Producteurs des Vins Mâcon
Place St-Pierre
tel: (85) 38 20 86
Daily 10–12h; 15–19h
Closed July 1–Sept 15
Max 50 pers.

Maison Mâconnaise des Vins à Mâcon
avenue de Lattre-de-Tassigny
tel: (85) 38 36 70
Daily 8–21h

71570 Chaintré

Cave Coopérative de Chaintré
tel: (85) 35 61 61
Mon pm–Sat am 8–11h30; 14–17h30
Max 4–5 pers.
Charge for *dégustation*.

71960 Solutré

Caveau Union des Producteurs de
Pouilly-Fuissé
tel: (85) 37 80 06
Daily except Jan; Feb
Appointment necessary.
Max 50 pers.
Charge for *dégustation*.

Beaujolais

69220 Belleville-sur-Saône

Château de Corcelles
Corcelles-en-Beaujolais
tel: (74) 66 00 24
Mon–Sat (except holidays) 10–12h;
14h30–18h30
Appointment necessary for groups over
30.
Max 200 pers.
Charge for *dégustation*.

St-Amour

Caveau de St-Amour
St-Amour
tel: (85) 37 15 98

Romanèche-Thorins

Maison de Dégustation du Moulin-à-Vent

There are 23 wine-tasting cellars along the
Route du Beaujolais, and in many *coopérative*
cellars, wine can be tasted in magnificent
settings: Bully, Chiroubles, Fleurie, Gleizé,
Juliénas, Lachassagne, Le Bois-d'Oingt,
Létra, Le Perréon,
St-Etienne-des-Oullières,
St-Laurent-d'Oingt, St-Vérand, & Thiezé.

Wine Museums

21200 Beaune

Musée du Vin de Bourgogne
Hôtel des Ducs de Bourgogne
Open daily with guided tours.
9–11h; 14–17h
Superb wine museum with displays
illustrating the history of wine-making in
Burgundy, as well as collections of vinous
paraphernalia.

Hôtel-Dieu
rue de l'Hôtel-Dieu
Guided tours daily.
Founded in 1443 by Nicolas Rolin,
Chancellor of Burgundy, as a charitable
hospital, the building was designed by a
Flemish architect whose unique style is
demonstrated by the yellow-green and
black varnished slate roof. The main ward,
or 'paupers' ward' is both hospital and
church, for it enabled the sick to attend
religious services while still in their beds.
The enormous kitchens are most
impressive, and there is a frightening
polyptic by Roger van der Weyden of the
Last Judgement.

21700 Vougeot

Le Château du Clos de Vougeot
Open daily – see Wine Producers for
opening hours
Owned by the Confrérie des Chevaliers du
Tastevin, a Burgundian brotherhood
which meets in this Renaissance château
monthly.

Igé (Mâconnais)

La Musée du Vin
Igé
tel: (85) 33 33 56
Open weekends and holidays

Wine Courses and Seminars

The *Comité Interprofessionnel des Vins de
Bourgogne* organize wine courses every
year. These often take place during the
week prior to Les Trois Glorieuses. The
programs include: lectures on vinification,
tasting appreciation, and *appellation
contrôlée* regulations, visits to the vineyards
of the Côte de Beaune, Côte de Nuits, and
Côte Chalonnaise, and specific wine
tastings covering the whole of Burgundy,
including Chablis and Beaujolais. For
further information, write to:

Comité Interprofessionnel de la Côte d'Or
et de l'Yonne pour les Vins AOC
Bourgogne,
rue Henri Dunant
21200 Beaune
tel: (80) 22 21 35

The *Institut International des Vins et
Spiritueux* in Bordeaux organizes a six-day
course in Beaujolais and Côtes du Rhône
which includes seminars, tastings, and
tours of vineyards. Three days are spent in
Beaujolais. For further information, write
to:

Institut International des Vins et
Spiritueux
10, place de la Bourse
33076 Bordeaux
tel: (56) 90 91 28

Wine Festivals

Sun following Jan 22	Feast of St Vincent, patron saint of wine growers. There is a service of Mass, processions, and free wine-tasting in the decorated village streets and cellars.	Held in different villages each year throughout the region, organized by the Chevaliers du Tastevin in conjunction with the St Vincent Friendly Societies.
Last Sat in March	Tastevinage	Clos de Vougeot

Last Sun in March	Wine Auction at Hospices de Nuits	Nuits-St-Georges
April 24	Wine Fair	Chiroubles
May	Wine Fair and National Wine Exhibition	Mâcon
1st to 2nd Sun in June	Wine Fair	Beaune
Sept	Wine Fair	Dijon
Oct 30	Fête Raclet – tasting and exhibition of wines of Beaujolais and Mâconnais	Romanèche-Thorins
Oct 31	Presentation of Beaujolais and Beaujolais-Villages *primeurs*	Venue varies
Nov 6	Exhibition of Beaujolais-Mâconnais	Fleurie
3rd Sat, Sun, Mon in Nov:	Les Trois Glorieuses:	
Sat	Exhibition of Burgundian wines (open to public) Banquet organized by the Chevaliers du Tastevin	Beaune Clos de Vougeot
Sun	Wine auction at the Hospices de Beaune: town festival with music, dancing and drinking	Beaune
Mon	La Paulée – shippers, workers, wine producers, guests and visitors gather for a traditional Burgundian feast	Meursault
4th Sun in Nov	Fête – wines, gastronomy and folklore	Chablis
Nov 14	Wine Fair	Julienas
Dec 4–5	Presentation of 'new' Beaujolais, Beaujolais-Villages, and Crus	Villefranche

Regional Gastronomy

Jambon persillé Ham in wine, parsley, and garlic gelatine – one of the many examples of excellent Burgundian *charcuterie*.

Cervelas truffé Pork sausage flavoured with truffle.

Rosette Sausage from Chalon flavoured with pimento and butter.

Jambon de Morvan Raw air-dried mountain ham.

Tourte bourguignonne Veal and pork pie, eaten hot or cold.

Gougères Light, puffy cheese balls that are superb hot from the baker's oven with a glass of red wine.

Boeuf bourguignon A classic regional speciality: beef stewed in Burgundy with baby onions, mushrooms, and bacon.

Charollais marchand du vin, or *maître d'hôtel* Charollais steak, grilled, with a wine sauce and shallot, or parsley butter.

Pochouse Pike, perch, tench, and/or river eel, stewed in white wine and herbs.

Escargots à la bourguignonne Snails in parsley, shallot, wine, and garlic butter.

Quenelles Pounded and sieved pike, mixed with *créme fraiche* and egg white, then poached in stock. Very light and delicate.

Charollais au poivre Pepper steak.

Jambon à Chablis Ham simmered in Chablis wine.

Jambon braisé à la lie de vin Slab of ham cooked on the wine lees (sediment left in the barrel after racking).

Queue de boeuf des vignerons Oxtail stewed with grapes: a vintager's favourite.

Oeufs en meurette Eggs poached in red wine sauce.

Coq au vin Country stew of chicken in red wine garnished with mushrooms and bacon. Variations include Coq au Beaujolais or Coq au Chambertin.

Poires au cassis Pears in Crème de Cassis (blackcurrant liqueur from Dijon).

Pain d'épices Spiced gingerbread from Dijon.

Dijon mustard Traditionally produced with mustard seed and *verjuice* (unripened grape juice).

Cheeses Époisses, St Florentin, Bleu de Bresse, Aisy-Cendré, *fromage à la crème, fromage de chevre* (goat's cheese), Soumaintrain.

Restaurants

Note: many of the listings in the Hotel section also have good restaurants.

Chablis and the Yonne

89800 Chablis

Au Vrai Chablis
place du Marché
tel: (86) 42 11 43
Charming 'bistro' serves regional specialities throughout the day.
Open daily except Tue 10–22h
Inexpensive

89200 Avallon

Restaurant Le Morvan
7, route de Paris
tel: (86) 34 18 20
Regional specialities and selections of fine Chablis and Aligotés.
Moderate

Les Capucins
6, avenue Paul-Doumer
tel: (86) 34 06 52
An **Inexpensive** restaurant serving house and regional specialities, and wines of Chablis and Irancy.
Closed Wed all year; Wed and Sun eve out of season; January

89000 Auxerre

Restaurant Le Jardin Gourmand
56, boulevard Vauban
tel: (86) 51 53 52
Dinner served in the garden of this **Expensive** restaurant in summer.
Closed Tue eve; Wed
Open 12–14h; 19h30–21h45

The Côte d'Or

21000 Dijon

Le Vinarium
23, place Bossuet
tel: (80) 30 36 23
Situated in a thirteenth-century crypt in the heart of Dijon, opposite Église St-Jean, this unique restaurant serves only Burgundian dishes such as *jambon persillé, oeufs en meurette, escargots, charlotte au cassis, sorbet au marc et cassis*, and others. Excellent selection of famous and not so famous Burgundies.
Open Mon–Sat 12–14h; 19h30–23h
Moderate

21220 Gevrey-Chambertin

La Rôtisserie du Chambertin
rue du Chambertin
tel: (80) 34 33 20
Highly rated restaurant serving traditional Burgundian cuisine.
Open Tue–Sun midday
Closed August
Expensive

Restaurant Le Richebourg
18, rue Richebourg
tel: (80) 34 30 37
Specialities include fish and *grillades au feu de bois*, and traditional Burgundian dishes such as *escargots, jambon persillé* and others.
Open Tue–Sun lunchtime 12h–13h45; 19–21h45
Inexpensive to **Moderate**

Chambolle-Musigny

Art & Vins Tradition
Route des Grands Crus
tel: (80) 61 86 26

Inexpensive small country restaurant conveniently located on the *Route des Grands Crus*. Wine from surrounding vineyards offered in the restaurant, and also for sale.

21670 Vosne-Romanée

La Toute Petite Auberge
RN74
tel: (80) 61 02 03
Inexpensive restaurant serving regional specialities.
Closed Wed eve; Thur; Dec–Jan

21700 Nuits-St-Georges

Restaurant Côte d'Or
1, rue Thurot
tel: (80) 61 06 10
Popular restaurant in this famous wine town with good selection of local wines. Bedrooms also available.
Closed Sun eve; August
Moderate

21200 Beaune

Rôtisserie de la Paix
47, Faubourg Madeleine
tel: (80) 22 33 33
Personal cooking and large wine list. Tables are limited, so advisable to book.
Open Tue–Sun midday 12–14h;
19h30–21h30
Moderate to **Expensive**

21200 Chorey-lès-Beaune

L'Ermitage de Corton
tel: (80) 22 05 28
Extensive menu and elegant regional cuisine served in luxurious atmosphere.
Open daily 12h30–14h; 19–21h15
Expensive

Restaurant Le Bareuzai
RN 74
tel: (80) 22 02 90
Burgundian specialities and fish dishes, and wines from Tollot-Voarick domaine.
Open daily
Moderate

21200 Montagne de Beaune

Restaurant Au Bon Accueil
tel: (80) 22 08 80
Situated 2 km from Beaune, this popular and **Inexpensive** restaurant can also be

reached on return to Beaune from the circuit of the Hautes Côtes. Regional specialities include *coq au vin, escargots à la bourguignonne*, and *terrine maison*. In summer dinner is served on the terrace. Advisable to book.
Open midday only during the week, Midday and evenings during weekends
Closed Fri

21190 Volnay

Le Cellier Volnaysien
place de l'Église
tel: (80) 22 00 93
Caveau de dégustation with restaurant serving traditional Burgundian dishes.
Closed Wed
Moderate

21190 Meursault

Le Relais de la Diligence
23, rue de la Gare
tel: (80) 21 21 32
This wine producers' favourite offers excellent cuisine, and over 100 *crus de Bourgogne*.
Closed Tue eve, Wed, January
Open 12–14h; 19–21h
Inexpensive to **Moderate**

21340 Nolay

Hôtel-Restaurant Ste Marie
38, rue de la République
tel: (80) 21 73 19
Inexpensive hotel-restaurant located at the start of the circuit of the Hautes Côtes.
Closed Mon (except in July & Aug), Jan 3–Feb 3

Mâconnais and Beaujolais

71000 Mâcon

Restaurant Au Rocher de Cancale
393, quai Jean-Jaurès
tel: (85) 38 07 50
Fish from the Saône, and other regional specialities.
Closed Mon, Sat lunch, Sun eve
Open 12–14h; 19h30–21h30
Moderate

Maison Mâconnaise des Vins
avenue de Lattre-de-Tassigny
tel: (85) 38 36 70
Limited menu of regional specialities and

simple cooking, together with an excellent selection of wines. Near the campsite.
Open daily 8–21h
Inexpensive

71960 Fuissé

Restaurant Au Pouilly-Fuissé
tel: (85) 35 60 68
Comfortable family-run restaurant serving regional menus in this quiet wine village.
Inexpensive

69820 Fleurie-en-Beaujolais

Auberge du Cep
place de l'Église
tel: (74) 04 10 77
Menu has Beaujolais specialities with seasonal dishes and a good selection of Beaujolais wines. Advisable to book.
Open Tue–Sun midday, except holidays and December
Expensive

69400 Villefranche-sur-Saône

Auberge du Faisan Doré
pont de Beauregard
tel: (74) 65 01 66
Specialities include *foie gras* and fish, and a good selection of *crus* Beaujolais.
Open Tue–Sun lunch
Moderate

Hotels

Chablis and the Yonne

89800 Chablis

Hôtel Étoile-Bergerand
4, rue des Moulins
tel: (86) 42 10 50
Well-liked hotel with good restaurant.
Inexpensive to **Moderate**
Closed Mon; Dec 15–Feb 15

89200 Avallon

Auberge Le Relais Fleuri
(exit autoroute at Nationale 6)
tel: (86) 34 02 85
Quaint auberge with a large garden and restaurant with regional specialities such as *le jambon à l'os bourguignonne* and *l'andouillette de Chablis grillée.*
Open daily
Moderate

The Côte D'or

21000 Dijon

Grésill Hotel
16, avenue Raymond-Poincaré
tel: (80) 71 10 56
Moderate hotel and restaurant
Hotel closed Aug 5–Aug 25
Restaurant closed Sun

Hôtel du Nord
2, rue de la Liberté et place Darcy
tel: (80) 30 55 20
A centrally located **Inexpensive** 24-room hotel with restaurant serving regional specialities.
Hotel closed Dec 23–Jan 14
Restaurant open daily 12–14h; 19h–22h30
Restaurant **Moderate**

21200 Fixin

Hôtel-Restaurant Chez Jeannette
21, rue Noisot
tel: (80) 34 31 08
Rustic auberge in the heart of the vineyards with atmospheric restaurant serving traditional Burgundian dishes, and a choice of 40 *crus* from the Côte de Nuits and Côte de Beaune. English spoken.
Hotel closed Nov 20–Dec 20; Jan 4–Jan 18
Restaurant closed Thur; open 12h15–13h30; 19h15–21h30
Inexpensive to **Moderate**

21220 Gevrey-Chambertin

Les Terroirs
28, route de Dijon
tel: (80) 34 30 76
Inexpensive to **Moderate** hotel in ancient building. No restaurant
Closed Dec 23–Jan 10

Hôtel-Restaurant aux Vendanges de Bourgogne
47, route de Beaune
tel: (80) 34 30 24
In the midst of some of the richest vineyards of the Côte de Nuits, an **Inexpensive** hotel/restaurant serving regional specialities.
Hotel closed Jan 27–March 1
Restaurant open Tue–Sun 12–14h; 19h30–21h

21200 Beaune

Hôtel Au Raisin de Bourgogne
164, route de Dijon
tel: (80) 24 69 48

A **Moderate** hotel/restaurant serving seasonal specialities and *foie gras maison* Hotel closed June 1–June 8; Dec 15–Jan 1 Restaurant closed Wed. Open 12–14h; 19h15–21h

Hôtel Le Cep
27, rue Maufoux
tel: (80) 22 35 48
Each of the 21 stylishly-decorated rooms is named after a prestigious *grand cru.*
Closed Dec 1–Feb 28
Expensive

Hôtel Central
2, rue Victor Millot
tel: (80) 24 77 24
Moderate hotel with restaurant.
Hotel closed Nov 20–March 20
Restaurant open daily 12–14h;
19h15–21h15

Hôtel de Bourgogne
avenue Charles-de-Gaulle
tel: (80) 22 22 00
Modern, comfortable hotel on outskirts of town with swimming pool, garden, 120 rooms, and restaurants.
Hotel closed Nov 20–April 1
Restaurants open daily 12–14h; 19h15–22h
Moderate

71150 Chagny

Lameloise
36, place d'Armes
tel: (85) 87 08 85
First-class hotel in ancient Burgundian house, with an elegant, highly-esteemed restaurant.
Restaurant closed Wed, Thur lunch
Hotel closed end of April–mid May; end of Nov–mid Dec
Very Expensive

Côte Chalonnaise, Mâconnais, and Beaujolais

71640 Givry

Hostellerie du Val d'Or
Grand Rue
tel: (85) 47 13 70
Regional specialities and wines of Mercurey and Rully.
Open Tue–Sun midday
Closed Nov 15–March 15
Inexpensive to **Moderate**

Hôtel-Restaurant de la Halle
place Halle
tel: (85) 44 32 45

Inexpensive hotel with restaurant serving specialities such as *mousseline de brochet, saumon au vin de Givry.*
Hotel closed end Oct–mid Nov
Restaurant closed Mon
Open 12–13h30; 19h30–21h

71700 Tournus

Hôtel-Restaurant Le Rempart
2/4, avenue Gambetta
tel: (85) 51 10 56
Modern and well-situated, with restaurant serving *ris de veau, écrevisses, turbot.*
Hotel open all year.
Restaurant open daily 12–14h30; 19–21h30
Moderate

71000 Mâcon

Hôtel Frantel
26, rue de Coubertin
tel: (85) 38 28 06
Modern, first-class chain hotel on the banks of the Saône with terrace and gardens. 63 rooms all with bathrooms; regional restaurant.
Hotel open all year.
Restaurant closed Sat lunch
English spoken
Hotel **Expensive**
Restaurant **Moderate**

(Outside Mâcon)

Hôtel Sofitel
Aire de St Albain
71260 Lugny
tel: (85) 38 16 17
Modern well-equipped 100-room hotel with swimming pool and restaurant.
Open all year. Restaurant open 19h–22h30
Moderate to **Expensive**

69400 Villefranche-sur-Saône

Hôtel Plaisance
96, avenue de la Libération
tel: (74) 65 33 62
68-room hotel located in the capital of the Beaujolais. Each room has bath or shower, and balcony. Restaurant serves specialities of the region such as *coq au Beaujolais* and *salade Lyonnaise* with good selection of Beaujolais wines.
Hotel closed Dec 24–Jan 2
Restaurant open daily 12–14h;
19h15–21h15
Hotel **Moderate**
Restaurant **Inexpensive**

Camping

Chablis Region

Auxerre
Camp Municipal, tel: (86) 52 11 15
Tonnerre
La Cascade, tel: (86) 55 15 44

Côte d'Or

Dijon
Le Lac, tel: (80) 43 54 72
Vougeot
Le Moulin, tel: (80) 61 86 77
Beaune
Les Cent Vignes, tel: (80) 22 03 91
Meursault
La Grappe d'Or, tel: (80) 21 22 48
Savigny-les-Beaune
Camping Municipal, tel: (80) 21 51 21

Côte Chalonnaise, Mâconnais, and Beaujolais

Chalon-sur-Saône
La Butte, tel: (85) 48 26 86
Mâcon
Camping Municipal, tel: (85) 38 16 22
Villefranche-sur-Saône
La Plage

Bibliography

Burgundy Vines and Wines by John Arlott and Christopher Fielden, Davis-Poynter, 1976

The Companion Guide to Burgundy by Robert Speaight, Collins, 1975

Monarch Guide to the Wines of Burgundy by Graham Chidgey, Monarch Press 1978

Where to Get Additional Information

Welcome Information Office
Pavillon du Tourisme
place Darcy
21000 Dijon
tel: (80) 43 42 12

Comité Interprofessionnel de la Côte d'Or et de l'Yonne pour les Vins AOC
Bourgogne
rue Henri Dunant
21200 Beaune
tel: (80) 22 21 35

Comité Interprofessionnel des Vins de Bourgogne et Mâcon
Maison du Tourisme
avenue du Maréchal de Lattre-de-Tassigny
71000 Mâcon
tel: (85) 38 20 15

Union Interprofessionnelle des Vins du Beaujolais
210, boulevard Vermorel
69400 Villefranche-sur-Saône
tel: (74) 65 45 55

Office du Tourisme de Beaune
rue de l'Hôtel-Dieu
21200 Beaune
tel: (80) 22 24 51

Burgundy Anthony Hanson, Faber & Faber, 1982

The Wines of Burgundy Pierre Poupon and Pierre Forgeot, Presses Universitaires de France, 1979

World Atlas of Wine by Hugh Johnson, Simon & Schuster 1978

CHAMPAGNE

The Champagne region, from which bubbles forth the world's most elegant, effervescent wine, is itself modest, quiet, and industrious. Lying between Paris and Lorraine, the Ardennes and Burgundy, it has been for centuries a crossroads rather than a stopping place for invaders and defenders, kings and pilgrims alike. Today it is the mecca for thousands of 'wine pilgrims' who come to pay homage to this great wine, to view at first-hand the laborious *méthode champenoise* in vast subterranean chalk cellars underneath Reims, and compact, busy Épernay, and to meander along sign-posted wine roads through gentle, undulating, perfectly-tended vineyards.

These vineyards form the heart of the region, curved over an idyllic stretch of rolling hills and valleys like two mirror-image horseshoes in the midst of the great Champagne plain (the name itself comes from the Latin *campus* which simply means an open field). The region was once the basin of a prehistoric inland sea which left behind vast and deep chalk deposits embedded with fossils. It is this chalky sub-soil – a block, in some places, some 600 feet thick and more – that nourishes the vines, assuring perfect drainage, storing and reflecting warmth, and above all, giving the wines of Champagne their delicacy, lightness, and finesse.

This massive substratum plays its part throughout in the production of champagne, for underground cellars carved out of the moist chalk provide ideal conditions for the making and storing of the wines. Some of the region's cellars were originally Roman excavations, massive conical-shaped *crayères* as much as 150 feet below the surface. Today there are no less than 120 miles of chalk cellar-galleries extending under the streets of Reims and Épernay, and under the prized vineyards of Champagne themselves. It is a strange, wonderful experience to venture down into the cool, damp caves to view thousands – indeed, millions – of bottles of wine ageing, either in horizontal racks, or slanted *pupitres*; stranger still to come upon vast, highly-mechanized bottling lines and other machinery furiously at work far underground in the dimly-lit, echoing passages of a Roman cave.

Champagne's great underground treasure of chalk, to which the region owes its present prosperity, has an impressive monument in the magnificent Gothic cathedral of Reims which still dominates this busy city, despite severe damage suffered during World War I. Indeed monuments from both wars abound: even the smallest wine villages have their centrally-placed statue to sons *'Morts pour la France'*; out of the same soil which nourishes the vines sprout row after row of identical white crosses; and nearby, famous and

How to Get There

By Car
From Paris take the A4 autoroute which runs from Paris to Metz (thus enabling a tour of Champagne to be made en route to Alsace, or to Germany's Rhineland). A slower (and less expensive route) follows the N3 to Meaux (centre for the production of 'farmhouse Brie' – one of the great cheeses of France), La Ferté-sous-Jouarre, and so on to Épernay, by way of the meandering Marne Valley.

By Plane
There is not an international airport in Reims, although there are direct flights from Lyons to Reims. The airport is called Aerodrome Reims-Champagne. The most accessible international airport is at Paris. Fly there and either rent a car, or else continue to Champagne by train.

By Train
There is a daily service from Paris-Est to Épernay and Reims. The fastest trains take only one hour and fifteen minutes to Épernay, and an hour and a half to Reims (so enabling day trips to be made from the capital). There are also daily trains from Paris-Est to Châlons-sur-Marne and on to Verdun.

Local Public Transport
Local bus network is good with services to most points of interest. There are also round-trip coach tours from Reims which follow the *Route du Champagne* and the Côte des Blancs; for details consult the tourist office in Reims.

Car Rental Information
Reims
  Avis: 14, boulevard du Maréchal Joffre
    tel: (26) 88 10 08
  Hertz: 26, boulevard du Maréchal Joffre
    tel: (26) 47 31 58
    Aerodrome Reims-Champagne
    tel: (26) 47 31 58
Châlons-sur-Marne
  Hertz: 7, avenue de la Gare
    tel: (26) 64 14 01
Troyes
  Avis: 4, avenue Pierre Brossolette
    tel: (25) 43 05 44
  Hertz: 31, rue Voltaire, tel: (25) 79 29 79

Michelin Maps 56, 61

infamous battlefields remain in mute testimony to an horrific age: Verdun, Soissons, Chemin des Dames, Belleau Wood, Hill 204, and many others.

But Champagne today is at peace, and indeed a more peaceful countryside is hard to find. Beyond the quietude of its wine country lie game-stocked forests and fish-laden rivers and streams, rolling fields of golden wheat, hills and valleys, and tiny French villages, each with its own story. Though the very name 'champagne' is synonymous throughout the world with gaiety, joy, and festivity, La Champagne, the region, remains quiet, modest, inward-looking. Certainly, the grand champagne houses are welcoming and hospitable, their mansions along the avenue de Champagne and elsewhere both sophisticated and elegant, like the wines themselves. But elsewhere, in the wine villages along the *Routes du Champagne*, or in the forests of the Ardennes and Aube, the essential character of the land is down-to-earth, hearty, and unpretentious (a character which is reflected in the country cooking of the region). From medieval Troyes, former capital of the Counts of Champagne, through the underground maze of welcoming cellars in Reims and Épernay, to the forests and lakes of the north and south, from elegant three-star restaurants to humble *relais routiers*, this essential duality makes La Champagne an absorbing land to visit.

The Wines of Champagne

Unlike wines from other French districts, champagne is defined by both a delimited geographical area of cultivation, and by a unique process by which the wine is made sparkling, the *méthode champenoise*. Additionally, stringent rules define the variety of vines allowed to be cultivated, methods of cultivation and pruning, maximum yield per hectare, vinification, minimum time aged in bottle before shipping, as well as many other aspects of wine production. There is also a complex system of grading vineyards, described briefly below.

Méthode Champenoise The process whereby still wines are made sparkling by secondary fermentation in the bottle. Basically, still wines from different vineyards throughout the region, each contributing its own particular character, are first blended together into a *cuvée*. In the case of non-vintage champagne, wines from the current vintage, as well as wine from older reserves, are blended together to produce a harmonious and balanced wine that conforms to the style of each particular house (it takes great skill on the part of the *chef du cave* as well as substantial reserves of older wine to produce a consistent style of non-vintage wine year after year). A small amount of *liqueur* made from variable amounts of pure cane sugar and natural yeasts dissolved in still wines, is added to the blended *cuvée*, which is then bottled; the yeast feeds on the sugar, causing a slow secondary fermentation that produces carbon dioxide which remains imprisoned in the wine, thus giving champagne its sparkle. If bubbles are a desired by-product, one undesired result of this process is a fine sediment which develops in the wine during secondary fermentation, and which must be removed in order to achieve the crystal-clear, bright product so loved throughout the world. The nature of the sediment is such that it can only be removed by a complex, delicate, and costly operation known as *remuage*. After the secondary fermentation is complete, the bottles are placed in slanted racks called *pupitres*. Gradually, over a period of months, the bottles are shaken, nudged, and gradually tilted from a near horizontal position to an almost vertical one. The deposit thus slides slowly into the neck of the bottle and collects on the cork where it must be removed, but without losing the precious sparkle. The next step is known as *dégorgement*; basically the procedure which most of the large firms employ consists of placing the necks of the bottles

in a freezing solution, thus trapping the sediment in a block of frozen wine. The bottles are then mechanically uncorked; a machine gives them a tap, the pressure in the wine expels the block of ice; afterwards, the wines are topped up with a *dosage* (a blend of pure cane sugar and old champagne). Finally they are corked again, wired down with a muzzle, and labelled.

Dosage The *dosage* determines the style of champagne – *brut* (very dry), *extra-sec* (dry), *sec* (slightly sweet), *demi-sec* (sweet), *demi-doux* (very sweet), and *doux* (exceptionally sweet). Though the prevailing taste in Britain is for *brut* champagne, the other styles have their place and should not be over-looked.

Premier & Grand Cru The essence of champagne (in addition to the wine's sparkle) lies in a unique blending of wines from grapes grown in various parts of the delimited Champagne region, each of which contributes particular characteristics and balance to the *cuvée*. While most of the great houses own their own vineyards, they must also buy grapes from individual *vignerons*. The finest vineyards have been classified into *premiers* and *grands crus* (the visitor to the region will see these designations in the vineyards themselves). Briefly, *grands crus* vineyards are rated 100%; *premiers crus* are given values between 99% and 90% while the remaining vineyards of Champagne are all given values down to 77%. Each year the *Comité Interprofessionnel du Vin de Champagne (CIVC)* sets a price per kilo-gram for the finest grapes; *vignerons* who sell to the great houses accordingly receive a percentage of this price depending on the quality rating of their vineyards. *Grand cru* champagne must be produced entirely from vineyards rated 100%; *premier cru* champagne, likewise, is produced from only those excellent vineyards with a rating between 99% and 90%.

Syndicat de Grandes Marques de Champagne A non-exclusive group of large firms who formed a syndicate to defend the interests of champagne, both in France and abroad. The following *grands noms* (in alphabetical order) are members:

Ayala
Billecart Salmon
J Bollinger
Canard Duchêne
Vve Clicquot Ponsardin
Deutz & Geldermann
Heidsieck & Co Monopole
Charles Heidsieck/Henriot
Krug & Co
Lanson P & F
Vve Laurent Perrier
Masse P & F
Mercier
Moët & Chandon
Montebello
G H Mumm & Co
Perrier Jouet
Joseph Perrier Fils & Co
Piper Heidsieck
Pol Roger & Co
Pommery & Greno
CH & A Prieur
Louis Roederer
Ruinart P & F
A Salon & Co
Tattinger/Irroy

Récoltant-Manipulant A grower who produces his own champagne (rather than sells his grapes entirely to one of the large firms). Such wines are generally considerably cheaper than those produced by the large firms and they can be very good. It is certainly worthwhile visiting such small producers to observe the contrasts between their operations, and those of the *grands noms* in Reims and Épernay, as well as to purchase wine direct. However, consistent high quality and the delicate balance of the *cuvée* are hallmarks of champagne. The *récoltant-manipulant*, since he generally produces his wines from grapes grown within his particular commune, cannot achieve the harmony which comes from blending wines from the various vineyards throughout the Champagne region. Moreover, the large firms keep substantial reserves of older and rare wines necessary

to produce a consistently high-quality non-vintage *cuvée*, of the same house style year after year, a practice impossible for most small growers to duplicate. However, in addition to the small grower who himself produces his own champagne, *coopératives* exist throughout the region, and they give their members both the technical expertise, and the marketing structure necessary to sell their wines once they are produced.

Vintage champagne Champagne produced from wines of a single, exceptional year; such champagne must age for a minimum of three years in the bottle (many firms, however, age such vintage wine for considerably longer: five or six years is quite normal).

Blanc de blancs Literally white wine from white grapes, i.e. champagne produced entirely from the Chardonnay, with no addition of the Pinots in the *cuvée*. Such champagne is characterized by its lightness and elegance.

Crémant Style of champagne with less pressure and 'fizz', produced by using a smaller amount of *liqueur* to induce the secondary fermentation.

Rosé champagne Pink champagne, produced only in limited quantities.

Coteaux Champenois The legal *appellation* for still wines of the region. Both red and white wines are produced, and should be tried while in the region (they are exported only in small quantity). Since they are produced from the same grapes used to make champagne itself, they remain necessarily relatively expensive, even in Champagne.

Ratafia A local aperitif produced by blending unfermented grape juice and brandy.

Fine Marne Local brandy.

Marc de Champagne Local spirit distilled from the grape skins, pips, and residue left after the grape-pressing. A pungent, powerful drink, it is also used in the kitchens of Champagne.

The Routes du Champagne

The vineyards of Champagne are comprised of four sections: the *Montagne de Reims, Vallée de la Marne, Côtes des Blancs* and to the south, separated by the vast Champagne Plain, the vineyards of the Aube. The first three, which comprise the heart of the vine-growing region, are each marked by sign-posted wine roads. They can be explored at leisure from either Reims or Épernay. The vineyards of the Aube, though not as widely visited, provide a contrast to the rest of the region and can be explored from Troyes. As well as following the wine roads of Champagne, a highlight of a visit to the region will certainly include visits to one or more of the welcoming *Maisons du Champagne* in Reims, Épernay, and elsewhere.

Reims The region's largest city, bombed severely during World War I, is today a modern, vital metropolis. Yet its thirteenth-century cathedral, damaged extensively in the wars though now restored, continues to dominate, as it always has in the past. It is one of the most important buildings in France, indeed in all of Christendom, for the country's kings were traditionally consecrated here (one of the most famous of many stirring moments occurred when the maiden warrior, Joan of Arc, led the young Dauphin to Reims to be crowned Charles VII). Many great and well-known wine firms are located in Reims, and miles of cellars extend underneath the city's streets (indeed, during the war, the local inhabitants had to take refuge in the champagne caves). With its numerous hotels and fine restaurants, cultural activities and lively nightlife, Reims is a city which every visitor to the region will want to explore.

Épernay Together with Reims, Épernay is the centre of the champagne trade, and home of many prestigious firms. Situated in the Marne Valley, in the very heart of the region's vineyards, this cosy, charming, bustling city lives and breathes wine. All three sign-posted wine roads begin or end here, while the eighteenth- and nineteenth-century mansions along the avenue de Champagne are witness to the prosperity and wealth which this most elegant wine has brought. The *Musée du Vin de Champagne et de la Préhistoire* is located along the avenue de Champagne, and there is pleasant camping along the river, as well as hotel-restaurants, bars, and numerous outdoor cafés where you can treat yourself to champagne by the glass, here as natural as taking a cup of coffee elsewhere.

Troyes Historic capital of the region, and former seat of the powerful Counts of Champagne, Troyes was also an important medieval trading centre for all of Europe. Today it retains that lively atmosphere, with its tilted, timbered houses with turrets and porch-roofs, its cobbled roads and flamboyant Gothic cathedral, its numerous churches and museums, and its hearty local gastronomy. Its location, apart from the rest of the region, by the natural parks and forests of the Aube and the lesser-known vineyards of Bar-sur-Seine and Bar-sur-Aube, makes Troyes less well-visited than the other main centres of Champagne. Yet the town deserves to be explored; its location on the road to Dijon and Burgundy provides a convenient link for exploring these two very different wine regions.

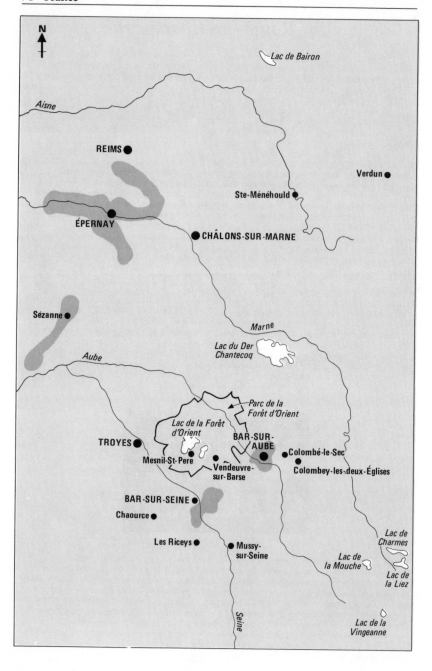

The Blue Route – Montagne de Reims

The gentle plateau of the Montagne de Reims, which forms part of the Ile-de-France cliff wall, extends around in an approximate horseshoe from Reims to Épernay. It is planted primarily with Pinot Noir and some Pinot Meunier grapes, and its vineyards are some of the region's finest. The *Blue Route* can begin from either Reims or Épernay. From Reims take the N31 (direction of Soissons) then turn left onto the D26 which climbs the flank of this 'petite Montagne'.

As the road climbs, the well-tended, low-lying, uniform rows of vines soon begin. *Vignerons* driving strange tractors with high bodies and wheels set at such a width so as to enable them to pass through the rows of vines rumble down little lanes, and through the vineyards. Meander along this pleasant *Blue Route* through Vrigny and Jouy, and then on to the small perched town of Villedommange; a detour to St-Lié, with its fifteenth-century chapel, provides a splendid view across the Champagne Plain. This looks down on the route used by the Gauls, linking the north of France with the corridor to the Rhône and the Mediterranean. Indeed, when Caesar founded Reims (he called it Durocortorum) in the first century BC, its central position made it the meeting point of eight great thoroughfares across Europe.

The sign-posted wine road continues, at times through surprisingly quiet, empty-looking, and ancient villages such as Sacy (with its twelfth-century church), Sermiers, and Montchenot (where there is another good view across to Reims). Rilly-la-Montagne is somewhat larger, a fashionable place for French tourists to gather in mid-summer to sip growers' champagne out of tall, cool glasses. This is the centre of some of the finest, most élite vineyards in Champagne, as signs near villages like Mailly and Verzenay (the windmill along the road, incidentally, was used as an observation post during World War I) boasting *Grands Crus* and *Premiers Crus* proclaim.

Additionally, located here and there and throughout the other vineyard regions of Champagne are the press-houses of many of the great wine firms. Because champagne is a white wine produced (often) from a large proportion of black grapes, it is essential that the grapes be pressed quickly to ensure that the must does not draw off the colour from the grape skins. The pressing thus takes place sometimes virtually on the spot, in massive, broad circular wooden presses which allow the grape juices to percolate rapidly. This grape juice is then drawn off into barrels (or, more commonly nowadays, modern tankers) and transported to the cellars of the great firms where it undergoes its first fermentation, resulting in a still wine which is then blended with other wines before undergoing the secondary fermentation which gives champagne its sparkle.

The wine road begins to turn back on itself at Verzy (former site of a Benedictine abbey). A short detour to the right on the D34 leads to a freak of nature, the so-called 'Faux-de-Verzy', a forest of stunted, twisted beech trees, some of which are 500 years old. Nearby is the highest point of the Montagne de Reims, the Observatory of Mt Sinai. Returning to Verzy, and continuing along the D26, the natural, vine-covered ridge turns south, and passes through Villers-Marmery, Trépail, Ambonnay, and, on the D19, Bouzy, a commune famous not only for the quality of its grapes used to make champagne, but also for a fragrant, popular still red wine which, along with other reds and whites, bears the *appellation* Coteaux Champenois. In Bouzy, the *Blue Route* splits, either towards the river at Tours-sur-Marne where it meets the *Red Route* of the Vallée de la Marne, or else towards Louvois, which has a twelfth-century church as well as a fine château in impressive grounds, formerly owned by Michel de Tellier, a French chancellor in the seventeenth century. The road from Louvois leads to the beautiful Val d'Or Valley and finally, along the *Red Route* through Ay-Champagne to Épernay.

The Red Route – Vallée de la Marne

Extending to the east and west of Épernay, the *Red Route* traverses a ridge of fine vineyards overlooking the Valley of the Marne. If coming from Reims along the *Blue Route*, turn left in Bouzy onto the D19 to Tours-sur-Marne, from where the *Red Route* commences. If beginning the tour from Épernay, cross the river and take the right fork (D201) to Ay-Champagne, an important and prestigious wine commune – so important that Henry IV was content to refer to himself simply as 'Lord of Ay'. Some large establishments have their headquarters here and visits can be arranged by appointment. The town, unfortunately, like so many others in the region, was seriously damaged in the war, but one wood-panelled house claims to have been the 'Pressoir' of Henry IV himself. The town also has a *Musée Champenois* which displays wine implements and tools, and tells the history of the village of Ay.

From Ay, continue to Dizy and turn northwards on the N51 to Champillon (excellent hôtel-restaurant) and, further on, climbing the hill, to Bellevue where there is a superb view of the Marne Valley, and the Pinot Noir and Meunier vineyards stretching out on either side. St-Imoges (D71) is a tiny, typical *champenois* village – an insular, silent, and self-contained hamlet. Pass through the dense woods to the N386 and turn left to arrive at the village of Hautvillers, perhaps the region's most famous. For it was here, in the Benedictine abbey above the village, that in the seventeenth century the blind cellar-master Dom Pérignon perfected the methods still used today for the production of champagne. Not only did he introduce the use of cork stoppers (tied down with string to keep them from popping out as the pressure within the bottles built up), he also experimented with blending different wines from vineyards throughout the region to form a

cuvée which possessed a finer character than any single vineyard wine had on its own. (The abbey itself, now owned by the firm of Moët et Chandon, has been wonderfully restored, particularly the abbey kitchens, and the cellars; it can be visited on application to that firm.) The abbey church contains the tombs of Dom Pérignon and Dom Ruinart (a friend and colleague). The village of Hautvillers, like so many others, may at first seem unforthcoming, its buff-coloured stone houses and buildings closed and impenetrable. Yet the arch of wicker baskets that spans the village streets during the annual Festival of St Vincent, the booming brass band, and the whimsical wrought-iron signs along the main street reflect a somewhat lighter, effervescent character.

From Hautvillers, the road descends to meet the D1 once more; turn right to Cumières and Damery (where Henry IV used to come to dally with Anne du Puy). Follow the D1 wine road through Venteuil and Reuil, passing vineyards as well as peaceful fields of wheat interspersed with clusters of wild poppies. Chatillon-sur-Marne was the birthplace of Pope Urban II (a huge statue proclaims this fact). At Verneuil, the D1 intersects with N380 (this is the quickest way back to Reims) and then continues on to Dormans on the opposite bank of the river. Dormans, an ancient town, commemorates the extremely fierce fighting of the two Battles of the Marne. The first, in 1914, took place during the vintage, which had to be harvested by old men, women, and children, since the men of the region were fighting and dying. The return to Épernay can be made directly via the N3 (on the right bank of the Marne now), while a pleasant detour into the vineyards of the south bank continues through the villages of Oeuilly, Boursault, and Vauciennes.

The Green Route – Côte des Blancs

The vineyards of the Côte des Blancs extend in a horseshoe shape similar to the arc formed by the Montagne de Reims. They are so named because they are planted almost exclusively with the Chardonnay, noble white grape of Champagne. The *Green Route*, shortest of

the three sign-posted wine roads, passes through more open, lower-lying country, presenting views of the vast and flat plains of Champagne.

From Épernay pass south through the town to pick up the N51 to Pierry and Moussy, and then take the D11 to the wine

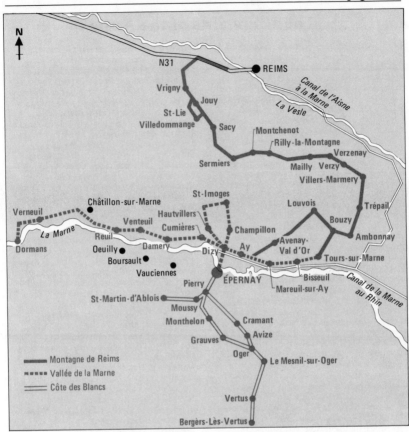

N

N31

Vrigny
Jouy
St-Lie
Villedommange   Sacy
Montchenot
Rilly-la-Montagne
Sermiers
Verzenay
Mailly Verzy
Villers-Marmery
St-Imoges
Louvois
Trépail
Châtillon-sur-Marne
Hautvillers
Bouzy
Verneuil
Venteuil
Cumières
Champillon
Ambonnay
La Marne
Reuil
Avenay-
Oeuilly   Damery   Ay   Val d'Or
Dormans
Dizy
Tours-sur-Marne
Boursault
Vauciennes
ÉPERNAY   Bisseuil
Pierry
Mareuil-sur-Ay
St-Martin-d'Ablois
Moussy
Monthelon   Cramant
Grauves   Avize
Oger
Le Mesnil-sur-Oger
REIMS
Canal de l'Aisne
à la Marne
La Vesle
Canal de la Marne
au Rhin
Vertus
Bergers-Lès-Vertus

— Montagne de Reims
---- Vallée de la Marne
== Côte des Blancs

village of St-Martin-d'Ablois. Return to
Pierry, and turn right on the D10 to
meander through renowned champagne
centres such as Cramant, Avize, Le
Mesnil-sur-Oger, and Vertus. Vertus is an
ancient fortified village with an
eleventh-century church of St-Martin. The
nearby cliffs of Falloises are a favourite
venue for rock climbers, while the Cave
des Falloises is an old chalk quarry that
provided the slabs of stone used to restore
Reims cathedral in the nineteenth century.
The wine road continues a short way to
Bergères-lès-Vertus (continuing on the D9
leads to the vineyards of the Aube and to
Troyes); in this short stretch, black grapes
are also grown.

Return along the D9 to Le Mesnil-sur-
Oger, and take the left fork to Oger
(direction of Épernay – this is the D10 once
more). A short detour on the D240 through

Grauves and Monthelon presents fine
views of the valley looking down towards
Épernay, which is soon reached via Pierry
and the N51.

There is no shortage of small producers
along the *Green Route* who make and sell
their own champagne. Such growers'
champagne produced in the Côte des
Blancs is excellent and perhaps better
balanced than growers' champagne
produced elsewhere from only black
grapes. This light *blanc des blancs* is superb
with a picnic of garlicky *pâté en croute*, thick
slabs of *jambon de Reims*, French bread and
runny, ripe Brie. Though because of its
cost and its image, champagne is often
drunk only on special occasions, one of the
luxuries of travelling in the region is being
able to indulge in this special wine on
picnics, for breakfast, or indeed, at any
time at all!

The Vineyards of the Aube

In the south of the region, far from the elegant mansions of Reims and Épernay and the élite vineyards of the Marne lie relatively small, but important pockets of vineyards – south of Sezanne and around Bar-sur-Seine and Bar-sur-Aube – that are legally allowed to bear the privileged *appellation* of champagne. The centre for exploring this less well-travelled but fascinating area is medieval Troyes; additionally, charming villages (and numerous campsites) in the nearby Regional Park also make useful bases.

From Épernay, take the N51 to Sezanne and the beginning of a brief but lush stretch of vineyards that extends to Villenauxe-le-Grande, an important market town well-known for its ceramics, china, and pottery. North of the village are the ruins of the Abbey of Nesle-la-Reposte, founded by Clovis in 501. Continue down to Troyes to explore the vineyards of Bar-sur-Seine and Bar-sur-Aube.

Take the N71 from Troyes to Bar-sur-Seine itself, a little town that lies between a cliff and the river. Perched on the top of the cliff is the Château of the Counts of Bar; this can be reached on foot, and provides a fine view of the town and the surrounding country. The vineyards lies to the south, east, and west. From Bar-sur-Seine, a short detour on the D444 leads to Chaource, nestled in the heart of the Chaource forest. This town is perhaps most famous for its rich, creamy, reddish cheese of the same name. The D17 leads to Les Riceys, a town whose position historically between the County of Champagne and the Duchy of Burgundy made it much fought over. Today the nearby vineyards produce neither champagne nor Burgundy, but a much-appreciated local wine, Rosé des Riceys. A bottle or two, together with some cheese from Chaource, and a freshly baked *baguette*, make a most enjoyable picnic.

Continue along the D17 to Mussy-sur-Seine, an historic town nestled in a bend of the river and a perfect spot to spin-out an hour or so with that aforementioned picnic. There is an interesting Museum of the Resistance in one of the town's many fine old houses. Return once more to Bar-sur-Seine on the N71, then meander along the D4 across to Bar-sur-Aube. In the Middle Ages, this town was one of the places where the great Fairs of Champagne were held, attracting dealers and traders from the entire Christian world. Today this attractive holiday resort remains the centre for the production of some excellent Coteaux Champenois wines, as well as some distinctive champagnes. (Admirers of de Gaulle, incidentally, will wish to pay homage to the great man in the nearby town of Colombey-les-Deux-Églises where the *Général* is buried.) Also nearby, the twelfth-century Cistercian cellars at Colombey-le-Sec may be visited by appointment; they are the home of the Confrérie St-Paul St-Vincent, an organization that represents the interests of wine producers in this southern area. A *chalet de dégustation du champagne de l'Aube* is located outside Bar-sur-Aube on the N19, open from the beginning of July to the end of September; it provides an opportunity to taste and purchase these often overlooked wines.

Return to Troyes along the N19, passing the regional *Parc de la Forêt d'Orient*. Excursions into this natural haven can be undertaken from centres such as Vendeuvre-sur-Barse, while Mesnil-St-Pere, and other villages offer camping facilities and bathing in the lake.

Champagne Producers

The hospitality and warmth afforded in this region, the fascination of viewing the complex and remarkable *méthode champenoise*, the vast extent of underground chalk cellars, some of them carved out in Roman days, combined with the elegance of the offices in Reims, Épernay and elsewhere, makes a visit to one of the great *Maisons du Champagne* a highlight of this wine tour. While the basic procedure and methods employed to produce champagne is similar in each, the *grands noms* all have their own histories, and stories to tell; a visit to more than one is recommended on even the shortest tour. Unless it is stated that an appointment is necessary, the champagne establishments keep 'open house' at the hours shown. For those firms requiring appointments, either write in advance, or telephone when in the region, giving as much notice as possible. In addition to the firms listed below (a complete list is available on application to the CIVC), make sure to visit a *récoltant-manipulant*, or a *coopérative* located in the vineyard regions along the *Routes du Champagne*.

51100 Reims

Besserat de Bellefon
allée du Vignoble
tel: (26) 06 09 18
Mon–Fri 9–12h; 14–17h
No appointment necessary for groups smaller than 20 pers.
English spoken.

Vve Clicquot-Ponsardin
1, place des Droits-de-l'Homme
tel: (26) 85 00 68
A. Jan 1–Jan 31; March 1–April 10
    Mon–Fri 14h 15–16h30
    Sun and holidays 14h15–17h30
B. April 6–Oct 31
    Mon–Fri 9–11h15; 14h15–17h
    Sat, Sun, and holidays 14h15–17h
C. February
    By appointment only.
English spoken.

Piper-Heidsieck
51, boulevard Henri-Vasnier
tel: (26) 85 01 94
A. Jan 1–April 2; Nov 12–Dec 31
    Mon–Fri 9–11h30; 14–17h30
    except holidays
B. April 3–Nov 11
    Daily 9–11h30; 14–17h30
Visit in electric train.
English spoken.
Charge for *dégustation*.

G H Mumm & Co.
34, rue du Champ-de-Mars
tel: (26) 40 22 73/88 29 27
Mon–Fri 9–11h15; 14–17h
except holidays
Max 12 pers.
English spoken.

Heidsieck & Co Monopole
83, rue Coquebert
tel: (26) 07 39 34
By appointment only.
Closed August
English spoken.

Krug
5, rue Coquebert
tel: (26) 47 28 15
By appointment only.
Closed July
English spoken.

Lanson Père et Fils
12, boulevard Lundy
tel: (26) 40 36 26
By appointment only.
English spoken.

Pommery & Greno
5, place Général-Gouraud
tel: (26) 05 05 01
Mon–Fri 9–11h; 14–17h
Sat, Sun, holidays by appointment only.
English spoken.

Louis Roederer S A
21, boulevard Lundy
tel: (26) 40 42 11
Mon–Fri 9–12h; 14–17h
Appointment necessary.
Max 12 pers.

Ruinart Père et Fils
4, rue des Crayères
tel: (26) 85 40 29
Daily 9h30–11h; 14h30–16h
Max 30 pers.
Appointment necessary.
Charge for *dégustation*.
English spoken.

Taittinger
9, place St-Nicaise
tel: (26) 85 45 35
Mon–Fri 9–11h15; 14–17h15
Closed Dec 1–Feb 28
English spoken in summer season.

51200 Épernay

Mercier
75, avenue de Champagne
tel: (26) 51 71 11
A. March 1–Oct 31
    Mon–Sat 9–12h; 14–17h30
    Sun and holidays 9–12h; 14–16h
B. Nov 1–Dec 12
    Daily
    Sat 9–12h; 14–17h30
    Sun and holidays 9–12h; 14–16h
Visit in electric train.
English spoken.

Moët et Chandon
18, avenue de Champagne
tel: (26) 51 71 11
A. Jan 4–March 31; Nov 1–Dec 31
    Mon–Fri 10–12h30; 14–17h30
    except holidays

B. April 1–Oct 31
      Mon–Fri 10–12h30; 14–17h30
      Sat 9h30–12; 14–18h
      Sun and holidays 9h30–12; 14–16h
Appointment necessary only for large groups.
English spoken.
Visit takes about 40 minutes.

Perrier-Jouet
26, avenue de Champagne
tel: (26) 51 20 53
By appointment only.
Max 10 pers.
English spoken.

Pol Roger & Cie S A
1, rue Henri-Lelarge
tel: (26) 51 41 95
Mon-Fri by appointment only.
English spoken.

51160 Ay-Champagne

Ayala
2, boulevard du Nord
tel: (26) 50 13 40
Mon–Fri 9–11h; 14–16h30
By appointment only.
Max 10 pers.

Bollinger
16, rue Jules-Lobet
tel: (26) 50 12 34
Mon–Fri
By appointment only.
Closed August
English spoken.

Collery
2, place de la Libération
tel: (26) 50 10 49
Daily 9–18h
Max 150 pers.
English spoken.
Audio-visual presentation.
Small restaurant 'Au Vieux Pressoir' serving regional *champenois* dishes and Collery champagne.

Deutz
16, rue Jeanson
tel: (26) 53 01 11
Mon–Fri 9–11h30; 13h30–17h
Appointment necessary.
Max 15 pers.
English spoken.

51500 Rilly-La-Montagne

Canard-Duchene
Ludes
tel: (26) 61 10 96 (weekdays)
tel: (26) 61 11 40 (weekends and holidays)
A. May 1–July 31; Sept 1–Sept 30
      Mon–Fri 9–11h30; 14–16h
B. Aug 1–Aug 31
      By appointment only.
English spoken.

51500 Mailly-Champagne

Société de Producteurs
tel: (26) 49 41 10
By appointment only.
Max 40 pers.
Charge for *dégustation*.

51000 Châlons-sur-Marne

Joseph Perrier Fils & Cie
69, avenue de Paris
tel: (26) 68 29 51
Mon–Fri 9–11h; 14h30–17h
Except holidays
By appointment only.
Closed August
Max 30 pers.
English spoken.

51150 Tours-sur-Marne

Laurent-Perrier
Boite Postale, 3
tel: (26) 59 91 22
Mon–Fri 9–11h; 14–16h
By appointment only.
Closed August
English spoken.

Wine Museums

Musée du Vin de Champagne et de la
Préhistoire
13, avenue de Champagne
Épernay
Open daily March 1–Nov 30 except Tue
and holidays
Hours: 9–12h; 14–18h; Sun 10–12h; 14–17h

Abbey of Hautvillers
Hautvillers
For information regarding visits contact:
Moët et Chandon
18, avenue de Champagne
51200 Épernay
tel: (26) 51 71 11

Le Musée Champenois d'Ay
4, rue Anatole-France
Ay-Champagne
tel: (26) 50 12 57
Open daily 10–12h; 14–17h

Musée Historique de Troyes et de la
Champagne
Hôtel de Vauluisant
rue de Vauluisant
Troyes
Mainly art, sculpture, and local history of
Champagne, in this impressive 16th
century mansion.
Open daily 10–12h; 14–18h except Tue and
holidays

Wine Seminars and Courses

Wine and food courses are organized by
the *Comité Regional de Tourisme*. These
range from basic weekends in 1-star
hôtel-restaurants learning about the basic
methods of champagne production, to
five-day tours exploring the wine roads,
learning about vinification, and
discovering and sampling typical
champenois cuisine while staying in a 4-star
hotel. For further information contact:

Comité Regional de Tourisme
'Champagne-Ardenne'
2 bis, boulevard Vaubécourt
51000 Châlons-sur-Marne
tel: (26) 68 37 52

The *Institut International des Vins et
Spiritueux* in Bordeaux organizes a six-day
course in Champagne and Alsace which
includes seminars, tastings, and tours of
vineyards. Three days are spent in
Champagne, based in Reims and Épernay.
For further information contact:

Institut International des Vins et
Spiritueux
10, place de la Bourse
33076 Bordeaux
tel: (56) 90 91 28

Wine Festivals

Jan 22 (in certain villages celebrated on the Sat before or after this date)	Festival of St Vincent	Villages throughout the region. Important manifestation at Ambonnay.

(St Vincent is the patron saint of wine growers. The new wine is blessed during a solemn
mass, and is then carried in procession through the streets of the town or village.
Afterwards there is a banquet, and much singing, drinking, and folk dancing.)

June 24 (or nearest Saturday)	Festival of St Jean	Reims, Épernay, Cumières, Hautvillers, and elsewhere
2nd Sun in Sept	Fair of the Wines of Champagne	Bar-sur-Aube
Last Sun in Aug – only every three years Next festival in 1984	Festival of Champagne of the Wine Growers of l'Aube	Takes place in different venues – write for details

There is no collective harvest festival in Champagne. At the end of the harvest each wine
grower celebrates with his family and grape pickers. Traditionally, this celebration of
another year's hard efforts centres around a sumptuous, hearty *champenois* feast, followed
by drinking and dancing. It is called *'Le Cochelet'*.

Regional Gastronomy

Salade aux lardons Salad of dandelion leaves dressed with hot bacon strips, bacon fat, and vinegar.

Pâté de pigeon, de grives Pigeon or thrush pâté.

Jambonneau de Reims Small hocks of ham breaded or enclosed in pastry.

Boudin blanc 'White sausage' made from pork or chicken.

Jambon d'Ardenne Country ham from the Ardennes.

Potée champenoise Hearty soup-cum-stew of rabbit, pork, sausage, cabbage, potato, and other vegetables – traditional *vignerons'* fare.

Andouillette de Troyes Highly-seasoned tripe and chitterling sausage from Troyes.

Pieds de porc à la Ste Ménéhould Pig's trotters poached, boned, then dipped in melted butter, rolled in breadcrumbs, and grilled until sizzling hot and served with mustard.

Matelote champenoise Pike, carp, trout, crayfish, and river eel simmered in the still white wines of the region.

Poulet au Champagne Elegant version of *coq au vin* – chicken stewed in champagne.

Canard au Bouzy Roast duck served with rich wine-sauce made from this distinguished red Coteaux Champenois wine, sometimes garnished with wild mushrooms or truffles.

Civet de lièvre Hare in rich winy sauce.

Blanquette de veau Hearty *vignerons'* stew of breast of veal and vegetables. Good with Coteaux Champenois *blanc*.

Truite au champagne rosé Trout cooked in a delicate *court bouillon* made with rosé champagne, the colour of the wine matching the pale colour of the fish.

Mousseline de brochet au champagne A *mousseline* of puréed pike mixed with *crème fraîche* and egg whites, poached, then served with *beurre blanc* made with champagne – a characteristic example of elegant *haute cuisine champenoise*.

Foie gras à la gelée de champagne Foie gras – whole goose liver – cooked in spices, then set in a shimmering aspic made with champagne.

Sorbet au marc de champagne Refreshing ice made with *marc de champagne*.

Tarte au sucre Sugar and egg tart.

Pâtisseries There are numerous beautifully-looking, and beautiful-to-eat, pastries which are delicious in accompaniment with this elegant wine. Try *biscuits de Reims, caissettes* (meringue), *massepains* (marzipan), *macarons, biscuits roses, croquettes de Bar-sur-Aube*, and much else.

Cheese A variety of cheeses come from the region, including Brie, as well as other fairly assertive and strong-flavoured varieties that accompany well the robust still wines of champagne.
Brie (the best comes from Meaux), Chaource, Dauphin, Langres, Coulommiers, Abbaye d'Igny, Maroille, 'Caprice des Dieux'.

Restaurants

Note: in addition to the listings below, some of the best restaurants in the region are attached to Hotels (see below).

51100 Reims

Boyer
184, avenue d'Épernay
tel: (26) 06 08 60
Well-known traditional restaurant serving seasonal specialities along with 100 varieties of champagne. Considered by many to be the best restaurant in the region.
Closed August; Dec 23–Jan 1; Sun eve; Mon
Open 12–14h30; 19–21h30
Very Expensive

Restaurant Le Vigneron
place Paul Jamot
tel: (26) 88 00 31
This favourite personally-run restaurant serves excellent hearty *champenoise* cuisine. Specialities include *salade aux lardons, andouillette de Troyes, canard*; good selection of Coteaux Champenois wines, and champagne.
Closed Sun
Moderate

Restaurant Grill Le Forum
34, place du Forum
tel: (26) 47 56 87

Grillades and *brochettes* a speciality in this **Inexpensive restaurant**.
Closed Mon eve; Thur eve
Open 12–14h; 19–22h

51160 Saint-Imoges

La Maison du Vigneron de Champagne
N 51
tel: (26) 51 23 62
Moderate family-style restaurant serving the proprietor's own champagne.
Closed Mon

51700 Dormans

Table Sourdet
6 rue du Docteur Moret
tel: (26) 50 20 57
Regional specialities, Coteaux Champenois wines and champagnes.
Closed Mon
Moderate

10000 Troyes

Restaurant Le Bourgogne
40, rue Général-de-Gaulle
tel: (25) 43 06 03
Situated in the heart of old Troyes in the ancient quarter, serving regional specialities such as *andouillette de Troyes, canard au Bouzy,* and *mousseline de brochet.*
Closed Sun, Mon
Open 12–13h30; 19h30–21h30
Moderate to **Expensive**

Hotels

51100 Reims

Frantel
31, boulevard Paul-Doumer
tel: (26) 88 53 54
Situated by the side of the canal, this modern 125-room hotel has excellent amenities, including a restaurant.
Open daily
Restaurant open 12h15–14h15; 19h15–22h15
Expensive

Hôtel-Restaurant de la Paix
9, rue Buirette
tel: (26) 40 04 08
Centrally situated, modern, and well equipped, each room with private bathroom.
Hotel open all year
Restaurant closed Sun
Moderate to **Expensive**

Hôtel Bristol
76, place Drouet-d'Erlon
tel: (26) 40 52 25
Inexpensive hotel without restaurant
Open daily

51500 Montechenot

Auberge du Grand Cerf
N51 Reims/Épernay
tel: (96) 97 60 07
7 km from Reims on the *Route du Champagne,* this hotel has an elegant restaurant serving refined *champenoise* dishes.
Hotel closed Aug
Restaurant open Thur–Mon 12–13h30; 19h30–21h
Expensive

51200 Épernay

Hôtel-Restaurant des Berceaux
13, rue des Berceaux
tel: (26) 51 28 84
Comfortable friendly family hotel under French/English management in the heart of Épernay. Restaurant serves fine *haute cuisine.*
Hotel open all year
Restaurant closed Sun eve
Moderate to **Expensive**

51400 Beaumont-sur-Vesle

La Maison du Champagne
2, rue du Port
tel: (26) 61 62 45
Inexpensive Restaurant/hotel serving good local dishes such as *tripe au champagne, canard aux griottes.*
Hotel closed Sun eve, Mon
Restaurant closed Mon

51130 Vertus

Hostellerie de la Reine Blanche
18, avenue Louis-Lenoir
tel: (26) 52 20 76
Modern **Inexpensive** to **Moderate** hotel/restaurant serving local dishes such as *poularde au champagne, saumon rosé au crèmant,* with Coteaux Champenois wines and champagne.
Restaurant open daily 12–14h; 19h30–21h

51160 Champillon

Royal-Champagne
tel: (26) 51 25 06
An elegant charming old coaching inn along the *Red Route du Champagne* with

bedrooms with verandas overlooking the vineyards. Highly-recommended restaurant serves regional *haute cuisine*.
Open daily
Expensive

51200 Vinay

Hostellerie La Briqueterie
tel: (26) 51 47 12
Well-situated with attractive gardens and 42 individually-decorated bedrooms. Tasteful, elegant restaurant with terrace serving refined cuisine.
Expensive

51150 Ambonnay

Auberge St-Vincent
tel: (26) 59 01 98
Inexpensive hotel with restaurant serving *champenois* and traditional dishes.
Hotel closed Jan 24–Feb 24
Restaurant closed Mon
Open 12–14h; 19h30–21h

51400 Sept-Saulx

Hôtel-Restaurant du Cheval Blanc
rue du Moulin
tel: (26) 61 60 27
Delightful country hotel surrounded by gardens and parkland with restaurant serving imaginative seasonal dishes.
Hotel closed mid Jan–mid Feb
Restaurant open daily 12–14h; 19–21h30
Moderate to **Expensive**

51000 L'Épine

Aux Armes de Champagne
place de la Basilique
tel: (26) 68 10 43
Elegant hotel with gardens and terraces. Restaurant serves sophisticated dishes freshly prepared.
Hotel closed Jan 10–Feb 15
Restaurant open daily 12–14h; 19h15–21h
Moderate

51150 Tours-sur-Marne

Hôtel-Restaurant La Touraine Champenoise
2, rue du Pont
tel: (26) 59 91 93
Champenois specialities at the restaurant of this comfortable hotel include *poulet au champagne, poire au Bouzy, sorbet au marc de champagne*. Good selection of Coteaux Champenois wines, and champagne.

Hotel and restaurant closed Nov 1–Easter
Restaurant closed Mon; open 12–15h; 19–21h
Inexpensive to **Moderate**

51000 Châlons-sur-Marne

Hôtel d'Angleterre
19, place Monseigneur-Tissier
tel: (26) 68 21 51
Comfortable hotel in the centre of town with 18 rooms, and restaurant with flowered terrace. Specialities include *canard sauvage au ratafia, feuilleté de sole au sabayon de champagne*.
Hotel closed Feb 15–March 15
Restaurant open daily
Moderate

Hôtel Pasteur
46, rue Pasteur
tel: (26) 68 10 00
Open all year round, without restaurant
Inexpensive

Where to Get Additional Information

Comité Regional de Tourisme Champagne-Ardenne
2 bis, boulevard Vaubécourt
51000 Châlons-sur-Marne
tel: (26) 64 21 74

Welcome Information Office
3, boulevard de la Paix
51100 Reims
tel: (26) 47 25 69

Office de Tourisme
place Thiers
51200 Épernay
tel: (26) 51 51 66

Comité Interprofessionnel du Vin de Champagne
5, rue Henri-Martin
51204 Épernay
tel: (26) 51 40 47

Champagne News & Information Bureau
220 E 42nd St
NY NY 10017
tel: (212) 907–9382

Camping

51100 Reims
Airotel de Champagne
tel: (26) 49 94 31
51200 Épernay
Camp Municipal
tel: (26) 51 50 71
51000 Châlons-sur-Marne
Camp Municipal
tel: (26) 68 38 00
51160 St-Imoges
Camping du Pré à l'Ane
tel: (26) 51 36 08

51700 Dormans
Au Clocher de Dormans
tel: (26) 50 21 79

Bibliography

Champagne: the Wine, the Land, and the People by Patrick Forbes, Gollancz, 1967

Guide to the Wines of Champagne by Pamela Vandyke Price, Pitman, 1979

——————— LOIRE ———————

The Loire Valley is vast, made up of numerous differing communities and provinces, united only by the longest river in France. The Sancerre hills for example lie far inland in the upper reaches several hundred miles from Nantes, which guards the river's mouth where it spills into the cold waters of the Atlantic. In between lie historic Anjou, Touraine, and Orléanais, each with its own unique catalogue of past and present glories, the former displayed in an unrivalled stretch of grandiose and magnificent châteaux set in forests and valleys, and on high strategic points above towns and villages.

The contrast between the wines of the Loire Valley equals the contrast between its various provinces. Almost every type and style possible is produced here, including pretty pink wines from Anjou; forceful, distinguished dry whites such as Savennières, Pouilly Blanc Fumé, and Sancerre; intensely-scented, rich reds from Chinon and Bourgueil; gay, effervescent sparklers from Saumur; seductive long-lived dessert wines such as Vouvray, Montlouis, Bonnezeaux, and others; and unashamedly short-lived ones like Gros Plant, and Touraine Gamay *primeur*.

If the regions themselves, and their wines, vary considerably, the Loire seems to unite them, exuding its subtle, mellow charm over what must be one of the most luxuriant and beautiful parts of France. It is a country, above all – this land of Rabelais – of refined good living, of relaxation, and of pleasure to be found in the best things in life: wine and supremely simple food (exemplified by the famous regional dish *brochet au beurre blanc* – no more than fresh river pike served with a simple, sublimely delicious sauce of shallots, wine vinegar, and butter); art and grandiose architecture; outdoor recreation in an unspoiled, beautiful preserve; and a tranquil, lazy riverscape which slows the world down to a peaceful, easy, always manageable pace.

Throughout its varied history, the region of the Loire has woven its seductive spell over all who come here. To appreciate the contrasts of this vast, important, and varied vineyard – its fairy-tale castles, natural, more remote beauty spots, and its wines and simple country cooking – the wine lover will travel at an easy, meandering gait, exploring the Loire Valley from Nantes way upriver to Sancerre and Pouilly-sur-Loire.

How to Get There

The Loire is the longest river in France, originating only a hundred miles or so north of the Mediterranean and spilling out into the Atlantic at Nantes some 600 miles later. Nantes and Angers can easily be explored from Brittany and Normandy. Orléans is only 70 miles from Paris, while Sancerre and Pouilly-sur-Loire are both nearer to Beaune than to Nantes. One logical and most pleasurable route meanders from the west, beginning in Nantes, and following the river through Angers, Tours, Blois, Orléans and finally to the upper reaches of the wine-producing valley at Sancerre and Pouilly-sur-Loire.

By Car

From Paris, the shortest, most direct route to the Loire is the A10 autoroute to Orléans. For Angers and Nantes, take the A11 to Le Mans, then the N23 to Angers. For the Upper Loire, take the N7 through Fontainebleau, Nemours, Montargis, Briare, to Pouilly-sur-Loire and Sancerre.

By Plane

The main French international airport is at Paris. The Loire is relatively near to the capital, so proceed from Paris either by car or train. There are internal flights to Nantes, useful for exploring the Muscadet region.

By Train

There are excellent connections between Paris and the Loire with direct routes to Nantes, Angers, Tours, Blois, and Orléans. To begin a tour in Nantes, take a *Rapide* or *Express* train from Paris-Montparnasse to Nantes. These run frequently daily, the quickest doing the journey in less than three and a half hours. For Sancerre and Pouilly-sur-Loire, the nearest principal station is at Cosne, which is on the main Paris–Lyons route.

Local Public Transport

Nantes, Angers, Saumur, and Tours are all connected by a main railway line, with trains running between these main centres frequently every day. Tours, Blois, and Orléans are all stops on the main Paris–Bordeaux route, so trains are both frequent and fast.

The local bus service is good, and there are numerous coach tours of the area from main centres such as Angers, Saumur, Tours, and Orléans (a variety of coach excursions to the region's châteaux are also offered).

A delightful tour on a steam train built at the turn of the century takes passengers from Chinon to Richelieu every Sat and Sun from May 16th to Sept 20th. It stops along the way for wine and goats' cheese tasting. For further information contact:

T.V.T.
Gare de Richelieu
37120 Richelieu
tel: (47) 58 12 97

Car Rental Information

Nantes
  Avis: Château-Bougon airport
      tel: (40) 75 84 60
      18, boulevard du Stalingrad
      tel: (40) 74 07 65
  Hertz: Château-Bougon airport
      tel: (40) 75 15 55
      6, allée du Com Charcot
      tel: (40) 74 18 29
Angers
  Avis: 13, rue Max Richard
      tel: (41) 88 20 24
  Hertz: place de la Gare
      tel: (41) 88 07 53
Saumur
  Avis: 5, rue de Rouen
      tel: (41) 50 48 68
  Hertz: 99, rue de Rouen
      tel: (41) 38 25 33
Tours
  Avis: 39 bis boulevard Heurteloup
      tel: (47) 05 59 33
  Hertz: 8, rue Fleming Galerie Marchande
      tel: (47) 61 02 54
Blois
  Avis: 6, rue Jean Moulin
      tel: (54) 45 24 28
Orléans
  Avis: 13, rue des Sansonnières
      tel: (78) 62 27 04
  Hertz: 47, avenue de Paris
      tel: (78) 62 60 60

Michelin Maps 63, 64, 65, 67

The Wines of the Loire

A remarkable range and variety of wines are produced along the length of the Loire. The following is a brief guide only to the principal wines that will be encountered.

Anjou Vast vineyard extending on both sides of the Loire around Angers, and down to Saumur. A variety of wines are produced here, including dry and sweet white, rosé, sparkling wine, and a small amount of light red. The simple *appellation* Anjou is generally applied to light red and white wines, while wines with more distinction bear qualified *appellations*. (See below.)

Anjou Coteaux de l'Aubance Vineyards which centre around the town of Brissac producing medium sweet rosé, and medium dry white wines.

Anjou Coteaux de la Loire Principally firm and delicate dry and medium dry white wines produced in vineyards north of the Loire, and west of Angers.

Anjou Gamay Light, fruity red wine produced from the Gamay, the great grape of Beaujolais.

Azay-le-Rideau White and rosé wine produced in vineyards around this town famous for its lovely castle on the banks of the Indre River.

Bonnezeaux Great growth of Anjou producing small quantity of sweet, highly perfumed, yet fresh and balanced wine from the Chenin Blanc grape.

Bourgueil and St-Nicolas-de-Bourgueil Red Touraine wines produced from the Cabernet Franc grape grown in sandy or chalk soil around these two well-known communes.

Cabernet d'Anjou Distinguished medium dry rosé from Anjou produced from the Cabernet Franc grape.

Chinon Red wine from vineyards around this beautiful medieval town – much loved by Chinon's favourite son, Rabelais.

Coteaux du Layon Anjou vineyard on the south side of the Loire producing primarily sweet wine from the versatile Chenin Blanc grape. Vineyards extend over 25 communes, the best of which are entitled

to the superior *appellation* Coteaux du Layon-Villages. Additionally, two great growths bear their own *appellations*: Bonnezeaux and Quarts de Chaume.

La Coulée de Serrant Great dry white wine produced in minute quantity within the commune of Savennières.

Gros Plant Sharp, crisp, dry white VDQS *(vin delimité qualité supèrieur)* from the Pays Nantais.

Menetou-Salon Sauvignon wine from the province of Berry.

Montlouis Wine commune on the opposite side of the Loire from Vouvray producing dry, medium dry, and sweet wines, as well as *pétillant* (slightly sparkling) and fully sparkling wines.

Muscadet Popular and well-loved dry white wine produced from vineyards near the mouth of the Loire. Crisp, dry, excellent with the shellfish and seafood of the region. Wine bottled *'sur lie'*, that is, while still on its barrel sediment, has a fresher, rounder flavour. Best known vineyards are located in Sèvre-et-Maine and Coteaux de la Loire.

Pouilly-sur-Loire Wine commune located on upper reaches of the Loire. Distinctive wine of the region is produced from the noble Sauvignon grape and bears the *appellation* Pouilly Blanc Fumé. Wine from the lesser Chasselas is known as Pouilly-sur-Loire.

Quarts de Chaume Great growth of Anjou producing honeyed, sweet wine, in the best years from Chenin Blanc grapes affected by noble rot.

Rosé d'Anjou Extremely popular medium-dry pink wine produced in vineyards around and between the towns of Angers and Saumur. Pretty to look at, easy to drink, it accounts for over half the production in Anjou.

Rosé de Loire *Appellation* for paler, dry rosé wine from the same region.

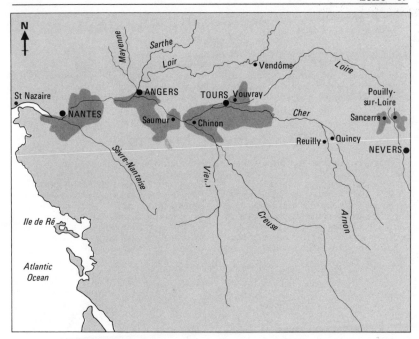

Reuilly, Quincy Two small regions in the Berry producing fine white wines from the distinctive Sauvignon grape.

Sancerre Well-known wine commune opposite Pouilly-sur-Loire producing similar white wine from Sauvignon grape. Wine has a pronounced earthy character, and a full-bodied flavour that allows it to stand up to a variety of full-flavoured foods. Small amounts of red and rosé Sancerre are produced from the Pinot Noir grape. They are entitled to the same *appellation* and, though popular locally, are rarely exported.

Savennières Wine commune west of Angers which produces fragrant, full-bodied dry white wine from the Chenin Blanc grape. Two great vineyards are entitled to their own *appellations*: La Coulée de Serrant, and La Roche aux Moines.

Saumur Best known for sparkling wines produced from grapes grown in the chalk tufa that resembles the soil of Champagne. The Chenin Blanc, Chardonnay, and Cabernet grapes are used to produce a

cuvée (blend of still wines) which undergoes secondary fermentation in the bottle *(méthode champenoise)*. A full range of styles of wine is produced by the firms who age their wines in deep chalk caves above the banks of the Loire.

Saumur-Champigny Light red wine with pronounced aroma of raspberries.

Touraine General *appellation* for white, rosé, and red wines produced in the vineyards of Touraine. Two wines, in particular, have recently been gaining favour: Touraine Gamay, a fruity young red wine, and Sauvignon de Touraine, a fresh, clean, dry white that is considerably less expensive than the distinguished Sauvignon wines from further upriver.

Vouvray Well-known wine commune producing famous sweet wines, and also dry, and medium dry still wines, and light sparkling wines by the *méthode champenoise*. The great sweet wines of Vouvray are known for their longevity, and for a rich, honeyed sweetness that is balanced by a firm, but unobtrusive acidity.

Wine Tours along the length of the Loire

As mentioned previously, the Loire Valley is not a single wine region, but many individual and distinctly different ones. Thus, beginning in Nantes and slowly proceeding upriver, various detours onto diverse *routes des vins* can be made, some of which provide little more than a pleasant circular interlude through vineyards and villages, while others allow greater opportunity to taste and purchase wines and tour cellars.

The Route du Muscadet

The Pays Nantais produces three wines, the first well-known – Muscadet – the other two less so – Gros Plant du Pays Nantais, and Coteaux d'Ancenis-Gamay. The area for the production of these wines virtually surrounds the region's capital city Nantes, extending along the Loire Valley both above and below that city, to the east, and to the south-west almost to the

Atlantic coast. The vineyards are influenced by the proximity of the ocean. One year in the early eighteenth century the winter was so savage that the sea actually froze near the coast, and the entire vineyard was destroyed. A hearty vine, the Melon de Bourgogne, was imported for replanting. Renamed Muscadet, it today accounts for nearly three-quarters of

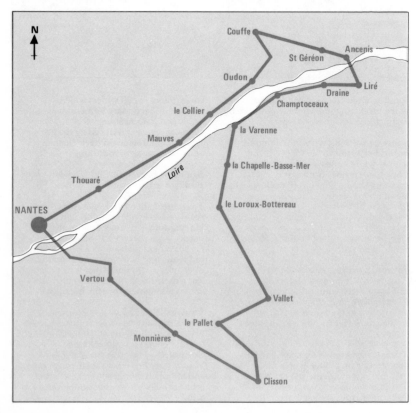

the region's production. The vineyards of the Pays Nantais are essentially cultivated by small family land-holders. As a consequence, there are few large properties with organized cellar tours.

Nevertheless, a sign-posted wine road appears frequently throughout the vineyard area, but it is not essential to follow it religiously from one point to another. The following is a suggested itinerary only; improvise and explore the region yourself, stopping to taste and purchase wine from producers who 'vente directe', or for a bite to eat in unpretentious restaurants where a *pichet* of tart Gros Plant, or Muscadet 'sur lie' washes down enormous platters of *fruits de mer*.

From Nantes, leave the city in the direction of Clisson, and find the D59 that leads to Vertou (whose vineyards were cultivated by monks in the eleventh century). This road leads soon into the heart of the Muscadet country, known as Sèvre et Maine, a pleasant, picturesque land of fields of vines, tended by horse-drawn machinery, leading on to surprising vistas such as the Byzantine-inspired tower that rises above St-Fiacre-sur-Maine or, from the hills above Monnières, no less than ten church steeples peeping out from the vine-covered fields.

Continue on to Clisson, nestled in a hollow formed by the confluence of the Sèvre-Nantaise and the Moine. The small town was burnt to the ground after the French Revolution, leaving only a fine, fifteenth-century covered market hall. A weekly gathering still takes place here. The town, curiously, was subsequently rebuilt in a rather grand Palladian style. Its central position in the midst of the vineyards makes Clisson a good base from which to explore the region.

Leave the town on the D763 north, and soon turn off left on the N149 to Le Pallet. This small village was once a fortress of the Dukes of Brittany, as well as the birthplace of Abelard – the Musée Pierre-Abelard is both a memorial to the life of that hapless theologian and philosopher, as well as a small museum depicting the folk art and traditions of the *vignobles*. From Le Pallet, find the D116 across to Vallet (the *Maison de Muscadet*, on the outskirts of the village, offers tastings and sells local producers' wines). Continue along the D37 to Le Loroux-Bottereau, another ancient town tired in continuously since the first century AD. Return to Nantes, or else skirt that city by finding the D7 which leads to La Chapelle-Basse-Mer, and on to the Loire itself.

There is a fine Turneresque view of the river valley above La Varenne. The D751 follows the river now, through Champtoceaux and Draine to Liré (pleasant camping along the river). Cross the suspension bridge at Liré, and so continue to Ancenis, a peaceful, historic town, whose fifteenth-century castle once guarded Brittany's border from the powerful and rapacious Dukes of Anjou. From Ancenis, the vineyards of the Coteaux d'Ancenis and Muscadet des Coteaux de la Loire can be explored by returning to Nantes on the D23 via St Gereon and Couffe, the D25 to Oudon and Le Cellier, and the D68 through Mauves and Thouaré. Otherwise, from Ancenis, continue upriver to Angers and the vineyards of Anjou.

Routes des Vins d'Anjou

The vineyards of Anjou, which extend around Angers in a moonshaped band downriver to Saumur, are some of the best known and varied along the length of the Loire. A wine tour of Anjou will include time in both Angers and Saumur, a meander along the sign-posted *Route du Vin* through the lovely Layon Valley, stops at *caveaux de dégustation* and a tour of a sparkling Saumur establishment to view the *méthode champenoise* in chalk caves remarkably reminiscent of those of Épernay and Reims.

Angers straddles the Maine River, its squat, massive seventeen-towered château dominating all that it overlooks.

Stone-paved, uneven streets without cars lead up to it and to the cathedral, and sunlight flickers off pale-grey slate roofs, highlighting boxes of red geraniums, aubretia, and strings of dish towels and drying washing. Before touring the château, refresh yourself with a glass of wine from *La Maison du Vin de l'Anjou* (located across from the castle – see hours below). The *Maison* serves to publicize the wines of Anjou, offers maps and other useful information and literature, as well as *dégustation*. A visit to the château itself is a must, to see the magnificent collection of tapestries, and to walk the broad ramparts which overlook the formal garden, chapel,

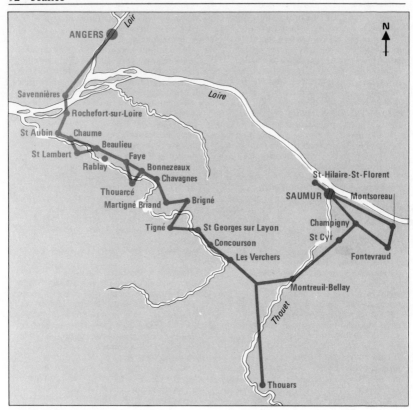

and the river itself.

Leave Angers on the D111 in the direction of Savennières, the wine commune that gives its name to superb, full-bodied dry white wines that partner so well the many fish dishes of the Loire. The Château de La Roche-aux-Moines, well sign-posted and reached before Savennières by turning left onto a small road towards the river, is the home of two of the finest wines of the Anjou vineyard, La Coulée de Serrant and La Roche-aux-Moines. From Savennières, cross the river towards Rochefort-sur-Loire, but before reaching the other bank, turn sharply down to the left to reach the agricultural island community of Béhuard, with its remarkable fifteenth-century church in the tiny village square which actually seems to be sculpted out of the rocks that surround its base.

Rochefort-sur-Loire is a small wine commune which lies alongside the Louet, one of many tributaries of the Loire (there are pleasant bathing spots along the river here). Though Rochefort is only just across the river from Savennières, and though the same grape, the Chenin Blanc, is cultivated on both sides, wine from this commune, and from others further along the Layon Valley, is virtually opposite in character: not dry, but luscious, honeyed and, in the best years, extremely sweet, yet with an essential underlying acidity which keeps it from cloying. The general *appellation* for such sweet wines is Coteaux du Layon; the following villages, which are all encountered while proceeding through this pleasant valley, produce wines with distinct characteristics and individuality, and are thus designated Coteaux du Layon-Villages: Rochefort, Chaume, Beaulieu, Rablay, Faye,

St-Aubin, and St-Lambert. These sweet wines, incidentally, are not drunk here solely as dessert wines, but are often taken as a favoured local aperitif or even to accompany rich foods such as the classic *canard à l'orange*.

There is a sign-posted *Route du Vin* which runs though the Layon Valley, though it is not essential – nor is it all that easy – to follow it rigorously. Simply pick your way through these communes enjoying the countryside, stopping when you want to, at Thouarce, or the Château de Tigne and so, eventually, come around to the vineyards of Saumur.

Montreuil-Bellay, some 8 miles south of Saumur itself, is perched on terraces which rise from the Thouet River, an interesting little town to explore on foot. The impressive ramparts remain mainly intact, and the château is well worth a visit. Additionally, there is a large, modern winery, La Compagnie de la Vallée de la Loire, located outside the town. From Montreuil-Bellay, continue downriver (that is, north, on D160) to St-Cyr-en-Bourg (wine can be tasted and purchased from the *coopératives* here), then continue on D405 to Champigny, a tiny hamlet which, within an almost overwhelming sea of white and pink wines, produces light but intensely-scented red wine known as Saumur-Champigny. A detour east along the D145 leads through the forest of Fontevraud to the famous Romanesque abbey of Fontevraud itself, which, apart from other carefully restored features,

boasts an unusual twelfth-century kitchen with twenty separate chimneys.

From Fontevraud, approach Saumur along the D947 that runs alongside the river, under a cliff of chalk tufa riddled with caves. Along the approach into the town, and on the other side, too, particularly in the town of St-Hilaire St-Florent, there are numerous establishments that specialize in the production of sparkling Saumur by the *méthode champenoise*. These fascinating firms, often located in caves carved out of the chalk tufa cliffs, are extremely welcoming; many have English-speaking guides, and the wines can be tasted and usually purchased. Keep an eye out, incidentally, for the curious troglodyte houses, cool, half-hidden in the cream-coloured hills, and for *caves champignons*, moist, damp caves in which literally tons of cultivated mushrooms are produced daily. These, too, can be visited, and provide a most interesting tour.

Saumur itself is one of the most lovely of all Loire Valley towns. Its château, splendidly grand, overlooking the river and town, provides a particularly beautiful vista over the blue slate roofs and across the peaceful valley. Apart from its wine and its castle, Saumur is known for its illustrious cavalry school, and for the Cadre Noir riding team which gives frequent skilful displays. There are hotels and restaurants here, as well as a large campsite on the island in the middle of the river.

Vineyards and Châteaux of Touraine

Touraine, *la douce Touraine*, with its grandiose Renaissance châteaux; its forests, green gardens, fruit orchards, and walnut groves; its many majestic, slow-flowing rivers, their names as beautiful as their aspects – Le Cher, L'Indre, La Vienne, La Choisille; and its verdant valleys whereon lie its famous vineyards, is a region of rare natural and man-made richness. A tour of this historic province combines wine tastings and meanders through vine-covered country with visits to some of the most famous and impressive châteaux in all of the Loire. As an added bonus Touraine, known as the Garden of France, is a province in which it is almost impossible not to eat well (indeed, would we expect any less in this land of François Rabelais?). Though there

are individual wine roads within Touraine, such as the *Route du Vouvray*, the following suggested tour leads through the most important vineyards of the region, as well as to some of its principal châteaux.

From Saumur, cross to the north side of the Loire and continue along the N147 for a few miles before branching right on the D10 to St-Nicolas-de-Bourgueil and Bourgueil. Both these picturesque communes are centres for the production of fragrant, delicate red wines made from the Breton grape which, despite its name, came several centuries ago from Bordeaux (it is, in fact, a variety of Cabernet Franc). As Rabelais wrote in the sixteenth century, 'This excellent Breton wine is not grown in Brittany, but comes from our own delightful countryside at Veron.' Bourgueil

itself was once the seat of a powerful
Benedictine abbey, though little of this
now remains. Just over a mile north of the
town, the Cave de la Dive Bouteille can be
visited; it is a *cave touristique* with an
interesting wine museum and a collection
of old wine presses; the local wines can be
tasted and purchased.

Return to the river on the D749, cross it
(passing the Avoine-Chinon nuclear
power station) and continue down to
Chinon, a superbly preserved, evocative
medieval town. A statue of satisfied,
well-fed Rabelais presides in the main
square (he was born just a mile or so away
at La Devinière, where there is now a
museum devoted to his life and work;
even the local Hostellerie is called 'La
Gargantua'). Vieux Chinon, the old part of
town below the sprawling castle, with its
leaning brick and timber houses, probably
has changed little since the stirring days
when Jeanne d'Arc first met and recognized
the Dauphin. Climb the steep, cobbled
streets up to the château for a magnificent
view over the roofs of the town and the
valley below. Chinon lies alongside the
Vienne River, and the Breton vines that
grow on the gentle slopes produce fine,
light, strawberry-scented wine. In Chinon
itself, along the riverfront, caves
have been carved into the soft tufa, some
of which can be visited, providing a cool
spot to taste these delectable wines.

From Chinon, it is possible to take a
pleasant train excursion to Richelieu (see
Local Transport). Make a detour to that
model town, or else follow the D751
through the forest of Chinon to yet
another lovely château and wine town,
Azay-le-Rideau. Set on the banks of the
placid Indre, many consider this elegant
yet individual castle to be the epitome of
the Renaissance ideal. With its pure white
stone walls, its graceful turrets, and
glimmering blue slate roof, all reflected in
the calm waters of its moat, it is virtually
the fairy-tale castle of every child's dreams
– except that it is real. There is a campsite
along the river near the château. A small
stretch of vineyards extends over the
slopes above the Indre towards its

confluence with the Loire, and both crisp,
fruity white, and rosé wine bears the
appellation Touraine Azay-le-Rideau. It is
perfect light holiday wine to while away
the hours.

From Azay-le-Rideau follow the river
north towards the Loire (D57) and at
Lignières-de-Touraine turn right on the D7
to Villandry (whose château is famous for
its triple-tiered formal gardens). An
impressive system of limestone caves can
be visited at Savonnières, while continuing
further along the same road brings us to
Tours.

Tours is a large and important provincial
capital. On first approach its flat, wide
boulevards, its industrial zone to the north,
and the fact that it was heavily bombed in
the last war, might tempt one to avoid it,

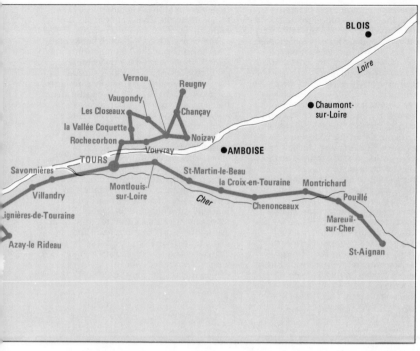

considering the numerous smaller beauty spots which literally abound along this particular stretch of the Loire. Certainly, it is not a 'picture postcard town', yet with its cathedral, its moody medieval quarter, its monasteries and museums (including an excellent one devoted to wine and viticulture), and its modern shops and University, it is a vital, living city that deserves to be visited.

Leave Tours on the N152 (river road along the north bank) to reach the start of the *Route du Vouvray*. About two and a half miles east of Tours lies the Monastère de Marmoutier (founded in the fourth century) and beyond, the first of the handful of communes that produce Vouvray: Rochecorbon which, like so many towns nestled under the tufa slopes whereon lie the vineyards, is noted for its curious troglodyte houses and cellars extending into the cliffs themselves. Vouvray is one of the great wines of the Loire, for the Chenin Blanc thrives in these splendid low-lying hills to produce a full range of dry, medium-dry, medium-sweet, and very sweet, still, *pétillant*, or fully sparkling wines. The

greatest are produced from grapes that have been affected by *pourriture noble*, lusciously sweet and extremely long-lived; youthful, fruity, dry and medium-dry wines, on the other hand, are more readily accessible, and partner such local specialities as *porc au pruneaux*, and rustic *charcuterie* such as *rillettes* and *rillons*, or simply just a handful of rich, oily walnuts and dry goats' cheese.

Vouvray itself is situated amidst its famed vineyards, an unimposing little town, proud of its wine and anxious to show it off. There are shops selling wine, local specialities, and distinctive glassware (some of the regions of the Loire, as elsewhere in France, have their own particularly-shaped glass which shows off the local wine at its best), and there are also a few local restaurants, hotels, and wine producers to visit. The *Route du Vouvray* continues east (D46) to Vernou; cross through the village, and carry on along the D1 to Noizay. At Noizay turn left on the D78 to rejoin the D46 at Chançay. Reugny is another wine commune further north up the Brenne Valley; either continue there, or else take the D46 south back towards Vernou then, before reaching that town again, find the D76 that leads into the hills above Vouvray – majestic, unspoiled vine-covered slopes interspersed with forests and other agriculture and grazing. In some small farms, both wine and home-produced goats' cheese can be purchased direct. At the hamlet of Les Closeaux, branch left; where the road forks, continue not to Vouvray, but right, across the D47, and down to the lovely Vallée Coquette. Reward yourself with a cool glass of wine at the *cave coopérative* there, and either return to Tours, or else continue further upriver to Amboise.

Alternatively, a tour of the vineyards of Montlouis and the Cher Valley (south side of the Loire) provides both more wine-tasting opportunities, as well as visits to châteaux. From Tours, follow the D751 to Montlouis-sur-Loire whose vineyards, virtually opposite those of Vouvray, produce a similar range of wines. There are numerous troglodyte houses and caves, some of which house wine cellars, as well as good regional restaurants, also located in

caves. From Montlouis, find the D40 that leads to the Cher Valley at St-Martin-le-Beau.

The vineyards on the south banks of the Cher form part of the Touraine wine region whose wines bear that simple *appellation*. Continue upriver, through La Croix-en-Touraine, to Chenonceaux. This celebrated château, with its graceful arches that actually span the Cher, its broad avenue of plane trees, its formal gardens and spacious park, and its chequered, romantic history, is one of the region's grandest and most grandiose. From Chenonceaux, continue through the Cher Valley, passing cellars and caves along the way, to pretty Montrichard; cross to the south bank and follow the smaller D17 through wine hamlets such as Pouillé, Mareuil-sur-Cher, and St-Aignan. From here, one can either return to Amboise or else continue to Chaumont-sur-Loire, to Blois, or to Chambord (largest of the Loire châteaux, and a former royal hunting lodge). The choice of beautiful places to visit in this magnificent stretch of the Loire is literally overwhelming.

The Upper Loire:
the Wine Roads of Sancerre and
Pouilly-sur-Loire

Well past the concentrated riches of Touraine, the wide Loire swings south towards its source. Upriver, here in the heart of France, lies yet another distinguished Loire Valley wine region, centring around two communes on opposing sides of the river: Sancerre and Pouilly-sur-Loire. Though often spoken of in the same breath, the river divides rather than unites them, and the communes remain distinct. The best wines from both – Sancerre and Pouilly Blanc Fumé – however, share a similar character that comes from the distinctive, intensely-scented Sauvignon grape, the climate, and the soils on which it ripens here in the Upper Loire. Both regions have sign-posted wine roads which lead into the surrounding slopes and wine communes.

The *Route du Sancerre et du Crottin de Chavignol* extends through the principal wine-making communes and vineyards of

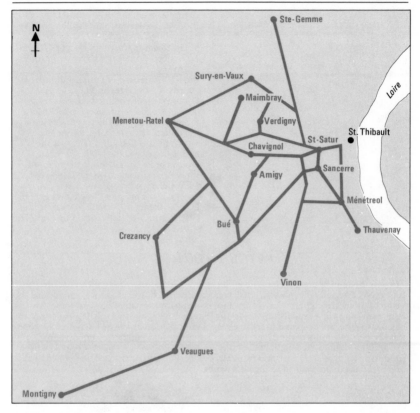

Sancerre, and also through majestic high fields where brown-furred goats nibble sweet grass. Their milk produces one of France's great goats' cheeses, Crottin du Chavignol, fresh, or dry and crumbly (depending on its age), pungent, and delicious with a glass of Sancerre wine (the name *'crottin'*, curiously, means dung). Sancerre itself is a fortified town located on an isolated hill overlooking the Loire, steep, remote, self-contained, with its old stone houses, winding, climbing streets, and fifteenth-century keep. The surrounding Sancerre hills are dotted with small wine communes where the *vignerons* and their families live, some 500 of them, though less than two dozen have holdings larger than 10 hectares. Because it is a region of small family proprietors, there are few large-scale facilities for the wine-loving tourist, though some producers both of wine and of cheese sell their products direct to the public. Nevertheless, the *Route du Sancerre et du Crottin du Chavignol* is most pleasant to follow, passing through remote hills, fields of well-exposed vines, and little communes such as St-Satur, Ste-Gemme, Sury-en-Vaux, Mainbré, Verdigny, Chavignol, Amigny, Ménétreol, Bué, Crézancy, Menetou-Ratel, Vinon, and others. Afterwards, relax in the *Caves de la Mignonne* with – what else – Sancerre and Crottin du Chavignol.

Pouilly-sur-Loire, as the name suggests, is actually sited along the river (Sancerre, on its sheltered perch, stands above it – the nearby suburb of St-Thibauld is along the river, and offers good restaurants and accommodation). The surrounding vine-covered slopes seem, if anything, less rugged and remote than those of Sancerre; and if, in Sancerre, the outlook is west, to the Berry and Poitou, in Pouilly it is

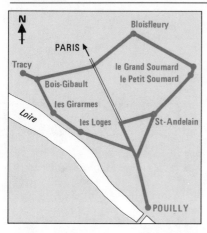

definitely east, to the forests of the
Morvan, to Vézelay and Avallon and to
rich, smug Burgundy.

The *Route du Vin* provides a brief circular
excursion into the wine country, through
charming little villages. From Pouilly, take
the RN7 (direction of Paris), and turn off
shortly to Les Loges and Les Girarmes.
Follow the gaily-painted wine road signs
on D243 to Tracy-sur-Loire, which has a
fifteenth-century castle set amidst some of
the region's finest estates. From Tracy,
return to Bois-Gibault, then cross the RN7
to Boisfleury, via the D247. Continue
around to Le Grand and Petit Soumard,
then turn right again on the D163 to
St-Andelain, a popular market town,
perched on a hill providing views over the
Loire to the west, and the Morvan to the
east. Return to Pouilly-sur-Loire via RN7.

Wine Producers

Though the Loire is a region famous for its grandiose châteaux, her wine producers, on
the whole, are generally modest, small concerns; many, however, do welcome casual
visitors, though a telephone call in advance is always appreciated. The exceptions are the
large sparkling wine establishments around Saumur who, like their distinguished cousins
in Champagne, are prepared to receive casual visitors; many have on hand multi-lingual
guides who give tours of the caves. Numerous tasting and purchasing opportunities
abound throughout the length of the Loire, in *caves touristiques*, or roadside stands, from
producers who *'vente directe'*, and from *Maisons des Vins* run by the various professional
organizations to promote their region's wines.

Muscadet

44000 Nantes

Caveau de Dégustation
Comité Interprofessionnel des Vins
d'Origine du Pays Nantais
17, rue des États
tel: (40) 47 15 58
Muscadet AOC, Gros Plant du Pays
Nantais, Coteaux d'Ancenis Gamay VDQS
Mon–Fri 10h30–12h; 16h30–18h
Max 40 pers.
English spoken.
(General explanations about the vineyards
of the Pays Nantais, literature and maps
available; visits to cellars and vineyards
can be arranged, if given sufficient
advance notice.)

44690 Monnières

Domaine des Moulins
tel: (40) 20 07 83
Muscadet de Sèvre et Maine AOC

Daily by appointment.
Max 30 pers.
English spoken.

44330 Le Pallet Vallet

Pierre Lusseaud
Château de la Galissonnière
tel: (40) 26 42 03
Muscadet AOC, Gros Plant du Pays
Nantais, Cabernet
Mon–Fri 9–19h
Appointment preferable.
Max 50 pers.
A little English spoken.
Buffet can be arranged for groups if given
advance notice.

Marcel Sautejea
Domaine de l'Hyvernière
tel: (40) 78 23 24
Muscadet de Sèvre et Maine
Mon–Thur 8–12h; 14–17h30
Fri 8–12h; 14–17h
English spoken.

44330 Vallet

Sauvion et Fils
Château du Cléray
tel: (40) 36 22 55
Muscadet de Sèvre et Maine 'sur lie'
Daily 9–12h; 14–17h
Appointment preferable.
Max 60 pers.
English spoken.

44330 La Chapelle-Heulin

Donatien Bahuaud et Co
tel: (40) 36 21 22
Muscadet AOC
Mon–Fri
By appointment.
Max 50 pers.
English spoken.

The Anjou Vineyard

49000 Angers

La Maison du Vin d'Anjou
5 bis, place Kennedy
tel: (41) 88 81 13
Daily except Tue 9–12h30; 14h30–18h30
Near the castle: free tastings and
information and literature about the
vineyards and wine roads of Anjou.

49800 St-Barthélémy d'Anjou

Cointreau SA
Carrefour Molière
tel: (41) 43 25 21
Mon–Fri 9–10h30; 13–15h30
Telephone or write in advance for an
appointment to visit the establishment
producing this famous orange-flavoured
liqueur.
Max 25 pers.
English spoken.

49710 Savennières

Château de la Roche aux Moines
tel: (41) 54 52 32
La Coulée de Serrant, La Roche aux
Moines
Mon–Fri 8h30–12h; 14–18h; Sat 8h30–12h
Max 40 pers.
English spoken.

49320 Brissac

Les Caves de la Loire
tel: (41) 91 22 71
Vins d'Anjou & Saumur

Appointment necessary for groups.
Max 50 pers.
English spoken.

49380 Thouarce

René Renou Fils
place du Champ de Foire
tel: (41) 54 04 05
Rosé de Loire, Rosé d'Anjou, Anjou
Rouge, Anjou Gamay, Anjou Blanc
Mon–Sat 9–12h; 14–18h
By appointment.
Max 40 pers.
English spoken.

49770 Tigne

Château de Tigne
tel: (41) 59 41 42
Coteaux du Layon, Vins d'Anjou,
Saumur-Champigny, St Nicolas de
Bourgueil, Quarts de Chaume, and others
Thur & Fri
Appointment necessary.
A little English spoken.

49260 Montreuil Bellay

Cave Coopérative des Vignerons de
Saumur
St-Cyr-en-Bourg
tel: (41) 51 61 09
Vins d'Anjou & Saumur
May 1–Sept 30 8–12h; 14–17h
Appointment necessary only for groups.
Max 100 pers.
English spoken.
Charge for *dégustation*.

49416 Saumur

Gratien & Meyer
Château de Beaulieu
route de Chinon
tel: (41) 51 01 54
méthode champenoise Saumur
Open daily 9–12h; 14–18h
English spoken.
Audio-visual.

Ackerman-Laurance
rue Léopold Palustre
St-Hilaire St-Florent
tel: (41) 50 25 33
méthode champenoise Saumur
Open daily
Appointment preferable.
English spoken.

S A de Neuville
EGVDN
St-Hilaire St-Florent
tel: (41) 50 16 43
méthode champenoise Saumur
Mon–Fri
Appointment necessary only for groups.
Max 50 pers.
English spoken.

Bouvet-Ladubay SA
rue Ackerman
St-Hilaire St-Florent
tel: (41) 50 11 12
méthode champenoise Saumur
Open daily June–Aug 9–12h; 14–17h
Appointment necessary only in low
season.
English spoken.
Audio-visual.

SCA Séjourné-Robineau
49730 Montsoreau
tel: (41) 51 70 30
Mushroom cave: 70% of the mushrooms
cultivated in France come from the caves in
the Saumur region. Séjourné-Robineau are
one such firm, located in a 15th-century
troglodyte house along the main D751
road upriver from Saumur.
Mon–Fri 9h30–11h45; 14–19h
English spoken.

Vineyards of Touraine

37140 Bourgueil

Cave Touristique de 'La Dive Bouteille' de
Bourgueil
tel: (47) 58 72 01
Bourgueil, St-Nicolas-de-Bourgueil
Open daily 10h–19h
Max 300 pers.
Charge for *dégustation*.

37500 Chinon

Plozeau & Fils
54 faubourg St-Jacques
tel: (47) 93 16 34
Chinon *rouge*, Touraine Sauvignon,
Touraine *rosé*
Open daily 10–12h; 14–18h
Appointment necessary.
Max 40 pers.
Charge for *dégustation*.

37210 Vouvray

Cave Coopérative de la Vallée Coquette
tel: (47) 52 70 03

Full range of Vouvray wines
Open daily 8h30–12h; 14–18h
Appointment necessary only for groups.

Cave des Viticulteurs du Vouvray
Château de Vaudenuits
route de Vernou
tel: (47) 52 70 50
Full range of Vouvray wines
Mon–Fri 9–12h; 14–17h30
Sat, Sun 9h30–12h; 14h30–18h

37270 Montlouis

Cave Coopérative des Producteurs de Vins
de Montlouis
tel: (47) 50 80 98
Full range of Montlouis wines
Daily 8–12h; 14–18h
June 15–Sept 15 open until 19h
Appointments necessary only for groups
of more than 50.

Cave Touristique du Montlouis
place Courtemanche
tel: (47) 50 82 26
Full range of Montlouis wines
Mon–Fri except holidays 10–12h; 14–19h
July–Sept open daily
English-speaking guides by arrangement
for groups.
Max 100 pers.

41400 Montrichard

Caves Monmousseau
73, rue de Vierzon
tel: (54) 32 07 04
Full range of wines of Touraine
Mon–Fri 9–12h; 14–18h except holidays
Appointment necessary only for groups.
Max 60 pers.
English spoken.

Upper Loire

18300 Sancerre

Caves de la Mignonne
(cave located off the route from Sancerre to
St-Satur)
tel: (48) 54 07 06
Sancerre AOC *blanc, rouge, rosé*
Daily March 15–Nov 15 10–12h; 14–18h
Max 600 pers.
Displays of old viticultural tools, and
tastings of wines together with Crottin du
Chavignol in this ancient quarry.
Charge for *dégustation*.

18300 St-Satur

Caves du Clos la Perrière
tel: (48) 54 16 93
Sancerre AOC *blanc, rouge, rosé*
Easter–end of Sept Sat, Sun only
July–August daily 14h30–19h30

58150 Pouilly-sur-Loire

Cellier de la Moynerie
N7
tel: (86) 39 14 72
Pouilly Blanc Fumé AOC
Daily 9–12h; 13h30–19h
Appointment preferable.

Domaine Saget
Caves St Vincent
tel: (86) 39 16 37
Vins de Pouilly & Sancerre
Open Mon–Sat 8–12h; 14h30–19h
Sun 10–12h; 14h30–19h30
Max 60 pers.
English spoken.

Caves de Pouilly-sur-Loire
Les Moulins à Vent
tel: (86) 39 10 99
Pouilly Blanc Fumé, Pouilly-sur-Loire
blanc, Coteaux du Giennois *rouge, rosé*
Groups only, by appointment.
A little English spoken.

Wine Museums

Musée des Vins de Touraine
Celliers St-Julien
16, rue Nationale
37000 Tours
tel: (47) 61 81 24
Daily except Tue, Jan 1, May 1, July 14,
Nov 11, and Dec 25

Le Musée Animé du Vin et de la
Tonnellerie
12, rue Voltaire
Chinon
tel: (47) 93 25 63

Musée du Vin
Chapelle St-Michel
Le Pallet
44330 Vallet
May–Nov Sat, Sun, and holidays only
14–16h
Appointment necessary for other times.

Wine Festivals

Jan 14, 15, 16	Wine Festival	Vouvray
2nd weekend in Jan	Wine Festival	Angers
End of Jan	Festivals celebrating St-Vincent, patron saint of vine growers	Angers, Nantes Vouvray, Tours, and Chinon
1st Sat in Feb	Wine Festival	Bourgueil, St-Nicolas-de-Bourgueil
2nd weekend in Feb	Wine Festival	Saumur
3rd Sat in Feb	Wine Festival	Montlouis
Last Sat in Feb	Wine Festival	Azay-le-Rideau
Last weekend in Feb	Wine Festival	Chalonnes-sur-Loire
1st weekend in March	Wine Festival	Loreoux Bottereau
1st Sat in March	Wine Festival	Chinon
2nd Sat in March	Wine Festival	Vallet
Easter Day	Wine Festival	Amboise, Bourgueil, St-Nicolas-de-Bourgueil, St-Georges-sur-Cher
4th Sun in March	Wine Festival	Machecoul
Sat, Sun, Mon of Pentecost	Wine Festival	Sancerre

May	Wine Festival	Clisson and Cravant-les-Coteaux
May 1	Wine Festival	Panzoult
Mid May	Wine Festival	Tours
May or June	Fête du Crottin and other cheeses of France	Sancerre
June	Wine Festival	Vertous
1st Sat in July	Wine Festival	Thésée
Sun after July 14	Wine Festival	St-Aubin-de-Luigne
1st Sun in Aug	Wine Festival	Montsoreau
Aug 11–15th	Wine Festival	Vouvray
Aug 15	Wine Festival	Amboise, Montlouis, and Bourgueil
Last weekend in Aug	Festival of French wines	Sancerre
Sept 19	Wine Festival	Chinon
Last weekend in Oct	Oyster festival – tastings of oysters from the Marennes	Sancerre
Last Sun in Nov	Vintage Festival	Nantes

Regional Gastronomy

The Loire is not one, but many regions, each with their own gastronomic traditions and specialities.

Crêpe Sweet, savoury, or *flambéed* pancake; speciality of Brittany available in Nantes and Muscadet region. *Crêpes aux fruits de mer* (seafood layered pancake) superb with Muscadet or Gros Plant.

Galette Buckwheat pancake, usually layered with smoked ham and egg.

Pâté aux pommes de terre Simple Sancerrois first-course: potato and cream purée.

Rillons Riblets of pork cooked slowly in their own fat until brown and caramelized.

Rillettes Potted paste, usually of pork, sometimes of pork and goose, bound in its own fat, and highly seasoned. Each of the various main centres, Angers, Saumur, Tours, and Blois, have their own versions.

Boudin blanc Pork and chicken sausage.

Pâté d'alouettes Lark pie.

Pâté de cailles Quail pie.

Truite à l'oseille Trout stuffed with sorrel and shallots.

Quenelles de brochet Sieved and pounded pike, mixed with *crème fraîche*, and egg whites, then poached in stock.

Matelote d'anguilles River eel stewed in wine.

Saumon de la Loire Loire salmon.

Beurre blanc Exquisite Loire sauce of whipped butter, reduced wine vinegar (or wine), and shallots, served over pike, salmon, shad, perch and other freshwater fish. Not to be missed.

Friture de la Loire Mixed fry of small river fish.

Canard au Muscadet Wild duck stewed in sauce of cream, Muscadet, and raisins.

Poulet d'Angevin Chicken pieces braised on a bed of vegetables, then served in a cream and egg yolk sauce flavoured with mustard.

Lapin au sang Rabbit cooked in red wine sauce thickened with blood. Speciality of Sancerre.

Porc aux pruneaux Pork and succulent prunes from Touraine in a rich wine and cream sauce.

Le veau au vin Veal braised in red or white Sancerre wine.

Champignons de Paris Fresh mushrooms cultivated in the moist caves of Saumur.

La salade à l'huile de noix Salad dressed with walnut oil.

Fruits Excellent plums (and prunes), pears, apricots, cherries, and strawberries grow in this 'Garden of France'.

Cheeses
Crottin de Chavignol Goats' milk cheese from the Sancerre region.
Crémets d'Anjou et Saumur Fresh cream cheese eaten with sugar and fresh cream.
Cendre Cheese that has been cured in ashes.
Ste-Maure Goats' milk cheese.
St-Benôit Round cows' milk cheese from Ste-Benôit-sur-Loire.
Port-Salut Round, mild cheese with distinctive orange rind.

Restaurants

Note: in addition to the following listings, many excellent restaurants are also found in the Hotel section.

Muscadet Region

44000 Nantes

Restaurant Le Nantais
161, rue des Hauts-Pavés
tel: (40) 76 59 54
Inexpensive restaurant serving regional specialities.
Open daily

Anjou

49170 Béhuard

Restaurant Au Rocher
tel: (41) 54 54 61
Located in a village on an island in the Loire opposite Savennières. Loire specialities including *brochet au beurre blanc*, and *saumon à l'oseille* are served on the terrace opposite the village chapel.
Closed Wed
Moderate

49000 Angers

Restaurant Le Quere
9, place du Ralliement
tel: (41) 87 64 94

Regional Angevin cooking, particularly fish specialities in this **Inexpensive** to **Moderate** restaurant.
Closed Tue eve; Wed
Open 12–14h; 19h15–21h30

Le Vert d'Eau
9, boulevard Gaston Dumesnil
tel: (41) 48 52 31
Specialities include *poisson de Loire au beurre blanc, poulet d'Angevin, crémets d'Anjou* together with a good selection of local wines.
Closed Sun eve; Mon; month of Aug
Open 12–14h30; 19–21h45
Moderate

49400 Saumur

Restaurant Le Gambetta
12, rue Gambetta
tel: (41) 51 11 13
Fish specialities, *coq au vin de Saumur*, and *soufflé maison au triple sec liqueur régionale*.
Closed Sun eve; Mon; Dec 20–Jan 20
Open summer 12–21h30
Open winter 12–20h30
Inexpensive to **Moderate**

49590 Fontevraud l'Abbaye

Restaurant La Licorne
31, rue Robert d'Arbrissel
tel: (41) 51 72 49
Regional specialities freshly prepared and served on the terrace in fine weather.
Open Tue–Sun lunch
Inexpensive to **Moderate**

Touraine

37500 Chinon

Restaurant Ste-Maxime
31, place du Général-de-Gaulle
tel: (47) 93 05 04
Regional dishes and wines of Chinon.
Closed Sun
Open 12–14h; 17h15–21h
Moderate

37130 Langeais

Restaurant Le Langeais
tel: (47) 96 70 63
Local specialities and wines from Vouvray, Chinon, and Bourgueil
Closed Mon
Open 12–14h30; 19–21h30
Moderate to **Expensive**

37022 Tours

Restaurant Charles Barrier
101, avenue de la Tranchée
tel: (47) 54 20 39
An elegant **Very Expensive** restaurant
with a good selection of Touraine wines
and sophisticated *tourangelle* specialities.
Closed Wed; Sun eve

Restaurant La Rôtisserie Tourangelle
23, rue du Commerce
tel: (47) 05 71 21
Near the medieval quarter, a **Moderate**
restaurant serving regional dishes
according to the season.
Closed Sun eve; Mon

37140 Bourgueil

Le Moulin Bleu
tel: (47) 97 71 41
An **Inexpensive** restaurant/hotel with a
good selection of Bourgueil and
St-Nicolas-de-Bourgueil wines and
regional cuisine.
Open all year

37270 Montlouis

Relais de Belle Roche
Belle Roche
tel: (47) 50 82 43
A **Moderate** restaurant serving regional
specialities, located in a *cave*, with open
fire.
Closed Wed

La Cave Restaurant
tel: (47) 45 05 05
Restaurant in troglodyte house with open
fire; *grillades au feu de bois* are the house
speciality, to accompany a full range of
Montlouis wines.
Closed Sun eve
Moderate

Upper Loire

18300 Sancerre

Auberge la Treille
Chavignol
tel: (48) 54 12 17
Local specialities such as *tourte au crottin de
chavignol, salade au crottin chaud, coq en
barbouille* accompanied by own-produced
Sancerre. English spoken.
Closed Mon eve, Tue eve, Wed in winter;
open daily in summer.
Inexpensive to **Moderate**

Hotels

Muscadet Region

44115 Haute-Goulaine (near Nantes)

La Lande Saint-Martin
route de Clisson (N149)
tel: (40) 80 00 80
Hotel with park and restaurant serving
Loire specialities such as *sandre beurre
blanc, cassolette de lotte*, and other fish
dishes, together with a good selection of
Muscadet.
Hotel open all year.
Restaurant open daily 12–15h; 19–21h30
Inexpensive to **Moderate**

Anjou

49000 Angers

Hôtel-Restaurant La Boule d'Or
27, boulevard Carnot
tel: (41) 43 76 56
Inexpensive hotel with restaurant.
Hotel open all year
Restaurant closed Fri eve; Sat midday

Hôtel d'Anjou
1, boulevard Foch
tel: (41) 88 24 82
Moderate hotel and restaurant serving
Loire specialities such as *brochet au beurre
blanc*, and *fricassé de volaille*.
Hotel open all year
Restaurant closed Sun
Open 12–16h; 19h30–22h

La Croix de Guerre
23, rue Châteaugontier
tel: (41) 88 66 59
Well-situated hotel within two minutes F
the cathedral and château. Comfortable
restaurant serves local specialities and
Loire wines.
Restaurant closed Sat; open 12–14h;
19h15–21h
Inexpensive to **Moderate**

49400 Saumur

Hôtel de la Gare
16, avenue David d'Angers
tel: (41) 50 34 24
Opposite the station with bar and
restaurant. English spoken.
Closed Oct 1–March 30
Restaurant open 11–23h
Inexpensive

49400 Chace

Auberge du Thouet
tel: (41) 50 12 04
Country *auberge* located in a village just
south of Saumur in the Thouet Valley.
Regional meals served in a typical *cave*,
including such specialities as *salade
champignons frais, papillotte brochet, sandre
châtelaine*.
Hotel and restaurant closed Sat, Sun from
Oct 1–April 1
Restaurant open 12–14h; 19h30–20h30
Inexpensive

49350 Gennes

Hostellerie du Prieuré
Chênehutte-les-Tuffeaux
tel: (41) 50 15 31
Situated on a hill overlooking the river, 4
miles west of Saumur, a 12th–15th century
priory surrounded by woodland, with
swimming pool, tennis courts, elegant
restaurant.
Hotel closed Jan; Feb
Restaurant open daily
Expensive

Touraine

49730 Montsoreau

Hostellerie Diane de Méridor le Bussy
tel: (41) 51 70 18
Inexpensive charming hotel with views of
the Loire and château. Fresh fish served in
the attractive rustic dining room.
Hotel closed Dec 15–Jan 31
Restaurant closed Mon eve; Tue

37500 Chinon

Hostellerie Gargantua
73, rue Voltaire
tel: (47) 93 04 71
Aptly named hotel-restaurant situated in
the centre of Vieux Chinon, in the
15th-century Bailliage Palais, with unique
medieval dining room. Restaurant serves
specialities such as *omelette gargantuenne,
matelote d'anguilles Rabelaisienne*.
Hotel closed Jan 15–March 1
Restaurant open daily in high season;
closed Wed in low season
Moderate

Auberge St-Jean
route de Tours
tel: (47) 93 09 29
Family-run hotel-restaurant serves
tourangelle country-cooking such as

*rillettes, rillons, porc aux pruneaux, matelote
d'anguilles* with full range of local wines.
English spoken.
Open daily 12h–19h30 April–Sept; closed
Sat in low season.
Inexpensive

Hôtel-Restaurant de la Boule d'Or
66, quai Jeanne d'Arc
tel: (47) 93 03 13
Inexpensive traditional hotel with terrace
restaurant serving local specialities: *coq au
vin de Chinon, brochet beurre blanc, matelote
d'anguilles*.
Hotel closed mid Dec–end of Jan
Restaurant closed Fri from Nov–Easter
Open 12h15–19h15

Château de Marcay
tel: (47) 93 03 47
A lovely old château hotel located in an
authentic 15th-century fortress in the heart
of the Touraine countryside (south of
Chinon off D116). 22 rooms, 4 apartments,
swimming pool, tennis courts, and
restaurant serving regional specialities.
Hotel closed Jan; Feb
Restaurant open daily
Expensive

37150 Langeais

Hôtel Hosten
2, rue Gambetta
tel: (47) 96 82 12
Close to the château, without restaurant.
Closed Nov–April
Moderate

37190 Azay-le-Rideau

Hôtel-Restaurant Le Grand Monarque
place de la République
tel: (47) 43 30 08
17th-century building with restaurant
serving regional dishes and local wines.
Hotel open all year
Restaurant closed Dec 1–Feb 29
Moderate to **Expensive**

37000 Tours

Hôtel-Restaurant le Bordeaux
3, place Maréchal-Leclerc
tel: (47) 05 04 32
Centrally situated and recently renovated.
Open all year.
Moderate

Hôtel des Châteaux de la Loire
12, rue Gambetta
tel: (47) 05 10 05
Inexpensive hotel without restaurant.
Closed Dec 15–Jan 15

37210 Vouvray

Hôtel-Bar-Restaurant Le Vouvrillon
14, avenue Brûlé
tel: (47) 52 78 80
Inexpensive hotel with bar and restaurant
serving local dishes and good selection of
Vouvray wines.
Hotel closed Sept
Restaurant open daily except Sun in winter
12–15h; 19h30–21h

Hôtel-Bar-Restaurant 'Le Gargantua'
N152
tel: (47) 52 70 53
Hotel located on the main road, along the
bank of the Loire.
Restaurant serves local dishes and wines.
Hotel open April 1–Sept 30
Restaurant open daily except Thur eve
Inexpensive

37400 Amboise

Auberge du Mail
32, quai du Général-de-Gaulle
tel: (47) 57 60 39
Comfortable, quaint hotel with restaurant
serving regional dishes, including *la tête de
veau à la tourangelle, le fois confit au Vouvray*.
Hotel closed Jan
Restaurant open daily
Inexpensive to **Moderate**

Château de Pray
tel: (47) 57 23 67
Surrounded by gardens and forest, this
turretted Loire château is peaceful and
comfortable.
Hotel closed Jan 1–Feb 7
Restaurant open daily 12–14h; 19–21h
Expensive

Hôtel du Lion d'Or
17, quai Charles Guinot
tel: (47) 57 00 23
Inexpensive hotel with **Moderate**
restaurant; *écrevisses* a speciality.
Hotel closed Nov 2–Feb 29
Restaurant open daily

Upper Loire

18300 Sancerre

Hôtel-Restaurant de l'Étoile
2, quai de Loire
St-Thibault
tel: (48) 54 13 15
Inexpensive hotel with restaurant serving
Sancerrois cuisine and a good choice of
Sancerre and Pouilly Blanc Fumé.

Hotel closed Nov 15–March 10; Wed in low
season
Restaurant closed Wed
Open 12–14h; 19–21h
Restaurant **Moderate**

L'Auberge
37, rue Jacques Combes
St-Thibault
tel: (48) 54 13 79
Comfortable 17th-century rustic hotel with
restaurant serving regional specialities.
Hotel closed end of May–mid March
Restaurant open daily, except Tue in low
season
Inexpensive

58150 Pouilly-sur-Loire

Hôtel-Restaurant Le Relais Fleuri
avenue de la Tuilerie
tel: (86) 39 12 99
Charming, comfortable hotel with terrace
and flowered garden on the banks of the
river.
Hotel closed Jan; Feb
Restaurant open daily except Thur in low
season
Inexpensive

Camping

The Loire Valley is one of the finest places
in France for a camping holiday, and sites
literally abound, along this great river, and
its numerous lovely tributaries. The
following is a brief selection only.

Muscadet Region

Nantes
Le Val du Cens, tel: (40) 74 47 94
Clisson
Le Moulin
Vallet
Les Dorices, tel: (40) 78 23 14

Anjou

Rochefort-sur-Loire (near Savennières)
Saint-Offange
Brissac-Quince
La Valière
Doue-la-Fontaine
Le Douet, tel: 59 14 47
Montreuil-Bellay
Les Nobis, tel: (41) 52 33 66
Saumur
Ile d'Offard, tel: (41) 50 45 00
Varennes-sur-Loire
Etang de la Brèche, tel: (41) 51 22 92

Where to Get
Additional Information

Comité Départemental du Tourisme de
Loire-Atlantique
4, rue d'Argentré
44305 Nantes

Comité Interprofessionnel des Vins
d'Origine du Pays Nantais
17, rue des États
44000 Nantes
tel: (40) 47 15 58

Syndicat d'Initiative d'Angers
71, rue Plantagenet
49000 Angers

Conseil Interprofessionnel des Vins
d'Anjou et de Saumur
21, boulevard Foch
49000 Angers
tel: (41) 87 62 57

L'Office du Tourisme et Maison du Vin
29, rue Beaurepaire
49400 Saumur
tel: (41) 51 03 06

Comité Interprofessionnel des Vins de
Touraine
19, square Prosper-Merimée
37000 Tours
tel: (47) 05 40 01

Office du Tourisme
place du Maréchal Leclerc
37042 Tours
tel: (47) 05 58 08

Départemental Tourist Directory
Préfecture d'Indre-et-Loire
16, rue de Buffon
37032 Tours
tel: (47) 61 61 23
(This office provides an official service of
interpreter/guides for Touraine, including
private guides for visits to the châteaux of
the Loire.)

Union Viticole-Sancerroise
Mairie de St-Satur
18300 Sancerre
tel: (48) 54 02 53

Syndicat d'Initiative et Comité des Fêtes de
Sancerre
L'Hôtel de Ville
18300 Sancerre
tel: (48) 54 00 26

Syndicat d'Initiative de Pouilly-sur-Loire et
de son Vignoble
Mairie de Pouilly
58150 Pouilly-sur-Loire
tel: (86) 39 12 55

Touraine

Bourgueil
Parc Capitaine, tel: (47) 58 73 79
Chinon
L'Ile-Auger, tel: (47) 93 08 35
Azay-le-Rideau
Le Sabot, tel: (47) 43 32 72
Langeais
Camp Municipal, tel: (47) 55 71 62
Joue-les-Tours
L'Alouette, tel: (47) 28 08 26
Rochecorbon
Le Moulin, tel: (47) 52 50 20
Montlouis-sur-Loire
Les Peupliers, tel: (47) 50 81 90
Amboise
L'Ile d'Or, tel: (47) 57 23 37

Blois
Camping Municipal 'La Boire'
tel: (54) 74 22 78

Upper Loire

Pouilly-sur-Loire
Malaga
Cosne-sur-Loire
L'Ile, tel: (86) 28 27 92

Bibliography

Châteaux of the Loire Michelin Green Guide,
1980
The Wines of France by Cyril Ray, Penguin
1978

RHÔNE AND PROVENCE

The wine region of the Côtes du Rhône extends along the valley of the Rhône from south of Lyons to Avignon through a landscape at times barren and even bleak. Yet if the Rhône is hardly picturesque (as is, for example, the Loire Valley), it is always impressively, majestically beautiful. The vineyards of the Côte Rôtie lie on tortuous, sunbaked granite terraces, some of which were carved out by the Romans; the 'soil' and landscape at southern Châteauneuf-du-Pape is bizarre: field after field of huge round stones – no earth in sight – out of which sprout stumpy, gnarled vines. The region is hot, sometimes overpoweringly so, and in winter as in summer an incessant dry wind, the *mistral*, blows cruelly from the north, ravaging the land and twisting the vines, the tall cypresses and buff green olive trees into strange, fantastic forms.

There is a timeless, elemental air to this region whose powerful wines are known as *vins du soleil*, wines of the sun. The southern half of the Côtes du Rhône lies in Provence, the *Provincia Romana* of antiquity, and throughout the region the remains of that splendid civilization – the magnificent aqueduct known as the Pont du Gard, the amphitheatre and triumphal arch at Orange, temples at Vaison la Romaine, Vienne, and elsewhere, and much else – merge with remnants from other great epochs – the ruined medieval Châteauneuf-du-Pape and the Palace of the Popes in Avignon – to impress upon us the importance of this region over the centuries. If in the past a centre of European civilization, the Rhône Valley today is far from moribund; in contrast to the parched, brown valley, the towns of the region are a riot of noise and colour and life. Overall, the heavy, heavenly scent of juniper and lavender, of heat and heady wine, and of garlic- and herb-laden food induces an easy indolence, a warm spell of utter relaxation and comfort.

The wines of the Côtes du Rhône and Provence are remarkably varied and the vineyards of this important valley produce a complete range, including distinguished and rare red and white wines (Côte Rôtie and Château Grillet); powerful, extremely long-lived wines from Hermitage, Châteauneuf-du-Pape, Gigondas, and elsewhere; possibly the best pink wines in France from Tavel and Lirac; sparkling *méthode champenoise* wines from St-Péray and Die; sturdy everyday reds and whites bearing the basic *appellation* Côtes du Rhône; and even magnificently fragrant sweet wines – the famous *vin doux natural* Muscat de Beaumes-de-Venise and Rasteau. And in the Côtes de Provence, vineyards along the coast and in the hills above the fabled French Riviera produce vast amounts of full-flavoured rosés, reds, and whites.

How to Get There

By Car
The main north/south autoroutes (A6/A7) extend down through the valley of the Rhône, thus making access to the region most convenient (though many may wish to make their own way here more slowly, perhaps en route through other regions such as Burgundy). The wine circuit of the northern Rhône begins at Vienne, south of Lyons, while those of the southern Rhône are best started from Avignon. For the Côtes de Provence wine road, continue from Avignon to Aix-en-Provence (A7/A8 autoroutes, or N7), then find the B52, or the N8 south to Toulon.

By Plane
The main French international airport is at Paris. Air Inter, the French internal airline, flies to Lyons, Marseilles, and Nice. A tour of the vineyards of the Northern Rhône begins at Lyons; either continue south by car to tour the Southern Rhône, or else proceed north from Marseilles to Avignon. The vineyards of the Côtes de Provence can be toured from Nice or from Marseilles.

By Train
The Rhône and Côte de Provence are on the main Paris–Riviera route with stops at Vienne, Valence, Montélimar, Orange, Avignon, Toulon, Les Arcs, and Fréjus. Trains run regularly every day from Paris Gare de Lyons; the trip to Avignon takes about six hours.

Local Transport
There are local bus and train services between the main towns, but getting off the beaten track into the vineyards requires the use of a car.

Car Rental Information
Lyons
Avis: 8, route de Vienne
    tel: (7) 85 83 344
    Perrache train station
    tel: (7) 92 83 64
    Satolas airport
    tel: (7) 71 95 25
Hertz: 95, avenue Roosevelt
    tel: (7) 84 93 234
    Perrache train station
    tel: (7) 84 22 485
    Satolas airport
    tel: (7) 87 19 451

Vienne
Avis: 29, quai Jean Jaurés
    tel: (74) 85 17 22
Hertz: 4, cours de Verdun
    tel: (74) 53 42 23

Valence
Avis: 1, avenue Pierre Semard
    tel: (75) 44 64 69
    164, avenue de Romans
    tel: (75) 42 58 91
Hertz: 11, rue Pasteur
    tel: (75) 44 39 45
    Valence airport
    tel: (75) 44 39 45

Avignon
Avis: 16, boulevard St-Dominique
    tel: (90) 82 26 33
Hertz: 6, route de Lyons
    tel: (90) 82 37 67
    Avignon airport
    tel: (90) 82 37 67

Toulon
Avis: 175, boulevard du Maréchal-Joffre
    tel: (94) 41 30 1
    14, boulevard Maréchal-Foch
    tel: (94) 89 62 67
Hertz: 60, avenue François
    tel: (94) 41 60 53
    Toulon airport
    tel: (94) 41 60 53

Michelin Maps 84, 93

The cuisine of the region, hand in hand with its wines, is equally varied, equally distinguished. Vienne, opposite the vineyards of the Côte Rôtie, boasts one of the greatest restaurants in the country, 'La Pyramide', made famous by the renowned chef Fernand Point. Further south, the herb-scented cuisine of Provence, which makes abundant use of its full-flavoured produce – vegetables and fruit, game and a colourful catch from the warm Mediterranean – is dominant: hearty, pungent, strong flavours of the land that go so well with the local wines, these *vins du soleil*.

The Côtes du Rhône, like Burgundy to the north, is a region that is easy to pass through since the A7 motorway, the *Autoroute du Soleil*, extends down to the sea. Thus, many anxious to reach those crowded glamour spots of St Tropez, or Cannes, or Nice, or, to the west, the vast, sandy beaches of the Languedoc, speed too quickly through. The wine regions of the Côtes du Rhône and Provence, however, remain for those who seek to encounter them at a relaxed and civilized pace.

The Wines of the Côtes du Rhône and Provence

The following is a brief guide to the principal *appellations* which the visitor will encounter on a tour of the vineyards of the Rhône and Provence.

Côtes du Rhône The basic *appellation* for the Rhône vineyard applies to forceful dry white wines, fresh rosé, and light- to full-bodied red wines. Much wine sold under the *appellation* is produced in *coopératives* which can be visited. The delimited region extends over six *départements*: Vaucluse, Gard, Drôme, Ardèche, Rhône, and Loire.

Côtes du Rhône-Villages Superior *appellation* that applies to red, white, and rosé wines that have been submitted to rigorous regulations regarding grape varieties, restricted yield, methods of cultivation, and compulsory testing, among other things. Such wines are produced in the following communes:

Drôme: Rochegude, Rousset, Saint-Maurice-sur-Aygues, Saint-Pantaléon-les-Vignes, Vinsobres.

Vaucluse: Cairanne, Rasteau, Roaix, Sablet, Séguret, Vacqueyras, Valréas, Visan, Beaumes-de-Venise.

Gard: Chusclan, Laudun, Saint-Gervais.

Beaumes-de-Venise Commune in the Vaucluse best known for an extraordinary *vin doux naturel* (slightly fortified sweet dessert wine) known as Muscat de Beaumes-de-Venise. At its best it is very fragrant and fresh – like drinking sweet table grapes – and is excellent as an aperitif. Beaumes-de-Venise is also one of the Côtes du Rhône-Villages of the Vaucluse producing vigorous red wines.

Château Grillet Minute estate within the delimited region of Condrieu producing one of the great dry white wines of France exclusively from the Viognier grape.

Châteauneuf-du-Pape One of the great classics of the southern Rhône: virile, full-bodied red wine produced from vineyards around the ruined former summer palace of the Popes, and in neighbouring communes such as Courthezon, Bedarrides, Sorgues, and Orange. Traditionally, it was a wine to lay down for several years, decades even, but younger, fresher styles of wine which can be consumed far earlier are now also being produced. White Châteauneuf-du-Pape, though not widely exported, should be tried when in the region.

Clairette de Die Luminous Muscat (predominantly) sparkling wine produced by traditional methods around this small commune in the Drôme Valley. The *appellation* also applies to still white wine produced from the Clairette grape.

Condrieu Distinguished dry to medium-dry white wine from Viognier grapes grown on granite terraces of the northern Rhône. Most distinguished example bears its own *appellation* Château Grillet (see above).

Cornas Rich deep-red wine produced from the mighty Syrah grape grown on vineyards around the village of Cornas, whose name, in Celtic, means 'scorched ground'.

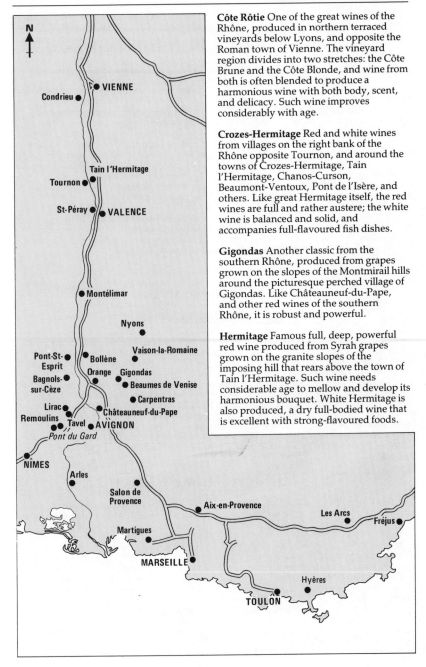

Côte Rôtie One of the great wines of the Rhône, produced in northern terraced vineyards below Lyons, and opposite the Roman town of Vienne. The vineyard region divides into two stretches: the Côte Brune and the Côte Blonde, and wine from both is often blended to produce a harmonious wine with both body, scent, and delicacy. Such wine improves considerably with age.

Crozes-Hermitage Red and white wines from villages on the right bank of the Rhône opposite Tournon, and around the towns of Crozes-Hermitage, Tain l'Hermitage, Chanos-Curson, Beaumont-Ventoux, Pont de l'Isère, and others. Like great Hermitage itself, the red wines are full and rather austere; the white wine is balanced and solid, and accompanies full-flavoured fish dishes.

Gigondas Another classic from the southern Rhône, produced from grapes grown on the slopes of the Montmirail hills around the picturesque perched village of Gigondas. Like Châteauneuf-du-Pape, and other red wines of the southern Rhône, it is robust and powerful.

Hermitage Famous full, deep, powerful red wine produced from Syrah grapes grown on the granite slopes of the imposing hill that rears above the town of Tain l'Hermitage. Such wine needs considerable age to mellow and develop its harmonious bouquet. White Hermitage is also produced, a dry full-bodied wine that is excellent with strong-flavoured foods.

Lirac Well-known rosé, as well as some red wine, is produced from grapes grown around this typical Gardienne village. The *appellation* applies to the vineyards of the neighbouring villages of Saint-Laurent-des-Arbres, Roquemaure, and Saint-Géniès-de-Comolas.

Rasteau Slightly fortified *vin doux naturel* produced from the black Grenache. The commune is also one of the Côtes du Rhône-Villages, producing mainly red wines in addition to the limited production of its dessert wines.

St-Joseph Red and white wines produced from vineyards on the left bank of the Rhône opposite Hermitage around the town of Tournon.

St-Péray *Blanc de blancs* sparkling wine produced by the *méthode champenoise*. Prior to 1929, however, the wines of this region

located opposite Valence were still whites which had enjoyed popularity through the ages, and had been drunk and praised by Plutarch, Henry IV, and Richard Wagner.

Tavel One of the finest rosés of France, produced from a blending of a variety of grapes; its pretty orange-pink colour belies a wine with strength and body which stands up well to the strong-flavoured, pungent foods of the region.

Côtes de Provence Generous rosé, red, and white wines produced from vineyards along and in the hills and mountains above the French Riviera: often sold in a distinctive wobbly-shaped bottle (or direct from the producer *en vrac*).

Costières du Gard Vineyards south of Nîmes and above the Camargue which produce a variety of robust red, dry white, and rosé wines.

The Wine Roads of Rhône and Provence

There is not, as yet, a sign-posted *route du vin* of the Côtes du Rhône; however, the following 'wine circuits' take in most of the principal communes of the region and give ample tasting and purchasing opportunities. The first two circuits begin in the south, at Avignon, exploring first the vineyards on the right bank of the Rhône (including Châteauneuf-du-Pape, Gigondas, Beaumes-de-Venise, and others), then those on the left bank, around the communes of Tavel, Lirac, Chusclan, and others up to the Ardèche gorge, before circling back for a detour to the Pont du Gard. A tour of the vineyards of the northern Rhône Valley commences in Valence and leads up to Vienne. For those coming from the north, follow the circuits southwards from Vienne to arrive eventually in Avignon. Additionally, a popular sign-posted holiday wine road, the *Route du Vin* of the Côtes de Provence can be followed (in whole or part) by those heading to the French Riviera.

The Southern Rhône – Circuit 1

The first tour of the southern Rhône stays on the east side of the river, and explores vineyards and cellars of the prestigious growths of Châteauneuf-du-Pape and Gigondas as well as those of the Côte du Rhône-Villages of the Vaucluse while making a circular trip which encompasses the fine Roman cities of Orange, Vaison-la-Romaine, and Carpentras. Both circuits of the southern Rhône begin in Avignon. Behind its fine and majestic machicolated walls that tower over the Rhône, itself half-spanned by its splendid Pont St-Bénézet of nursery fame ('Sur le pont d'Avignon . . .'), lies a town of

considerable charm and elegance, dominated since the fourteenth century by the monumental Palace of the Popes. Indeed, it was their presence that turned a provincial market town into one of the religious (and political) capitals of Europe. Avignon today, with street cafés dappled with light streaming through canopies of plane trees, numerous hotels and restaurants, and pleasant (though in mid-season crowded) campsites on an island in the Rhône, serves as an excellent base for touring the region. As well as visiting the Palais des Papes (site of an annual summer drama festival), climb up to the Rocher des Doms for a superb view over the town, the river valley, and the Pont St-Bénézet; and simply stroll around the wonderful ramparts, soaking in the atmosphere, and exploring the medieval trades and crafts quarters. The town information centre, incidentally, (41, cours Jean-Jaurés) is also the headquarters of the *Comité Interprofessionnel des Vins des Côtes du Rhône*, and much useful information is available from the *Maison du Vin* there (maps, wine literature, complete list of addresses of wine producers who welcome visitors, and much else – ask for the booklet *Parcours du Vignoble*).

Leave Avignon on the N7 to Sorgues, and there branch left on the D117 to

Châteauneuf-du-Pape, centre for the production of a noble and powerful wine that bears its name, and also a village which, like Avignon, has a distinguished and grandiose past. Indeed, as the village is approached, the imposing silhouette of the ruined twelfth-century château itself is soon visible, proud and majestic in its decay, sprouting from stony earth on hills above the Rhône. Wander through the village on foot up the old stone streets that lead to the castle, relax in the square, or lunch in one of the fine restaurants where regional foods such as *soupe au pistou* and *caillettes* accompany distinguished local wines. Producers in the surrounding vine-covered country are hospitable and

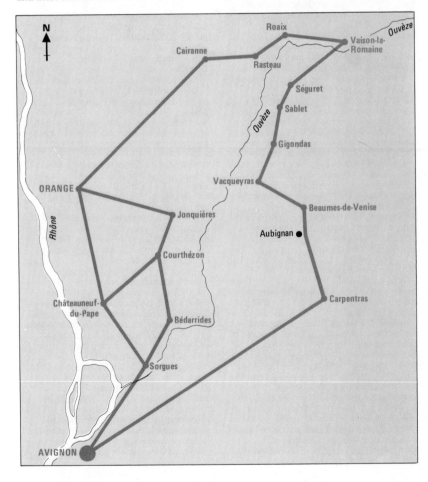

welcoming, and the wine museum of Père Anselme is worth a visit.

The vineyards of Châteauneuf-du-Pape and other nearby communes, Bédarrides, Courthézon, Orange, and Sorgues, are striking, for though the soil varies, here are some of the most amazing and distinctive vineyards in Europe: stumpy, free-standing vines sprouting from fields of smooth, large round stones. These stones accumulate heat by day, and release it at night, thus warming the vines on spring evenings that are sometimes surprisingly cold. The wine itself, which has the highest minimum alcohol level of any table wine in France (12.5%), is produced from a blending of up to 13 permitted varieties of grapes which gives Châteauneuf-du-Pape a rare balance of vigour and strength, together with fragrance and a certain delicacy. Though most exported Châteauneuf-du-Pape is red, the *appellation* also applies to a dry, full-bodied white wine.

After exploring vineyards and visiting cellars, continue through Châteauneuf-du-Pape along the D17 towards the river, and then take the D976 to Orange. Orange is a fascinating city, with its well-preserved triumphal arch (commemorating Caesar's victory over Pompey in 49 BC), and its superb Roman amphitheatre that is still used for dramatic and musical productions (during summer months, there is a small stand in the amphitheatre grotto where local wines can be sampled). Orange, too, makes an interesting base from which to explore the region. From Orange leave the town on the D975 in the direction of Vaison-la-Romaine. After about 12 km turn left on the D8 to Cairanne, one of nine villages in the Vaucluse region that produces wine that is subjected to rigorous tests regarding yield, method of cultivation, minimum alcohol content, and other factors, and which is thus allowed to bear the superior *appellation* Côtes du Rhône-Villages. Cairanne is a typical Rhône villages, with its mixture of Roman and medieval heritage; the heady wines produced in the local *coopérative* (which can be purchased direct) are typical too: warm, full-bodied, and honest *vins du soleil*. From Cairanne continue on the secondary road (D69) to Rasteau, and then on to Roaix, both of whose vineyards are also entitled to the Côtes du Rhône-Villages *appellation*, and whose wines can be sampled and purchased in the cellars of their respective *cave coopératives*. As well as full-bodied red,

white, and rosé wines, Rasteau also produces a sweet, slightly fortified dessert wine.

Continue from Roaix on the D975 to reach Vaison-la-Romaine, and allow enough time off from wine sampling to explore the important and well-preserved Roman ruins of this ancient town. Vaison in Roman times was an opulent centre of relaxation and leisure, as the remains of comfortable and wealthy villas indicate; one could do far worse than to stop in this lovely town set under the wooded Mont Ventoux to contemplate the centuries of Provençal civilization – Gallic, Roman, medieval – while sampling fine local wines and foods that have been praised and enjoyed for millennia.

From Vaison-la-Romaine return following the south bank of the Ouvèze briefly along the D977 before branching left on the D88 to meander through superb wine country spread out along the *Dentelles de Montmirail* through the picturesque villages of Séguret and, on the D23, Sablet (both Côte du Rhône-Villages), and so on to Gigondas. Gigondas, like Séguret, is nestled against the steep Montmirail; climb up to the ruined castle for a magnificent vista over the village to the gentle, well-exposed vine-covered slopes of the Côtes du Rhône. Gigondas is without doubt one of the great wines of the southern Rhône, rich in flavour and alcohol, and an ample, robust partner to full-flavoured foods such as game or the Provençal stew known as the *daube*.

Vacqueyras, the next wine town encountered, is on the D7, another Côtes du Rhône-Villages as is nearby Beaumes-de-Venise (continue briefly south on the D7 towards Carpentras before turning left on the D81). Though red and white table wines are produced in the latter, the wine commune is most famous for its Muscat wine, which is remarkably and intensely fragrant, a golden, fortified wine as fresh and appetizing as a bunch of cool dessert grapes. The village itself is most attractive, also perched under the Montmirail, its houses and shops climbing in terraces up the steep slopes. From Beaumes-de-Venise continue on the D7 to Carpentras (particularly lively on market day when stalls wind their way through tight streets in the centre of the town, and the abundance and colour of the Provençal garden is gaily displayed). Don't miss, too, sampling the *berlingots*, caramel sweets produced here, before returning to Avignon.

The Southern Rhône – Circuit 2

The second tour of the southern Rhône concentrates on the vineyards on the west bank of the Rhône, those of Tavel and Lirac, as well as the Côte du Rhône-Villages of the Gard: Chusclan, Laudun, and St-Gervais. In addition, excursions can be made to the monumental Pont du Gard (a three-tiered Roman aqueduct) en route to Nîmes, while to the north the dramatic Ardèche gorge

can be explored from Pont St-Esprit. This tour, like our first, begins and ends in Avignon (see above).

From Avignon, cross the Rhône to the adjoining suburb of Villeneuve-les-Avignon; though the two towns are virtually contiguous, divided only by the river, they in fact developed both in conjunction and in opposition. For when the papal court settled in Avignon, the

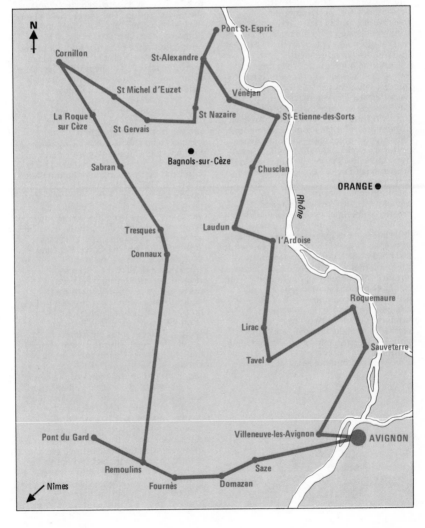

town eventually spilled over the river, and Villeneuve became a fashionable suburb where Cardinals built substantial villas; the river, on the other hand, also served to delineate the boundary between the Holy Roman Empire and the secular realm of the kings and counts of France. The tower of Philippe le Bel, for example, constructed at the end of the thirteenth century was built as a watch point from which to survey enemy territory; the stout St-André fortress above the town looks calmly and confidently across to the Palais des Papes. Villeneuve today offers alternative accommodation, and numerous restaurants, and so can also serve as a base from which to explore the region. A lively market often takes place on the D980 road that follows the river north.

Continue north on this road through Sauveterre to Roquemaure, which stands opposite Châteauneuf-du-Pape (both Sauveterre and Roquemaure, incidentally, have *caves coopératives*; wines produced from vineyards around Roquemaure bear the *appellation* Lirac). From Roquemaure, once an important wine-shipping river port, turn back on the D976, which leads through fields of free-standing vines to the little town of Tavel, located just off the main road. Tavel stands like an island, surrounded by a sea of intensively-cultivated vines, tended, pruned, sometimes even harvested by modern machinery, not man. A range of different types of grapes grows on these slopes, and a skilful blending of both white and black – the latter are pressed only briefly on their skins to yield their colour – produces a shimmering, pink-orange wine that has deceptive stamina, body, and alcohol. Tavel is certainly one of the best rosé wines in France. Taste – then purchase a bottle or two – from the *coopérative* outside the town, and drink it with the pungent, and full-flavoured foods of the Gard.

From Tavel, find the small secondary

road (D26) which leads to Lirac, continues to the walled village of St-Laurent-des-Arbres and, towards the river once more, to St-Géniès-de-Comolas. Both of the latter villages, together with Roquemaure, share the *appellation* Lirac, and the firm, vigorous rosé produced in this neighbouring vineyard shares the distinction, if not the renown of Tavel. In addition, sound red, and some white wines are also produced from this abundant and fertile Provençal garden. The wine tour follows the river road north to l'Ardoise, and there branches away on the D9 to Laudun. The village, nestled on the *plateau du camp de César* where the Roman general stopped on one of his campaigns in the region, is another of the Côtes du Rhône-Villages, as is Chusclan, some five km or so to the north. The wines of the various Côtes du Rhône-Villages, incidentally, do vary considerably, displaying not only the unique character of each commune, but also reflecting differences in style and priority, and ranging from fruity, youthful *vins de primeur*, to be imbibed, like Beaujolais, within weeks of the vintage, to longer-lived, fuller wines that need both barrel and bottle ageing to bring out their character. The *cave coopérative* at Chusclan is particularly worth a visit. This pleasant, meandering tour returns to the Rhône once more, by-passing the atomic power station of Marcoule. Pause at the *belvédère* above the river before continuing on the D138 to St-Etienne-des-Sorts, Vénéjan, St-Alexandre, and so, eventually, (N86) to Pont St-Esprit. All of the villages encountered are set amidst glorious, sun-baked wine country; there are producers along the way who offer tasting and purchasing opportunities.

Pont St-Esprit, located where the winding Ardèche joins the Rhône, is named after the thirteenth-century bridge built by the Frères Pontifs (a brotherhood of bridge-builders) which still spans the river. Pont St-Esprit is both a convenient halting-place, and also an excellent base from which to explore the rugged and majestic Ardèche gorge. The wine tour, however, returns south once more, following the N86 through St-Nazaire before, just short of Bagnols-sur-Cèze, turning right on the D980 to St-Gervais, the third commune in the Gard entitled to the *appellation* Côtes du Rhône-Villages. Continue to the little wine villages of St-Michel-d'Euzet and, further on, Cornillon, perched atop a hill, or else turn

off on the winding D166 to La
Roque-sur-Cèze. The cascade is worth
seeing, as is the Château de Sabran,
reached after much more twisting and
turning on the same road. Continue south
along the D166 to the D9, and there return
to the N86 near Connaux.

Follow the N86 south for some ten miles
to Remoulins, another wine commune,
then make a detour to the Pont du Gard.
Built nearly 2000 years ago to supply the
nearby city of Nîmes with fresh water, it
stands today in near perfect condition (it
was restored in the nineteenth century), a
monument to Roman engineering and
civilization. After visiting the Pont du
Gard, (there are campsites along the river),
either continue to Nîmes and the
Camargue, or else return to
Villeneuve-les-Avignon by way of
wine-tasting villages such as Fournès,
Domazan, and Saze.

The Northern Rhône

Many of the greatest wines of the Rhône
are produced on the northern stretch of
the river, from vineyards extending from
Valence to Vienne, just south of Lyons.
This route takes in all the great growths of
the northern Rhône, and offers ample and
varied tasting opportunities; there is much
else of interest, too, including ancient and
medieval monuments, as well as visits to
modern temples of gastronomy.

If approaching from the south, continue
from Pont St-Esprit north, pausing in the
nougat town of Montélimar as well as
climbing up to the Château de
Rochemaure on the opposite bank of the
river for a superb view of the Rhône
Valley. At Le Pouzin a detour can be
made, following the valley of the Drôme,
to Die where a popular sparkling Muscat
wine is produced by traditional methods.
It is known as Clairette de Die and it can be
sampled there in the local *cave coopérative*.
This circuit of the northern Rhône,
however, commences in Valence, itself a
large and busy town with a long history
dating back before Roman times; the
young Napoleon spent a year here as a
military cadet. Today it is an energetic
market town, a centre for the sale and
distribution of the luscious fruits and
vegetables that grow in this fertile valley.

From Valence, cross the Rhône to the
west bank, following the N532 to St-Péray,
a small town whose splendid wines were
praised by Plutarch and enjoyed by
Richard Wagner. Those wines of the past,
however, were no doubt still, for it was
only in 1929 that the local producers began
applying the *méthode champenoise* to the
assertive white wines of the region that are
produced from the Marsanne and
Roussette grapes. After St-Péray, continue
north briefly on the N86 to the
neighbouring village of Cornas. Though
the vineyards of St-Péray and Cornas are
virtually adjoining, the wines produced

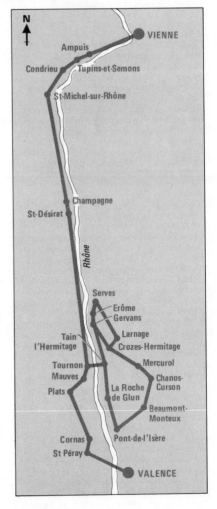

from each are strikingly different. For in contrast to that refreshing, effervescent sparkler, the wine of Cornas, produced from the rich, mighty Syrah grape – the same grape which, across the river, produces the famous wines of Hermitage – is a deep, rasping red wine, tough, even unforthcoming at first, but which mellows and softens with age. Go through the village and climb the steep, sun-burnt slopes (the name, in Celtic, means 'burnt ground') to find the winding road that leads to the ruined sixteenth-century feudal castle of Crussol where impressive views extend over the vineyards and valley.

From Mont Crussol continue briefly along the D287, then find the road right to Plats, continue through the village, and wind down slowly on the D219 back towards the Rhône at Mauves. The vineyards which stretch to the north, hugging the slopes above the river from Mauves to Tournon and, beyond that market town, through St-Jean-de-Muzols, Lemps, and Vion, produce both white and red wines which are sold under the *appellation* St-Joseph. Like the wines of Cornas, those of St-Joseph, though not as well known, perhaps, as the other great growths of the Rhône, display the full character of this vast and prestigious vineyard.

Tournon is worth stopping in, if only to climb up to the old castle above the town. From the castle, the village of Tain l'Hermitage is clearly visible, dominated by the rearing granite rock that rises from the river; on a clear day, too, the jagged cut-out shapes of the Alps can be seen, pasted against the eastern horizon. Cross the river to Tain to explore the important Rhône vineyards of Hermitage and Crozes-Hermitage, which extend both north and south of the town. A circular tour through the surrounding villages and vineyards provides opportunities to taste the wine, while climbing the rugged granite hills on foot demonstrates the unique geographical factors that give rise to this rich and harsh wine, once as popular and as well known as either claret or Burgundy. In addition to deep, extremely long-lived red wines produced from the uncompromising Syrah, the vineyards of Hermitage and Crozes-Hermitage also yield fine and full-bodied white wines. The vineyards, incidentally, gained their name from a local hermit who settled in the area – religious ascetics, it seems, retiring from the cares and tribulations of the world, often and inevitably seemed to gravitate to where the wine was good (St-Emilion, for example, and Santo Domingo de la Calzada, who settled in the Spanish Rioja).

From Tain, make a brief circular tour on the right bank of the Rhône to explore this important vineyard: follow the river road (D220) south to La Roche de Glun, then continue to Pont de-l'Isère and up the Isère river valley to Beaumont-Monteux. Cut north once more across the hills to Chanos-Curson and Mercurol, and then up to Crozes-Hermitage, Larnage, and Serves, before returning back through Erôme and Gervans to Tain.

Recross the Rhône to Tournon, and continue upriver along the N86. Vineyards stretch over most of the slopes to the north, and refreshment can be had at the *cave coopérative* of St-Désirat Champagne, and elsewhere. The next great area of vine growing, however, begins at the little village of St-Michel and extends north almost to Vienne itself. Within this narrow gorge, on steep, terraced, and sun-baked slopes lie the vineyards of Condrieu, Côte-Rôtie, and tiny, prestigious Château-Grillet. The village of Condrieu was settled by Caesar, who stationed a legion of Swiss Helvetians there; the vineyards have thus probably been producing wine since the first century BC. Condrieu is a fragrant dry white wine that is only produced in small quantity exclusively from the Viognier grape. Even more exclusive is the tiny property of Château-Grillet, the smallest in France to be entitled to its own *appellation*. Like the surrounding vineyards of Condrieu, Château-Grillet produces intensely fragrant, compact white wine; it is one of the great white wines of France. It is produced in minute quantity and is naturally correspondingly expensive; the owners of this prestigious vineyard are most welcoming, though understandably, it is not possible to offer tastings of this rarity to all and sundry. However, the finest wines of Condriu can be sampled in the excellent restaurants of this locality (such as the highly-recommended Beau Rivage).

North of Condrieu, the vineyards of the aptly named Côte Rôtie rise steeply, the slopes themselves carved into a patchwork by retaining walls that make the land cultivatable. Some of these stone walls, known as *cheys* and *murgeys*, date back to Roman times. If the vineyards and the village of Condrieu can boast of a history

dating back to Caesar's time, little Ampuis, located in the heart of the Côte Rôtie, precedes it by some 600 years, for it was actually founded by the Greeks who at the same time probably brought with them the Viognier and the Syrah vines. The Côte Rôtie is divided into two sub-regions, the Côte Blônde and the Côte Brune. Local legend has it that a nobleman of Ampuis left his lands to his two daughters, one fair, the other dark. In fact, as one can see, the soil of both regions corresponds with the legend; likewise, the wine from the former is somewhat lighter, that from the latter deeper and longer-lived. Both are often blended to produce one of the great red wines of the Rhône, fragrant, powerful, yet at the same time well-balanced, delicate, and complex.

The tour of the Rhône ends at Vienne, a famous old Roman town where two thousand years ago the local wines were enjoyed and praised by consuls and poets alike. The Roman ruins that remain are impressive – the temples of Augusta and Livia, a magnificent theatre even larger than that at Orange, and of course, the Roman 'pyramide', almost as famous, perhaps, as the gastronomic temple of the same name.

The *Route du Vin* of the Côtes de Provence

The *Route du Vin* of the Côtes de Provence extends along the coast of the Riviera and into the mountains of the Massif des Maures and the Esterel. The rosé, red, and white wines, sold in their distinctive bottles or *'en vrac'*, that is, in your own jug, demi-john, barrel or camp canteen, direct from the farmer who has grown, harvested, pressed and vinified it himself, are uncomplicated and straightforward, in total harmony with this holiday landscape, its way of life, and its cuisine.

The sign-posted wine road extends through old and historic villages along the winding corniche road, through the sandy isthmuses of the Maures coast and the porphyry rocks of the Esterel, into the mountain masses above the coast, covered in scrub and vines, lavender and heather, pine and cork trees. Though the Riviera is one of the most popular – and crowded – holiday destinations in the South of France, the wine road leads to places off the beaten track. There are ample opportunities to taste and to purchase wine, and there are plenty of good places to stay and to eat. The wine road needn't be traversed in its entirety. Simply pick it up wherever it is convenient; meander through the vineyards, taste and purchase, then head back to the beach; do, however, make an effort to traverse sections of both the coastal and the inland stretches.

The *Route du Vin* actually begins in Toulon, a lovely old port down the coast from Marseilles, and still an important naval town. The old town, with its busy market, and its colourful *poissonnerie* is particularly worth exploring. From the outskirts of Toulon, find the wine road that leads to La Valette. Follow the N98 briefly in the direction of Hyères (itself an old and fashionable Riviera resort, with popular islands such as Porquerolles and Port-Cros sheltering its harbour), then branch off on the smaller D29 to La Crau. The wine road cuts back once more on the N98 to La Londe-les-Maures and Bormes-les-Mimosas. Bormes is a pretty, old town, located on the steep flanks of the Massif; follow the winding road through the Col de Caguo-Ven (a memorable viewpoint) to reach the N98 once more which continues to La Môle. Descend back to the coast via the precarious Col du Canadel, and continue through Le Rayol-Canadel and Cavalaire-sur-Mer (both of which have extensive sandy beaches sheltered by pine forests). Branch off right through the charming and characteristic Provençal village of Ramatuelle to St Tropez.

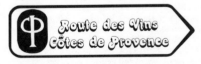

St Tropez and nearby Port Grimaud are legendary and (still) ultra-fashionable resorts, and some may wish to stop to goggle at the luxury yachts and beautiful people posing on the promenade. The wine road, however, beats a hasty retreat from this over-popular coast to ascend into the Massif once more, following the D61 to Grimaud (perched protectively on its hill below the ruins of its sixteenth-century castle), then (along the D558) to La

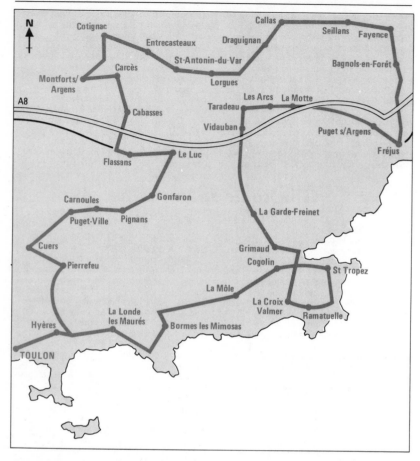

Garde-Freinet, located in the very heart of the Maures. Its Saracen castle is a reminder of those marauders who once pillaged Provence. After La Garde-Freinet, branch off onto the D48 to Vidauban, and then continue across the river to the little wine village of Taradeau (which also has reminders of the Saracens) before carrying on to Les Arcs, centre of the wine trade of the Côtes de Provence. The *Comité Interprofessionnel* for the wines of the region is located here, and will answer any questions from curious wine lovers as well as provide literature, maps, and a complete list of wine producers who welcome visitors (address below). From Les Arcs, the wine road continues along the secondary D91 to La Motte, then (D54)

to Le Muy, before returning to the coast once more at Fréjus, a former Roman port which still boasts impressive ruins worth visiting.

From Fréjus, either carry on to St-Raphaël, Cannes, and Nice, or else continue the circular wine tour by striking out from the coast into high Provence. Follow the D4 through Bagnols-en-Forêt, St-Paul-en-Forêt, then continue (across the D562 to the D563) to Fayence, and around to Seillans and Callas before returning down to Draguignan. These wine villages of the interior Massif are an interesting contrast to the resorts and fishing villages of the coast and present an equally characteristic and important face of Provence. Draguignan is a particularly lovely medieval town, lively and colourful on market days. From Draguignan, the wine road (D562) continues to Lorgues, then branches right on the secondary D50 through the wine villages of St-Antonin-du-Var, Entrecasteaux, and Cotignac (with its numerous cool caves).

After Cotignac it descends, like the numerous rivers that inevitably force their way to the warm waters of the Mediterranean, once more to Toulon, passing through wine villages such as Carcès, Cabasse, Flassans-sur-Issole, Carnoules, Puget-Ville, and Cuers.

Wine Producers

Southern Rhône – Circuit 1

84320 Châteauneuf-du-Pape

Père Anselme
avenue Bx-Pierre-de-Luxembourg
tel: (90) 39 70 07
Châteauneuf-du-Pape, Gigondas, Tavel, Hermitage, Côtes du Rhône-Villages and other Rhône wines.
Open Mon–Sat
Appointment preferable.
English spoken.
Wine museum open Sundays and holidays only, or by appointment.

Caves Reflets
3 Chemin du Bois-de-la-Ville
tel: (90) 39 71 07
Châteauneuf-du-Pape *rouge, blanc*
Open Mon–Sat midday 9–12h; 14–18h
Appointment necessary only for groups.
Max 20 pers.

Jean Pierre Brotte
tel: (90) 39 70 07
Châteauneuf-du-Pape, and other Rhône wines.
Open daily.
English spoken.

Caves Saint-Pierre
Pierre-de-Luxembourg
tel: (90) 39 72 14
Châteauneuf-du-Pape, Gigondas, Tavel, and other Rhône wines.
Open Mon–Fri 8–12h; 14–17h
Appointment preferable.
Max 24 pers.
English spoken.

84370 Bédarrides

Bérard Père et Fils
'Terre Ferme'
tel: (90) 39 14 24
Côtes du Rhône-Villages, Gigondas, Tavel & Lirac, Châteauneuf-du-Pape
Open Mon–Fri 9–12h; 14–18h
Appointment necessary.
Max 18 pers.

84110 Vaison-la-Romaine

Coopérative Vinicole de Vaison et du Haut-Comtat
tel: (90) 36 00 43
Mon–Sat 8–12h; 14–18h
Appointment necessary.
Max 50 pers.

84110 Sablet près l'Ouvèze

Societe Coopèrative
Le Gravillas
tel: (90) 36 90 20
Côtes du Rhône-Villages, Gigondas, *vins de table*
Mon–Fri by appointment.
Max 40 pers.
English spoken.

84190 Gigondas

Cave des Vignerons
tel: (90) 65 86 27
Gigondas, Côtes du Rhône
Daily (tasting and buying only)

84190 Vacqueyras

Lambert Frères, Domaine les Lambertins
la Grande Fontaine
tel: (90) 65 85 54
Côtes du Rhône-Villages, Côtes du Rhône *rouge, blanc, rosé*
Open daily 8–12h; 14–20h
Appointment necessary only for groups.
Max 15 pers.

Cave des Vignerons
tel: (90) 65 84 54
Vacqueyras, Gigondas, Côtes du Rhône
Open Mon–Fri 8–12h; 14–18h
Appointment preferable.
Max 50 pers.
English spoken.

84190 Beaumes-de-Venise

Cave des Vignerons de Beaumes-de-Venise
tel: (90) 62 94 45

Muscat de Beaumes-de-Venise *(vin doux
natural)*, Côtes du Rhône-Villages, Côtes
du Rhône, Côtes du Ventoux
Daily (tasting and buying only)

Southern Rhône – Circuit 2

30150 Roquemaure

Antoine Sarl Verda et Fils
Domaine Viticole du Château St-Roch
tel: (66) 50 12 59
Lirac *rosé, rouge, blanc*, Côtes du Rhône
rouge
Mon–Sat by appointment.
Max 30 pers.
A little English spoken.

30126 Tavel

Association des Producteurs
Les Vignerons de Tavel
tel: (66) 50 03 57
Tavel *rosé*
Open daily.
Appointment necessary for groups.
Max 50 pers.

30126 Lirac

Domaine du Château de Ségriès
tel: (66) 50 10 53
Lirac *rosé, rouge, blanc*
Open daily 9–20h
Appointment necessary.
Max 40 pers.

30290 Laudun

Caves des Vignerons
route de l'Ardoise
tel: (66) 50 02 07
Mon–Fri 8–12h; 14–18h
Sat 8–12h
Appointment necessary.
Max 30 pers.

30200 Chusclan

Cave des Vignerons de Chusclan
tel: (66) 89 63 03
Côtes du Rhône-Villages, Côtes du Rhône
Open Mon–Sat
Appointment necessary only for groups
larger than 10.
Max 50 pers.

30200 Vénéjan

Cave Coopérative de Vénéjan
tel: (66) 89 65 04
Côtes du Rhône *rouge, rosé*

Open Mon–Fri 8–12h; 14–18h
Appointment preferable for groups.
A little English spoken.

30210 Fournès

Cave Coopérative 'Les Coteaux de
Fournès'
tel: (66) 37 02 36
Côtes du Rhône *rouge*
Open Mon–Fri

30130 Saint-Alexandre

Alain Robert et Fils
Vieux Manoir du Frigoulas
tel: (66) 39 18 71
Côtes du Rhône
Mon–Fri
Appointment preferable.
Max 40 pers.
A little English spoken.

30130 Pont St-Esprit

Cave Coopérative
tel: (66) 39 08 65
Côtes du Rhône, *vins de table*
Open Mon–Fri 8–12h; 14–18h
Max 35 pers.
A little English spoken.

30970 Saint-Nazaire

Dominique Pons
Domaine des Cedres
tel: (66) 89 66 09
Côtes du Rhône *rouge, rosé*
Open daily by appointment.
Max 25 pers.

30630 Cornillon

Mme Castor et Fils
Domaine Saint-Nabor
tel: (66) 82 20 30
Côtes du Rhône
Open daily 9–12h; 14–18h
Appointment necessary.
Max 20 pers.
English spoken.

30200 Sabran

Bernard de Sérésin
Domaine de Bruthel
tel: (66) 89 69 06
Côtes du Rhône *rouge, blanc*
Daily 9–20h
Appointment preferable.
Max 40 pers.

Northern Rhône

Die

Caveau de Dégustation
Cave Coopérative de Clairette de Die

07130 Saint-Péray

Jean-François Chaboud
21, rue Ferdinand-Malet
tel: (75) 60 31 63
St-Péray *méthode champenoise brut & demi-sec*
By appointment.
Max 50 pers.

07300 Mauves

Pierre Coursodon
place du Marché
tel: (75) 08 29 27
St-Joseph AOC
Mon–Sat
Appointment preferable.
Max 10 pers.
A little English spoken.

Bernard Gripa
RN86
tel: (75) 08 14 96
St-Joseph AOC, St-Péray AOC
Mon–Sat 9–19h
Appointment preferable.
Max 10 pers.

07300 Tournon

Jean-Louis Grippat
quartier La Suava
tel: (75) 08 15 51
St-Joseph AOC, Hermitage AOC
Mon–Sat 9–12h; 15–19h
Appointment preferable.
Max 10 pers.

26600 Tain l'Hermitage

Cave Coopérative de Vins Fins
22, route de Larnage
tel: (75) 08 20 87
Hermitage, Crozes-Hermitage, St-Joseph,
Cornas, St-Péray *méthode champenoise*
Mon–Sat 8–12h; 14–18h
Sun 9–12h; 14–18h
Appointment necessary.
Max 50 pers.

M Chapoutier SA
18, avenue de la Republique
tel: (75) 08 28 65
Hermitage AOC
Mon–Fri by appointment.

Max 15 pers.
English spoken.

26600 Mercurol

Desmeure Père et Fils
route de Romans
tel: (75) 08 10 56
Hermitage, Crozes-Hermitage AOC
Daily by appointment.
Max 40 pers.

26600 Serves

Albert Bégot
tel: (75) 03 30 27
Crozes-Hermitage AOC
Saturday 14–18h
Appointment necessary.

07340 Serrières

Cave Coopérative St-Désirat Champagne
St-Désirat
tel: (75) 34 22 05
St-Joseph AOC
Daily by appointment.
Max 50 pers.

42410 Chavanay

Caveau de Boisseyt
Chol et Fils
tel: (74) 59 10 53
Côte Rôtie, St-Joseph, Côtes du Rhône
Open daily except Mon
Max 50 pers.

69420 Condrieu

Georges Vernay
1, rue Nationale
tel: (74) 59 52 22
Condrieu, Côte Rôtie, St-Joseph, Côtes du
Rhône
Daily 9–12h; 14h30–19h
Appointment preferable.
Max 25 pers.

42410 Verin

Neyrey-Gachet
Château-Grillet
tel: (74) 59 51 56
Château Grillet AOC
Open daily.
(note: it is not usually possible to taste this
rare wine, but small quantities of bottles
may be available for sale)
Max 12 pers.
English spoken.

Côtes de Provence

Many producers in this sunny vineyard sell their wines 'en vrac', that is, where you bring your own container, and fill it directly from the barrel, or 'au pistolet' – irreverently pumped out of a nozzle; we have indicated those establishments that sell either in bottles (bouteilles) or en vrac. Appointments are not generally necessary. Do bear in mind, however, that many places close for a couple of hours (sometimes longer!) at midday.

83160 La Valette

Château Redon
route d'Hyères
tel: (94) 27 02 10
Open Sat
Vente en bouteilles et en vrac

83260 La Crau

Domaine de la Castille
tel: (94) 66 71 48
Open Mon–Sat morning
Vente en bouteilles et en vrac

83250 La Londe-les-Maures

Domaine de la Source Sainte-Marguerite
tel: (94) 66 81 46
Open daily
Vente en bouteilles et en vrac

83230 Bormes-les-Mimosas

Domaine de Leoube
tel: (94) 64 80 03
Open daily
Vente en bouteilles et en vrac

83350 Ramatuelle

Domaine de Valderian
tel: (94) 97 34 06
Open daily
Vente en bouteilles et en vrac

83990 St-Tropez

Cave Coopérative du Golfe de St-Tropez
tel: (94) 97 01 60
Open Tue–Sun
Vente en bouteilles et en vrac

83310 Cogolin

Domaine des Garcinières
tel: (94) 56 02 85
Open Mon–Sat

83360 Grimaud

Cave Coopérative Vinicole
tel: (94) 43 20 14
Open Mon–Sat
Vente en bouteilles et en vrac

83680 La Garde-Freinet

Domaine des Launes
tel: (94) 73 06 09
Open daily
Vente en bouteilles et en vrac

83550 Vidauban

Cave Coopérative la Vidaubannaise
tel: (94) 73 00 12
Open Mon–Sat
Vente en bouteilles et en vrac

83460 Taradeau

Château de Selle
tel: (94) 68 86 86
Open daily 8–12h; 14–18h

83460 Les Arcs-sur-Argens

Comité Interprofessionnel des Vins Côtes de Provence
3, avenue Jean Jaurès
tel: (94) 73 33 38
Professional organization for the wines of the region; literature, maps, and other information available

Cave Coopérative l'Arcoise
tel: (94) 73 30 29
Open Mon–Sat
Vente en bouteilles et en vrac

S.A.R.L Domaines de Rasque de Laval
Château Sainte-Roseline
tel: (94) 73 32 57
Open Mon–Fri
Vente en bouteilles

83920 La Motte

Domaine les Demoiselles
tel: (94) 70 82 03
Open Mon–Sat
Vente en bouteilles et en vrac

83490 Le Muy

Cave Coopérative l'Ancienne
tel: (94) 44 40 42
Open Mon–Sat
Vente en bouteilles et en vrac

83600 Fréjus

Cave Coopérative La Fréjussienne
tel: (94) 51 01 81
Open Mon–Sat
Vente en bouteilles et en vrac

83600 Bagnols-en-Forêt

Cave Coopérative La Bagnolaise
tel: (94) 40 60 13
Open Tue–Sat
Vente en bouteilles et en vrac

83300 Draguignan

Domaine Christiane Rabiega
Clos Dière Méridional
tel: (94) 68 44 22
Open daily
Vente en bouteilles et en vrac

83510 Lorgues

Domaine du Clos
tel: (94) 73 70 21
Vente en bouteilles et en vrac

83960 Entrecasteaux

Cave Coopérative Vinicole
tel: (94) 04 42 68
Open Mon–Sat
Vente en bouteilles et en vrac

83850 Cotignac

Cave Coopérative Agricole 'Les Vignerons
de Cotignac'
tel: (94) 04 60 04
Open Mon–Sat
Vente en bouteilles et en vrac

83340 Flassans-sur-Issole

Commanderie de Peyrassol
tel: (94) 69 71 02
Open daily
Vente en bouteilles et en vrac

83890 Besse-sur-Issole

Château de la Croix de Bontar
tel: (94) 69 70 20
Open daily

83750 Puget-Ville

Cave Coopérative Vinicole La
Pugétoise
tel: (94) 48 31 05
Open Mon–Sat morn.
Vente en bouteilles et en vrac

83390 Cuers

Château de Gairoird
tel: (94) 28 60 84
Open daily
Vente en bouteilles et en vrac

Camargue

30220 Aigues-Mortes

Domaines Viticoles des Salins du Midi
Domaine de Jarras-Listel
Easter–Oct 1 daily 9–11h30; 14–18h30
Oct 1–Easter: Mon–Sat morning 9–11h30;
14–17h30
English guide in summer.

Wine Festivals

Weekend closest to Jan 20	Professional tasting of new wines in amphitheatre grotto	Orange
Around April 25th	Festival of St Mark, patron saint of the village	Châteauneuf-du-Pape
End of April	Festival of St Vincent, patron saint of vine growers	Tavel
May	Festival of Côtes du Rhônes-Villages wines	Vacqueyras
July/Aug	Small permanent exhibition of Côtes du Rhône wine in the amphitheatre grotto	Orange
Sept 24/25	Vintage Festival	Châteauneuf-du-Pape
Mid-November	Tasting of Côtes du Rhône *primeurs*	Vaison-la-Romaine

Regional Gastronomy

The cuisine of the northern Rhône reflects the gastronomic influence of the Lyonnais, but by the middle of the valley, the distinctive herb-scented cuisine of Provence becomes dominant. Many of the specialities listed below are Provençal – full-flavoured foods that go so well with the robust, full-bodied *vins du soleil*.

Brandade de morue Salt cod boiled, then pounded to a thick paste with olive oil, garlic, and milk.

Anchoïade Dip or sauce of pounded anchovies, garlic, and olive oil, generally served with raw vegetables such as celery, fennel, carrots, and lettuce, or else spread onto rounds of bread that have been toasted over an open fire.

Saucisson d'Arles Large pork and beef sausage.

Tapénade Purée of stoned black olives, capers, anchovy fillets, olive oil, and lemon juice.

Pissaladière Thin bread dough, spread with virgin olive oil, sliced sweet onions, olives, and anchovies, then baked in a *'feu de bois'* – a wood-fired oven.

Tian de provence Egg and vegetable casserole cooked in an earthenware dish of the same name.

Salade niçoise Salad of tomatoes, lettuce, olives, anchovies.

Ratatouille Aubergines, courgettes, onions, tomatoes, peppers, and garlic, sliced or coarsely chopped into chunks, and stewed in rich olive oil.

Soupe au pistou Fresh vegetable soup enriched with an exquisite sauce of basil, garlic, olive oil, and ground pine nuts.

Aigo bouido Garlic soup.

Bourride Fish soup flavoured with saffron, garlic, and parsley. Sometimes a dollop of hot red-pepper sauce called *rouille* is first spooned into the bowl.

Bisquebouille Shellfish soup.

Bouillabaisse Famous Mediterranean fish soup produced, authentically, with gurnet, red mullet, eel, *racasse*, sea perch, crabs, and other shellfish. It is a main (and often expensive) meal.

Quenelles de brochet Sieved pike, mixed with *crème fraîche* and egg whites, then poached gently in stock. Very light and delicious when freshly prepared.

Le grand aïoli Poached whiting, salt cod, red mullet and other fish, hard-boiled eggs, boiled potatoes, carrots, artichokes, and beans, eaten with an extremely pungent garlic mayonnaise, itself called *aïoli*.

Daube de boeuf provençale Beef marinated in red wine flavoured with herbs, bitter orange peel, and mushrooms, then slowly braised in an earthenware pot.

Caillette aux herbes 'Meatball' of pork, vegetables, and herbs baked in an oven.

Grillades au feu de bois Meats or fish grilled over a wood fire.

Civet de lapin Rabbit stewed in wine flavoured with juniper berries and thyme.

Couscous North African dish of semolina steamed over stew (usually lamb or chicken), then served with a thick sauce. Much loved in the South of France.

Poularde demi-deuil Lyonnais favourite of chicken stuffed first with slivers of truffle, boiled in stock, then served with a *sauce velouté*.

Poulet au vinaigre Another favourite from gastronomic Lyons: chicken cooked in white wine, wine vinegar, cream, and shallots.

Pieds et paquets Tripe made into little 'packets' and simmered in white wine.

Truffes du Ventoux Truffles from the forests of the Ventoux range.

Cèpes Large-capped, highly-prized wild mushrooms.

Jambon de montagne Air-cured ham from the mountains.

Marrons glacés Candied chestnuts from the Ardèche.

Nougat de Montélimar Even the air around this town is perfumed with the irresistible scent of honey and almonds which produce this delicious nougat.

Berlingots Caramel candies from Carpentras.

Calissons Marzipan sweets from Aix-en-Provence.

Cheeses:
Fromage fort du Mt Ventoux Strong-smelling and -tasting cheese flavoured with herbs and (sometimes) *marc*.

Banon Small sheeps' or goats' milk cheese wrapped in moist leaves.
Brousse Fresh, mild sheeps' or goats' milk cheese.
Rigotte de Condrieu Reddish cheese made on farms around Condrieu.

Restaurants

Note: In addition to the restaurants below, see Hotel section.

Southern Rhône – Circuit 1

84000 Avignon

Hiely Lucullus
5, rue de la République
tel: (90) 86 17 07
In the centre of old Avignon, near the Palais des Papes, serving elegant classic and regional dishes.
Closed Tue; also Mon in low season
Expensive

Restaurant La Fourchette
7, rue Racine
tel: (90) 82 56 01
Inexpensive restaurant serving regional wines and personally-cooked dishes.
Open Tue–Sat 12h30–14h; 19h30–21h30

Le Vernet
58, rue Joseph-Vernet
tel: (90) 86 64 53
Regional and *nouvelle cuisine* and a full range of French wines.
May 1–Aug 31 open daily
Winter closed Sun
Open 12–14h; 19–21h30
Moderate

Restaurant La Marmite
3, boulevard du Mal-de-Lattre-de-Tassigny
tel: (90) 82 44 94
Family restaurant serving Provençal dishes such as *civet de porcelet* and *pieds et paquets*.
Closed Sun
Inexpensive

84140 Montfavet (5 km east of Avignon on D53)

La Ferme St-Pierre
1551, avenue d'Avignon
tel: (90) 87 12 86
Regional dishes and wines and home-made *pâtisseries*.
Open Tue–Sat 12–14h; 19h30–21h30
Inexpensive

84230 Châteauneuf-du-Pape

Restaurant 'La Mule du Pape'
rue de la République
tel: (90) 39 73 30
Well-loved by the local *vignerons*, this restaurant is located in a typical Provençal *maison* with views over the vineyards and serves local specialities and wines.
Closed Mon eve; Tue
Moderate

Restaurant Le Pistou
15, rue Joseph Ducos
tel: (90) 39 71 75
Provençal specialities served in a comfortable family restaurant.
Closed Mon
Open 12–14h; 19h30–21h
Inexpensive

84190 Gigondas

Hostellerie Les Florets
tel: (90) 65 85 01
On the edge of the Montmirail hills, a charming and peaceful hotel/restaurant serving local dishes. Shady terrace.
Hotel closed Jan; Feb
Restaurant closed Wed
Inexpensive to **Moderate**

Southern Rhône – Circuit 2

30150 Sauveterre

Hostellerie la Crémaillère
route 980
Regional specialities and the wines of Lirac, Tavel, and Châteauneuf-du-Pape.
Closed Tue eve; Wed
Moderate

Northern Rhône

26000 Valence

Restaurant Pic
285, avenue Victor-Hugo
tel: (75) 44 15 32
Elegant **Very Expensive** restaurant serving *haute cuisine*.
Closed Wed; Sun eve; 10 days in Jan; Aug
Accommodation in 4 rooms and 1 apartment is **Moderate**

69420 Condrieu

Hostellerie Beau Rivage
tel: (74) 59 52 24
Highly-recommended restaurant serving specialities such as *le pintadeau* (guinea

fowl) *au poivre vert, matelote d'anguilles,
mousse de brochet* and an excellent selection
of Condrieu and Côte Rôtie wines and
others from the Côtes du Rhône.
Open daily
Expensive
Also **Moderate** accommodation
Hotel closed Jan 5–Feb 15

38200 Vienne

La Pyramide
14, boulevard Fernand-Point
tel: (74) 53 01 96
Quite simply one of the greatest
restaurants in France. Essential to book
well in advance.
Closed Mon eve; Tue; Nov 1–Dec 15
Very Expensive

Le Bec Fin
7, place St-Maurice
tel: (74) 85 76 72
Good comfortable restaurant serving
Lyonnais dishes and wines from the
northern Rhône.
Closed Sun eve; Mon; two weeks at end of
Jan
Moderate

69560 St-Romain-en-Gal

Chez René
tel: (74) 53 19 72
Situated on the banks of the river, serving
regional dishes such as *assiette du pêcheur*
and *aiguillette de caneton aux olives* (duckling
breast with olives).
Closed Sun eve; Mon
Moderate

Côtes de Provence

83000 Toulon

Restaurant Madeleine
7, rue Tombades
tel: (94) 92 67 85
Family-run restaurant serving local dishes.
Closed Wed
Open 12h15–13h30; 19h15–21h30
Moderate

83230 Bormes-les-Mimosas

Restaurant La Tonnelle des Délices
place Gambetta
tel: (94) 71 34 84
Family restaurant open evenings only.
Moderate

83990 St Tropez

Restaurant Leï Mouscardins
extremité du Port
tel: (94) 97 01 53
Elegant seafood specialities, including
bouillabaise, bourride, and *langoustines.*
Open daily except Nov 1–Feb 1
Expensive

Restaurant L'Escale
quai Jean-Jaurès
tel: (94) 97 00 63
Fish and shellfish in this **Inexpensive** to
Moderate restaurant on the quay.
Open daily.

Camargue

30220 Aigues-Mortes

La Camargue
rue République
tel: (66) 88 31 57
Gypsy music and specialities of the
Camargue and the Gard.
Inexpensive to **Moderate**

Hotels

Southern Rhône – Circuit 1

84000 Avignon

Hôtel Cité des Papes
1, rue Jean Vilar
tel: (90) 86 22 45
Moderate hotel without restaurant.
Closed Dec 17–Jan 18

Hôtel Mercure
route de Marseille
2, rue Marie-de-Médicis
tel: (90) 88 91 10
Moderate riverside hotel with attractive
garden and **Inexpensive** to **Moderate**
restaurant.
Hotel open all year
Restaurant open daily 12–24h

84130 Le Pontet

Auberge de Cassagne
(exit Avignon Nord)
tel: (90) 31 04 18
5 km north of Avignon, a country hotel
with a swimming pool, tennis courts, and
a restaurant that serves imaginative
specialities.
Hotel open all year.
Restaurant open daily 12–13h30;
19h30–21h30
Moderate to **Expensive**

30400 Villeneuve-les-Avignon

Hostellerie Le Prieuré
7, place du Chapitre
tel: (90) 25 18 20
14th-century priory surrounded by trees
with swimming pool, tennis court, and
restaurant with meals served in gardens in
summer.
Hotel closed Nov 1–March 3
Restaurant open daily 12h15–13h30;
19h15–21h15
Very Expensive

La Magnaraie Hostellerie
37, rue Camp-de-Bataille
tel: (90) 25 11 11
Elegant 15th-century hotel surrounded by
gardens with swimming pool and tennis
courts. Specialities of the restaurant
include *feuilletés aux truffes* and *la lotte
camarguaise.*
Hotel closed Jan 15–March 1
Restaurant open daily
Moderate to **Expensive**

Hôtel Les Cèdres
39, boulevard Pasteur
tel: (90) 25 43 92
Hotel set amidst ancient cedars, with
restaurant serving *grillades au feu de bois.*
Open all year.
Inexpensive

Hôtel de l'Atelier
5, rue de la Foire
tel: (90) 25 01 84
Inexpensive hotel without restaurant set
in a medieval building.
Closed Dec 20–Feb 4

84230 Châteauneuf-du-Pape

Hostellerie des Fines Roches
(3 km south-east on the D17)
tel: (90) 39 70 23
In the heart of the vineyards, a château
hotel owned by a prominent wine
producer, with restaurant serving regional
and gastronomic menus.
Hotel closed Jan
Moderate to **Expensive**

84110 Vaison-la-Romaine

Le Logis du Château
Les Hauts de Vaison
tel: (90) 36 09 98
Comfortable, quiet hotel with swimming
pool and restaurant.
Closed Nov 1–March 15
Moderate

Hostellerie Le Beffroi
rue de l'Evêché Haute Ville
tel: (90) 36 04 71
17th-century building with comfortable
rooms, antique furniture, terraced
gardens, and views of surrounding
country. Restaurant serves many fish
specialities.
Hotel closed Nov 15–March 10
Restaurant closed Mon; Tue midday
Moderate

84110 Séguret

Domaine de Cabasse
tel: (90) 36 91 12
Farmhouse *auberge* set within olive and
pine groves and vineyards. Limited
number of rooms let on a half-board basis
only. Simple local cuisine is accompanied
by Côtes du Rhône-Villages wines from
the proprietor's own vineyards. Cellar
visits and wine tasting can be arranged,
and wines can be purchased direct.
Closed Sept 25–March 20
Moderate

Southern Rhône – Circuit 2

Avignon and Villeneuve-les-Avignon

(see Circuit 1 above)

30150 Roquemaure

Château de Cubières
route d'Avignon
tel: (66) 50 14 28
Grand 18th-century hotel in parkland with
restaurant serving regional food and wine
in the garden in fine weather.
Hotel closed Jan 1–March 20
Restaurant closed Tue
Moderate

30126 Tavel

L'Auberge de Tavel
tel: (66) 50 03 41
Hotel with swimming pool, gardens, and
restaurant serving mainly fish and
shellfish. Wine tastings, and visits to
cellars can be arranged.
Hotel closed Feb
Restaurant open daily except Mon in low
season
Moderate

Hostellerie du Seigneur
tel: (66) 50 04 26

Inexpensive family hotel with restaurant serving Provençal specialities and Tavel and Lirac wines in a medieval building. Open all year.

30200 Vénéjan

Ferme Auberge
tel: (66) 89 65 16
Inexpensive *auberge* with restaurant serving *grillades au feu de sarments* and Côtes du Rhône wines.
Open all year.

30210 Remoulins

Hôtel Moderne
tel: (66) 37 20 13
Hotel with restaurant serving local wines and foods.
Hotel closed Nov
Restaurant closed Sat in low season; open 12–14h; 19h30–21h
Inexpensive

Northern Rhône

07130 Soyons

Hostellerie La Musardière
RN86
tel: (75) 60 83 55
Moderate hotel with swimming pool, tennis courts, sauna, and restaurant.
Hotel closed Dec 11–Jan 3
Restaurant closed Sat in low season

07130 St-Romain-de-Lerps

Château du Besset
tel: (75) 44 41 63
Château hotel within 50 hectares of parkland, with swimming pool, tennis courts, and restaurant serving regional dishes.
Restaurant open daily 12h30–14h; 19h30–21h30
Hotel **Moderate**
Restaurant **Expensive**

07300 Tournon

Hôtel de Paris
place du Lycée
tel: (75) 08 01 11
Hotel facing the Rhône, and, across the river, the vineyards of Hermitage, with restaurant serving country specialities such as *caillette ardèchoise* and local wines.
Open daily
Moderate

26600 Tain l'Hermitage

Inter Hôtel du Commerce
69 avenue Jean Jaurès
tel: (75) 08 65 00
Thirty-room hotel, each with bathroom, and restaurant that serves regional dishes such as *terrine de caneton truffée, écrevisses gratines, pintadeau de la Drôme.*
Closed Nov 15–Dec 15
Moderate

Hotel les Deux Coteaux
18, rue Joseph Peala
tel: (75) 08 33 01
Peaceful **Inexpensive** hotel on banks of the Rhône without restaurant.
Closed Nov

26600 Pont de l'Isère

Michel Chabran
tel: (75) 84 60 09
Modern comfortable hotel with restaurant.
Hotel open all year.
Restaurant closed Mon; Sun eve in low season
Expensive

Côtes de Provence

83200 Toulon

Frantel La Tour Blanche
boulevard Amiral-Vence
tel: (94) 24 41 57
Modern luxury hotel overlooking the harbour. 96 rooms, each with bathroom, and balcony facing the sea. Swimming pool and restaurant.
Hotel open all year.
Restaurant open daily 12h30–14h30; 19h30–22h30 except Sun in low season
Expensive

83230 Bormes-les-Mimosas

Paradis Hotel
Mont-des-Roses
tel: (94) 71 06 85
Peaceful hotel in park, without restaurant.
Closed Oct 15–March 30
Moderate

83350 Ramatuelle

Hostellerie Le Baou
tel: (94) 79 20 48
Expensive hotel with swimming pool and panoramic views.
Hotel open all year.
Restaurant open daily 12–15h; 19h30–22h

La Ferme d'Augustin
route de Tahiti
tel: (94) 97 23 83
Quiet hotel with gardens, close to Tahiti
beach. No restaurant.
Open Easter–mid Oct
Moderate

83360 Grimaud

La Boulangerie
route de Collobrières
tel: (94) 43 23 16
Hotel with swimming pool, tennis courts,
gardens, and superb views of the Massif
des Maures.
Hotel closed Oct 1–March 15
Restaurant open daily 12–14h; 20–23h
Expensive

83460 Les Arcs

Le Logis du Guetteur
place du Château
tel: (94) 73 30 82
Hotel-restaurant set in an 11th-century
fort. Restaurant has various **Inexpensive**
to **Moderate** menus.
Hotel closed Nov 15–Dec 15
Restaurant closed Fri

83600 Frejus

Auberge du Vieux Four
57, rue Grisolle
tel: (94) 51 56 38
Comfortable rustic *auberge* with restaurant
serving both regional and classic cuisine.
Hotel closed Sept 20–Oct 20
Restaurant closed Sun, Mon eve
Moderate

Les Residences du Colombier
route de Bagnols
tel: (94) 51 45 92
Set within a nature reserve, this 60-room
hotel has excellent facilities and a
restaurant serving Provençal specialities.
Hotel closed Oct–April
Restaurant closed Tue
Expensive

83440 Seillans

Hôtel de France
place du Thouron
tel: (94) 76 96 10
Comfortable hotel with panoramic views,
and restaurant 'Clariond' serving game
and other specialities.
Hotel closed 3 weeks in Jan
Restaurant closed Wed in low season
Moderate

Hôtel-Restaurant Les Deux Rocs
place d'Amont
tel: (94) 76 05 33
Charming hotel in old Provençal village.
Hotel closed Nov 1–March 20
Restaurant closed Tue in low season
Moderate

83850 Cotignac

Lou Calen
1, cours Gambetta
tel: (94) 04 60 40
Typical and charming Provençal
hotel-restaurant.
Hotel closed end of Oct
Restaurant closed Thur
Moderate

Camping

The South of France is one of the most
popular camping destinations in Europe,
and there are sites throughout, particularly
along the coast. The following is a brief
selection only of campsites in the wine
regions:

84000 Avignon
Bagatelle
tel: (90) 86 30 39
Pont St-Bénézet
tel: (90) 82 63 50
84190 Beaumes-de-Venise
Camp Municipal
tel: (90) 65 02 01
84200 Carpentras
Villemarie
tel: (90) 63 09 55
84110 Vaison-la-Romaine
Le Moulin de César
tel: (90) 36 00 78
84270 Vedene
Flory
tel: (90) 31 00 51
84130 Le Pontet
Grand Bois La Tapy
tel: (90) 31 37 44
84100 Orange
St-Eutrope
tel: (90) 34 09 22
30200 Bagnols-sur-Cèze
Les Genêts d'Or
tel: (66) 89 58 67
26000 Valence
L'Epervière
tel: (75) 43 63 01

26600 Tain l'Hermitage
Les Lucs
tel: (75) 08 32 82
07300 Tournon
Le Manoir
Camping Municipal
tel: (75) 08 05 28

Where to Get Additional Information

Maison du Vin
Comité Interprofessionnel des Vins des
Côtes du Rhône
41, cours Jean Jaurès
84000 Avignon
tel: (90) 86 47 09

Comité Interprofessionnel des Vins des
Côtes de Provence
3, avenue Jean Jaurès
83460 Les Arcs-sur-Argens
tel: (94) 73 33 38

Office de Tourisme et Accueil de France
41, cours Jean Jaurès
84000 Avignon
tel: (90) 82 65 11

Syndicat d'Initiative
place Portail
Châteauneuf-du-Pape
tel: (90) 39 71 08

Office de Tourisme
place Chanoine Sautel
Vaison-la-Romaine
tel: (90) 36 02 11

Office de Tourisme
place Gen-Leclerc
Valence
tel: (75) 43 04 88

Syndicat d'Initiative
place Église
Tain l'Hermitage
tel: (75) 08 06 81

Office de Tourisme
3, cours Brillier
Vienne
tel: (74) 85 12 62

Office de Tourisme et Accueil de France
8, avenue Colbert
Toulon
tel: (94) 92 37 64

Les Foulons
tel: (75) 08 22 72
Les Sables
tel: (75) 08 20 05
07760 Peyraud
Camp du Château
tel: (75) 34 01 04
38200 Vienne
Piscine de Leveau
tel: (74) 85 23 15

Along the Côte d'Azur there are literally
hundreds of campsites. Even so, they can
get extremely crowded in high season so it
is essential to book if you want to stay
along the coast. Here are a few inland sites
along the *Route du Vin des Côtes de Provence*.

83460 Les Arcs
L'Eau Vive
tel: (94) 73 30 66
83490 Le Muy
Les Cigales
tel: (94) 44 42 08
Sellig
tel: (94) 44 41 71
Domaine de la Noguière
tel: (94) 44 43 78
La Prairie
tel: (94) 44 42 22
83440 St-Paul-en-Forêt
Le Parc
tel: (94) 76 15 35
83830 Callas
Notre-Dame-de-Pennafort
tel: (94) 76 62 71
83000 Draguignan
La Foux
tel: (94) 66 18 27
83340 Flassans-sur-Issole
Camp Municipal
tel: (94) 69 71 13

Bibliography

Guide to the Wines of the Rhône by Peter
Hallgarten, Pitman 1979

The Wines of the Rhône by John
Livingstone-Learmouth and Melvyn C. H.
Master, Faber & Faber, 1978

Michelin Green Guides: *Provence; French
Riviera; La Vallée du Rhône* (French edition
only)

—GERMANY—

—THE RHINE AND— MOSEL

The vineyards of Germany are concentrated in the west of the country, along the slopes and valleys that descend down to the Rhine and Mosel Rivers, their tributaries, and tributaries of their tributaries. This is Germany's Rhineland. The wine country varies considerably, from the hot, Upper Rhenish lowlands of the Rheinpfalz to the grey-green slopes of the Mosel, the wooded expanses

How to Get There

By Car
Germany's Rhineland is a compact area in the western corner of Germany, with excellent approaches from Belgium, Luxembourg, France, and Holland. From Ostend take the E5 autoroute (ring road north around Brussels) via Liège and Aachen (by-passing Cologne and Bonn, and optionally making a brief detour down the Ahr Valley) to Koblenz. From Koblenz commence tours of the Mosel-Saar-Ruwer, Mittelrhein, and Rheingau. Alternatively, from Brussels, head south on E40 across Luxembourg to Trier to commence a tour of the Mosel-Saar-Ruwer downriver to Koblenz.

From Paris take the A4 autoroute to Reims and Metz. From Metz head north to Thionville on the E9. Take the N153 along the east bank of the Moselle (Mosel) River into Germany. Continue to Trier. Alternatively from Metz, continue on E12 autoroute to cross the border at Saarbrücken. From Saarbrücken either continue on the E12 east to the Rheinpfalz, north-east to the Nahe Valley, or else follow the Saar downriver to Saarburg, Konz, and the Mosel.

If touring the Alsatian *Route du Vin* continue north through the massive *Weintor* ('wine gate') to join the *Deutsche Weinstrasse* which leads through wine towns and vineyards of the Rheinpfalz.

Alternatively cross the Rhine at Strasbourg on B28 to Appenweier to tour the Ortenau wine region of Baden, stretched out on the lower slopes of the Black Forest.

By Plane
There are direct, non-stop flights from the US to Frankfurt, which is an ideal centre for commencing tours of the German wine regions. The eleven quality-wine regions are all in relative close proximity (unlike, for example, the numerous wine regions of France). Another convenient centre for commencing tours of the Rhineland is Cologne, which also has an international airport. There are international airports a Zurich and Basle, and these may prove convenient for touring the southern wine regions of Baden and Württemberg. Industrial Stuttgart, a familiar businessman's destination, also provides an entry into the beautiful wine lands of Germany.

By Train
From Paris Est there is an excellent regular service to Frankfurt via Metz, Saarbrücken, Bad Kreuznach, and Mainz.

of the Schwarzwald to the steeply terraced vineyards of the Ahr, yet the region as a whole is continuous: rich, beautiful, and welcoming.

Germany's overall wine production compared to France, Italy, Spain, or Portugal, is relatively small. Yet it is one of the most important wine-producing countries in the world. Each of the eleven designated quality-wine regions produces unique and distinctive products. On the whole, however, the classic wines of Germany do bear certain family resemblances. The greatest (all white) are elegant and stylish wines that balance the fresh acidity and ripe, complex scent of the Riesling grape with a natural degree of residual grape sugar. On a more basic level, too, good inexpensive *Deutscher Tafelwein* (German table wine) displays the flowery bouquet and character of distinctive German grape varieties, allied with a firm, underlying acidity. These characteristics – at their most fundamental or most complex – result in unmistakable and exciting products from these most northerly quality vineyards in Europe.

Though there are eleven separate quality-wine regions, the entire German vineyard can be approached as an entity. This simplifies matters practically, too, for, if in France or Italy, for example, the vineyards stretch from the far

Local Public Transport
Trains Local train services are efficient, serving most of the wine regions. There is a frequent daily service between Trier and Koblenz with stops at Bullay and Cochem. Regular service also between Trier and Saarbrücken, stopping at Saarburg. Good service connecting Cologne and Frankfurt with stops at Koblenz, Niederlahnstein, St Goarshausen, Assmannshausen, Rüdesheim, Wiesbaden, and Mainz. For exploration of the Rheinhessen there are trains from Frankfurt to Ludwigshafen, via Mainz, Nierstein, and Worms. For the Rheinpfalz, take the train from Frankfurt to Ludwigshafen and Neustadt, then change at Neustadt for local service to Landau. The Baden wine region is on the main Frankfurt/Basle route, with stops at Rastatt and Baden-Baden.
River boat Köln-Düsseldorfer German Rhine Line offers numerous services along the Rhine and Mosel Rivers, ranging from single journeys in an afternoon, to 10-day cruises beginning in Amsterdam. The boats are modern and comfortable, and have good restaurants and (often) live entertainment. Other companies offer river cruises in summer season. For further information contact:

K-D German Rhine Line
Frankenwerft 15
5000 Cologne, West Germany
tel: (0221) 20 881

Car Rental Information
Frankfurt
  Avis: Niddastrasse 46–48
    tel: (0611) 23 01 01
  Airport
    tel: (0611) 69 02 777
  Hanauer Landstr. 66
    tel: (0611) 49 00 36
  Frankenallee 41
    tel: (0611) 73 03 91
  Hertz: Airport
    tel: (0611) 69 05 011
  Hanauer Landstr. 106
    tel: (0611) 43 92 48
  Mainzer Landstr. 139
    tel: (0611) 23 31 51
Trier
  Avis: Herzogenbuscher Str.
    tel: (0651) 12 722
Koblenz
  Avis: Moselweisser Str.
    tel: (0261) 44 050
Mannheim
  Avis: Augartenstr. 112–114
    tel: (0621) 40 20 51
  Hertz: Friedrichsring 36
    tel: (0621) 12 29 97
Baden-Baden
  Hertz: Lichtentalerstr.
    39 Augusta Parkhaus
    tel: (07221) 22 471

Michelin Map Numbers 203, 204, 205

north to the far south of the countries, here they are all in relative proximity, and can be reached and explored from basically similar routes. Indeed, so compact is her wine country, that it is perfectly possible (though not necessarily desirable) to tour all eleven German quality-wine regions within, say, a few weeks. Moreover, while in other great wine countries the contrast between various wine regions is dramatic, reflecting cultural, historic, and gastronomic differences, these western lands are basically contiguous and homogeneous. That is not to say that local differences do not exist, or that Swabians would feel affinity with people from Trier. Nevertheless, the great contrasts in attitudes and character between, for example, southern Bavarians and northern Hamburgers, are not found in the Rhineland.

For the visitor, the Rhineland is above all a land of enjoyment, exuding an atmosphere of an all-year party to which all are invited. Wine festivals take place throughout the year, and especially during late summer. Little wine villages in all the eleven regions drape colourful bunting from their town fountains to the *Rathaus*, from leaning, gothic shops to half-timbered houses. Stands are set up in cobbled streets, and local producers offer a full range of their varied wines. They are served in small measures and thus one is able to taste a full range of different styles and quality levels of wine from near and adjoining vineyards. (One particular festival, Bad Dürkheim's *Wurstmarkt* (Sausage Festival) makes such comparative tasting a Herculean feat, for the local wines are only served in half-litre glasses known as *Schoppen!*) Such wine festivals are gay, happy affairs, for when Germans get together it is not long before the sentimental singing and dancing begins. The wail of electric accordions sounds from the depths of dimly-lit *Weinkeller*, while in the town square, a local brass band puffs and oomphs. And if there is no shortage of wines to sample, there is also on hand a vast array of simple, well-prepared foods such as various types of sausage, roast chickens, knuckles of veal, *Schwenkbraten* (pork steaks roasted over open fires), *Spiessbraten* (spit-roasted beef) and *Eisbein mit sauerkraut* (pickled knuckle of pork and sauerkraut), all served in Wagnerian portions.

Apart from these numerous festivals, there are countless other opportunities to sample wine. Many of Germany's wine producers are small family concerns who offer informal tastings of their products in their own premises, at outdoor tables set up in the front or back garden or in the cellar itself. A sign which proclaims *'Weinproben'* indicates that the casual visitor is welcome, and that an interesting range of open wines, that is, wines that can be sampled by the glass, are available. This allows a comparative tasting of the higher quality levels *(Spätlese, Auslese, Beerenauslese, Trockenbeerenauslese)*. Sensibly for everyone involved, the wine producers make reasonable charges for wines offered, and thus one may taste as much or as little as one likes, without feeling any compulsion to purchase. Such wine producers, incidentally, sometimes offer simple foods to accompany wine tastings; others, too, rent out rooms, thus providing opportunities of actually staying with a wine-producing family, and being able to view the cellars and wine-making processes in action.

Germany's Rhineland is an ideal place for a relaxing family holiday. There are numerous quiet spots deep in forests or atop hills where one can come just to get away from it all. Spa towns such as Bad Dürkheim (Rheinpfalz), Baden-Baden (Baden), Bad Kreuznach (Nahe), and others abound. For those

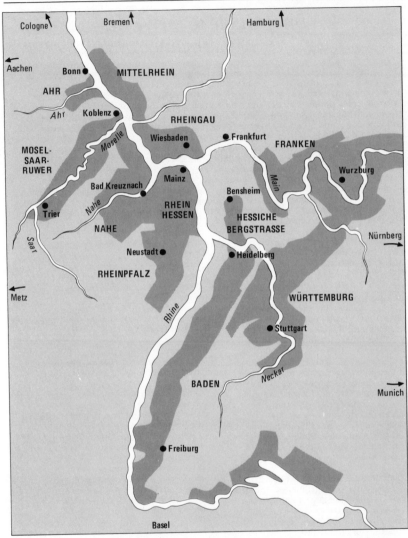

who like to combine hiking with wine-tasting, there are plenty of vineyard footpaths *(Weinwanderweg)* that lead through the vines to the welcoming cellars of local wine producers (the 30-mile *Rotweinwanderweg* in the Ahr is one of the most famous). Additionally, one can take 'wine tours' that pass by (if not through) vineyards without ever stepping foot on land, for the renowned Köln-Dusseldorfer steamers that chug slowly up the Rhine and Mosel Rivers pass by some of Germany's most beautiful and famous vineyards (don't worry about missing wine tastings, either, for the boats are well-stocked with wine, food, and German *Gemütlichkeit*).

Brief Guide to the Wines of Germany

The wines of Germany (85% white) are unique, prized for their delicate balance of ripe fruit, and fresh acidity, characteristics that are the result of the northerly position of the wine lands and the climate (both factors which cause the grapes to have a lengthy, slow ripening time); of the types of grapes cultivated; and of the variety of soils in which they grow, such as fertile loam and loess, heat-storing slate, mineral-rich volcanic stone, clay and limestone, and others. Each of the eleven quality-wine regions produces wines with distinct and individual character. Within the broad regions themselves, which must always be indicated on bottles of *Qualitätswein*, the origins of a particular wine can be further pin-pointed: either as a large sub-region *(Bereich)* within the designated region (i.e. Bereich Bernkastel, one of four large sub-regions within Mosel-Saar-Ruwer) or, more exactly, by the name of a wine commune and vineyard (i.e. Wehlener Sonnenuhr). Confusingly, however, certain vineyard names refer to broad and large collective sites *(Grosslagen)*, while others, the finest, are actual individual plots *(Einzellagen)*. In addition to their origin, wines in Germany are also categorized by a remarkable hierarchy of grape ripeness, based on must weight.

Deutscher Tafelwein Light, everyday wines from one of the following German table wine districts: Neckar, Oberrhein, Main, Rhine, and Mosel.

Qualitätswein bestimmter Anbaugebiete (QbA) 'Quality wine from one of the eleven designated quality-wine regions'. To qualify for this designation the grape juice must reach a minimum weight of between 60–72 degrees on the Oechsle scale (this scale, developed by a physicist of the same name, measures the sugar content in the grape juice, for in the German priority of wine-making, riper, sweeter grapes produce better wines). The eleven quality-wine regions are Mosel-Saar-Ruwer, Rheingau, Rheinpfalz, Nahe, Rheinhessen, Baden, Württemberg, Franken, Hessische Bergstrasse, Mittelrhein, Ahr.

Qualitätswein mit Prädikat (QmP) 'Quality wine with distinction'. Indicates wines with higher degrees of ripeness. This is further classified into the following hierarchy, indicating progressively riper, sweeter, and rarer wines.
Kabinett Elegant, mature wines produced from grapes that are riper than average.
Spätlese Term means 'late-picked' and indicates full-bodied, rich wines produced from ripe grapes picked after the main harvest.
Auslese Wines produced from over-ripe bunches of grapes that have been individually selected by hand.
Beerenauslese Exceptional quality wines produced from extremely ripe and over-ripe grapes affected by *Edelfäule* ('noble rot') that have actually been individually selected.
Trockenbeerenauslese The triumph of German wine, produced from individually selected, dried, raisin-like grapes that have been affected by *Edelfäule* to produce intense, extremely concentrated and heavy dessert wines.

Eiswein Rare wine produced from grapes that have been harvested while frozen, then quickly pressed and fermented.

Grape varieties The most important grape varieties (often indicated on the bottle label) are Riesling (late-ripener producing the finest, most elegant wines), Sylvaner (higher yield, producing mild, fruity wines), Müller-Thurgau (cross between Riesling and Sylvaner, and widely planted in most wine regions, producing tasty, mild wines), Ruländer (full-bodied and aromatic). Other grape varieties encountered include Gewürztraminer, Morio-Muskat, Kerner, Scheurebe, Bacchus, Faber and others. The principal

grape varieties producing Germany's red wines are Spätburgunder, Portugieser, and Trollinger.

Other important terms include:

Erzeugerabfüllung A guarantee of quality, indicating that the grower or cooperative has bottled and matured the wine in his own cellar.

Trocken Dry wine, generally with less than 4 g/l residual sugar.

Halbtrocken 'Half dry', or medium-dry wine.

Sekt German quality sparkling wine produced from a specific German wine region.

German Wine Tours

Moselweinstrasse – Tour of the Mosel-Saar-Ruwer

The steep, winding Mosel Valley, which twists and turns so sharply on its way from Trier north to Koblenz where the river joins the Rhine, is a breathtakingly beautiful and dramatic wine region. The sign-posted *Moselweinstrasse* follows the river along its looping path through wine towns known throughout the world, some of which, like pretty Piesport, are little more than a cluster of houses set around the village church, its slender steeple pointing up to the famous vineyards. There are a remarkable number of bridges that span the Mosel; this wine route, therefore, meanders back and forth on both sides. The Mosel Valley is wine country to savour slowly, like the complex bouquet – at once fresh and piquant, ripe and racy – of the wines produced here.

Our tour of the Mosel-Saar-Ruwer begins in Trier. Trier is an atmospheric old Roman town, and its connections with wine go back at least two thousand years and probably far longer. Numerous viticultural ornaments and tools which date from the first century AD attest to the extensive vine cultivation of that period; in the fourth century the poet Ausonius, a tutor in the Imperial Court of Trier (who came from and owned vineyards in Bordeaux), enthusiastically sang his praise of the valley's wine in his hymn 'Mosella'. Today Trier remains an important centre of the wine trade. As well as being surrounded by vineyards, Trier is the headquarters of many important producers and shippers. A vast network of cellars extends below the city, and there is certainly no shortage of cosy wine taverns.

Trier was an important medieval town; Sancta Treveris, as it was known then, was

the episcopal see and capital of the Electorate of Trier which oversaw the Mosel Valley up to Koblenz. The power and wealth of the church is reflected in the fact that three religious establishments continue to administer some of the finest estates not only around Trier, but elsewhere in the Mosel-Saar-Ruwer (Hohe Domkirche, Priesterseminar, and Bischöfliches Konvikt).

Germans are great walkers, and footpaths lead through many of the country's vineyards. In particular, many regions have sign-posted *'Weinlehrpfad'* – wine-teaching paths – and one such path is found in Trier, beginning near the Roman amphitheatre. As it leads through pleasant vineyards, overlooking the city and the valley, occasional displays and exhibits give information about production, grape varieties, disease, and other aspects of viticulture. It is a brief and enjoyable stroll and, best of all, it ends near the premises of local producers who offer tastings, open their cellars, and willingly discuss any and all aspects of German wine-making (a map of the path, together with the addresses of the participating producers, who are open to visitors on a rotating basis, is available from the town information centre).

Before proceeding from Trier north, brief excursions can be made along two other river valleys whose vineyards produce important wines that share the essential characteristics of the wines of the Mosel. For this reason, their names are hyphenated to the name of the quality-wine *Gebiet* (region): Mosel-Saar-Ruwer.

The valley of the Saar lies south of Trier. Its finest vineyards, like those of the

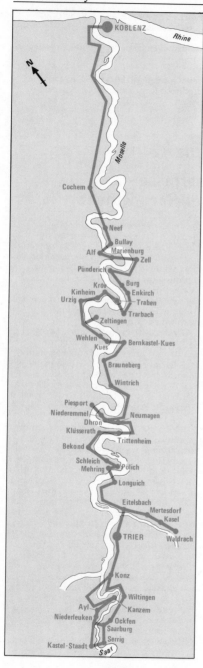

Mittelmosel, are extraordinarily steep, covered in a heat-storing layer of grey, scraggy slate. Though in mediocre years the wines of the Saar tend to be overly acidic and thin, in the finest hot years they balance the magnificent and elegant scent of the Riesling with a steely, firm acidity that is the epitome of the best of the region. The main communes of the Saar – Wiltingen, Kanzem, Ockfen, Ayl, and Serrig – are easily visited from Trier. The Ruwer, hardly more than a stream, enters the Mosel at Trier-Ruwer, north of Trier. Wines produced from vineyards above little-heard of villages such as Eitelsbach, Mertesdorf, Kasel, and Waldrach, are also important and fine examples of the best from the Mosel-Saar-Ruwer.

Follow the *Moselweinstrasse* north, downriver, along the right bank to Longuich, then cross over to pass through Mehring, Pölich, Schleich, and Bekond, small villages rich in Roman remains, which produce considerable and fine wines that are much appreciated both locally and further afield. For this is the beginning of the great stretch of distinguished vineyards known as the Mittelmosel. The *Bereich* (sub-region) of the Mittelmosel is known as *Bereich Bernkastel*. Finer wines are identified more specifically, by the name of a village, followed by either the name of a *grosslage* (collective site) or, best of all, an *einzellage*, that is, a specific individual vineyard.

The wine road continues to Klüsserath and Trittenheim (Trittenheimer Apotheke is an elixir almost as famous as the legendary Doktor of Bernkastel; Klüsserath's great vineyard is Bruderschaft). Cross the river at Trittenheim, and follow the right bank to Neumagen-Dhron (another important Roman village where the famous stone 'wine ship', now in the Landesmuseum, Trier, was discovered). At one time the Emperor Constantine had his summer residence here. Niederemmel is the next village encountered; follow the road left through the village to arrive at the bridge, and look across to the little village of Piesport, the fine steeple of its Baroque church pointing up to the well-exposed slopes of its best vineyard, Goldtröpfchen – little drop of gold. Piesport, like Bernkastel, is an evocative, easily-remembered name and much wine from neighbouring and less well-known communes is bottled and sold under its aegis. Piesporter Michelsberg, for example, refers to wines from the collective *grosslage* Michelsberg which extends from the village of Minheim upriver to Trittenheim. As always, the finest wines will bear individual site names, such as the previously mentioned Goldtröpfchen, Falkenberg, and Schubertslay.

Return to the right bank, continue through Wintrich, Brauneberg, and Mülheim (this village has fine patrician houses with extensive cellars, evidence of an important and prosperous wine trade), and so come to the jewel of the Mittelmosel, a town both famous and totally charming, Bernkastel-Kues. With its fairy-tale town square and Michaelsbrunnen fountain, its Gothic and Renaissance gabled half-timbered houses, its famous autumn wine festival, its location in the very heart of the region's finest vineyards, and its numerous wine taverns and places to stay, Bernkastel is one of the best towns to use as a base for exploration of the Mittelmosel.

The ruined Landshut castle (follow the road to Longkamp), perched on its conical hilltop, provides a superb vista of the vineyards of the Mosel; an even keener impression of the unique features of viticulture here is gained by walking through the town and up the very steep road that leads to the region's finest vineyards. Indeed, from up here the exposure and favoured situation of the famed Doktor vineyard is apparent, for it nestles in its sheltered cup of land high above the town, and thus manages to catch virtually every available ray of sun in morning, afternoon, and evening. The vineyards here are frighteningly steep, the topsoil a layer of dark, slippery, loose slate. These factors make tending the vines extremely difficult and labour-intensive. But the rewards in the best years are great, for the rich, honeyed *Auslesen* and *Beerenauslesen* wines produced from the finest vineyards here and in adjoining communes are some of the greatest wines in Germany. As well as the Doktor vineyard, which gained its name in the fourteenth century because a glass (or, more likely, several) is said to have cured an important archbishop on the verge of death, four other neighbouring vineyards that produce the best wines of Bernkastel – Graben, Bratenhöfchen, Matheisbildchen, and Lay – are grouped together in a small, but élite *grosslage*, Badstube. Kues, on the opposite side the river, was the birthplace of a great scholar and theologian, Nikolaus von Cusanus, who founded in Kues the

charitable St Nicholas Hospital for the care of the sick and needy.

Continue on the *Moselweinstrasse* downriver to Wehlen. Opposite the little village lies a vast and impressive slope entirely covered in vines, those of Graach, Wehlen, and, further downriver, Zeltingen, all of which produce consistently fine and, in the best years, great wines. Wehlener Sonnenuhr is the name of that village's finest vineyard, and the sundial can actually be seen amidst the precious Riesling vines. Zeltingen, too, has its Sonnenuhr vineyard, while the best in Graach are Himmelreich and Domprobst. Follow the wine road around the great loop in the river, through Ürzig, Kinheim, and Kröv, pleasant villages all, with attractive prosperous merchants' houses. They, too, all produce fine and interesting wines; indeed, in this brief, aristocratic stretch of the Mosel, there are few indifferent vineyards.

Traben-Trarbach spans the river, a spa town overlooked on one side by Mont Royal (built under Louis XIV), and, on the opposite bank, the ruined castle of Grevenburg. Cross to the right bank and follow the road through Enkirch, Burg, and Pünderich to Zell. Zell lends its name to another sub-region of the Mosel-Saar-Ruwer, Bereich Zell, which includes those vineyards on the lower stretch of the river extending up to Koblenz. Though there are fine wines produced in this lower district, generally speaking, the concentration of elegance so apparent in the Mittelmosel is not so high here. But that does not mean that the final stretch of the *Moselweinstrasse* is any less inviting, the numerous cellars offering *Weinproben* any less welcoming.

Zell itself is an extremely pretty village, its vineyards dominated by the *Runder Turm* (Round Tower) that is a familiar landmark. In the town square near the fountain there is a statue of the *Schwartze Katz* (Black Cat) which is the name of the area's best-known collective site. Cross the river at Zell, and drive up to the castle of Marienburg for an extraordinary view of the incredibly sharp bend that the river takes here; continue down to Alf, or cross to Bullay, and on to Neef. As the river is recrossed, cast a glance at the almost sheer wall of vines that towers above the bend. This is the Calmont vineyard of Bremm, the steepest in Germany. The river, on its lazy, winding, unhurried way north, takes another wide bend. A short cut through the Kaiser Wilhelm tunnel (only 4 km long, while the bend itself is over 21 km) leads to Cochem.

Cochem is to the Lower Mosel what Bernkastel is to the middle stretch: a lively and enjoyable centre from which to explore the region. There are numerous hotels, homes that offer private rooms for rent (the German equivalent of B & B), restaurants, and plenty of taverns in which to sample wine. As elsewhere, the town is dominated by yet another impressive castle, the Reichsburg Cochem, built at the beginning of the eleventh century. Don't miss the curious statue along the river promenade of a goat in a wine press. Legend has it that a goat was accused of stealing wine. Because he stubbornly refused to answer the charge, one of the town's magistrates came up with a bright idea: the goat would be pressed, and the wine yielded would be proof of the crime. But when the goat began to bleed under this grisly form of Germanic justice, the townsfolk realized their error. The goat's blood was red; since only white wines are produced in Cochem, the goat could not have been the culprit. And so he was set free.

From Cochem, follow the river further north to Koblenz, which derives its name from the Latin *confluentia* since it is here that the beautiful Mosel River finally expires into the mightier Rhine.

Rheingauer Riesling Route

The Rhine River, which from Basle has been flowing ever north, sharply, suddenly, and briefly turns west at Mainz to Rüdesheim, before again resuming its northward direction through Koblenz and Cologne to the North Sea. This 30 km interlude, however, is most fortunate, for on the gentle slopes of the north bank of the river lies a virtually continuous band of favoured vineyards, extending from Lorch east to Hochheim (actually located along an adjacent stretch of the Main River). These south-facing vineyards are sheltered by the Taunus Mountains; the fertile, complex loam and loess soils are generous and rich; and the broad Rhine reflects warmth and sun, and also gives rise to morning mists that encourage the formation of *Edelfäule*. This is the Rheingau, miniscule compared to prolific wine regions such as the Rheinhessen, just across the river, or the Rheinpfalz, further south, yet the home, undoubtedly, of some of the finest classic wines of Germany, from famous communes such as Rüdesheim, Rauenthal, Johannisberg,

Oestrich-Winkel, Hochheim, and many others.

A short but important wine road, the *Rheingauer Riesling Route*, extends through this distinguished region, sometimes following the river, then zig-zagging into the hills and wine villages above it. Its name indicates the predominance here of the noblest white wine grape in the world. The *Route* can easily be traversed beginning from major centres such as Frankfurt, Wiesbaden, or Mainz, or else, coming from the other direction, Koblenz.

From Koblenz, take the B42 road which follows the right bank of the Rhine south through the Rhine Gorge. This road leads through a separate wine region, the Mittelrhein, and indeed, the journey from Koblenz to Lorch is itself spectacular, providing panoramic vistas of vineyards and romantic castles, all of which have their own legend or tale of gods and heroes.

The sign-posted *Rheingauer Riesling Route* (white goblet on a green background) begins at Lorch, a town

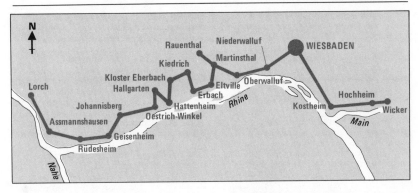

typical of the region with its painted
timber houses and Gothic church of St
Martin. From Lorch, continue on B42 to
Assmannshausen, nestled in the river
bend just before it begins its uninterrupted
stretch east. Assmannshausen is full of
poky narrow streets and charming houses
and taverns, and many will find it much
quieter than nearby Rüdesheim and thus
preferable as a place to base a stay
(additionally, there is an excellent
first-class hotel here with a notable
restaurant, as well as numerous wine
taverns to visit). Behind the town lie the
sunbaked slopes of Höllenberg ('hellish
hill'), the town's most famous vineyard.
Surprisingly, the soil here is bluish-red
phyllite slate, quite different to that found
in most other parts of the Rheingau, and it
produces from Spätburgunder grapes one
of the best red wines in Germany. Low in
tannin, pale, and fragrant, it should not be
compared with weighty, full-bodied red
wines from European vineyards further
south, for the northern climate and unique
conditions result in an entirely different
type of wine. Indeed, the usual German
Prädikaten, such as *Kabinett, Spätlese,* even
Auslese can apply to the red wines of
Assmannshausen.

From Assmannshausen, rather than
travelling the short distance along the river
to nearby Rüdesheim am Rhein, make a
detour through the town, and into the
wooded hills above the bizarre Niederwald
Monument, erected in the late nineteenth
century in commemoration of the
reestablishment of the German Empire.
The view from the Niederwald itself is
particularly impressive, down to the
vineyards of Rüdesheim, the village, the
Rhine, and, across the river, the mouth of
the Nahe. There are numerous footpaths

that lead through the forests of the
Niederwald National Park.

Descend to Rüdesheim, noisy, happy
Rüdesheim. Probably one of the
best-known and most popular wine towns
in Germany, it is fashionable to dismiss it
simply as a rude and gaudy tourist trap.
Certainly the riverfront is massed with
shops selling souvenirs and nicknacks;
true, the music that emanates from the
narrow, famous (infamous?) Drosselgasse
is rather brash and inebriated. Yet
nevertheless, Rüdesheim is undeniably
full of the welcome, good cheer, and
Gemütlichkeit so characteristic of
Germany's wine regions. There is much to
offer here to the serious wine lover, too.
The vineyards that rise above and on
either side of Rüdesheim are well-known,
and the wines produced, such as
Rüdesheimer Berg Rottland, Rüdesheimer
Rosengarten and Rüdesheimer Berg
Schlossberg, are superb: weighty, full
wines with the complex, ripe scent of the
Riesling. There are local *Weinguten* away
from the town centre where such wines
can be tasted (and at much more
reasonable prices than along the
Drosselgasse). The town boasts a superb
wine museum, located in the
Brömserburg, which is the oldest and best
preserved of Rüdesheim's three castles.
Additionally, a well-known brandy
distillery, Asbach & Co., offers tours and
tastings to all.

Follow the signs of the *Rheingauer
Riesling Route* to the next village,
Geisenheim, best known, perhaps, for its
viticultural and horticultural research
institute, founded some 100 years ago,
where much important and detailed study
takes place. In the Institute's vineyards
behind the village, numerous varieties of

experimental vines can be seen growing. Many new and successful vines have been developed here. From Geisenheim, take the road left at the end of the village, away from the river, and into the hills that lead to the Taunus Mountains. This brings us, shortly, to one of the most famous monuments in the Rheingau, the great Schloss Johannisberg, which from its sunny perch high on the vine-covered slopes dominates the entire valley. The vineyards that extend around the impressive yellow castle owned by the Metternich family (the Austrian Emperor gave it to the Prince in 1816 after the Congress of Vienna) are certainly some of the finest in the region. Moreover, it was at Schloss Johannisberg that, in 1775, an important and remarkable discovery was made quite by accident. The grapes at this time could never be harvested annually without permission from the Bishop of Fulda. This year, however, that permission arrived too late. The grapes had withered on the vine to a useless-looking, rotten, shrivelled state.

RHEINGAUER RIESLING ROUTE

The despondent monks harvested them and made the wine nevertheless. To their wonder and amazement, it was glorious! For the rot, known now as *Edelfäule* ('noble rot') had concentrated the natural grape sugars, and also lent its unique, unmistakable, heavy scent to result in wines that were more luscious and rich than ever before. Thus, from these shivelled grapes came the first *Spätlese* wine (the word, after all, simply means 'late-picked').

Descend from Schloss Johannisberg to Oestrich-Winkel, passing the prettily-named Winkeler Hasensprung (hare leap) vineyard. The moated tower of

Schloss Vollrads, another well-known, distinguished and aristocratic estate, stands a mile or so behind Winkel, peeping out of the hollow in which it sits, surrounded by over a hundred acres of its prized Riesling vines. The property has been owned by the Greiffenclau family for some 800 years; it is recorded that the knights of Greiffenclau sold wines to the St Victor Monastery in Mainz as long ago as 1211. Oestrich and Winkel are pretty little towns, virtually continuous; don't miss the old wine crane along the river, or the Graues Haus in Winkel, the oldest tavern of its type in Germany.

From Oestrich-Winkel, the *Rheingauer Riesling Route* again leaves the river road to ascend to Hallgarten, whose vineyards are the highest in the Rheingau. The wine road descends from Hallgarten once more to the river, and the village of Hattenheim, with its timbered houses and attractive village square. Its finest vineyards, which rise above the village and extend towards Erbach, are Hattenheimer Nüssbrunnen and Wisselbrunnen and, further up the slopes, Steinberg and Heiligenberg. The latter two are passed en route to the important Cistercian monastery, Kloster Eberbach. A visit to its magnificent twelfth- and fourteenth-century buildings is one of the highlights of a tour of the Rheingau, for it is one of the most important medieval monuments in the region. The refectory houses an impressive collection of monumental old wine presses, demonstrating the continued importance of viticulture at Kloster Eberbach for over 800 years. Today Kloster Eberbach is the home of the German Wine Academy, which offers various levels of wine seminars (in English) to improve knowledge and enjoyment of German wines. Tastings and lectures take place in the old work rooms of the monks. A wine shop is open to all, offering a varied selection of wines produced from the numerous estates of the *Staatsweingut*. The wine-making premises may be visited by appointment.

From Kloster Eberbach, cross over to Kiedrich, with its lovely fifteenth-century Gothic St Valentin Kirche, and then continue down to Erbach. Nearly every vineyard encountered along this glorious and continuous stretch is superb, the Gräfenberg and Klosterberg vineyards of Kiedrich and the Marcobrunn of Erbach deserving special mention. But any estate-bottled wine from these and neighbouring towns is likely to be a fine, classic example of the Rheingau at its most elegant. Eltville, somewhat larger than most other towns in the Rheingau, was once the residence of the Archbishops and Electors of Mainz, and the Electoral Castle along the river, today home of the Gutenberg Museum (the great German printing pioneer once lived here), is still an important landmark. Two miles further east are the two villages of Oberwalluf and Niederwalluf, but before proceeding further along the river, the *Rheingauer Riesling Route* leaves Eltville to swing sharply into the hills again, first to Martinsthal, and then to Rauenthal. The wines of Rauenthal, produced from grapes grown in richer, heavier soils, are correspondingly weighty and intense. From Rauenthal, return along the B260 to the Wallufs.

Finally, skirting around the sprawling spa town of Wiesbaden, the *Rheingauer Riesling Route* commences again for a brief spell through vineyards that front the Main, not the Rhine, River. Both historically and geographically, the vineyards of Hochheim are an extension of the Rheingau. Hochheim itself resiliently remains a pleasant and separate wine

village, despite its proximity to both Wiesbaden and Frankfurt. The annual wine festival which takes place in June is a lively and joyous occasion.

Though there are several fine vineyards in and around Hochheim, such as Domdechaney and Kirchenstück, for English visitors one in particular deserves special mention: Hochheimer Königin Viktoria Berg. This curious vineyard received its name by special royal permission after the Queen and Prince Albert visited the estate in 1850 while on a train tour. Afterwards the owner petitioned Queen Victoria to be allowed to rename the vineyard, a request that was granted, presumably because she had enjoyed the wines there. Thus, Königin Viktoria Berg was officially entered on the Hochheim Land Register, and the owner erected a charming memorial which still stands today amidst the treasured vineyards, below the town and facing the Main River. Indeed, the wines of Hochheim, with their balance of residual sweetness allied to fruity acidity, and their rich, spicy finish, are superb – or, as the Queen herself put it, so much more succinctly: 'Good hock keeps off the doc'.

Naheweinstrasse – The Nahe Wine Road

The small wine region of the Nahe is proudly known as the *Probierstübchen der deutschen Weinlande* – 'the tasting-room of the German wine lands'. This is true on two accounts. Firstly, the central location of the Nahe, between the classic wine regions of Mosel-Saar-Ruwer, Rheingau, Rheinhessen, and Rheinpfalz, combined with the region's diverse microclimates and, in particular, its varying soil conditions, ranging from slate to sandstone, clay, and loam and loess, results in an intriguing and broad range of wines that demonstrate traits or characteristics found in wines from those other regions. Nahe wine, for example, can sometimes display the racy, crisp acidity of the Mosel-Saar-Ruwer or the elegant depth of flavour found in the wines of the Rheingau; other samples, though, may evoke the warm, spicy scent of the Rheinpfalz, where figs and lemons ripen as well as grapes, or the robust generosity of the Rheinhessen, whose heavy-soiled vineyards are a virtual

extension of the Nahe. The Nahe, therefore, is 'the tasting room of the German wine lands' because all the finest characteristics and the variety of the classic wines of Germany can be found in her wines. And there is no shortage of

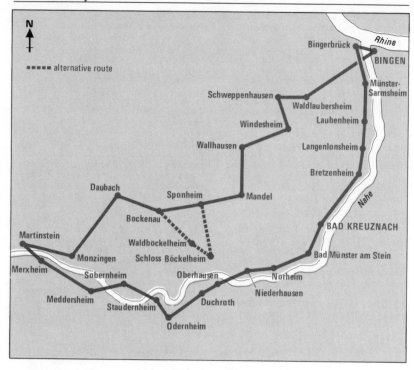

welcoming *Probierstübchen* – tasting-rooms – in the many romantic wine villages along the brief, but lovely *Naheweinstrasse*.

Despite the attractions of its wines, the region itself is perhaps less well-known than others. Yet its central location makes it easily accessible from popular centres such as Rüdesheim am Rhein (there is, confusingly, another Rüdesheim in the Nahe), or Koblenz, or Mainz, or from Trier, via the beautiful Hunsrück. Begin a tour of the region at Bingen, which lies opposite Rüdesheim am Rhein at the mouth of the Nahe (the Rhine can be crossed here, incidentally, by a ferry). Bingen is an old Roman trading town located just before the bend in the Rhine which marks the end of the south-facing vineyards of the Rheingau, and the commencement of the castle-lined Rhine Gorge that extends northwards to Koblenz. The Burg Klopp, a castle that overlooks the town and the Nahe River, is an important landmark as is the pretty Mäuseturm, located just opposite the mouth of the Nahe on an island in the Rhine. This gaily-painted,

fairy-tale fortification was built in the thirteenth century; legend has it that a suitably evil person, one Bishop Hatto of Mainz, was devoured in the tower by a host of angry, hungry mice! Cross the Nahe to Bingerbrück, and then commence the journey upriver along the north bank, following the B48.

The first wine-growing communities are soon encountered: Münster-Sarmsheim, Laubenheim, Langenlonsheim, and Bretzenheim, though the sign-posted *Naheweinstrasse* does not actually begin until just after Bad Kreuznach, a spa town as famous for its waters as for its wines. This popular holiday resort is an excellent place to base a stay, as is Bad Münster am Stein, which is further up river. In both there are numerous wine producers who welcome visitors, as well as taverns, inns, and restaurants – nothing particularly luxurious or elegant, just pockets of happy, cosy family-run places that are warm and welcoming. Bad Kreuznach is the centre of the Nahe wine trade, and weekend seminars (in German) for wine lovers can be arranged here. The town, as well, gives its name to one of the two large sub-regions of the Nahe, Bereich Kreuznach, the other being Bereich Schloss Böckelheim after the small village of that name further up the river. The vineyards between the two towns are among the finest in the region. Cross the 600-year-old Nahebrücke in Bad Kreuznach to the south bank of the river and continue to Bad Münster am Stein, following the signs of the *Naheweinstrasse*. In both of the above spa towns one of the most striking sights is the high wooden scaffoldings propped up on their sides with oak buttresses. Thermal waters run over this basic but effective 'humidifier', thus enriching the air for all those taking the cure. Another fortifier, apart from the waters, is a favourite of the local inhabitants: *Federweisser*, a young, still-fermenting wine that is known for its health-giving properties, and which is traditionally drunk in autumn, accompanied by warm slices of *Zwiebelkuchen* – local onion tart.

Just outside Bad Münster the sheer, red porphyry rock formation known as Rotenfels rises, at the foot of which lies a narrow band of sheltered vines sprouting from the red earth. The Ebernburg quarter, a former wine village dominated by its eleventh-century castle, is also worth a visit for in medieval times it was important in the creation of the German State. The *Naheweinstrasse* continues through Norheim and Niederhausen but not yet to Schloss Böckelheim itself, for the wine road crosses the river once more for a short stretch through villages along the south bank. The wine road continues to meander

through unspoiled rural countryside, crossing and recrossing the little Nahe, from Staudernheim to Sobernheim, and back across to Meddersheim and Merxheim. Each of these villages, with their old and quiet houses, have numerous *Weinguten* with *Probierstübchen* to provide opportunities of tasting the excellent local Müller-Thurgau, Sylvaner, and Riesling wines on the spot. Moreover, many wine producers in this region (and indeed, in all German wine regions) do not live solely by the vine; thus, as well as offering wine to be tasted or purchased, some rent out rooms – *Privatzimmern* – as well as serving simple, tasty local fare. It can be a very enjoyable, as well as educational, experience to stop for a day or two at such a place.

The farthest point upriver is reached at Martinstein, and here the *Naheweinstrasse* begins its circular journey back to the Rhine, this time through wine villages located in the hills and valleys somewhat above the river. Monzingen has been famous for its wines since Roman days, (the Romans, here as elsewhere, brought the vine to the valley) and the village is also known for its lovely old houses, such as the sixteenth-century *Alte Haus*. It is one of many picturesque villages encountered in this brief region. At Bockenau, leave the sign-posted wine road to visit Waldböckelheim, then continue on to Schloss Böckelheim, where it is pleasant to stop for awhile, to taste local wines and foods, or just to relax in this peaceful rural village. From Schloss Böckelheim, either return to Bad Kreuznach via Rüdesheim, or else rejoin the *Naheweinstrasse* at Mandel or Hargesheim, and so return to Bingerbrück.

Rheinhessen

Rheinhessen is the largest wine region in Germany in terms of area of vines under cultivation, as well as the country's largest wine-exporting region. It is rich, fertile agricultural country, sheltered in the west by the Hunsrück Mountains and the forests of the Rheinpfalz, and bounded on the east and north by the Rhine River. It is one of the most historically rich of all of Germany's wine regions, for its capital city Mainz was the former capital of the Roman province. Naturally, wherever the Romans went, so went the vine. Thus, the vineyards of Rheinhessen have been continuously cultivated for at least 2000 years. Though the wines of the

Rheinhessen do not generally reach the elevated heights of the finest from such classic regions as the Rheingau or Mosel-Saar-Ruwer, nevertheless it remains one of the greatest and most important of all Germany's wine regions as a producer of consistent and large quantities of mild, fruity wines primarily from the Müller-Thurgau and Sylvaner grapes, as well as for its distinguished, estate-bottled wines from individual vineyards, wines that are prized for their robust ripe character. Many newcomers' first experience of German wines is through imbibing the soft, easy-to-drink wines of the Rheinhessen, such as Liebfraumilch

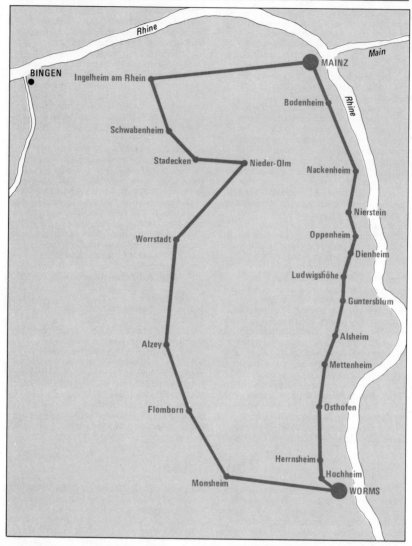

(originally wine produced from the vineyards of the Liebfrauenkirche in Worms), or wines from well-known large sub-regions such as Bereich Nierstein. The central location of the Rheinhessen in the heart of the Rhineland makes the region easily accessible from main centres such as Wiesbaden, Frankfurt, Koblenz, or the region's own capital, Mainz. Moreover, the region can be explored en route to or

from other regions, such as the Rheingau, Rheinpfalz, or Nahe.

Begin a tour of the Rheinhessen in Mainz itself, today capital of the Rheinland-Pfalz and an important centre of the German wine trade. Located at the confluence of the Rhine and the Main Rivers, it was the home of Johannes Gutenberg and an important historical town since Roman times. The former

Prince Electors' palace should be visited as well as the Romanesque, Gothic, and Baroque cathedral and the city's numerous museums that trace the history and prehistory of the region. Mainz, too, is a lively and important industrial city, and there is no shortage either of fine restaurants or of comfortable hotels in which to stay. Worth experiencing, as well, is Mainz at Carnival time, when the traditional and lively *Rosenmontagzug* procession takes place (Monday before Lent).

From Mainz, find the B9 road that follows the west bank of the Rhine through some of the region's most important wine villages. Turn off to meander through Bodenheim, return to the river at Nackenheim, and continue on to Nierstein, Oppenheim, and Guntersblum. These wine villages along the Rhine front are extremely peaceful and beautiful, while the high road above the Rhine gives particularly fine views over the villages to the river and the Odenwald. Explore the hills and wine towns above the river. At Guntersblum turn right off the B9 to drive through picturesque wine villages such as Alsheim, Mettenheim, Osthofen, and Herrnsheim. There are roadside wine booths, wine cellars and taverns, restaurants, hotels and campsites that provide facilities for relaxation and the enjoyment of simple eating and drinking. And, like the rest of Germany's wine regions, the local inhabitants celebrate their fortunate, generous land with a series of lively and happy wine festivals, including a red wine festival in Ingelheim, a fried fish festival in Worms, the *Mainzer Weinmarkt*, and many others. Don't miss the Roman baths at Nierstein and the wine-tasting cellars in the Oppenheim town hall.

Worms is much larger than the preceding wine villages, but it remains a wine town famous throughout the world for its Liebfrauenkirche that has given its name to one of the best-known and popular of all wines, Liebfraumilch. Liebfraumilch was originally wine produced fron the vineyards which today still surround the church. The evocative name, however, soon spread to wines produced well beyond this favoured plot, and today it can legally apply to wine from the Rheinhessen, Rheinpfalz, Rheingau, or Nahe which has passed certain quality tests, and has a characteristic 'mild' taste (the region, incidentally, must now be indicated on the bottle). As well as its Liebfrauenkirche, Worms is famous as the former capital of the Duchy of Burgundy (the Burgundians are the Niebelungen of the Rhine legends), and as the town from which Charles V convened the Diet denouncing Martin Luther as an heretic.

From Worms, leave the Rhine Valley by taking the B47 to Monsheim, and then the B271 to Alzey (or else join the *Deutsche Weinstrasse* of the Rheinpfalz at Bockenheim). Alzey is the centre of the Wonnegau – land of bliss – and wines produced in nearby villages along the way, such as Pfeddersheim, Flörsheim, Flomborn, and Dintesheim are ripe, mild, and immediately appealing; they go well with such ample regional specialities as *Rippchen mit Kraut* (pork cutlets with sauerkraut), potato soup, dumplings, *Handkäse mit Musik* (strong, hand-moulded cheese, garnished with pickles and onions), and much else. Though traditionally the wines of the Rheinhessen are produced primarily from Sylvaner and Müller-Thurgau, grape varieties such as Morio-Muskat, Scheurebe, Bacchus, and Sieggerebe are finding increasing favour. Leave Alzey on the B40 to Wörrstadt, and either return to Mainz, or else, cut through the heart of the Rheinhessen to Ingelheim (famous for its red wine) and to Bingen (see Nahe).

Deutsche Weinstrasse
– the Rheinpfalz

Germany's first wine road, the *Deutsche Weinstrasse*, begins at the border with French Alsace, and meanders north through the vineyards of the historic Rheinpfalz almost up to Worms. An actual 'wine gate', the massive *Deutsches Weintor*, erected in 1936, welcomes visitors at Schweigen, and for some 80 km the sign-posted wine road (depicted by a stylized bunch of grapes) leads through some of the most picturesque country and wine villages in Germany. The Rheinpfalz (or Rhenish Palatinate) has a remarkably mild climate and along the lush *Deutsche Weinstrasse*, where lemon, almond, and fig trees grow alongside vines, the atmosphere is bright, happy and decidedly southern. The Haardt Mountains shelter the region and regulate its climate; a near-continuous crest of vineyards stretches over their foothills, producing an unashamed profusion of fresh, quaffable everyday wines from grapes such as Müller-Thurgau, Sylvaner, Ruländer, Morio-Muskat, Scheurebe, Kerner, and others. In addition, the Rheinpfalz, with its warm, humid, benevolent climate, also yields enormous, raisiny dessert wines of *Auslese, Beerenauslese*, and *Trockenbeerenauslese* standard, while from the Mittelhaardt – the heart of the Haardt – come exciting, fine, elegant wines produced from the noble Riesling. The wine region of the Rheinpfalz is divided into two large sub-regions: in the north Bereich Mittelhaardt/Deutsche Weinstrasse (extending from Zellertal down to Neustadt) and, further south, Bereich Südliche Weinstrasse, (from Maikammer down to the border at Schweigen).

A tour of the Rheinpfalz can be linked with a tour of the Alsatian *Route du Vin*; or, if coming from the north, excursions can easily be made into the region from main centres such as Mainz, Frankfurt, Mannheim, Heidelberg, or Stuttgart. From the north, begin a tour at the start (or finish) of the *Deutsche Weinstrasse* at Bockenheim, near Worms. Bockenheim, and nearby villages such as Kindenheim, Zell and, further down the wine road (B271), Grünstadt, Kirchheim, Dackenheim, and Herxheim, though part of the sub-region Bereich Mittelhaardt,

actually form a distinct district known as the Unterhaardt (Lower Haardt). This district, bordering the fertile, flatter plains of the Rheinhessen, has rich heavy soil, and yields big, soft white wines, as well as some surprisingly deep red ones. Grünstadt, former residence of the Counts of Leiningen, is the centre of this northern district.

From Grünstadt, make a brief but worthwhile detour off the *Weinstrasse* through nearby Sausenheim to the medieval hill village of Neuleiningen, then continue down the wine road, moving ever-closer to the great, looming barrier of the Haardt Mountains. Kallstadt and neighbouring Freinsheim, with its graceful Baroque town hall and impressive ramparts, are soon reached. Saumagen, incidentally, is the name for a *grosslage* (collective site) near Kallstadt, as well as the name of a regional food speciality, Pfälzer Saumagen (a sort of Palatinate 'haggis' – the name actually means 'sow's stomach'). Both this local sausage and the wine can be sampled at unpretentious wine taverns located along the wine road, or – along with hundreds of other German sausages, hundreds of other local wines – at the annual *Wurstmarkt* in Bad Dürkheim.

The *Wurstmarkt* is Germany's greatest wine festival, celebrated annually in September, an important, traditional event in the lives of the Pfälzers. The wine drunk at the *Wurstmarkt* is generally from the previous vintage; it is only served in imposing, straight-sided *Schoppen* which hold no less than a half litre. Everything is big at the *Wurstmarkt*, including an enormous 40-metre-long wine cask which can hold a mind-boggling 1,700,000 litres; today it serves as a unique wine tavern. During the rest of the year, Bad Dürkheim regains its sanity and is a most pleasant spa town, lying in the midst of its vineyards which produce both white and mild red wines, and protected by the nearby Pfälzerwald, into which excursions can be made. (A cable-car, open from April to October, runs from the fairground up to the Ringwald-Teufelstein recreation area.)

The *Deutsche Weinstrasse* below Bad Dürkheim leads to a concentration of the

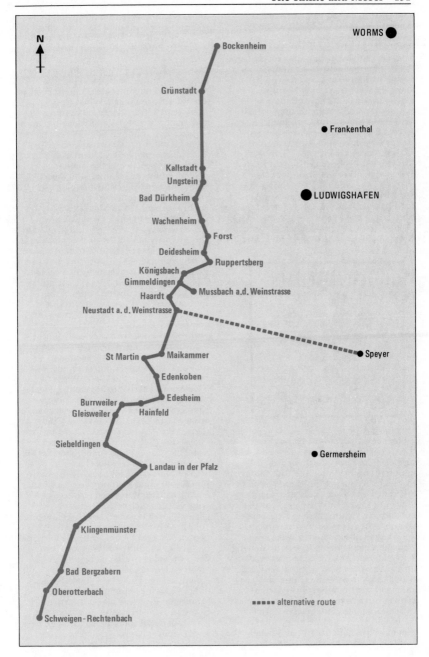

N

WORMS

Bockenheim

Grünstadt

Frankenthal

Kallstadt
Ungstein
Bad Dürkheim

LUDWIGSHAFEN

Wachenheim
Forst
Deidesheim
Königsbach
Ruppertsberg
Gimmeldingen
Haardt
Mussbach a.d. Weinstrasse
Neustadt a. d. Weinstrasse

Speyer

St Martin
Maikammer
Edenkoben
Burrweiler
Edesheim
Gleisweiler
Hainfeld
Siebeldingen
Germersheim
Landau in der Pfalz

Klingenmünster

Bad Bergzabern
Oberotterbach
Schweigen-Rechtenbach

===== alternative route

most distinguished vineyards of the Rheinpfalz, those of the Mittelhaardt. Indeed, the vineyards of wine villages such as Wachenheim, Forst, Deidesheim and Ruppertsberg, with their lovely names such as Mandelgarten ('almond garden'), Jesuitengarten, Paradiesgarten, Hergottsacker ('acre of the Lord'), Linsenbusch, and many others, are planted primarily with Riesling, which here gains a pithy, forceful character at once full-bodied and stylishly elegant – quite different in character to the Rieslings of the Mosel-Saar-Ruwer or Rheingau. Deidesheim is one of the most attractive towns along the wine road, with its painted town fountain, and the lush, surprising Feigengasse, lined with fruit-bearing fig trees. Other important wine villages along, or just off, the *Deutsche Weinstrasse* include Mussbach, Königsbach, Gimmeldingen, and Haardt.

Neustadt an der Weinstrasse, nestled at the foot of the mountains, is the wine capital of the Rheinpfalz, not only an important centre of trade, but also home of the region's wine-teaching and research institute, and an ancient historical town. Like most towns and villages in the Pfalz it is extremely picturesque, and it is a joy to wander down its twisting little streets lined with half-timbered houses. From Neustadt, incidentally, it is worth making a detour some 20 km east to Speyer, if only to visit the *Historisches Museum der Pfalz*, with its superb wine museum that boasts, among numerous other wine-related exhibits, an amazing, multi-coloured glass amphora, said to contain wine from the third century.

Below Neustadt, the sub-region Bereich Südliche Weinstrasse begins. It is an important and prolific wine region, and

there is a further continuous band of charming, welcoming Palatinate wine villages. Maikammer is one of the larger wine communities along the *Südliche Weinstrasse*, and a vast range of different types and styles of wine are produced here from vineyards that extend along the foothills below the Kalmit, highest point of the Haardt Mountains. Wines from Maikammer, from nearby St Martin, dominated by the craggy Kropsburg, from Edenkoben, and from Edesheim, range from plentiful everyday wines to *Qualitätswein mit Prädikaten* produced from grape varieties such as the familiar Müller-Thurgau, Sylvaner, and Riesling (though this noble grape does not predominate here) as well as the highly-scented Morio-Muskat, spicy Gewürztraminer, and warm Ruländer. Lesser-known varieties are also planted in this prolific vineyard, such as Scheurebe, Siegerrebe, Huxelrebe and Kerner; it is worth trying wines produced from such grapes, for each has its own character and flavour. Because of the hot climate and rich soil, deep, sweet dessert wines of the highest quality categories are produced here. Worth seeking, too are *Trocken* (dry) and *Halbtrocken* (half-dry) styles of wine, particularly good with the hearty fare of the Rheinpfalz. Edenkoben, incidentally, has a *Weinlehrpfad* (wine-teaching footpath) through its vineyards and also hosts the popular and lively *Weinfest der Südlichen Weinstrasse* in September. Nearby Schloss Ludwigshöhe, summer home of King Ludwig I of Bavaria, can be visited, while a chair-lift to the Rietburg, where there is the *Aussichtsterrasse der Deutschen Weinstrasse* ('viewpoint of the German Wine Road'), provides superb views of the surrounding countryside.

Continue on the wine road (B38) south past Rhodt unter Rietburg, and Hainfeld, and turn off right through picturesque wine villages such as Burrweiler, Gleisweiler, Birkweiler, and Siebeldingen. Take the B10 to Landau, an attractive garden city, and a main centre for the wine trade of this southern sub-region. Bad Bergzabern lies further along the *Südliche Weinstrasse*, a popular spa town and holiday resort. The lovely, meandering, unhurried wine road finally ends at Schweigen-Rechtenbach, at the mighty *Deutsches Weintor*. However, should you wish to carry on south through yet more lovely vineyards and wine villages, the Alsatian *Route du Vin* begins not far over the border.

Badische Weinstrasse
– The Wine Road of Baden

The wine region of Baden, though less well-known abroad than classic regions such as Mosel-Saar-Ruwer, Rheingau, and Rheinpfalz, is nevertheless one of Germany's most important, stretching over 400 km from the Main Valley in the north to the Swiss border and the Bodensee (Lake Constance) in the south. It is the third largest of the eleven German quality-wine regions, and a large proportion of its wine is produced in the region's 120 wine cooperatives. Though it is considered a single wine region, Baden is in fact divided into seven distinct sub-regions. A well sign-posted wine road, the *Badische Weinstrasse* runs through some of the region's loveliest countryside.

The seven sub-regions produce wines that are strikingly different in character. The character of the lands and the people, too, differ greatly. Badisches Frankenland, for example, lies below Würzburg, its vineyards extending through the Tauber Valley until its intersection with the Main River. As such, they virtually adjoin the vineyards of Franken, and not surprisingly, Müller-Thurgau and Sylvaner wines from Badisches Frankenland share the same pithy, aromatic qualities as wine from Franken itself. Like the wines of Franken, those from Badisches Frankenland are allowed to be sold in the distinctive flagon-shaped *Bocksbeutel*. The wine road follows the Tauber Valley from where the river enters the Main at Wertheim, through villages such as Werbach and Impfingen to Tauberbischofsheim, home of Boniface when he was Archbishop and Primate of Germany in the eighth century.

Badisches Frankenland is a small 'wine island', rather like Chablis, separated from the vast and almost continuous stretch of vineyards that extend in a narrow band from north to south. From Tauberbischofsheim, therefore, it is necessary to drive along the B27 through Walldürn across to the Neckar Valley, and so follow it downriver to Heidelberg through a gentle landscape of woods and orchards, of vineyards and hillocks crowned with impressive ruined or restored castles such as Hirschhorn am Neckar. Further downriver at Neckarsteinach four castles dominate the valley. (Incidentally, upon reaching the

Neckar from Tauberbischofsheim, a tour upriver leads to the *Swabische Weinstrasse* and the vineyards of Württemberg. Heilbronn, in particular, is worth visiting; while there sample local specialities such as *Spätzle* – a light dumpling served as a side dish with meat and gravy – washed down with a carafe of pale, pink *Schillerwein*.)

Heidelberg, centre of the Baden sub-region known as Badische Bergstrasse/Kraichgau, is an ever-popular university town, which, if no longer a political centre (from the thirteenth to the seventeenth centuries it was the home of the Prince Electors), remains an important cultural centre. The University, founded in 1386, is one of the oldest in Europe; its students today, as always, continue to amuse themselves in uproarious fashion in the town's many popular wine taverns and beer halls. The Heidelberg Schloss which overlooks the town is an important and impressive monument that should be visited; wine lovers, too, will no doubt wish to view the *Grosses Fass* – the Great Vat – in the castle interior. This enormous wine barrel holds 220,000 litres of wine. Follow the *Badische Bergstrasse* north of Heidelberg, sampling the wines of Leutershausen, Lützelsachsen, and Weinheim an der Bergstrasse, an old fortified town, with its ruined Windeck castle, timbered houses and lush, exotic gardens. If you are in the area in May or June it is worth making a trip either to Schwetzingen or to Lampertheim (near

Mannheim) to sample the famous white asparagus *(Spargel)* that is grown there in earth mounds. The classic way to eat this delicacy is with shavings of air-dried ham *(Schinken)*, boiled potatoes, and hollandaise sauce, though some local restaurants have amazing 'asparagus menus' offering up to forty different methods of preparation. However prepared, it is superb with a rich, insistent local wine such as a Badische Ruländer or Gewürztraminer. Wiesloch, to the south of Heidelberg, is another important wine town; here the *Badische Weinstrasse* leaves the B3 to branch off into the hills and valleys of the Kraichgau, through wine villages such as Eichelberg, Tiefenbach, and Odenheim. Return to the main road at Grotzingen, and continue down to Baden-Baden.

Baden-Baden, nestled in the Oos Valley under the Black Forest, is one of the most fashionable and luxurious resorts in Germany, an elegant thermal spa popular ever since Roman times. As well as its *Trinkhalle* (Pump Room), the town boasts a glittering casino, and there is no shortage of luxury hotels or restaurants. Just south of Baden-Baden, lying on the foothills of the Black Forest, are the distinguished vineyards of another Badische wine sub-region, the Ortenau. The sign-posted *Badische Weinstrasse* begins again outside Baden-Baden and makes brief excursions into the hills through tiny wine villages such as Steinbach, Neuweier (nearby Yburg is a popular holiday centre), Altschweier, Bühlertal and Waldulm. The Ortenau is the third most important wine-producing sub-region in the Baden vineyard (after Kaiserstühl-Tuniberg, and Markgräflerland) and the Riesling wines that are produced here are particularly prized. The taste, too, is often for the drier styles of wine *(Trocken* and *Halbtrocken).* The best-known wine of the Ortenau, however, is a curiosity, a red wine from Affental, sold in its unique *'Affen'* – 'monkey' – bottle. As well as Baden-Baden, other chief towns in the Ortenau include Bühl (a centre of fruit-growing, famous for its superb plums), and Offenburg, a former free Imperial town with many fine houses.

The *Badische Weinstrasse* continues south leading eventually to Freiburg im Breisgau. Freiburg, with the famous pierced spire of its *Münster* (said to be the most beautiful in Christendom), its pleasant *Rathausplatz*, sixteenth-century burghers' houses, and other reminders of

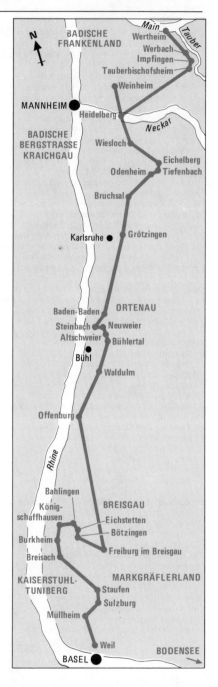

its important medieval and Renaissance past, is also in the fortunate position of being located at the intersection of three Badische wine sub-regions: Breisgau to the north, Markgräflerland to the south and, to the west, the rich district of Kaiserstühl-Tuniberg. Freiburg itself makes a superb holiday centre, for excursions can be made not only into these three wine districts, but also into the Upper Black Forest, and the Hollentaler.

The Kaiserstühl is a great volcanic spur that rises above the Rhine west of Freiburg, while the loess slopes of Tuniberg rise to the south. The mineral-rich volcanic soil of the Kaiserstühl, combined with its sheltered aspect, results in strong, intensely aromatic and fiery wines produced from insistent grape varieties such as Ruländer, Gewürztraminer, and Traminer. Indeed, this small, sunniest corner in Germany is fascinating, at times barren yet elsewhere lush, with an exotic, hot-house atmosphere. The *Zentralkellerei Badischer Winzergenossenschaften* (Central Wine Cellar of Baden) is located in picturesque Breisach. This vast, modern winery is one of the largest and most up-to-date in Europe; it is worth visiting to contrast this highly efficient and organized operation with that of any numerous smaller growers/producers visited elsewhere.

Other wine villages to visit include Ihringen, Bötzingen, Eichstetten, and Bahlingen, and, overlooking the Rhine, Sasbach, Jechtingen, and Burkheim. In addition to its warm, fiery white wines, this sub-region also produces a forceful pink wine known as Weissherbst.

The *Badische Weinstrasse* continues south of Freiburg into Markgräflerland. This pleasant, fertile country, extending from Freiburg south to Basle was formerly the ancestral seat of the Margrave of Baden. Medieval towns such as Staufen and Sulzburg are worth visiting, while Müllheim is the centre of the district's wine trade. Much of the wine from the Bereich Markgräflerland is produced from an old grape variety, the mild, fruity Gutedel, not surprising considering the district's proximity to Switzerland, where the same grape, under its French name Chasselas thrives so well to produce wines such as Fendant, Dorin, and others. The *Badische Weinstrasse* ends at Weil near the Swiss–German border.

One other district should be mentioned, that of the Bodensee (Lake Constance), where grapes ripen not only near the lake shores, but also on the 535m-high Hohentwiel, highest vine-growing point in Germany. The ancient castle of Hohentwiel that stands near the lake was ravaged by Napoleon.

Other German Wine Tours

Ahr Rotweinwanderweg A 30-km footpath begins at Lohrsdorf, and passes through the vineyards of some of the 11 wine villages in this brief valley, famous for its red wine produced from the Spätburgunder and Portugieser grapes.

Bocksbeutelstrasse This wine road, named after the distinctive flagon-shaped bottle used for Franken wines, begins in Aschaffenburg and follows the Main Valley to Wertheim, Karlstadt, Würzburg, and Öchsenfurt, before branching north to Volkach and Schweinfurt, and south to the spa towns of Bad Mergentheim and Bad Windsheim. The pithy Sylvaner wines of Franken are particularly worth seeking.

Swabische Weinstrasse The Swabian Wine Road follows the lovely Neckar Valley from Gundelsheim to Heilbronn, Lauffen, Mundelsheim, almost to the outskirts of industrial Stuttgart. Both red and white

wines are produced in the Württemberg vineyard, as well as a pale pink speciality known as Schillerwein.

Hessische Bergstrasse North of Heidelberg, the *Badische Bergstrasse* leads to the brief *Hessische Bergstrasse*, which continues from Weinheim to Heppenheim and Bensheim.

Rheingoldstrasse One of the most dramatic stretches of the Rhine Valley follows the vineyards of the Mittelrhein through the precarious and dramatic Rhine Gorge that runs from Koblenz down to Bingen (where the river turns briefly but sharply to Mainz, before continuing its north–south flow). The *Rheingoldstrasse*, which extends at times on both sides of the river, runs through towns such as St Goarshausen (near the famous Loreley rock), Kaub, and Bacharach, with its old timber houses and fourteenth-century fortifications.

Wine Producers

There are literally hundreds of wine producers throughout Germany's wine regions who welcome casual visitors without appointments, and many visitors will wish to simply meander along the wine roads of Germany, stopping when and where one likes. A 'Weinproben' sign indicates that wines can be tasted, usually for a small charge that depends on the number and quality of wines selected; if there is time, the interested visitor can also sometimes visit cellars. Most of the wine producers listed below ask for an appointment to be made in advance: either a postcard indicating time of arrival, or a telephone call when in the area.

Mosel-Saar-Ruwer

5500 Trier

Weingut Thiergarten – Georg Fritz von Nell
Thiergarten 12
tel: (0651) 3 23 97
Open daily.
Appointment necessary.
Max 170 pers.
English spoken.
Charge for *Weinproben*. If arranged in advance, Trier speciality of *Schwenkbraten* (pork cooked over an open fire), can be prepared in atmospheric *Weinkeller*.

Weingut-Weinstuben Deutschherren-hof
Geschw. Schieben Oberbillig
Olewiger Str 181
tel: (0651) 3 11 13

5511 Ockfen-Saar

Weingüter Dr Fischer
tel: (065 81) 2150
Open daily 10–12h; 15–17h
Appointment preferable.
Max 15 pers.
English spoken.

5511 Wiltingen-Saar

Weingut Neu-Karges
tel: (065 01) 6563
Appointment necessary.
Max 20 pers.

Saar-Winzerverein
am Schlossberg 345
tel: (065 01) 2061
Appointment necessary.
Max 70 pers.
Charge for *Weinproben*.

5511 Wawern-Saar

Weingüter Dr Fischer
tel: (065 01) 3459

Open daily 10–12h; 15–17h
Appointment preferable.
Max 30 pers.

5512 Serrig-Saar

Weingut Schloss Saarstein
tel: (065 81) 2324
Open daily 8–18h
Appointment necessary.
Max 25 pers.
English spoken.
Charge for *Weinproben*.

5501 Kasel-Ruwer

Weingut Christoph von Nell
tel: (0651) 5 20 20
Open Mon–Fri
Appointment necessary at weekends, and for large groups.
Max 80 pers.
Charge for *Weinproben*.
A little English spoken.
If given advance notice, meals with music can be arranged.

5559 Trittenheim

Weingut Günther Bollig-Lehnert
Joh. Trithemiusstr. 62
tel: (065 07) 5077
Weekends only, by appointment.
Max 40 pers.

5550 Bernkastel-Kues

Zentralkellerei Mosel-Saar-Ruwer eG
tel: (065 31) 6063
Open Mon–Sat 8–10h; 13–15h
Appointment necessary.
Max 15 pers.
English spoken.
Charge for *Weinproben*.

Weingut Peter Meyer-Horne KG
Cusanusstr. 14
tel: (065 31) 3071

Open by appointment only.
Min 15 pers.
English spoken.

Weingut Peter Kropf
Kardinalstr. 1
tel: (065 31) 6632
By appointment only.
Max 50 pers.
English spoken.
Talk and tasting lasts about 1½ hours.
Charge for *Weinproben*.

5550 Graach

Weingut Bernard Weiskopf
Fischerstr 9
tel: (065 31) 3442
Open May–Oct by appointment.
Max 80 pers.
English spoken.
Charge for *Weinproben*.
Schwenkbraten grill prepared if arranged in
advance.

5550 Wehlen

Weingut S A Prum Erben
Uferallee 25–26
tel: (065 31) 3110
Appointment necessary.
Max 30 pers.
English spoken.
Charge for *Weinproben* of quality wines
exclusively from Riesling grapes.

'Winzerkeller' der Winzergenossenschaft
Mittelmosel
Hauptstr 159
tel: (065 31) 6065
Appointment necessary.

5564 Ürzig

Weingut Peter Nicolay KG
Würzgartenstr. 41
tel: (065 32) 2026
Mon–Fri 8–12h; 13–17h
Appointment necessary only for groups.
Max 60 pers.
English spoken.
Charge for *Weinproben* of quality wines
exclusively from Riesling grapes.

5580 Traben-Trarbach

Weingut C A Haussmann Erben
Wilhelmstr. 13
tel: (065 41) 1543
Open daily by appointment.
Max 25 pers.

5585 Enkirch

Enkircher Winzergenossenschaft eG
Weingasse 12–14
tel: (065 41) 9957
Appointment necessary.
Max 70 pers.
English spoken.

Weingut Adolf Jung
Priesterstr. 11
tel: (065 41) 6373
Appointment necessary.
Max 35 pers.
English spoken.

5583 Zell

Klaus Bremm & Sohn
Winzermeister
tel: (065 42) 4459
Appointment necessary.
Max 20 pers.

5590 Cochem

Moselweinkellerie Koll & Cie
Ravenestr. 35
tel: (026 71) 7066
Open daily 8–17h
Appointment necessary.
Max 40 pers.
English spoken.
Charge for *Weinproben*.

5400 Koblenz

Deinhard & Co
Deinhardplatz 3
tel: (0261) 1041
Visits to Deinhard's impressive
cross-vaulted cellars, wine museum, and
modern Sekt plant must be arranged in
advance by writing for letter of
introduction to:
Deinhard & Co Ltd
29 Addington Street
London SE1 7XT
tel: 01-261 1111

Rheingau

6220 Rüdesheim am Rhein

Weingut Dr Heinr. Nägler
Friedrichstr. 22
tel: (067 22) 2835
Appointment necessary.
Max 50 pers.
English spoken.
Charge for *Weinproben*.
Visit with tasting takes about 1–1½ hours.

Staatsweingut Assmannshausen
Aulhauser Str 19
tel: (067 22) 2273
Appointment necessary.
Max 25 pers.
English spoken.

Asbach & Co
tel: (067 22) 120
Mon–Thurs 8–11h; 13h30–15h30; Fri 8–11h
This well-known brandy distillery receives
150,000 visitors a year.
Appointment preferred for large groups.
Max 25 pers.
English spoken.

Geisenheim

Weingut Freiherr V. Zwierlein
Schloss Kosakenberg
Bahnstr. 1
tel: (067 22) 8307
Appointment necessary.
Max 45 pers.
Charge for *Weinproben*.

6222 Johannisberg

Schloss Johannisberg
tel: (067 22) 8027
Open daily 9–12h; 14–16h
Appointment necessary to see cellars, not
vineyards.
English spoken.
Charge for *Weinproben*.

6227 Oestrich-Winkel

Schloss Vollrads
tel: (067 23) 3314
By appointment only.
English spoken.

Weingut des Hauses Deinhard
Friedensplatz 9–11
tel: (067 23) 3071
Appointment necessary.
Max 20 pers.
English spoken.
(This is the Rheingau estate for the firm of
Deinhard & Co – see above)

Kloster Eberbach

Staatsweingut Kloster Eberbach
tel: (067 23) 4228
Open daily 10–18h by appointment.
Max 1000 pers.
English spoken.
Charge for *Weinproben*.

6228 Eltville-Erbach

Administration Schloss Reinhartshausen
Hauptstr. 41
tel: (061 23) 4009
Open Mon–Fri 8–12h; 13–17h
Sat 8h30–11h30
Appointment necessary only for groups
larger than 12.
Max 60 pers.
English spoken.
Charge for *Weinproben*.

Staatsweinkellerei
Schwalbacher Str. 62
tel: (061 23) 61 055
Open 8–16h by appointment.
Max 50 pers.
English spoken.

Freiherrlich Langwerth von
Simmern'sches Rentamt
Langwerther Hof
tel: (061 23) 3008
Appointment necessary.
English spoken.

Staatsweingut Rauenthal
Wagenkehr
tel: (061 23) 2538
Appointment necessary.
Max 50 pers.
English spoken.

Staatsweingut Steinberg
tel: (067 23) 2093
Appointment necessary.
Max 50 pers.
English spoken.

6203 Hochheim am Main

Weingutsverwaltung Geh. Rat
Aschrolt'sche Erben
Kirchstr. 38
tel: (061 46) 2207
Open Mon–Fri 7–17h
Appointment necessary.
A little English spoken.
Charge for *Weinproben*.

Nahe

6550 Bad Kreuznach

Weingut Ökonomierat August E Anheuser
Brückes 53
tel: (0671) 2077
Open 9–15h by appointment.
Max 25 pers.
English spoken.

Weingut Paul Anheuser
Stromberger Str. 15–19
tel: (0671) 2 87 48
Open Mon–Fri 10–12h; 14–17h
Sat and Sun by appointment only.
Max 30 pers.
English spoken.
Charge for *Weinproben*.

Reichsgräflich von Plettenberg'sche
Verwaltung
Winzenheimer Str.
Open Mon–Fri by appointment only.
Max 25 pers.
English spoken.

6551 Oberhausen

Verwaltung der Staatlichen
Weinbaudomänen
Niederhausen-Schlossböckelheim
tel: (067 58) 6215
Open daily 7h30–12h; 13–16h30 by
appointment.
Max 40 pers.
English spoken.

Rheinhessen

6505 Nierstein

Weingut Freiherr Heyl Zu Herrnsheim
Langgasse 3
tel: (061 33) 5120
Open daily 8–12h; 14–18h
Appointment necessary.
English spoken.
Charge for *Weinproben*.

Weingut Geschwister Schuch
Oberdorfstr. 22
tel: (061 33) 5652
Mon–Sat 9–18h
Appointment preferable but not
essential.
Max 150 pers.
English spoken.
Charge for *Weinproben*. *Winzerplatte* or spit
roasts available by pre-arrangement.

6526 Alsheim

Weingut Rappenhof
tel: (062 49) 4015
Open Mon–Sat by appointment.
Max 60 pers.
English spoken.
Charge for *Weinproben*.

6501 Gaubischofsheim

Weingut Oberst Schultz-Werner
Bahnhofstr. 10
tel: (061 35) 2222
Appointment necessary.
Max 25 pers.
English spoken.

6507 Ingelheim am Rhein

J Neus Weingut Sonnenburg
Bahnhofstr. 96, Postfach 1520
tel: (061 32) 7003
Appointment necessary.
Max 40 pers.
English spoken.
Charge for *Weinproben*.

Rheinpfalz

6701 Kallstadt

Weingut Koehler-Ruprecht
tel: (063 22) 1829
Open daily 9h30–18h
Appointment necessary.
English spoken.
Charge for *Weinproben*.
Adjoining Hotel-Restaurant.

6706 Wachenheim

Weingut Dr Bürklin-Wolf
tel: (063 22) 8956
Open Mon–Fri 9h30–12h; 13–16h
Appointment necessary only for large
groups.
Max 120 pers.
English-speaking guide if pre-arranged.
Charge for *Weinproben*.
9th-century ruined Wachtenburg belongs
to the estate. When the flag is flying on the
tower then there are special *Weinproben* of
quality wines available at reasonable
prices.

6705 Deidesheim

Weingut Dr Deinhard
Weinstr. 10
tel: (063 26) 221
Open 8–11h; 13–17h
Appointment necessary only for groups.
Max 50 pers.
Charge for *Weinproben*.

Weingut Reichsrat von Buhl
Weinstr. 16
tel: (063 26) 1851
Open daily 8–17h

Appointment necessary only for groups.
Max 60 pers.
English spoken.

Weingut Dr Kern – Schloss Deidesheim
tel: (063 26) 260
Appointment necessary.
Max 30 pers.
English spoken.
From April–Nov *Weinstube* serving Pfälzer
specialities is open to the public.

Weingut Josef Biffar
Niederkirchener Str. 13
tel: (063 26) 1928
Appointment necessary.
Charge for *Weinproben*.

Baden

Badische Frankenland

6970 Lauda-Königshofen

Winzergenossenschaft Beckstein eG
Weinstrasse 30
tel: (093 43) 611
Open Tue and Thur working hours.
Appointment necessary only for large
groups, and for other times.
Max 200 pers.
English spoken.
Charge for *Weinproben*.

Badische Bergstrasse/Kraichgau

6140 Bensheim

Staatsweingut Bensheim
Grieselstr. 34–36
tel: (062 51) 3107
Appointment necessary.
Max 30 pers.
English spoken.
(note: Bensheim is one of the main wine
towns of the small and separate wine
region of Hessische Bergstrasse, which
continues north of Badische Bergstrasse.)

7519 Sulzfeld (Kraichgau)

Frhr v Göler'sche Verwaltung
Hauptstr. 44
tel: (072 69) 231
Open Mon–Fri by appointment.
Max 50 pers.
Wines are sampled in the Knight's Room
of the magnificent ruined castle of
Ravensburg.

Ortenau

7601 Durbach

Markgräflich Bad. Weingut Schloss
Staufenberg
tel: (0781) 42 778
Mon–Fri 8–12h; 13–17h by appointment.
Max 50 pers.
Charge for *Weinproben*.

Breisgau

7800 Freiburg

Staatliches Weinbauinstitut
Merzhauser Str 119
tel: (0761) 40 026
This is a scientific research institute; visits
only from members of the wine trade,
experts, or scientists.
Open 8–12h; 14–16h by appointment for
the above.
Max 50 pers.
English spoken.

Kaiserstühl-Tuniberg

7814 Breisach am Rhein

Zentralkellerei Badischer
Winzergenossenschaften eG
Kupfertorstr.
tel: (076 67) 820
Open daily by appointment.
Max 150 pers.
English spoken.
Charge for *Weinproben*.
A tour of these vast, extremely modern,
and important central cellars of the Baden
Wine-Growers Cooperatives (there are
over 23,000 vintners who belong to the
region's 92 cooperatives) takes about 2½
hours (including wine-tasting).

Gräflich von Kageneck'sche
Erzeuger Weinvertriebsgesellschaft mbH
Bürohaus W & V
tel: (076 67) 513
Open daily 8–12h; 13–17h
Appointment necessary.
Max 10 pers.
English spoken.

7817 Ihringen

Kaiserstühler Winzergenossenschaft eG
Winzerstr. 6
tel: (076 68) 622
Appointment necessary.
Charge for *Weinproben*.

7805 Bötzingen

Winzergenossenschaft Bötzingen am
Kaiserstühl eG
Hauptstrasse 13
tel: (076 63) 2066
Appointment necessary.
Max 100 pers.
Charge for *Weinproben*.

7831 Eichstetten

Kaiserstühlkellerei Friedrich Kiefer KG
Bötzinger Str 13
tel: (076 63) 1207
Open daily 8–12h; 13–17h
Max 6 pers.
A little English spoken.

7836 Bahlingen

Weingut und Weinkellerei August Häuber
Hauptstrasse 2
tel: (076 33) 1221
Open Mon–Fri 8–12h; 14–17h

Appointment necessary.
Max 50 pers.
English spoken.
Charge for *Weinproben*.

7831 Jechtingen

Weingut Adolf Weber, Inh Felix Domke
Rutzenstr. 19
tel: (076 62) 6302
Appointment necessary.
Max 55 pers.

Bodensee

7759 Hagnau

Winzergenossenschaft eG
im Hof 5
tel: (075 32) 6217
Open Mon–Fri by appointment.
Max 45 pers.
Charge for *Weinproben* of wines produced
in this cooperative with 103 members.

—— Wine Museums ——

Trier

Landesmuseum
Ostalle 44
Open Mon–Fri 10–16h
Sun 9–13h
Pre-historic, Roman, and early Christian
artifacts, including the Neumagener 'Wine
Ship' – tomb of a Roman wine merchant
which was found at Neumagen, one of the
oldest German wine-producing
communities.

Traben-Trarbach

Mittelmoselmuseum
Haus Böcking
Enkircherstr. 2
Museum in an 18th-century patrician's
house showing, among other exhibits,
historical aspects of viticulture in the
Middle Moselle.

Koblenz

Wine Museum
Deinhard & Co
Deinhardplatz 3
tel: (0261) 1041
Excellent little wine museum in Deinhard
cellars which can be visited on

appointment only. Write to Deinhard &
Co., London (address above p. 157)

Rüdesheim am Rhein

Brömserburg
Rheingau-und-Wein-Museum
Rheinstr. 2
tel: (067 22) 2348
Open Feb 1–Nov 30 daily except Mon
9–12h; 14–17h
The Brömserburg castle houses one of the
best wine museums in Germany, with
about 30 rooms of exhibits, ranging from
massive old wine presses to delicate wine
glasses, tools, and many other artifacts.

Speyer

Historisches Museum der Pfalz
Grosse Pfaffengasse 7
tel: (062 32) 75 185
Open daily 9–12h; 14–17h
Closed Dec 24, 25, 31, and Jan 1
The wine museum here contains
implements, artifacts, drinking vessels,
decorated barrels, and old wine presses.
The most impressive exhibit is a glass
amphora dating fron the 3rd century AD
which contains a residue of cloudy, thick
wine.

Wine Courses and Seminars

The German Wine Academy

6-day courses for wine lovers and experts are run in English 7 times a year by the German Wine Academy, at their headquarters in historic Kloster Eberbach in the heart of the Rheingau. The courses include seminars and lectures on vinification, the German Wine Law, and other aspects of German viticulture; visits to estates in the principal wine regions; and numerous tutored tastings. The course ends with a festive dinner at Kloster Eberbach, and the awarding of certificates. A Postgraduate Course which includes advanced lectures and tastings is offered in October. For more information write to:

German Wine Academy
Postfach 1705
6500 Mainz 1
tel: (061 31) 25 818

German Wine Seminars

A variety of wine seminars are offered in each of the 11 quality-wine regions ranging from non-residential weekend seminars, to residential week-long courses. Most, however, are only run in German, though some of the regions do offer weekend courses in English, such as: 3-day wine seminar in Bacharach (Mittelrhein), and weekend wine seminars in Trier (Mosel-Saar-Ruwer). For full details write for the booklet *'Deutsche Weinseminare'* available from:

German Wine Institute
Gutenbergplatz 3–5
D-6500 Mainz
tel: (061 31) 25 818

Schloss Vollrads

'Lucullan winetastings' in this historic estate, presented by Graf Matuschka-Greiffenclau, with 12 to 14 wines and a 4- to 5-course dinner. For further information write to:

Gutsverwaltung Graf
Matuschka-Greiffenclau
Schloss Vollrads
D-6227 Oestrich-Winkel
tel: (067 23) 3418

———————— Wine Festivals ————————

There are hundreds of wine festivals which take place in the 11 quality-wine regions throughout the year. They are much more than just outdoor communal parties, for they provide opportunities to taste a broad selection of local quality wines served, generally, in small tasting measures. A brochure with full list and precise dates (*'Deutsche Winzerfest'*) is available from: Deutsche Wein-Information, Postfach 1707, D-6500 Mainz. The following are some of the most important ones:

Mosel-Saar-Ruwer

beginning of June	Moselweinwoche	Cochem
beginning of Sept	Weinfest der Mittelmosel	Bernkastel-Kues
beginning of Sept	Saarweinfest	Saarburg
Rheingau		
end of June	Hilchenfest	Lorch
end of June	Weinfest	Hochheim
middle of July	Lindenfest	Geisenheim
middle of August	Weinfest	Rüdesheim
end of August	Weinfest	Eltville, Stadtteil Hattenheim

Nahe

end of Aug/beginning of Sept	'Fest rund um die Naheweinstrasse' – takes place in each of the well-known communities along Nahe Wine Road.	

Rheinhessen

beginning of August	Winzerfest	Nierstein
end of August	Kellerwegfest	Guntersblum
end of August/beginning of September	Backfischfest	Worms
beginning of Sept	Mainzer Weinmarkt	Mainz
end of Sept/beginning of Oct	Rotweinfest	Ingelheim

Rheinpfalz

2nd–3rd weeks of Sept	Wurstmarkt	Bad Dürkheim
end of Sept	Weinfest der Südlichen Weinstrasse	Edenkoben
beginning of Oct	Deutsches Weinlesefest	Neustadt
3rd week of Oct	Fest des Federweissen	Landau

Baden

end of June	Freiburger Weintag	Freiburg
end of Aug/beginning of Sept	Kurpfälzisches Winzerfest	Wiesloch

Württemberg

beginning of Sept	Heilbronner Herbst	Heilbronn
October	Fellbacher Herbst	Fellbach

Ahr

end of May/beginning of June	Gebietsweinmarkt der Ahr	Ahrweiler
end of Sept	Winzerfest	Dernau

Franken

middle of August	Wein-und-Winzerfest	Volkach
middle of August	Wein-und-Winzerfest	Sulzfeld
end of Sept/beginning of Oct	Wein-und-Winzerfest	Würzburg

Hessische Bergstrasse

end of June/beginning of July	Bergsträsse Weinmarkt	Heppenheim
middle of Sept	Bergsträsser Winzerfest	Bensheim

Mittelrhein

end of June	Weinblütenfest	Bacharach
middle of Sept	Weinwoche	St Goarshausen
end of Sept/beginning of Oct	Weinfest	Boppard
beginning of Oct	Weinlesefest	Bacharach

Regional Gastronomy

German Wurst Throughout Germany, and particularly in the Rhineland, an excellent variety of German sausages is served, both as a cold array of sliced meats, and as hot sausages that are picked up with the fingers and dipped into mustard.

Bratwurst, Frankfurters, Leberwurst (coarse home-made liver sausage), *Weisswurst* (small veal sausages) and *Bockwurst* are all served hot; cold platters often consist of a variety of such sausages as *Fleischwurst, Blutwurst, Sülzwurst* (a type of brawn) and others.

Handkäse mit Musik Hand-moulded, strong cheese served covered with vinegar, oil, raw onions: speciality of Rheinpfalz and Rheinhessen.

Pfälzer Saumagen Speciality of the Rheinpfalz: sow's stomach stuffed with meat and seasonings, boiled, and cut into thick slices.

Bauernspeck Smoked bacon.

Schinken Ham. Air-dried ham from the Black Forest is served raw in razor-thin slices.

Zwiebelkuchen Onion tart – often served in the Nahe with *Federweisser* (newly fermented wine).

Frankfurter Linsensuppe Lentil soup with sausage.

Pfälzer Zwiebelsuppe Onion soup from the Rheinpfalz.

Maultaschen 'Mouth pockets' of dough stuffed with spinach or meat, and served in broth. Speciality of Swabia.

Rotweinsuppe Red wine soup: speciality of the Ahr.

Halber Hahn Rye roll topped with cheese and good German mustard.

Rippchen mit Kraut Thick pork chops served with sauerkraut and mustard: speciality of Frankfurt and the Rheinhessen.

Eisbein mit Kraut Pickled pig's knuckle, stewed for several hours with sauerkraut.

Spiessbraten Spit-roasted beef.

Schwenkbraten Pork steaks roasted over an open wood fire: speciality of Mosel-Saar-Ruwer.

Rinderrouladen Beef olives stuffed with bacon, parsley, and German mustard.

Schweinshaxen and *Kalbshaxen* Roasted knuckles of pork and veal.

Rehrücken Saddle of venison, often served with a rich fruit gravy.

Sauerbraten Beef marinated in vinegar, wine, and spices for several days, then braised in its liquid, and served with sauerkraut, potatoes, or dumplings.

Spätzle 'Little sparrows': tiny, flour and egg dumplings, poached, then fried in butter and served with meat and gravy. Best, it is said, made by housewives in Baden-Württemberg.

Schnitzel Pork or veal escalope, usually served garnished in a variety of ways (*Jagerschnitzel*, with sliced mushrooms; *Zigeunerschnitzel*, in a paprika sauce, etc).

Himmel und Erde Favourite Rhineland purée of potatoes and apples.

Spargel Large, white asparagus grown in mounds of earth around Schweigen and Lampertheim (near Mannheim); in June local restaurants serve this speciality – which is worth a detour – in a variety of imaginative ways, though the local favourite is with hollandaise sauce, boiled potatoes, and slices of air-dried *Schinken*.

Räucheraal Smoked eel – very popular in Mosel region.

Blau Forelle Trout cooked in vinegary *court bouillon*, a method which turns extremely fresh fish a striking shade of blue.

Käseteller Platter of thinly sliced cheeses, served with good German breads. Cheeses include Allgäuer, Emmenthaler, Kummelkäse (with caraway seeds), Limburger, Weisslacker (highly aromatic), and others.

Schwarzwalder Kirschtorte Chocolate and cherry cake: try the real thing while touring Badische vineyards on the slopes of the Black Forest.

Dampfknödeln Steamed yeast dumplings served with Weincreme.

Weincreme Wine, sugar, and eggs whipped together and gently cooked to a thick, frothy sauce.

Restaurants

Note: in addition to the mainly inexpensive *Weinstuben* and local restaurants listed below, many hotels in the following section also have restaurants. They are generally a little bit more expensive, and offer a wider range of international dishes as well as hearty German fare.

Mosel-Saar-Ruwer

5550 Trier

Weinstube 'Zum Domstein'
Hauptmarkt 5
tel: (0651) 7 44 90
Inexpensive *Weinstube* located in the
historic market square, serving regional
specialities, as well as some dishes cooked
from recipes after the Roman cook
Apicius.
Open daily 9–24h

Speiserestaurant 'Zum Krokodil'
Justizplatz
tel: (0651) 7 31 07
Near the city centre, with 3 different
dining rooms, all with good selection of
local wines.
Daily 8h30–23h30
Inexpensive to **Moderate**

5503 Konz

Ratskeller Fam. Lukosch
am Markt
tel: (065 01) 2258
Family-run restaurant with good
home-cooking and a selection of
Mosel-Saar-Ruwer wines.
Mon–Sat 10–22h
Inexpensive

5550 Bernkastel-Kues

Rôtisserie Royale
Burgstrasse 19
tel: (065 31) 6572
350-year-old building houses this
restaurant specializing in grills.
Advisable to book.
Closed Tue
Open 19–24h
Inexpensive to **Moderate**

Rheingau

6222 Johannisberg

Gutsschenke der Domäne Schloss
Johannisberg
Schloss Johannisberger wines served with
mainly cold platters.
Closed Tue
Inexpensive

Burg Schwarzenstein
Weingutsausschank des G H v
Mumm'schen Weingutes

Typical hot and cold dishes served with
own-produced wines.
Closed Nov–Jan; Mon
Inexpensive

6228 Eltville

Restaurant Weinhaus Weinpump
Rheingauer Str. 3
tel: (061 23) 2389
Dining room with open fire and tiled
stove, and a lovely arboured garden.
Venison and fish dishes.
Closed Tue
Open 11h30–14h; 17–1h
Inexpensive to **Moderate**

Rheingauer Hof
Burgplatz 3
tel: (061 23) 5170
Near the castle, a comfortable, typical inn
serving local foods and wines.
Closed Wed
Inexpensive

Nahe

6531 Guldental

Restaurant le Val d'Or
Haupstr. 3
tel: (067 07) 1707
Moderate restaurant serving German
dishes with local wines.
Open Tue–Sat after 18h
Sun 12–14h; after 18h

6550 Bad Kreuznach

Die Kauzenburg
tel: (0671) 2 54 61
Views over the town and the Nahe River
from this bizarre-looking restaurant – a
mixture of the ultra-modern and the
medieval. Three different eating areas: a
sophisticated dining room, an atmospheric
Weinkeller, and the Knight's Hall where
grand medieval feasts take place
accompanied by minstrels.
Closed Mon
Open from 11h30 onwards.
Moderate to **Expensive**

Rheinhessen

6500 Mainz

Restaurant Walderdorff
Karmeliterplatz 4
tel: (061 31) 22 25 15

Elegant restaurant serving 'new style of
German cuisine' with wide selection of
Riesling wines.
Closed Mon
Open 12h15–14h; 18h30–22h
Sun lunch only.
Moderate

Haus des Deutschen Weines
Gutenbergplatz 3–5
tel: (061 31) 2 86 76
An impressive selection of German wines
to accompany simple foods served outside
in summer.
Closed Sun
Open 10–24h
Inexpensive

Gebert's Weinstuben
Frauenlobstr. 94
tel: (061 31) 61 16 19
Popular *Weinstube* with fish and venison
cooked by the owner.
Advisable to book.
Closed Sat
Open Mon–Fri 11h30–14h; 18–22h
Sun lunch only.
Inexpensive to **Moderate**

Rheinpfalz

6702 Bad Dürkheim

Weinakademie
Holzweg 76
tel: (063 22) 2414
Inexpensive restaurant specializing in
steaks and grills.
Mon–Sat 12–15h; 18–23h
Sun and holidays 18–23h30

Gaststätte Dürkheimer Riesenfass
tel: (063 22) 2143
At the fairground of the Wurstmarkt, this
wine tavern is located in the world's
largest wine barrel. Room for 1,700,000
litres, or 500 people. Pfälzer specialities
such as *Saumagen*, *Rippchen*, and local
wines.
Closed Dec 1–Feb 6; Wed
Inexpensive

6706 Wachenheim a.d.
Weinstrasse

Gaststätte 'Luginsland'
Weinstr. 2
tel: (063 22) 8102
Pfälzer specialities and quality wine in this
Inexpensive restaurant.

6705 Deidesheim

Gasthaus 'Zur Kanne'
Weinstr. 31
tel: (063 26) 396
The oldest *Gasthaus* in the Rheinpfalz,
serving Pfälzer specialities and wines.
Closed Wed.
Open 12–14h; 18–22h
Inexpensive

6701 Forst

Hausgaststätte Forster Winzerverein
Weinstr. 57
tel: (063 26) 259
Very Inexpensive inn open all day
(11h–23h), serving own quality wines.

6735 Maikammer

Gutsausschank Weingut Straub
Bahnhofstr. 20
tel: (063 21) 5143
Pfälzer specialities and local wines in this
simple inn.
Closed July 15–Aug 15; Dec 20–Jan 20
Inexpensive

6740 Landau in der Pfalz

Restaurant-Café Festhallen
Mahlastr. 3
tel: (063 41) 2 09 33
Modern restaurant with terraces
overlooking the lake. Local specialities and
wines.
Closed Wed
Open all year 10–24h
Inexpensive to **Moderate**

Baden

(see Hotels)

Hotels

Mosel-Saar-Ruwer

5500 Trier

Hotel Petrisberg
Sickingenstr. 11
tel: (0651) 4 11 81
Modern, comfortable hotel set within
parkland and good walking country.
Attractive dining room.
Open all year.
Moderate

Holiday Inn
Zurmaienerstr. 164
tel: (0651) 2 30 91
Comfortable, reliable chain hotel with all
the facilities, including swimming pool,
sauna, bar, and restaurant.
Hotel open all year.
Restaurant open daily 7–23h30
Hotel **Expensive**
Restaurant **Moderate**

5550 Bernkastel-Kues

Doctor Weinstuben
Hebegasse 5
tel: (065 31) 6081
Built in 1652, this quaint, rustically
furnished hotel is comfortable and
atmospheric. Each room has private
facilities.
Restaurant serves local foods and wines.
Closed Dec–Feb
Moderate

Hotel-Restaurant Römischer Kaiser
Markt 29
tel: (065 31) 3038
60-room comfortable hotel along the
Mosel promenade. Restaurant serves
international and regional cuisine.
Weinkeller with daily (and nightly!)
dancing.
Hotel closed Nov 15–Dec 15
Restaurant open daily 7h30–22h
Moderate

Hotel Burg Landshut
Gestade 11
tel: (065 31) 3019
Family-run hotel with restaurant.
Hotel closed Nov 15–Dec 22
Restaurant open daily 12–14h30; 18–22h
Moderate

Hotel 'Zur Post'
Gestade 17
tel: (065 31) 3001
Rustic atmosphere with comfortable
rooms, and restaurant offering regional
and international foods, and over 100
different own-produced Mosel wines.
Closed Dec–Jan
Inexpensive

Hotel-Restaurant Hubertusklause
Cusanusstr. 26
tel: (065 31) 8045
Situated in Kues, each room with private
facilities. Well-known restaurant serves
fine cuisine; game a speciality in season.
Restaurant closed Wed
Open 11–14h30; 17h30–23h
Moderate

Hotel Älteste Weinstube
am Kreuz
tel: (065 31) 2443
Hotel with typical restaurant.
Hotel closed Jan–March
Restaurant closed Wed
Moderate

5564 Ürzig

Hotel-Weinhaus Moselschild
Moselufer 12–14
tel: (065 32) 3001
Hotel overlooking Mosel with pretty
flowered terrace. 17 rooms, each with
shower. Own vineyards produce quality
wines served in restaurant.
Closed Jan 10–31
Restaurant open daily
Moderate

5580 Traben-Trarbach

Hotel Krone
An der Mosel 93
tel: (065 41) 6363
Peaceful position directly on the Mosel
riverfront, with restaurant serving a wide
selection of dishes, and a good selection of
Trocken and *Halbtrocken* wines.
Hotel closed Jan 15–March 15
Restaurant open daily 8–22h
Moderate

Hotel-Restaurant Altes Gasthaus Moseltor
Moselstr. 1
tel: (065 41) 6551
Hotel with comfortable restaurant serving
dishes using only fresh products.
Advisable to book.
Closed Dec 24
Restaurant closed Tue; open 12–14h;
18–22h
Moderate

Kur-und-Sport Hotel Gonzlay
am Moselufer
tel: (065 41) 6921
Well-situated hotel overlooking Mosel,
with indoor swimming pool, sauna,
solarium, terrace, and restaurant.
Hotel closed Jan–March
Restaurant open daily 11h30–14h;
18h30–21h
Moderate to **Expensive**

5583 Zell

Hotel Schloss Zell
tel: (065 42) 4084
In a 700-year-old castle, with its own
vineyards. Restaurant serves own wines

and local dishes using only fresh products.
Hotel and restaurant closed Dec 15–Jan 15
Restaurant closed Tue
Expensive

5590 Cochem

Hotel Alte Thorschenke
Brückenstr. 3
tel: (026 71) 7059
Dating from 1332, this historic inn has 51
comfortable rooms, all with baths. There is
a dining room, and also a 'hunting lodge'
where grills and game are served.
Closed Jan 5–March 15
Restaurant open daily 7h30–24h
Moderate

Hotel-Restaurant Lohspeicher
Obergasse 1
tel: (026 71) 3976
Well-situated, quiet, and comfortable.
Each room is uniquely furnished.
Restaurant serves grills from the open fire.
Closed Jan
Restaurant open Tue–Sat 11–23h
Moderate

Parkhotel Landenberg
Sehler Anlagen 1
tel: (026 71) 7110
Peaceful hotel with gardens, large terrace,
indoor swimming pool, sauna, and
solarium. Ideal spot for walking in woods
and hills.
Restaurant serves regional specialities
such as venison, fresh trout, Mosel eel,
and snails.
Closed Jan 5–March 15
Restaurant open daily 7h30–24h
Moderate

Rheingau

6220 Assmanshausen

Hotel Krone
Rheinuferstr. 10
tel: (067 22) 2036
16th-century half-timbered hotel,
considered one of the finest in the region,
with superb position overlooking Rhine.
Terrace, swimming pool, conference
rooms, and elegant restaurant with high
standard of cuisine. Good selection of
Rheingau and Mosel-Saar-Ruwer wines, as
well as the local red wines of
Assmannshausen, produced from
vineyards that belong to the hotel.
Hotel closed Nov 10–15; March
Restaurant open daily 12–22h
Expensive

Hotel Café Post
Rheinuferstr. 2
tel: (067 22) 2326
Situated on the Rhine front, a **Moderate**
40-room hotel with garden-terrace and
restaurant.
Closed Dec 1–March 1

Altes Haus
Lorcher Str. 5
tel: (067 22) 2686
Built in 1578, and retaining its original
16th-century style. Half-timbered exterior
and comfortable, atmospheric interior.
Cellar bar, historical wine restaurant
and modern bedrooms, each with
bathroom.
Closed Jan–Feb
Moderate

6220 Rüdesheim am Rhein

Hotel Jagdschloss Niederwald
Auf dem Niederwald
tel: (067 22) 1004
Surrounded by the nature reserve in the
hills above Rüdesheim, near the
Niederwald monument, this comfortable
hotel has indoor swimming pool, sauna,
solarium, and 50 rooms, each with
bathroom.
Restaurant with spectacular views serves
venison in season, and fresh fish, to
accompany wines from the Rheingau.
Closed Dec 12–March 1
Restaurant open daily
Expensive

6227 Oestrich-Winkel

Romantik-Hotel Schwan
Rheinallee 5–7
tel: (067 23) 3001
Charming, elegant, and **Very Expensive**
hotel, with restaurant specializing in fish
and game, and an atmospheric wine cellar
where a full range of wines from the
Rheingau can be sampled.
Hotel & restaurant closed Dec–Feb
Restaurant **Moderate**

Hotel Weinhaus Nägler
Hauptstr 1
tel: (067 23) 5051
Modern luxury hotel with views across
vineyards to the Rhine. Sun terrace,
sauna, and restaurant.
Hotel closed Nov 8–Dec 2
Restaurant closed Tue; open 7–23h
Expensive

6225 Johannisberg

Hotel-Restaurant Haus Neugebauer
tel: (067 22) 8827
Idyllic position in heart of the forest.
Peaceful, and with views from the terrace
down the valley to the river. Restaurant
specializes in venison, and Johannisberger
Rieslings.
Hotel closed Dec 20–Feb 15
Restaurant closed Tue
Inexpensive to **Moderate**

6228 Hattenheim

Hotel-Weinhaus 'Zum Krug'
Hauptstr. 34
tel: (067 23) 2812
Atmospheric old hotel in the centre of the
village with restaurant serving seasonal
specialities, simple foods, and
own-produced wines.
Hotel closed 2 weeks in Jan, 2 weeks in
July
Restaurant closed Sun eve, Mon
Moderate

6228 Eltville

Hotel-Restaurant Burg Crass
tel: (061 23) 3635
Directly on the Rhine, in peaceful position,
with restaurant and *Winzerstube*.
Hotel open all year.
Restaurant closed Mon in winter.
Moderate

6229 Erbach im Rheingau

Hotel Schloss Reinhartshausen
tel: (061 23) 4081
Palatial building with gardens and terraces
extending down to the Rhine. 40
comfortable rooms, each with bathroom.
Conference rooms, *Schlosskeller*, and
extremely elegant restaurant serving
international cuisine.
Open all year.
Very Expensive

6200 Wiesbaden

Aukamm-Hotel
Aukamm-Allee 31
tel: (061 21) 5 68 41
Modern, first-class hotel near the spa
parklands. 160 rooms, each with
bathroom. Restaurant serving
international dishes, and unusual grills.
Hotel open all year.
Restaurant open daily 12–23h
Very Expensive

6203 Hochheim am Main

Hotel-Restaurant Frankfurter Hof
tel: (061 46) 2252
Traditional old hotel with restaurant
serving home-made dishes, accompanied
by good selection of Hochheimer wines.
Hotel closed Jan
Restaurant closed Thur; open
11h30–14h30; 17h30 onwards
Moderate

Nahe

6530 Bingen

Rheinhotel Starkenburger Hof
Rheinkai 1–2
tel: (067 21) 1 43 41
Moderate hotel near the ships' landing
stages, without restaurant.
Closed Jan

6531 Münster-Sarmsheim

Hotel-Restaurant Trollmühle
Trollmühle
Trollbachstr. 10
tel: (067 21) 3 28 04
Hotel with restaurant serving venison in
season and Nahe wines.
Hotel open all year.
Restaurant closed Mon
Inexpensive

6536 Langenlonsheim

Hotel Garni
Naheweinstr. 195
tel: (067 04) 700
Small, pretty hotel, with private facilities
for each room. Located next to owner's
Weingut where wines can be sampled in
the *Bacchuskeller*.
Closed Jan
Inexpensive

6552 Bad Münster

Weinhaus 'Deutsches Haus'
Berliner Str. 29
tel: (067 08) 1851
Inexpensive, unpretentious hotel with
restaurant serving simple foods such as
Spiessbraten to acoompany local wines.
Closed Dec 15–Jan 15
Restaurant closed Mon

Caravelle Hotel
Im Orianienpark
tel: (0671) 2495

Hotel with swimming pool, sauna, conference rooms, rustic *Weinstube*, and restaurant.
Hotel open all year.
Restaurant open daily 7–23h
Expensive

6551 Schlossböckelheim

Weinhotel Niederthaler Hof
tel: (067 58) 6996
A 'wine hotel' in idyllic position overlooking the Nahe.
Weinproben can be arranged, there is a small wine museum, and wine weekends are often run here.
Restaurant serves simple roast meats as a speciality.
Hotel closed Jan
Restaurant open daily.
Moderate

Rheinhessen

6500 Mainz

Hotel Mainzer Hof
Kaiserstr. 98
tel: (061 31) 2 84 71
Luxury hotel in central position. 72 rooms all with private facilities. Roof-top restaurant with views of the Rhine and the city.
Very Expensive

Hotel Am Römerwall
am Römerwall 53–55
tel: (061 31) 23 21 35
Quiet hotel situated in large park.
No restaurant.
Open all year.
Moderate

Hotel Hammer
Bahnhofsplatz 6
tel: (061 31) 6 28 47
Modern hotel opposite main rail station within walking distance of the cathedral.
No restaurant.
Open all year.
Moderate

6508 Alzey

Massa Hotel
am Massa Markt
tel: (067 31) 4030
Hotel with tennis and squash courts, conference rooms, and a **Moderate** restaurant.
Hotel open all year.
Restaurant open daily 18h30–1h

6504 Oppenheim

Hotel-Restaurant Oppenheimer Hof
Fried-Ebert Str. 84
tel: (061 33) 2495
Inexpensive to **Moderate** hotel with restaurant serving *nouvelle cuisine*.
Open all year.

6520 Worms

Dom-Hotel
Am Obermarkt 10
tel: (062 41) 6913
Well-kept hotel with restaurant serving regional specialities and wines of the Rheinhessen.
Hotel open all year.
Restaurant open Mon–Fri 12–15h; 18–24h
Sat 18–24h
Moderate

Rheinpfalz

6701 Kallstadt

Weincastell 'Zum Weissen Ross'
Weinstr. 80
tel: (063 22) 2240
Hotel with 22 rooms and restaurant.
Own-produced estate wines served with Pfälzer specialities.
Hotel & restaurant closed Jan–Feb
Restaurant closed Thur; open 11h30–14h; 18–23h
Inexpensive

6702 Bad Dürkheim

Gartenhotel Heusser
Seebacherstr. 50–52
tel: (063 22) 2066
Quiet, comfortable hotel with outdoor and indoor swimming pools, sauna, solarium, gardens, and terrace. Restaurant serves mainly Pfälzer wines, and local specialities.
Hotel & restaurant closed Dec 20–Jan 20
Moderate

6706 Wachenheim

Hotel-Café-Weinstube Goldbächel
Waldstr. 101
tel: (063 22) 7314
Quiet position in woodland with tennis courts and garden.
Traditional *Weinstube* with lively entertainment.
Closed Dec–Jan
Inexpensive to **Moderate**

6705 Deidesheim

Hotel Reichsrat von Buhl
Weinstr. 12
tel: (063 26) 1916
Hotel owned by a well-known producer of
quality wines. Restaurant serves wide
range of dishes and excellent wines,
naturally from the Reichsrat von Buhl
estates.
Hotel open all year
Restaurant open daily 9–24h
Moderate

6730 Neustadt an der Weinstrasse

Hotel-Restaurant Kurfürst
Mussbacher Landstr. 2
tel: (063 21) 7441
Hotel well-situated for walks and drives
through beautiful surrounding
countryside of Pfälzerwald. Restaurant on
eighth floor has panoramic views.
Hotel open all year.
Restaurant open daily.
Moderate

6730 Neustadt-Haardt

Hotel Garni Tenner
Mandelring 216
tel: (063 21) 6541
Set within parkland, a comfortable hotel
with indoor swimming pool and sauna.
Open all year.
Moderate

6740 Landau in der Pfalz

Hotel Körber
Reiterstr. 11
tel: (063 41) 4050
Hotel with restaurant serving local foods
and wines.
Restaurant closed Fri
Moderate

6748 Bad Bergzabern

Kurhotel am Wonneberg
Am Wonneberg 9
tel: (063 43) 2023
Hotel with indoor swimming pool, tennis
courts, and restaurant.
Open all year.
Restaurant open daily 8–22h30
Moderate

Park Hotel
Kurtalstr. 83
tel: (063 43) 2415

Luxury hotel set within parkland, with
swimming pools, sauna, solarium, terrace,
gardens, and restaurant. Numerous
different recipes for fresh trout from their
own pools.
Hotel closed Jan–March
Restaurant closed Jan–Feb
Moderate

Hotel Pfälzer Wald
Kurtalstr. 77
tel: (063 43) 1056
Inexpensive family-run hotel situated in
parkland with terraces, gardens, and
restaurant.
Closed Nov 15–Dec 15; Feb

6749 Gleiszellen

Südpfalzterrassen
Winzergasse 42
tel: (063 43) 2066
Hotel with pool, and restaurant serving
mainly international cuisine. Dancing
nightly.
Hotel closed Dec 1–23
Restaurant closed Mon
Moderate

6749 Schweigen-Rechtenbach

Hotel-Restaurant Leiling
Hauptstr. 2
tel: (063 42) 244
Inexpensive to **Moderate** hotel located in
the first – or last – town on the *Deutsche
Weinstrasse*. Restaurant serves Pfälzer
specialities and wines.
Closed Jan
Restaurant closed Mon

Baden

6970 Lauda-Königshofen

Gästehaus Birgit
tel: (093 43) 998
Inexpensive *Gästhof* with full buffet
breakfast and lively *Weinstube*.
Closed Jan; Wed

6900 Heidelberg

Europäische Hof
Friedrich-Ebert-Anlage 1
tel: (062 21) 2 71 01
Centrally situated, a luxury hotel with
elegant restaurant and atmospheric
Weinstube.
Very Expensive

Romantik-Hotel 'Zum Ritter' St George
Hauptstr. 178
tel: (062 21) 2 42 72
Charming 16th-century building in the
heart of the city. Roof garden with views of
old city, castle, and mountains. Rustic
Ritterstube (Knight's Room) and elegant
main restaurant.
Open all year except Dec 24
Advisable to book.
Expensive

6840 Lampertheim bei Mannheim

Hotel Deutsches Haus
Kaiserstr. 47
tel: (062 06) 2022
Not on the wine road, but worth a detour
in June when the asparagus is in season.
Special *'Spargelkarte'* (asparagus menu)
offers this delicacy in over 40 different
ways. Hotel is comfortable and
well-equipped, with 31 rooms.
Closed Dec–Jan
Restaurant closed Fri; Sat lunchtime
Moderate

6830 Schwetzingen

Hotel Adler-Post
Schlossstr. 3
tel: (062 02) 1 00 36
Like Lampertheim, Schwetzingen is on the
'asparagus road', and well worth a detour
in season. This well-kept hotel has a
restaurant serving that speciality, as well
as fish and venison.
Hotel and restaurant closed 3 weeks in July
and August, and Tue
Restaurant closed Tue
Open 12–14h15; 18–22h
Inexpensive to **Moderate**

6909 Rauenberg

Hotel-Restaurant Winzerhof
Bahnhofstr. 6–8
tel: (062 22) 6 20 67
Hotel with swimming pool, sauna, and
solarium, and restaurant serving wines
produced from own vineyards.
Open all year.
Hotel **Expensive**
Restaurant **Moderate**

7602 Oberkirch-Ödsbach

Waldhotel Grüner Baum
tel: (078 02) 2801
Modern 55-room hotel with indoor
swimming pool and restaurant.
Closed Jan.
Moderate

7570 Baden-Baden

Hotel Am Markt
Marktplatz 17–18
tel: (072 21) 2 27 47
Hotel situated in old town near thermal
baths. Restaurant serves local specialities,
and offers a good range of Badische wines.
Open all year.
Restaurant open 8–21h
Inexpensive to **Moderate**

7590 Achern

Hotel Götz Sonne-Eintracht Achern
Hauptstr. 112
tel: (078 41) 5055
Modern hotel in this village on the wine
road, with swimming pool, restaurant and
Badische Weinstube.
Restaurant closed Sun.
Expensive

7600 Offenburg

Hotel Palmengarten
Okenstr. 17
tel: (0781) 2 50 31
Moderate hotel with restaurant.
Closed Dec 22–Jan 15
Restaurant closed Sun; open 12–14h;
18–22h

Hotel Drei Könige
Klosterstrasse 9
Modern family-run hotel situated in quiet
part of town. No restaurant.
Open all year.
Moderate

7800 Freiburg

Hotel 'Zum Roten Bären'
Oberlinden 12
am Schwabentor
tel: (0761) 3 69 69
Hotel with restaurant serving seasonal
Badische specialities, and local Badische
wines.
Open all year.
Restaurant open daily 12–14h; 18–22h
Expensive

7814 Breisach am Rhein

Hotel am Münster
Münsterbergstr. 23
tel: (076 67) 7071
Comfortable 42-room hotel with
swimming pool, and restaurant.
Open all year except Dec 24
Moderate to **Expensive**

7817 Ihringen

Hotel-Restaurant Winzerstube Ihringen
Wasenweiler Str. 36
tel: (076 68) 5051
Comfortable, rustic *Gasthof*; each room has
private bathroom.
Regional specialities and Ihringener wines
are served in the atmospheric *Winzerstube*.
Closed Tue
Inexpensive

7847 Badenweiler

Romantik-Hotel 'Sonne'
tel: (076 32) 5053
Attractive, comfortable hotel in this
2000-year old spa town.
Restaurant serves local wines and food.
Hotel closed mid-Nov–Feb
Restaurant closed Wed
Expensive hotel with **Moderate** restaurant

Camping

Mosel-Saar-Ruwer

Trier
'Schloss Monaise'
tel: (0651) 8 62 10
Saarburg
'Im Leukbachtal'
tel: (065 81) 2228
ENNIA-Ferienzentrum 'Warsburg'
tel: (065 81) 2037
'Waldfrieden'
tel: (065 81) 2255
Leiwen
'Sonnenberg'
tel: (065 07) 3414
Bernkastel-Kues
'Sonnenuhr'
Kröv
'Ferienzentrum Mont Royal'
tel: (065 41) 9234
Zell
'Mosella'
tel: (065 42) 4222
Bullay
'Moselstrand'
tel: (065 42) 2 17 21
Cochem
'Schausten'
tel: (026 71) 7528
Pommern/Mosel
A Lenz
tel: (026 72) 227
Koblenz
'Rhein-Mosel'
tel: (0261) 8 27 19

Where to Get Additional Information

German National Tourist Office
747 3rd Ave
NY NY 10017
tel: (212) 308–3300

German Wine Information Bureau
99 Park Ave
NY NY 10016
tel: (212) 599 6900

Deutsche Wein-Information
Postfach 1707
D-6500 Mainz 1
W. Germany

Rheingau

Rüdesheim am Rhein
'Ponyhof Ebental'
tel: (067 22) 2518
Geisenheim
'Stadt'
tel: (067 22) 8021
Wiesbaden
Wiesbadener Kanuverein
tel: (061 21) 6 67 81
Kostheim (near Hochheim)
'Maaru' (on island in river)
tel: (061 43) 4383

Nahe

Sobernheim
'Nahetal'
tel: (067 51) 2555

Rheinhessen

Gerbach
Campingplatz 'Platz'-ARAL
tel: (063 61) 8287
Guldental
HuG Faust
tel: (067 07) 633

Rheinpfalz

Bad Dürkheim
Camping Knaus
tel: (063 22) 6 13 56
Dahn
'Buttelwoog'
tel: (063 91) 622

Ludwigswinkel
'Waldcamp Schönetal'
tel: (063 31) 7 45 58
Ochsenbusch
Campingplatz des DCC
tel: (063 51) 8563

Baden

Bühl-Oberbruch
'Erholungsparadies-ADAM'
tel: (072 23) 2 31 94
Kehl am Rhein
'Camping der Freundschaft'
tel: (078 51) 2603
Rheinmünster-Stollhofen
Freizeitcenter Oberrhein GmbH
tel: (072 27) 2500

Achern
'Seeho el'
tel: (078 41) 2 13 53

Bibliography

Guide to the Wines of Germany by H.
Siegel, Cornerstone 1979.

The Wines of Germany by Cyril Ray,
Penguin, 1979

German Wine Atlas and Vineyard Register
Stabilisierungsfonds für Wein, revised
English edition 1979

The Wines of Germany: Completely Revised
Edition of Frank Schoonmaker's Classic by
Peter Sichel, Hastings House 1982

ITALY

‒PIEDMONT‒

'Piedmont' means foot of the mountain, for the Alps crown this region of north-west Italy along its borders with Switzerland to the north, and with France to the north and west. It is a stunningly beautiful land. In the hills of Alba, isolated little villages such as Barolo, Serralunga, Barbaresco, Castiglione Falletto and others, face each other across valleys covered with precious vines. The Po River winds its way from the mountains down to the plains and on its flatter, fertile shores lie watery-green paddies where *arborio* rice, the staple food of the north, is cultivated; the jagged, snow-covered alpine peaks are often reflected in their grassy, glassy surfaces near centres such as Vercelli and Novara. The forests of the Langhe and Monferrato, meanwhile, are densely covered with poplar, oak, birch and willow trees which colour the region with their myriad autumnal hues as the days shorten, and the cold winds bring tidings of another winter.

Indeed, autumn is the time to visit this rich and varied land, for at this time of the year only it yields not only its valuable harvest of grapes, but also an abundance of highly-prized foods: *tartufi bianchi* (white truffles), and *funghi porcini* (large-capped mushrooms that are both eaten fresh and used dried as a pungent flavouring), as well as numerous other varieties of wild mushrooms. In restaurants and homes throughout Piedmont local and regional dishes are prepared which make ample use of these unmistakable and luxurious specialities, and which are fit partners to one of the finest – and most varied – range of wines in Italy. The world's favourite *aperitivo*, vermouth, is a product of Piedmont, though the region's finest wines are robust, red aristocrats such as Barolo, Barbaresco, Gattinara and others, all produced from the noble yet temperamental Nebbiolo. Honest, everyday reds and whites also come from here, such as Barbera d'Asti, Grignolino, and Cortese di Gavi, while the great Italian wine for celebrations, Asti Spumante, comes from the province of Asti. There are 38 official DOC (*denominazione d'origine controllata*) wines from this prolific region, though many are rarely encountered outside their own locality or commune, let alone the region itself or the country.

If Piedmont produces both aristocratic and plentiful everyday wines, its essential character is a mixture of the noble and the down-to-earth. Simple, humble stone houses are neighbours to great castles and fortresses of former counts and barons (Italy's first King, Vittorio Emmanuele, came from the Piedmontese family of Savoy). Yet, as in other naturally abundant and richly-endowed lands, the everyday man here does not live at all badly. The distinctive *cucina piemontese* reflects this duality, ranging from such robust (and delicious) simple fare as *bagna cauda* (a pungent, hot anchovy and garlic dip, flavoured – like everything else – with truffles in season), and *bollito misto*, to creamy rich creations (such as *finanziera*) which indicate the region's proximity to France.

Throughout this stunningly beautiful land run a series of sign-posted *Strade del Vino*; exceedingly proud of its natural abundance, the region's inhabitants celebrate their prosperity with festivals that take place throughout the year – harvest and vintage celebrations in countless villages, truffle festivals and auctions in Asti and Alba, the historic *Palio* in Asti, even a *polenta* festival in Molare, and many more. There is a high concentration of excellent restaurants serving regional specialities, and there are also regional *enoteche* which display, promote, and sell their locality's wines; some, too, have restaurants and bars offering sophisticated and simple foods to accompany wine tastings. There are, on the other hand, fewer wine producers here who directly welcome visitors, but the visitor will find ample opportunity to sample and to enjoy the flavours of this rich and abundant land.

How to Get There

By Car
The best approach to Piedmont is by way of either the Mont Blanc tunnel, or the Great St Bernard pass. If approaching from the South of France, cross the border at the Colle di Tenda, then continue on through the resort town of Limone Piemonte, and so on to Cuneo and Alba. The A4 autostrada quickly connects the region with centres to the east such as Milan and Venice, while the A21 and A1 autostrade, link it with Piacenza, Parma, and Bologna. Piedmont (and the adjoining area of Valle d'Aosta) is a land of mountains and hills, known to many who have encountered this region through its popular ski resorts (Courmayeur, Val d'Isère, Bardonécchia, Limone Piemonte, and many others). It is perhaps also surprising to discover that the region is so close to the sea; as mentioned above, it is within easy reach of the South of France, while the A26 autostrada which begins north of Genoa leads to Alessandria and Asti, thus linking Piedmont with the Italian Riviera.

By Plane
There are direct non-stop flights from the US to Milan, and connecting flights from the US to Turin. Also numerous internal flights daily from Rome to Turin on Alitalia.

By Train
There are numerous trains to Turin from all major cities such as Rome, Milan, Venice, and Florence. The 'Palatino Express' runs from Paris to Turin daily, making the trip in under nine hours.

Local Public Transport
There is a good local train service that links Turin with Asti, Alessandria, and Acqui Terme, but in order to explore the wine country in full, the use of a car is essential.

Car Rental Information
Turin
Avis: Corso Turati, 15 g
  tel: (011) 50 11 07
  Porta Nuova FS
  tel: (011) 50 55 68
  Caselle Airport
  tel: (011) 47 01 528
Hertz: Corso Marconi, 19
  tel: (011) 65 04 504
  Porta Nuova FS
  tel: (011) 65 96 58
  Caselle Airport
  tel: (011) 47 01 103

Maps Touring Club Italiano no. 1 (Piemonte e Valle d'Aosta)

The Wines of Piedmont

Wines in Piedmont are named, confusingly, both after grape varieties (Barbera, Cortese, Moscato, Spanna) and also after wine communes where they are produced (Barolo, Barbaresco, Gattinara, for instance). The following are the most important wines that will be encountered in this prolific region.

Asti Spumante Sparkling wine produced (primarily) from the Moscato grape, which gives this popular wine its characteristic fragrant, grapy bouquet. It is produced by the *cuvée close* method, whereby the secondary fermentation takes place in a sealed stainless steel tank; afterwards the wines are bottled under pressure. This method is not only considerably less expensive than the *méthode champenoise* (whereby secondary fermentation takes place in the bottle itself), it also preserves the distinctive character and freshness of the Moscato.

Barbaresco Wine commune east of Alba that produces dry, full-bodied red wine from the Nebbiolo grape.

Barbera Prolific grape variety which is the most widely grown in the Piedmont. Austere, dry red wine which develops with age, but much is often drunk young, high in acid and tannin, as the everyday wine of the region. Such *vino da tavola* is often sold in 2-litre screw-capped bottles and even much larger containers, but the finer examples of Barbera are sold in 75cl bottles with a geographical qualification indicated on the label, such as Barbera d'Alba, Barbera d'Asti, and Barbera di Monferrato. Barbera is not only a wine to drink with pungent, full-flavoured country cooking, it is also an important ingredient in the kitchen for such dishes as *risotto al Barbera*, and *gallo al Barbera*.

Barolo Intense, robust wine produced in communes of Alba, including Barolo, Castiglione Falletto, La Morra, Serralunga d'Alba, and others. Such rich, full-flavoured wine needs at least three years ageing to mellow and develop its complex bouquet (many connoisseurs detect a distinctive scent of violets). Barolo is without doubt one of the greatest red wines in Italy.

Brachetto Lively, semi-sparkling sweetish red wine, often drunk while young, fresh, and frothy. Good as an *aperitivo*.

Caluso Passito As is the method elsewhere in Italy, this sweet wine is produced by partially drying grapes after the harvest. In this case the fragrant Erbaluce grape produces just such a concentrated, heavy dessert wine.

Cortese Prolific white grape that produces pale, dry, everyday white wines.

Dolcetto Dry red wine produced from local grape of the same name. Sometimes made into semi-sparkling version.

Erbaluce di Caluso Light, dry white wine produced from the Erbaluce grape grown in the provinces of Torino and Vercelli. Good with fried frogs' legs. Sample it in the regional *enoteca* at Roppolo.

Freisa Garnet, light red wine that should be drunk while young and fresh.

Gattinara In the northern wine districts of Piedmont, the noble Nebbiolo, confusingly, is locally known as the Spanna. Here, around the village of Gattinara, it produces superb and highly-valued intense red wines which rank with the greatest from Barolo. Like Barolo, it needs at least three to four years ageing in oak or chestnut casks, and in the bottle, to develop its full potential and character.

Gavi Dry white wine produced from the Cortese grape. Rare, but superb white wine produced in limited quantity only is known as Gavi di Gavi. Everyday wines sold as Cortese di Gavi.

Grignolino Light, garnet-coloured wine produced in Asti and Monferrato.

Malvasia di Casorzo Fragrant, sweet red wine from vineyards of Monferrato above Asti.

Moscato Either still (Moscato *naturale*), or sparkling (Moscato Spumante) wines are produced from this distinctive grape.

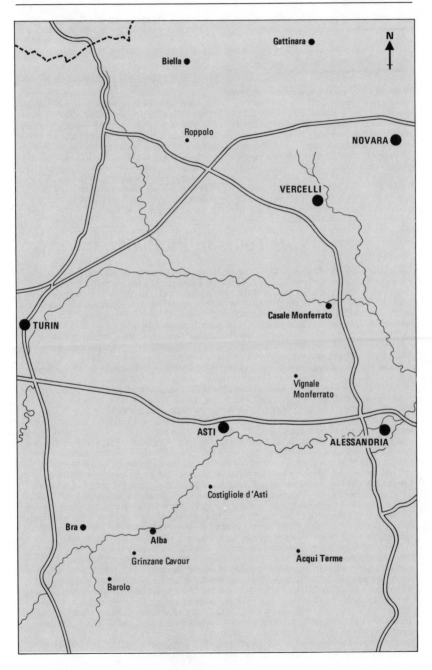

While Moscato Spumante is often a cheaper version of Asti Spumante, Moscato *naturale*, produced in regions such as Alba, is a dry, intensely perfumed wine of considerable distinction which makes a most appetizing *aperitivo*.

Nebbiolo The great grape of the Piedmont produces wines which bear their own *denominazione*; wines are also sold under the varietal name, Nebbiolo, or Nebbiolo d'Alba. While they may be neither as profound nor as intense as, say, Barolo or Barbaresco, they nevertheless display the grape's essential character.

Spanna North of Turin, the Nebbiolo is locally called the Spanna. Wine is sold under this name, while in addition, wines produced in restricted and superior zones bear their own *denominazione* such as Lessona, Carema, Sizzano, Fara, Ghemme, and the above-mentioned Gattinara.

Vermouth A manufactured wine made from a base of neutral white wines (often imported in bulk from the south of Italy) to which is added a concentrated infusion of herbs and spices, quinine, bitters, orange and lemon peel, and other aromatic flavourings, as well as fragrant wine (such as Moscato), and finally, sugar and spirits. Various styles are produced by large firms in Turin and elsewhere, including *bianco* (sweet white), *rosso* (sweet red, coloured with caramel), *secco* (dry white), and *rosé* (pink, semi-sweet).

Wine Tours in Piedmont

Piedmont is a vast wine region, with no less than 38 wine zones qualifying for *denominazione d'origine controllata (DOC)* status. These range from intensive areas of cultivation, such as those areas centring around Alba and Asti (the two most important and well-known zones of production), to isolated pockets of vineyards found in the north, around Ivrea, Gattinara, Lessona, and other communes. Throughout this important wine region run a series of sign-posted wine roads. These *Strade del Vino* are identified by a sign designed with crenellated corners, representing the many castles found throughout the region, a brown wine glass, a bunch of grapes, and a winding road, all on a yellow background.

These wine roads of Piedmont, however, do not proceed from one point to another. Rather, they serve as important points of reference within a total complex of landscape of which the grapes are a part. Thus as one travels the maze of small roads that extends over the hills of Monferrato between Asti and Acqui Terme, wine roads and vineyards merge one into another: first the *Strada del Asti Spumante*, extending through vineyards bearing the plump Moscato grapes that will be turned into that fragrant sparkler; then, further south (and often even overlapping), the signs proclaim other zones of production, Freisa and Barbera d'Asti, Brachetto d'Aqui and Barbera del Monferrato. Travel between Asti and Alba, then south of that important wine town, and the signs indicate that we have entered other wine realms. The *Strada del Barolo* thus winds its way down into low valleys, and up high hills topped by watchful towers, as it leads through important communes like Barolo, Serralunga d'Alba, La Morra, Castiglione Falletto, Novello, and Grinzane. Elsewhere, further up the Tanaro Valley, the *Strada del Barbaresco* indicates that we have entered the demarcated limits of the zone of production for this important wine. To the north, a network of tiny wine roads, like myriad arteries, extends from Alessandria up to Casale Monferrato, while further north still, beyond Novara they connect isolated (and little visited) wine villages such as Fara, Sizzano, Ghemme, and Gattinara.

Along the wine roads, producers and *cantine cooperative* display the wine road logo. Often, if one does not come at an awkwardly busy time (such as the vintage) or at midday, when everything and everybody stops for the main meal of the day, it is possible for the interested visitor to have a look around the establishment with or without a guide. Some producers also sell their wine direct, others do not. While it is our experience that most Italian wine producers do not have the facilities nor indeed the necessity to make provision for casual foreign visitors, it is equally our experience that many are extremely devoted to their occupation, and eager to discuss it, to talk about wine production here compared to elsewhere in Europe, and to listen, too. We do include a brief list of producers whose premises can be visited, mostly by appointment, but do make an effort to stop along the wine roads where you see the sign displayed.

One important (and extremely pleasant) way to learn about the wines of the different districts is to plan routes along the wine roads which lead to the five regional *enoteche* of Piedmont. These establishments, located in historic and splendid castles and villas, are integral to the concept of the *Strade del Vino* of Piedmont, for they serve as central 'wine libraries', displaying, offering for taste and sale, wines from their particular localities, housing artifacts of past viticulture and local history and, in some cases, serving excellent regional dishes (and, of course, wines) for reasonable prices in adjoining restaurants or *trattorie*. Two *enoteche* are located in Alba, in Barolo and in Grinzane Cavour. Two are in the province of Asti, in Costigliole and Vignale Monferrato. The fifth lies to the north, at Roppolo, overlooking Lake Viverone. For those visitors driving to Piedmont via the Mont Blanc or Great St Bernard tunnels, it is the first that is encountered, for it is just off the A5 autostrada (exit Santhia).

The wine roads of Piedmont are not meant to be followed consecutively, but the following suggested routes will help make touring this diverse and vast wine region more manageable.

Asti and Monferrato

The vineyards and wine villages of Asti and Monferrato can be explored from Asti itself, capital of the province, and at once a busy industrial town, a local agricultural centre, and a medieval municipality rich in history and art, culture and folklore. In September its past is celebrated with the *Palio*, a colourful and historic festival which has taken place annually since the thirteenth century and during which the men of the town compete in a horserace around the Campo del Palio. Yet if this lively event looks back on the town's illustrious history, further events take place in the autumn which celebrate the present. The *Douja d'Or* is an important wine festival which takes place annually for fifteen days in September, during which there is naturally much singing, dancing, drinking and eating, as well as

important competitions and awards for the finest wines. The following month, the province's other most famous product, the *tartufo bianco* – white truffle – is honoured with the *Grande Festa del Tartufo* which lasts for over a month, with local festivals, truffle auctions and other festivities. Restaurants on designated itineraries participate by preparing regional dishes that make use of this magical, prized fungus.

The following two routes take the wine tourist through the heart of much of the wine country of Asti, however, they are suggestions only, so do explore other parts of this fascinating province.

Route 1 Asti; (N456) Isola d'Asti; Costigliole d'Asti (Castello di Costigliole is the magnificent setting for a regional *enoteca* with restaurant); Nizza Monferrato (truffle centre, particularly worth visiting in autumn – see *Ristoranti del Buon Vino* below in Restaurant section); follow Belbo Valley to Canelli (centre of production of Asti Spumante); continue through the lovely, low hills of Monferrato to Búbbio, then follow Bormida Valley to Céssole and Vésime; cross river and continue on small, winding road around to Roccaverano, an ancient little village, centre for the production of Robiole cheese (*Ristorante del Buon Vino*); continue east to reach N30 which leads to Acqui Terme, famous for its hot springs and mud cures since Roman days.

Route 2 Asti; north (N457); brief detour to Castell'Alfero perched on its high hill; Calliano; Penango; Moncalvo, agricultural and commercial centre of the locality

(*Ristorante del Buon Vino*); find small road east to Grazzano Badóglio (*Ristorante del Buon Vino*); Casorzo, centre for the production of a highly-regarded local sweet red Malvasia wine; Vignale Monferrato (one of the five important regional *enoteche* is located here in the Palazzo Callori – see below, p. 184); return to Asti, or else continue north to Casale Monferrato, and, if touring the northern Vercellese and Novarese vineyards, to Vercelli and Novara.

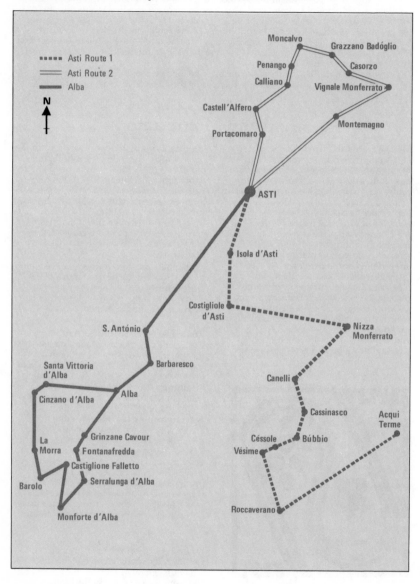

Alba

The region known as the Langhe has good reason to be proud of the products of its land, for from these rich, isolated, and beautiful hills come some of the finest wines not only of Italy, but of Europe. A brief tour of the area begins from Asti, passes through dramatic wine country and modest, unassuming villages whose names are known by wine lovers throughout the world, such as Barolo and Barbaresco. Additionally, there are two regional *enoteche* which should be visited, one with a fine restaurant, while a circular return to Alba leads to Santa Vittoria d'Alba, a town with a secret, and home of the famous vermouth company Cinzano. Alba itself is a fine old town, and a visit in autumn or winter to the daily *mercato dei tartufi* (truffle market) in the medieval Piazza di San Giovanni is a rare experience. The following suggested route cuts and winds its way over hills, down into deep valleys, and back again; the nature of the terrain necessitates the vineyards and wine villages of Alba being explored in such an unhurried manner.

From Asti, take the N456 west to N231 direction of Alba; turn off left (crossing the Tanaro River) to climb up to the perched wine village of Barbaresco; continue through hills, then down to Alba, an unspoiled medieval town and centre of this rich region known as the Langhe; from Alba continue south (direction of Diano d'Alba), then turn off right to Grinzane Cavour (the *Castello di Cavour* is the home of the important and prestigious regional *enoteca* with restaurant); follow the road further down to the Talloria Valley, then go left to reach the heart of the *terra del Barolo*: Fontanafredda (well-known producer) and Serralunga d'Alba; when road meets junction, turn right to Monforte d'Alba; continue on to Castiglione Falletto, then cut back to Barolo (another regional *enoteca* is found in this tiny, unpretentious wine village); return north to La Morra (at Annunziata, 2 km from La Morra, visit the wine museum of Renato Ratti); continue further north to meet N231; turn right, direction of Alba, to Cinzano d'Alba, Santa Vittoria d'Alba (even if an appointment has not been arranged to visit this fascinating establishment, stop for refreshment at the company's good restaurant located along the main road); then back via Alba to Asti.

Northern vineyards

While much pleasurable time can be spent in Asti and Alba, sniffing out (like trained truffle dogs) small family wine producers and good local restaurants, a tour of the vineyards of Piedmont is not complete without visiting the towns, villages, and vineyards of the north, those of the Vercellese and Novarese. Because the Nebbiolo wines from those wine communes and vineyards north of Novara are sold under so many different and little-known names, they generally do not command the same top prices as, say, Barolo and Barbaresco, yet the wines are in no way inferior. Additionally, the atmosphere here, on the more open stretches of land, literally in the shadow of the dominating, majestic Alps, is quite a contrast to the close, compact, even claustrophobic atmosphere of the hills of the Langhe and Monferrato. The following suggested route takes in some of the great wine communes, and ends at the fifth

regional *enoteca* at Roppolo, a good centre for relaxing outdoor-pursuits as well as for eating and drinking:

Vercelli (an interesting town with a medieval quarter, centre of the important rice industry); Novara; then north (direction of Romagnano/Varallo) to Briona; Fara Novarese; Sizzano; Ghemme; Romagnano; cross river to Gattinara (Fara, Sizzano, Ghemme, and Gattinara are all

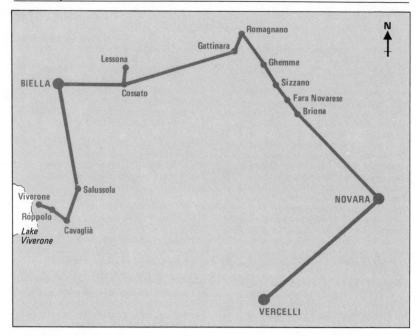

DOC wines, produced from the Spanna grape); from Gattinara, take N142 west to Cossato, turn right to vineyards and village of Lessona (another distinguished wine produced from the Spanna grape); continue to Biella (take the funicular to Biella Piazzo, for medieval houses and superb view of the mountains); south on

N143 to Cavaglià; nearby regional *enoteca* with restaurant at Roppolo located above Lake Viverone; sports and recreation facilities on this and other lakes; this is a good position for either leaving the region on the A5 to France or Switzerland, or for exploration of the autonomous region known as the Valle d'Aosta.

The Five Regional *Enoteche* of Piedmont

Costigliole d'Asti The marvellous Castello di Costigliole (Asti route 1), which dominates this small wine village as it is approached, is today used in part as an *enoteca* dedicated to furthering knowledge of the wines of Asti. A broad range of wines is displayed and is available for tasting and purchase. The wines chosen for display, and also those that are served in the adjoining restaurant, have all been selected at the important annual wine fair, the *Douja d'Or*, which takes place annually in September in Asti. The restaurant has

been designated one of Asti's *Ristoranti del Buon Vino* (see below), and takes pride in honouring and safeguarding country cooking by serving local specialities with wines, at reasonable prices.
Closed Mon
tel: (0141) 96 60 15

Vignale Monferrato The Palazzo di Callori in Vignale Monferrato, (north of Asti – Asti route 2), serves as the regional *enoteca* for the wines of Monferrato. This eastern section is primarily a zone for the

production of Barbera di Monferrato and Grignolino (nearby Casorzo is the centre for the production of a locally popular sweet red Malvasia). The palace is situated in the midst of gently rolling land characterized by fields of haphazard vines, interspersed with rambling *aziende* (farmhouses), and small cottages made of turf. The area is also rich in prehistoric remains. While selected wines from the region are on show in the *enoteca*, other rooms are used for technical and educational displays. A restaurant serves elegant Piedmontese food with wines selected from the *enoteca* and in summer the palace is the setting for many cultural and folk art events.
Closed Tue
tel: (0142) 92 31 30

Grinzane Cavour The austere, majestic Castello di Cavour is situated on an isolated peak overlooking the magnificent countryside of the Langhe. Just a few miles from Alba (see Alba route above), it is among the most prestigious of Italy's regional *enoteche*. It is administered by the Order of the Cavaliers of Truffles and Wines of Alba, and it is this important gastronomic body that selects and offers sample bottles from some of the best producers from the region. In addition there are permanent exhibitions of artifacts that give a historical picture of the castle, as well as of wine-making in Alba since Roman times. Tools and implements, as well as collections of wine glasses, plates, etc. are displayed. Adjacent to the *enoteca* is a *ristorante* which serves traditional foods in conjunction with the wines of the *enoteca*. Special programmes are held periodically on wine-related themes.
Closed Mon eve, Tue
tel: (0173) 62 159

Barolo The *enoteca* of Barolo (see Alba route above) is the oldest in Piedmont, and was started by the people of the area to protect its artistic and architectural heritage, as well as to honour its great wine. Bottles of wine from over fifty producers are displayed and are available for purchase at reasonable prices. The castle of Barolo houses a rich museum of peasant and country life, with agricultural artifacts, and a collection of unusual glasses, corks, and old photographs.
Hours: 9h30–12h30; 15–18h30
Closed Tue
(Holidays open by appointment only)
tel: (0173) 56 106

Roppolo The fifth regional *enoteca* of Piedmont is at Roppolo (Northern vineyards route – see above), in a fourteenth-century castle that provides splendid panoramic views of Lake Viverone. It is called the *Enoteca della Serra*, and is dedicated to furthering knowledge of the wines of the Vercellese. A museum in the castle tower displays local farming tools and other artifacts. A regional restaurant is located in another part of the castle, and serves Piedmontese specialities together with wines from the *enoteca*. Roppolo is an important *enoteca* not only because it is integral to this important (and little-visited) northern section of the Piedmont vineyard, but also because its central location near three autostrade connects it directly with France, Switzerland and central Europe.
tel: (0161) 98 501

Wine Producers

Many producers in Piedmont are small family farmers who either sell their grapes or wine to local cooperatives, or else produce limited amounts of quality products which are earmarked for traditional customers. Most do not, therefore, have the time or the resources to welcome casual visitors; moreover, the various regional *enoteche* serve as a link between consumer and producer. As a result the wine tourist will certainly wish to plan itineraries around visits to the *enoteche*. The following producers welcome interested visitors, but by appointment only. While the serious connoisseurs' wines from Piedmont are the great, robust reds, the visitor should also arrange to tour one of the large vermouth factories to see the fascinating process of producing this fragrant, herbal-scented wine. Martini & Rossi have an interesting wine museum, *Il Museo di Storia dell'Enologia*, located, along with that company's main plant, in Pessione. Santa Vittoria d'Alba, home of Cinzano, is a fascinating perched village whose World War II 'secret' – its hidden wine – was the subject of a delightful film.

Asti

14053 Canelli

Luigi Bosca & Figli SpA
Via Luigi Bosca, 2
tel: (0141) 82 95 5
Asti Spumante, vermouth, and table wines
of the Piedmont.
Mon–Fri 9–11h; 15–17h
Appointment necessary.
English spoken.

14049 Nizza Monferrato

Bersano Antico Podere Conti della
Cremosina SpA
Piazza Dante, 21
tel: (0141) 72 12 73
Barbera d'Asti, Freisa d'Asti, Moscato
d'Asti, Grignolino d'Asti, Dolcetto and
other quality table wines.
Mon–Fri 8–11h; 14–17h
Appointment necessary.
Max 40 pers.
English spoken.

Guasti Clemente & Figli SpA
Via IV Novembre, no. 80
tel: (0141) 72 13 50
Moscato *naturale* d'Asti, Barbera d'Asti,
Barbera del Monferrato, Grignolino d'Asti,
Dolcetto d'Alba, Cortese di Gavi, Malvasia
di Casorzo, Brachetto d'Acqui, Asti
Spumante
Mon–Fri by appointment.
English spoken.

Alba

12051 Alba

Casa Vinicola Ceretto
Corso Langhe, 3
tel: (0173) 2484
Barolo, Barbaresco, Nebbiolo d'Alba,
Dolcetto d'Alba
Daily 9–11h; 15–17h
Appointment necessary.
Max 4 pers.
English spoken.

12064 La Morra

F.lli Dogliani SpA
Località Batasiolo, 87
tel: (0173) 50 13 1
Open Mon–Fri 8–12h; 14–16h

Appointment necessary.
Max 50 pers.
English spoken

12051 Fontanafredda

Tenimenti di Barolo e di Fontanafredda
Casella postale 29
tel: (0173) 5300/5392
Open Sat & Sun 9–12h; 15–18h from
April–Oct
Closed August.
Weekdays and group visits by
appointment only.
English-speaking guide for groups by
pre-arrangement.

12060 Santa Vittoria d'Alba

Cinzano e Cia SpA
Stabilimente di Santa Vittoria
tel: (0172) 47 041
Vermouth, Asti Spumante
Open daily, by appointment only.
English spoken.
For appointment, write to: Cinzano U.K.,
20 Buckingham Gate, London SW1.
This famous firm owns an excellent
restaurant, 'L Muscatel, in the village of
Cinzano d'Alba.

Pessione

Martini e Rossi SpA
tel: (011) 57 451
Open Mon–Fri 9–12h30; 14–17h
Appointment necessary by letter or
telephone at least 15 days in advance.
Write to the Public Relations Dept., Casella
Postale 475, 10100 Turin. No visits can be
arranged for groups smaller than five
persons. English spoken. Write in advance
to confirm visits to the important wine
museum.

Cantine Cooperative The following wine
cooperatives are located along the region's
wine roads; though they lack the
organization for in-depth tours (English is
rarely spoken, for example), the interested
visitor is usually welcomed.

Asti and Monferrato

14100 Fraz. San Marzanotto (near Asti)

Cantina Sociale Asti Barbera
tel: (0141) 51 22 1

14049 Nizza Monferrato

Cantina Sociale di Nizza Monferrato
Via Alessandria, 57
tel: (0141) 72 13 48

14053 Canelli

Cantina Sociale di Canelli
Via Loazzolo, 12
tel: (0141) 81 34 7

15011 Acqui Terme

Società Cooperativa Cantina Sociale di
Acqui Terme
Via IV Novembre, 14
tel: (0144) 20 08

15049 Vignale Monferrato

Cantina Sociale di Vignale Monferrato
Via Mazzucco, 2
tel: (0142) 92 30 15

Alba

12050 Barbaresco

Società Cooperativa Produttori del
Barbaresco·
Piazza Parrocchia
tel: (0173) 63 51 39

12060 Castiglione Falletto

Cantina Sociale Terre del Barolo
Via Barolo-Alba, 5
tel: (0173) 62 053

Monforte d'Alba

Cooperativa Vinicola Pavitim
tel: (0173) 79 93 24

Novarese Vineyards

13045 Gattinara

Società Cooperativa Cantina Sociale di
Gattinara
Via Montegrappa, 7
tel: (0163) 81 56 8

28073 Fara Novarese

Società Cooperativa Cantina Sociale dei
Colli Novaresi
Via C Battisti, 60
tel: (0321) 81 23 4

28070 Sizzano

Società Cooperativa Cantina Sociale
Vini Pregiati di Sizzano e Ghemme
Corso Italia, 44
tel: (0321) 81 02 68

--- Wine Festivals ---

September (lasts for fifteen days)	Douja d'Or – important annual wine festival.	Asti
Mid Oct–Nov	Grande Feste del Tartufo. Manifestations include truffle auctions, while local restaurants participate by preparing dishes to honour this magnificent fungus	Various towns throughout Asti and Alba – write to regional tourist offices for further details
	Polentone	Molare
September	Palio	Asti
September	Festa dell'Uva	Castello d'Annone (Asti)

Regional Gastronomy

Antipasti piemontese Virtually a meal in itself: a vast trolley of 'appetizers', including raw meat served with lemon juice and grated truffles; meatballs; trout in aspic; beans served with chopped onion and anchovy; roasted red peppers bathed in *bagna cauda*, and much else.

Bagna cauda Pungent hot anchovy, olive oil, and garlic dip, served with grated truffles in season. Raw vegetables such as celery, *cardi* (an edible thistle much loved here), and strips of red pepper, as well as bread and *grissini* are dipped into the bubbling pot.
Grissini Breadsticks, an ubiquitous Italian staple which originated in

Piedmont. Here they often are laid out on the table fresh from the baker's oven, over a foot long, and still soft and warm.

Agnolotti Favourite local pasta similar to ravioli, stuffed with meat or spinach.

Risotto al Barbera Rice (*arborio*) cooked with good home-made stock, Barbera wine, and *funghi porcini*.

Gnocchi alla Fontina Small dumplings made from potatoes and flour, poached, then baked with creamy Fontina cheese.

Polenta A corn mush staple much loved in northern Italy.

Funghi porcini Wild mushrooms that are excellent eaten fresh (in season only), or else used dried as a flavourful addition to stews and rice dishes.

Tartufi bianchi White truffles: generally grated into very thin slivers with a special knife and sprinkled over virtually everything. A rare delicacy is small whole truffles cooked in Asti Spumante, then dressed with olive oil, lemon juice, and Parmesan cheese.

Rane dorato Frogs' legs, dipped in flour and fried in olive oil – speciality of Vercelli.

Fonduta Piedmontese 'fondue' made from melted Fontina cheese, cream, and grated truffles.

Bollito misto Gargantuan trolley of boiled meats, including beef, chicken, veal, and tongue, served with vegetables and two types of sauce: *verde* (anchovies and parsley), and *rossa* (piquant tomato).

Gallo al Barbera Chicken stewed in Barbera wine.

Trotelle alla Savoia Trout baked with wild mushrooms.

Finanziera Extremely rich speciality: chicken giblets, calves' sweetbreads, cock's comb cooked separately, then mixed with cream and truffles.

Zabaione Favourite dessert invented by cooks of the House of Savoy, made of beaten egg yolks, sugar, and Marsala (some local cooks use Barbera wine rather than Marsala).

Bonet Characteristic rum-flavoured dessert.

Dolce torinese Chocolate-almond biscuits.

Cunesi Chocolate and liqueur sweets.

Astigiani Large chocolates with rum and other flavours.

Palio Characteristic hard cake which is a speciality of Asti.

Cheeses:
Fontina creamy, from the Valle d'Aosta.
Toma veja strong-flavoured fermented cheese from Gressoney Valley.
Robiela spicy, creamy, strong-flavoured.

Restaurants

Asti and Monferrato

The province of Asti has plenty of regional restaurants. Some of the best, chosen both for their food and their wine, have been designated 'Ristoranti del Buon Vino'. We have mentioned them on the suggested routes. They are often worth a detour.

14100 Asti

Il Falcone Vecchio
Via San Secondo, 8
tel: (0141) 53 10 6
Comfortable and intimate, this *Ristorante del Buon Vino* is located in an old section of the town, and serves *astigiana* specialities and wines.
Closed Mon
Essential to book on Sun.
Moderate

Il Reale
Piazza Alfieri, 6
tel: (0141) 50 24 0
Elegant *Ristorante del Buon Vino* annexed to the Albergo Reale, one of the oldest and best known hotels in town. Restaurant serves traditional Piedmontese specialities, including *finanziera, arrostini*, and *risotto alla Reale.*
Closed Thur
Moderate
Hotel **Moderate** to **Expensive**

Il Moro
tel: (0141) 32 51 3
Located along the banks of the Tanaro River, a characteristic *simpatico* restaurant serving meals outdoors in summer. Family cooking, including *pasta e fagioli, minestrone, gli agnolotti. Ristorante del Buon Vino.*
Closed Mon
Essential to book.
Inexpensive to **Moderate**

14055 Costigliole d'Asti

Ristorante Enoteca
Castello di Costigliole
tel: (0141) 96 60 15
Part of the important regional *enoteca*, and also a designated *Ristorante del Buon Vino*: elegant, refined dining room, and regional specialities such as *antipasti caldi piemontese* (hot *antipasti*), *risotto del castello, galletto al Barbera, bonet*. Wines from the *enoteca* are all selected from the *Douja d'Or*.
Closed Mon
Advisable to book
Moderate to **Expensive**

Ristorante da Guido
Piazza Umberto I, 27
tel: (0141) 96 60 12
Elegant restaurant serving classic *cucina piemontese*.
Closed Sun, July 15–August 15; end of Dec to mid Jan
Open only for dinner.
Very Expensive

14049 Nizza Monferrato

Ristorante Da Italo
Piazza Garibaldi, 52
tel: (0141) 72 11 28
Typical Monferrato atmosphere in this friendly, family-run *Ristorante del Buon Vino*. Faithful traditional cooking, including *fonduta con tartufi, gallo al Barbera, risotto al Barbera, zabaione al Barbera*.
Closed Tue
Inexpensive to **Moderate**

Ristorante Savona
Via Carlo Alberto 127
tel: (0141) 72 573
Comfortable traditional restaurant with excellent selection of wines and many dishes using *funghi porcini*.
Closed Wed
Advisable to book.
Moderate

Roccaverano

Ristorante Aurora
(near Piazza)
tel: (0144) 93 02 3
Panoramic position with terrace overlooking the Langhe, this intimate, comfortable restaurant serves home-made salami, *agnolotti con funghi porcini, coniglio al Barbera* (rabbit stewed in Barbera) and other local dishes, as well as excellent locally-produced cheese.
Closed Tue
Moderate

15100 Alessandria

Ristorante Grappolo
Via Casale, 28
tel: (0131) 53 21 7
Inexpensive restaurant serving Piedmontese dishes and local wines.
Closed Tue; Aug; early Jan

15066 Gavi

Ristorante Cantine del Gavi
Via Mameli, 60
tel: (0143) 64 24 58
Closed Mon
Open 12h30–20h
Located in an old house in the historic centre of the village, serving regional dishes and the wines of Gavi. Booking advisable.
Moderate

Moncalvo

Il Centrale
(main Piazza)
tel: (0141) 91 12 6
Comfortable, familiar atmosphere in this typical Monferrato *Ristorante del Buon Vino*. Speciality of the house is *'il gran bollito misto'*.
Closed Mon
Essential to book.
Moderate

Grazzano Badoglio

Il Giardinetto
tel: (0141) 92 51 14
Refined, elegant restaurant located in a little house in this quiet old village. Simple, but excellent cooking using fresh local ingredients.
Closed Tue
Essential to book.
Moderate to **Expensive**

15049 Vignale Monferrato

Ristorante dell'Enoteca
Palazzo Callori
Piazza del Popolo, 7
tel: (0142) 92 31 30
The restaurant of this regional *enoteca* of Monferrato is set in the 14th-century palace, serving local foods and wines in a refined and elegant venue.
Closed Tue
Open 12h30–14h30; 19h30–21h
Moderate

Alba

12051 Alba

Ristorante La Capannina di Flli Gallina
Borgo Moretta
tel: (0173) 43 95 2
Family-run restaurant serving only wines
of Alba, to accompany Piedmontese dishes
such as *antipasti, risotto al Barolo, fonduta,
nocciolata delle Langhe.*
Closed Mon
Moderate to **Expensive**

12060 Grinzane Cavour

Ristorante dell'Enoteca del Regionale
Piemontese Cavour
Castello di Grinzane Cavour
tel: (0173) 62 15 9
An integral part of the important regional
enoteca, this superb *ristorante* is located in
the castle, with impressive views over the
hills of the Langhe. Regional foods
accompany wines from the *enoteca*, chosen
by the esteemed gastronomic body, the
*Órdine dei Cavalieri dei Vini e dei Tartufi
d'Alba.*
Closed Mon eve, Tue
Essential to book.
Moderate to **Expensive**

12064 La Morra

Ristorante Belvedere
Piazza Castello, 5
tel: (0173) 50 19 0
Classic, elegant foods of Piedmont in this
traditional **Expensive** restaurant.
Closed Sun eve, Mon; Jan

12060 Barolo

Del Buon Padre
località Vergne
Via Narzole, 50
tel: (0173) 56 19 2
An *antica locanda* in the Barolo countryside
serving home-made salami, *bagna cauda,
brasato al Barolo*, and other local specialities,
together with the great wines of Barolo.
Closed Wed
Essential to book.
Moderate to **Expensive**

12042 Bra

Ristorante dell'Arcangelo
Strada San Michele, 28
tel: (0172) 42 21 63

An **Expensive** restaurant serving
traditional and imaginative foods, and
wines of the Piedmont and the other
classic wine regions of Italy.
Closed Wed

12060 Santa Vittoria d'Alba

Ristorante 'L Muscatel
Via Statale, 68
Cinzano d'Alba
tel: (0172) 47 03 9
Regional cuisine and wines in this
restaurant located along the main road,
and owned (like virtually everything in
Cinzano d'Alba) by the great vermouth
firm of Cinzano.
Closed Sun eve; Mon
Moderate

Northern Vineyards –
Vercellese and Novarese

28100 Novara

Ristorante Caglieri
Via Tadini, 12
tel: (0321) 45 63 73
Local and regional dishes, and Novarese
wines in this **Moderate** restaurant.
Closed Fri
Open 12–14h30; 19h30–24h

28072 Briona

Trattoria del Ponte
località Proh
Via per Oleggio, 1
tel: (0321) 82 62 82
The small wine communes of this northern
vineyard produce excellent Nebbiola
wines that are rarely encountered outside
the locality: Briona, Fara, Sizzano,
Ghemme, and others. They can be
sampled in this country *trattoria*
together with Piedmontese specialities
such as home-made salami, and *rane
dorata.*
Closed Tue
Moderate

13040 Roppolo

Enoteca Regionale della Serra
Via al Castello, no. 2
tel: (0161) 98 501

Hotels

Asti

14100 Asti

Il Reale
(see above)

Salera
Via Monsignor Marello, 19
tel: (0141) 21 18 15
First-class hotel with restaurant.
Expensive

Hotel Palio
Via Cavour, 106
tel: (0141) 34 37 1
Centrally located, without restaurant.
Closed Dec 25–Jan 1
Moderate

14049 Nizza Monferrato

Moderno
Via Tripoli, 17
tel: (0141) 72 19 29
Inexpensive hotel with restaurant.

Alba

12051 Alba

Hotel Savona
Via Roma, 2
tel: (0173) 2381
Comfortable **Moderate** hotel with restaurant.

12050 Barbaresco

Tre Stelle
tel: (0173) 63 19 8
Small **Inexpensive** family hotel with good restaurant serving regional foods and wines. Isolated, in the heart of the wine country.

12050 Serralunga d'Alba

Albergo Ristorante Italia
tel: (0173) 53 12 4
Inexpensive hotel with restaurant in a commanding position in the high, fortified old town in the midst of the Barolo hills overlooking valleys and vineyards.

Where to Get Additional Information

Italian Government Tourist Office
(E.N.I.T.)
630 5th Ave
NY NY 10111
tel: (212) 245–4822

Regional Tourist Offices:

Ente Provinciale per il Turismo
Piazza Alfieri, 34
14100 Asti

Ente Provinciale per il Turismo
Via Savona, 26
15100 Alessandria

Ente Provinciale per il Turismo
Corso Bagni, 8
15011 Acqui Terme

Ente Provinciale per il Turismo
Corso Cavour, 2
28100 Novara

Ente Provinciale per il Turismo
Viale Garibaldi, 92
13100 Vercelli

Ente Provinciale per il Turismo (for information on Alba and the Langhe)
Corso Nizza 17
12100 Cuneo

Ente Provinciale per il Turismo
Via Roma, 226
10100 Torino

For further information on wine and truffle festivals in Asti write to:

Camera di Commercio di Asti
Piazza Medici, 8
14100 Asti

12042 Bra

Hotel Elizabeth
Piazza Giolitti, 8
tel: (0172) 42 24 86
Moderate hotel with bar, but no
restaurant.

Hotel Cavalieri
Piazza Carlo Alberto, 29
tel: (0172) 43 30 4
Albergo with 30 rooms, each with
bathroom. No restaurant.
Inexpensive

12069 Santa Vittoria d'Alba

Soggiorno Santa Vittoria,
al Castello di Santa Vittoria d'Alba
tel: (0172) 47 19 8
Spectacular situation in 11th-century
castle, in this dramatic village above the
hills of the Langhe. 45 rooms, all with
balconies. Restaurant serves regional
specialities and wines.
Hotel closed Jan
Hotel **Inexpensive**
Restaurant **Moderate**

Novarese Vineyards

28100 Novara

La Rotonda
rotonda Massimo d'Azeglio
tel: (0321) 23 69 1
Hotel with garden, bar, and restaurant.
Expensive

13045 Gattinara

Albergo Ristorante Impero
Corso Garibaldi, 83
tel: (0163) 81 23 2
A comfortable hotel/restaurant serving
good country cooking and wines of
Gattinara and other nearby communes.
Closed Fri
Moderate

Camping

14100 Asti
Umberto Cagni, tel: (0141) 27 12 38
Castel Boglione
Antica Contea, tel: (0141) 76 10 0
15100 Alessandria
Val Milana, tel: (0131) 50 24 5
Bastía Mondoví
La Cascina, tel: (0174) 60 18 1
12100 Cuneo
Campeggio Bisalta, tel: (0171) 49 13 34
Agip, tel: (0171) 61 96 1
Galliate (near Novara)
Valverde, tel: (0321) 62 75 6

Bibliography

The Wines of Italy by Cyril Ray, Penguin
1971
Vino by Burton Anderson, Atlantic,
Little, Brown 1980.

───TUSCANY───

The region between Florence and Sienna, interspersed with groves of silver-grey olive trees, punctuated by rows of moody cypress, and over-seen by still-noble estates and farmhouses, is one of the most idyllic, gently harmonious, and timeless of all of Europe's varied wine countries. This is the heart of the Chianti, the region known as Chianti Classico. A tour here offers visits to wine estates and castles; historic villages and medieval towns unchanged since the days when the region's two principal cities were dire rivals, as often as not at war; art and architecture (in this cradle of the Italian Renaissance); and ample opportunities to enjoy regional and local specialities in both humble *trattorie* and elegant and sophisticated restaurants alike.

The region itself is a blend of rural simplicity and refined urbanity. The overwhelming magnificence of both Florence and Sienna stands in contrast to the gentle, quiet, timeless outlook of the surrounding countryside. The

How to Get There

By Car
Tuscany is extremely well served by *autostrade*, making access to the region convenient. The A1, running from Bologna to Rome, passes through Florence, and the A11 from Lucca connects north-west Italy and Livorno with Florence. There are also excellent non-toll roads between Florence and Sienna, and Florence and Arezzo, though the wine tourist will wish to travel less direct routes through the vineyards.

By Plane
Rome or Milan are the two most convenient international airports offering direct, non-stop services from the US. The nearest airport serving Florence is at Pisa; there are direct internal flights to Pisa from both Rome and Milan. There is a direct train from the Pisa airport to Florence. Alternatively, fly to Rome or Milan and continue by train to Florence or Sienna.

By Train
Florence is on the main Paris–Rome route of the 'Palatino' express. TEE trains from Milan reach Florence in about 3 hours 15 minutes.

Local Public Transport
There are frequent trains daily running between Florence, Empoli, Poggibonsi, Sienna, and Montepulciano.

Car Rental Information
Florence
 Avis: Via Borgognissanti, 128/R
  tel: (055) 213629
 Hertz: Via Maso Finiquerra, 33
  tel: (055) 298205
Pisa
 Avis: S Giusto Airport
  tel: (050) 42028
 Hertz: Via Mascagni, 10
  tel: (050) 40878

Maps Touring Club Italiano No 7 (Tuscany and Umbria)

countryside too retains a regal and noble bearing, not simply because the aristocratic estates that once dominated it still remain, but also from an inbred confidence that comes from living in a generous land that provides an abundance of natural riches. For Tuscany, in all its classic beauty, remains a land of almost overwhelming richness. The best beef in Italy comes from the massive, white Chianina cattle bred in valleys south of Arezzo. Vegetables that grow in this fertile garden of Italy – fennel, artichokes, beans, peas, and zucchini – are full-flavoured, and vividly coloured. The hand-made production of sausages such as *finocchiona* (pork salami flavoured with wild fennel seeds) is considered virtually a fine art. The best olive oil in the country, thick and fragrant and an indispensable accessory to fine Tuscan cooking, comes from Lucca. And of course, the best-known wine in Italy comes from these same beautiful hills: Chianti.

The wine itself is a mixture of the humble and the sophisticated. Young Chianti, often sold in its gay rafia-covered flask, is an honest everyday beverage; in its simplicity, it embodies the essence of wine-drinking. Indeed, with a bowl of home-made egg noodles covered with a hearty sauce made from left-over hare *(pappardelle con la lepre)*, with rounds of bread spread with a paste of chicken liver and anchovies, then toasted over the *carbone* (traditional wood-fired oven-stove), with lively conversation and company, or the beauty of the romantic, timeless Tuscan landscape, one could ask for little more. Finer wines are produced from aristocratic estates, some of them owned and run by the same families for generations. Such oak-aged *riserve* Chiantis, produced by traditional methods and in small quantity, are without doubt some of the most noble of all Italian wines.

A tour of the region, and of the other important Tuscan wine towns (the lovely, many-towered San Gimignano, Montalcino, and Montepulciano) can be combined with holidays in Florence or Sienna. One alternative, which gives both greater insight into the land and its people, as well as allows one to relax after the unavoidable hectic rush of sightseeing in important cultural centres, is to rent a self-catering farmhouse or villa in the heart of the wine country. Purchase your wine direct from farmers, and visit cooperatives where virgin olive oil is scooped out from immense terracotta urns; make an evening *passeggiata* through quiet, unspoiled medieval villages like Greve in Chianti, Radda, and Panzano, or simply sit on your veranda, drinking vivid, warm Chianti as the sun dips coolly, quietly over the rich, classic umber hills of Tuscany.

The Wines of Central Tuscany

Brunello di Montalcino The Brunello grape is a variety of the Sangiovese, principal grape of Chianti. In the hills around Montalcino, south of Sienna, it produces magnificent red wine – one of the finest in Italy: robust, intense, and in need of lengthy ageing to bring out its full character and bouquet. One of the finest and most welcoming producers is the family-run estate of Biondi-Santi.

Chianti The *denominazione* of Chianti covers a vast zone spreading over the provinces of Arezzo, Florence, Pisa, Pistoia, and Sienna, and both styles of wine produced, and quality varies considerably. Chianti, however, is always red (there is no such thing as white Chianti), and it is produced from a blend of the following grapes: Sangiovese (50–80%), Caniaolo (10–30%), Trebbiano Toscano and Malvasia di Chianti (10–30%). Additionally, the following regional qualifications indicate superior wines: Chianti Classico, Chianti Putto, Chianti Colli Fiorentini, Chianti Rufina, Chianti Montalbano, Chianti Colli Senesi, Chianti Colli Aretini, and Chianti Colline Pisane.

Chianti Classico The heart of the Chianti country, and the oldest traditional area of production. Approved wines from this central region are always recognizable by the *gallo nero* (black cockerel) symbol affixed around the neck of the bottle. *Riserva* wines must age a minimum of three years; such robust, slightly tannic, mellow red wines accompany roast meats, game, *bistecca fiorentina* and other simple, classic foods of the region.

Chianti Putto While the wines from the Classico region are generally considered some of the finest, they are not exclusively the best of the region. Indeed, because of this, some growers outside the élite Classico zone banded together to form their own *Consorzio* to maintain quality, to protect members' interests, and to promote their wines at home and abroad. Their symbol, the *putto* (a rosy-cheeked cherub), is found on members' approved wines.

Moscatello di Montalcino Sweet, light, sparkling wine from the same area as Brunello.

Vernaccia di San Gimignano Dry, fresh white wine with a characteristic slightly bitter aftertaste, produced from vineyards around this lovely, walled medieval town.

Vino novello, 'novembrino' Fresh, new wine, drunk within weeks or months of the vintage.

Vino Nobile di Montepulciano Fine, dark-red wine from the province of Sienna, blended from the same variety of grapes used to produce Chianti.

Vinsanto Toscano Sweet dessert wine made by the Italian method of drying grapes after they have been harvested to concentrate their sugar content.

Wine Tours

Tours of Tuscany's wine country can begin from either Florence or Sienna. There is not space here to elaborate on all the two cities have to offer, and visitors will no doubt have their own priorities when planning a visit. The wine lover, however, will certainly wish to put aside ample time to spend in the *Enoteca Permanente* for Italian Wines, located in the ancient Fortezza Medicea in Sienna. This remarkable 'wine library' permanently displays an exhaustive range of regional Italian wines to enable both native and foreign visitors to gain a greater appreciation of the wealth and variety of wines produced not just in this region but throughout the country. Fine wines can be sampled by the glass or bottle; wines can be purchased; and snacks such as *crostini, tramezzini, panini*, etc are usually available. The *Enoteca* provides one of the best opportunities for learning about Italian wines; indeed, it is a most pleasant task to make your way through its vast list comparing both different vintages, and wines from different regions, against one another.

Il Mondo del Chianti Classico
– La Via del Chianti

Though the *Via Chiantigiana* extends through the Classico wine region, to tour the wine country one does not necessarily have to follow a wine road from one point to another. Rather, here, as the signs proclaim, one enters *'nel mondo del gallo nero'* – into the world of the black cockerel, symbol of Chianti Classico wine. Due to the nature of the terrain, the area is characterized by a fine network of roads which link small villages and towns with one another. Part of the charm of travelling this timeless wine region lies in simply exploring it at one's own pace.

Our suggested tour extends through the vine-covered hills from Sienna up to Florence. From Sienna, take the N408 which leads, eventually, to Gaiole in Chianti. Before reaching this central town, however, branch off on the N84 to visit the famous Castello di Brolio, not only an important and majestic national monument and home of the noble Ricasoli family since the twelfth century, but also an important landmark in the history of Chianti wine. The castle stands in a dramatic position atop a hill, regally surveying its superb surrounding vineyards and olive groves (and, on a clear day, Sienna in the distance), while below, in the valley of the Arbia, lie stretches of rocky, wild land (the background of a Leonardo canvas), as well as forests of oak, the wood from which is used to make the immense traditional *botti* – barrels – in which this classic wine ages.

While the wines of Brolio have been produced for over a thousand years, and were already appreciated in Britain by the early eighteenth century, the Ricasoli family made its most lasting contribution to the wines that we enjoy today in the nineteenth century. For it was at this time that Barone Bettino Ricasoli, who later became Prime Minister of Italy after Cavour, devoted much time to perfecting methods used to produce Chianti, including discovering the proportions and particular blends of various grapes that give the best result. The Castello di Brolio can be visited without appointment. Unfortunately, however, visits to the winery are only possible for members of the wine trade or other related professionals.

From Brolio, rejoin the N408 and continue north to Gaiole in Chianti, a medieval village which in 1308 fell under Florentine rule. The numerous castles and parish churches which encircle Gaiole bear witness to the village's agricultural and commercial prosperity over the centuries; indeed, it is still an important market centre for the surrounding area, and interesting excursions can be made from Gaiole into the nearby hills. Castagnoli, for example, is an unspoiled village straight out of the Middle Ages (return south on the N408 before branching left on the secondary road that leads past the ancient, angular Castello di Meleto en route to Monte Luco). The Castello di Vertine is also worth a visit.

Continue north on the N408 to Badia a Coltibuono (reached by branching left off the main road). This superb stone compound, parts of which are eight centuries old, consists of a church, convent, farmhouse, and extensive cellars surrounded by vineyards, pine and chestnut woods. The lands surrounding the abbey of Coltibuono were exchanged in 1141 for the Castello di Brolio, a deal struck between the Ricasoli family and the Vallombrosian monks who had settled there. The monks of the abbey are thought to have been the first to cultivate vines in the region, and they have continued to produce fine wines for centuries. The earliest part of the abbey was built in 770, but nothing of this now remains. The bell-tower, built in 1160, is the oldest remaining structure. Today, in addition to fine Chianti Classico, the estate produces its own olive oil, wine vinegar and honey, all of which can be purchased. There is also an excellent adjoining restaurant serving authentic Tuscan dishes.

After visiting Coltibuono, return to the main road, then almost immediately look for another secondary road to the right which leads over the Chianti hills across to Radda in Chianti. Radda, located on the border between the old territories of Florence and Sienna, was often the scene of conflict between the two; in 1415, however, the town was declared capital of the League of Chianti, and thus enjoyed much local influence as the judicial and commercial centre of the surrounding area

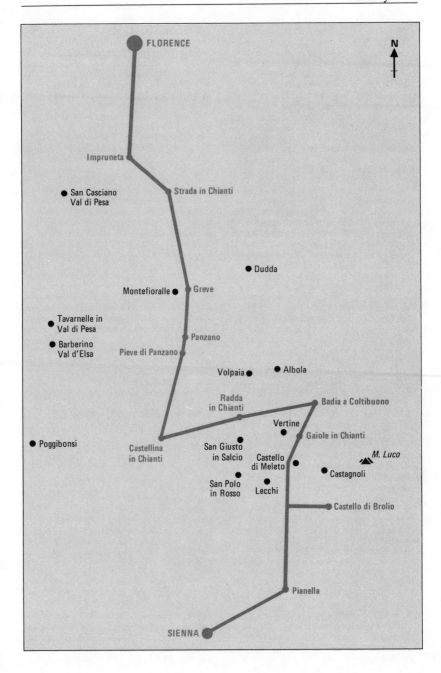

(the self-important town hall, adorned with various coats of arms, dates from this time). Today, the town remains a most important centre of wine production; its central position, now as in the past, makes Radda a junction for surrounding communities and isolated estates and small farms alike. It is interesting to strike out on the minor roads that branch out from Radda to travel through beautiful and isolated wine country to small wine communities such as Volpaia, with its ancient castle and fortifications, to Albola, on the slopes of Monte La Guardia or, to the south, through San Giusto in Salcio, San Polo in Rosso, and Lecchi, and so back to the N408. There are numerous wine producers located in this heart of the region, and it is usually possible to stop and purchase wine direct; the interested visitor who speaks even just a bit of Italian will undoubtedly find a warm welcome.

From Radda in Chianti continue along the N429 that leads eventually to Castellina in Chianti, whose fortified walls that enclose the town were erected at the beginning of the fifteenth century, after it fell under Florentine rule. So recurrent were the wars that ravaged this peaceful region that one can clearly understand why so many fortified towns and villages are perched high on strategic hills. Castellina, dominated by its medieval fortress (from the top there are splendid panoramas) illustrates this most graphically; stroll along the Via delle Volte to observe other characteristic features of that age, such as former residences, as well as the covered walkway which once formed part of the town fortifications. Castellina, like both Radda and Gaiole, was a judicial and commercial centre and today it remains an important town for the surrounding small communities, isolated from one another by the region's rugged yet beautiful hills.

The N429 continues on to Poggibonsi; from there one can visit the important wine town of San Gimignano (see below), before continuing north to Florence by way of Barberino Val d'Elsa and San Casciano Val di Pesa (both important wine towns). Our tour of the Chianti, however, continues along the *Via Chiantigiana*, north through intensely cultivated wine country, and towns such as Pieve di Panzano, Panzano itself (this town's castle was razed by the Ghibellines in 1260; even today, this and other distant events are relived annually in vivid and lively festivals) and so on to Greve in Chianti.

Greve is one of the most important towns in the region, dominated by its superb seventeenth-century piazza *Il Mercatale*, which is surrounded by pleasant arcades and terraces. A great exhibition of the wines of Chianti Classico is held here each September, *Il Mostro Mercato del Chianti Classico*. The importance of this event, traditionally, is more than just commercial, for Greve, which grew up around its market square, has always been a centre where the people from the surrounding communities and countryside gather every week to exchange opinions and compare ideas concerning agricultural methods, as well as to discuss political and economic problems. These meetings, the so-called *riunioni di Greve*, continue to be important. There is a small *enoteca* in Greve which permanently displays an exhaustive range of Chianti Classico; the wines can be purchased.

Excursions from Greve can be made to nearby Montefioralle (which boasts the house of Amerigo Vespucci, as proud inhabitants like to point out) and to Dudda, while continuing north on the *Via Chiantigiana* (N222) leads to Strada in Chianti. After Strada, branch off left to Impruneta, an interesting town with Etruscan origins. The town gained importance in the sixteenth century as a shrine to the Virgin Mary; the Basilica to the Virgin is an important monument. The town is also well known for its distinctive terracotta work, and visitors may wish to purchase pieces.

Either continue on to Florence (the outskirts of that great city are soon reached) or else make a circular tour back in the direction of Sienna via San Casciano Val di Pesa, Tavarnelle Val di Pesa, and Poggibonsi.

Additional Wine Tours

Chianti Classico is only one of seven types of Chianti produced in Tuscany, though it is generally considered the finest. The other Chianti regions are Chianti Colli Aretini (from the hills north and west of Arezzo); Chianti Colli Fiorentini (from the hills south of Florence and north of the Classico region); Chianti Colline Pisane (an area of vineyards south of Pisa and Pontedera); Chianti Colli Senesi (from the hills both to the east and west of Sienna, and south of the Classico region); Chianti Montalbano (from vineyards south of Pistoia); and Chianti Rufina (a small but highly-regarded areas east of Florence and centred around the little town of Rufina). In addition to Chianti, other notable Tuscan wine tours encompass the area producing Vernaccia di San Gimignano, Brunello di Montalcino, and Vino Nobile di Montepulciano.

The following suggested tours begin in either Florence or Sienna.

1. **Chianti Colli Fiorentini and Chianti Rufina** Florence, Fiesole, Santa Brigida, Molin del Piano, Rufina, Pomino, Borselli, Florence (approximately 90 km/56 miles).

2. **Chianti Colli Fiorentini, Chianti, Chianti Colli Pisane** Florence, Roveta, Lastra a Signa, Montelupo, Empoli, San Miniato, Palaia, Peccioli, Terricciola,

Casciana Terme, Crespina, Pisa (approximately 139 km/87 miles).

3. **Chianti Montalbano** Florence, Montelupo, Empoli, Cerreto Guidi, Lazzeretto, Lamporecchio, San Baronto, Pistoia (approximately 72 km/45 miles).

4. **Chianti Colli Senesi** Sienna, Monteriggioni, Colle di Val d'Elsa, Poggibonsi (visit the Castello di Strozzavolpe), San Gimignano (approximately 52 km/32 miles).

5. **Chianti Colli Senesi, Chianti, Vino Nobile di Montepulciano** Sienna, San Gusmè, Castelnuove Berardenga, Lucignano, Sinalunga, Torrita di Sienna, Montepulciano, Chianciano Terme (fashionable spa) (approximately 104 km/65 miles).

6. **Chianti, Brunello di Montalcino** Sienna, Asciano, Abbey of Monte Oliveto, Torrenieri, Montalcino, Sienna (approximately 136 km/85 miles).

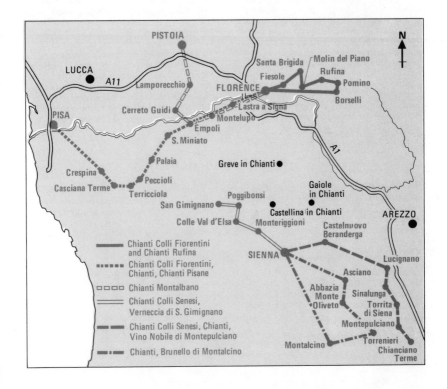

The wine tourist will certainly want to visit these three important centres:

San Gimignano The hills around this lovely and popular town are covered in vines that produces dry, slightly bitter Vernaccia di San Gimignano, possibly the best white wine in Tuscany. The town itself, like so many others in this compact and wonderful area, has managed to keep the appearance and atmosphere of the fourteenth century – it is a singular and marvellous example of medieval town planning. Encircled by its ramparts, its moody, narrow streets are lined with old villas and palaces; of the 72 towers that once stood in the town, 15 still remain, tribute to the glorious age of the city-states of central Italy. While there are numerous monuments, churches, and examples of Florentine architecture to explore, what is most striking about San Gimignano is that the town itself is in total harmony with the surrounding Tuscan countryside.

Montalcino The town of Montalcino lies some thirty miles south-east of Sienna, a noble and fitting home for one of Italy's greatest wines, Brunello di Montalcino, a rich, intense red wine that is exceptionally long-lived (even the youngest examples must legally be aged in wood for a minimum of four years; the greatest vintages last upwards of 50 years, while bottles over 100 years old are said to be still excellent). 'Il Greppo', the estate of the Biondi-Santi family, one of the finest producers in the region, can be visited, though, as with most producers here, an appointment is necessary. Montalcino itself is perched on top of a hill that dominates the valleys of Orcia, Arbia, and Ombrone, a former Etruscan and Roman town with a strongly medieval character. Indeed, in the fourteenth to sixteenth centuries, the walled town, with its powerful Rocca fortress, was one of the strongholds of the Siennese Republic. Like so many of the other hill towns of Tuscany, Montalcino should be explored on foot. The views that extend over the countryside from streets that ascend and descend from the old town within the existing ramparts, are magnificent, and buildings such as the Town Hall are both atmospheric and characteristic of medieval Siennese architecture. A lively festival takes place on the last Sunday in October: the Festival of the Thrush, during which an archery contest takes place between the ancient districts of the town. At that time, too, there are of course numerous gastronomic 'manifestations' to accompany the town's finest, as well as its everyday, wines. The nearby Cistercian abbey of Sant'Antonio is worth a visit.

Montepulciano Vino Nobile di Montepulciano is another celebrated Tuscan red wine produced from grapes grown on the slopes of the municipality of Montepulciano, south-east of Sienna. Like Montalcino, it is a fortified town, and it is a pleasant task to sample the wine in old bars in the *città antica*, or while sitting out in the irregular-shaped Piazza Grande.

Wine Producers

The Chianti is primarily a region of small estates producing quality wines in limited quantity; most of the following producers request that an appointment be made in advance. Either telephone, notify by postcard, or have your hotel make arrangements. In addition to the wine producers listed below (some of whom also produce and sell their own Tuscan olive oil), the region's *enoteche* provide tasting and purchasing opportunities.

53010 Castagnoli in Chianti

Fattoria Valtellina
tel: (0577) 73 10 05
Chianti Classico *riserva*, Chianti Classico, Vin Santo, *vino bianco, extra vergine* olive oil.
Open daily 9–20h
Appointment preferable.
Max 6 pers.
English spoken.

Castello di Brolio

Casa Vinicola Barone Ricasoli
Piazza Vittorio Veneto, 1
Florence
tel: (055) 26 36 81
Visits to the winery of this famous estate are possible only for people connected with the wine trade in some way, though the castle, a national monument, is open to all.

Mon–Fri 8–17h by appointment.
Max 50 pers.
English spoken.

53013 Gaiole in Chianti

Agricoltori del Chianti Geografico
tel: (0577) 74 94 89
Chianti Classico, Vernaccia di San
Gimignano, Vin Santo, *vino bianco*
Mon–Fri 9–12h; 15–17h
Appointment preferable.
Min 3, max 50 pers.
English spoken.

Badia a Coltibuono
tel: (0577) 74 94 98
Chianti Classico *riserva*, Chianti Classico,
Vin Santo, *grappa, extra vergine* olive oil,
honey, and red wine vinegar.
Open daily. Visits to the wine cellars by
appointment.
Max 20 pers.
English spoken.
Charge for *degustazione*.

53017 Radda in Chianti

Cantina della Fattoria di Castelvecchi
tel: (0577) 73 80 50
Chianti Classico, *vino bianco*
Open daily.
Appointment preferable.
Max 20 pers.

50020 San Polo in Chianti

Azienda Agraria Fattoria Vitiano
Via Vitiano, 44
tel: (055) 85 50 37
Chianti Classico, Vin Santo, *vino bianco*
Open Mon–Fri 16–18h
Appointment necessary.
Max 30 pers.
Charge for *degustazione*.

50028 Tavarnelle Val di Pesa

Fattoria Poggio Romita
Via della Commenda, 10
tel: (055) 80 77 253
Chianti DOC, *vino bianco*, Vin Santo, *extra
vergine* olive oil
Open Saturday afternoon by appointment.
Max 10 pers.

50021 Barberino Val d'Elsa

Fattoria Pasolini dall'Onda Borghese
tel: (055) 80 75 019
Chianti *riserva*, Chianti DOC, Bianco delle
Colline Toscane
Mon–Fri 10–12h; 15–17h

Appointment necessary.
Max 50 pers.
English spoken.

56034 Casciana Terme

Casa Vinicola Barone Ostini
Sant'Ermo
tel: (0587) 64 62 88
Chianti DOC, *vino novello*
Open Mon–Sat
Appointment necessary.
Max 10 pers.

53100 Castelnuovo Berardenga

Casa Vinicola Pagni S.r.l.
tel: (0577) 35 90 67
Chianti Classico, Chianti DOC
Open Mon–Fri 9–12h30; 15–18h30
Appointment necessary.
Max 20 pers.

50065 Pontassieve

Chianti Ruffino SpA
Via Aretina, 42/44
tel: (055) 83 02 307
Chianti Classico, Chianti, Orvieto
Tuesday and Thursday 8–12h; 14–17h
Appointment preferable.
Max 50 pers.
English spoken.
Charge for *degustazione*.
Chianti Ruffino have their own tavern in
the village, Ristorante 'Girarrosto', serving
local foods with, of course, their own
wines.

53048 Sinalunga

Azienda Agricola Farneta dei F.lli Pomarici
Scrofiano – località Farneta, 161
tel: (0577) 60 485
Chianti Putto, *vino bianco*
Mon–Fri 8–17h
Appointment necessary.
English spoken.

50042 Carmignano

Casa Contini Bonacossi
Tenuta di Capezzana
Via Capezzana
tel: (055) 87 06 005
Villa di Capezzana, Chianti Montalbano
DOC, *vino bianco & rosato*, Vin Santo
Mon–Fri.
Appointment necessary.
Max 60 pers.
English spoken.
Charge for *degustazione*.

53010 Vagliagli

Fattoria Le Lodoline
tel: (0577) 32 26 19
Chianti Classico, *vino bianco, extra vergine*
olive oil
Open daily.
English spoken.

50059 Vinci

Fattoria Montalbano
Via Provinciale Petroio, 25
tel: (0571) 50 82 57
Chianti DOC, *vino bianco*, Vin Santo, *extra
vergine* olive oil
Open daily by appointment.
Max 100 pers.
English spoken.

50050 Marcignana per Bassa

Tenuta di Colle Alberti
Cerreto Guidi
tel: (0571) 58 10 23
Chianti DOC
Open by appointment.
Max 20 pers.

53032 Castellina Scalo

Casa Vinicola Alberto Bartali e Figli
Via E Berrettini, 5
tel: (0577) 30 40 49
Chianti Classico, Chianti, Bianco
Toscano
Open Mon–Fri
Appointment necessary.
Max 10 pers.

52025 Montevarchi

Agricola Scráfana
Via Vicinale della Consuma, 14
tel: (055) 98 14 19
Chianti DOC, *vino bianco*
Open daily by appointment.
English spoken.

50054 Fucecchio

Fattoria Montèllori
Via Pistoiese, 136
tel: (0571) 20 041
Chianti DOC, Trebbiano, *'novembrino' (vino
giovane), vino spumante (méthode
champenoise)*
Mon–Sat 8–17h
Appointment preferable.
English spoken.

50060 Molin del Piano

Fattoria Torre a Decima SpA
tel: 83 17 804
Chianti DOC, *vino bianco & rosato*
Saturday 9–17h
Appointment necessary.
Max 40 pers.
English spoken.

51039 Quarrata

Fattoria di Lucciano
tel: (0573) 72 009
Chianti Montalbano DOC, Vin Santo, *vino
bianco*
By appointment.
English spoken.

50025 Montespertoli

Fattoria Castello di Poppiano
tel: (055) 82 315
Chianti Colli Fiorentini, Vin Santo, *vino
bianco*
Open daily
Appointment necessary.
Max 200 pers.
English spoken.
Charge for *degustazione*.

53037 San Gimignano

Fattoria Ponte a Rondolino
Località Casale, 19
tel: (0577) 94 01 43
Vernaccia di San Gimignano, Chianti, *vino
spumante*
Open Mon–Fri.
Appointment preferable.
The *fattoria* also runs a restaurant, open
daily except Mon eve, Tue.
tel: (0577) 94 10 29 for reservations.

Azienda Agricola Pietraserena di Arrigoni
Località Casale, No 5
tel: (0577) 94 00 83
Vernaccia di San Gimignano, Chianti
Open daily by appointment.
Max 30 pers.

Casa Vinicola Bruni
Porta al Cerchio, 61
tel: (0577) 94 04 42
Vernaccia di San Gimignano, Chianti
Classico, Chianti DOC
Mon–Fri 9–12h; 14–18h
Appointment necessary.
Min 5, max 40 pers.

S A P Società Agricola Pietrafitta
Fattoria di Pietrafitta
Località Cortennano
tel: (0577) 94 03 32

Vernaccia di San Gimignano, Chianti
Putto, Vin Santo, *extra vergine* olive oil
Mon–Fri 8–17h
Appointment necessary.
English spoken.

53024 Montalcino

Fattoria dei Barbi e del Casato
tel: (0577) 84 82 77
Brunello di Montalcino *gran riserve, riserve,*
Vin Santo, *vino da tavola, grappa*
Open Mon–Fri 8–12h; 13h30–17h30
Appointment necessary.
Max 20 pers.
English-speaking guide by arrangement.

Azienda Agraria 'Il Greppo'
Biondi-Santi
tel: (0577) 84 80 87
Brunello di Montalcino *gran riserve, riserve,*
vino da tavola
Open Mon–Fri 10–12h

Max 20 pers.
Appointment necessary.
Charge for *degustazione*.

53045 Montepulciano

Cantina Contucci
Via del Teatro, 1
tel: (0578) 77 00 6
Vino Nobile di Montepulciano, Chianti
Colli Senesi, Vin Santo, own-produced
olive oil.
Open daily.
Appointment necessary.
Max 30 pers.

Tenuta S Agnese di Fanetti
Via Antica Chiusina, 15
tel: (0578) 77 26 6
Vino Nobile di Montepulciano, Chianti
Colli Senesi, Vin Santo
Open April–Sept; Mon–Fri 9–12h; 15–18h
Appointment necessary.
Max 30 pers.

Enoteche

53100 Sienna

Enoteca Italica Permanente
Fortezza Medicea
tel: (0577) 28 84 97
Open daily 15–24h
Exhibition of over 500 wines; vast range of
wines for tasting and sale; light snacks
available.
Some English spoken.

Fattorie Associate del Gallo Nero
Bottega del Vino
Via della Sapienza, 35
also adjoining Ristorante Al Marsili
Enoteca del Gallo Nero (restaurant of the
Fattorie Associate), Via del Castoro, 3

53013 Gaiole in Chianti

Enoteca Montagnani
Via Baccio Bandinelli, 9
tel: (0577) 74 95 17

53011 Castellina in Chianti

Bottega del Vino Gallo Nero
Via della Rocca, 10
tel: (0577) 74 02 47

50020 Panzano

Enoteca del Chianti Classico
Via G da Verrazzano, 8–10
tel: (055) 85 21 10

50022 Greve in Chianti

Enoteca del Gallo Nero
Piazzetta S Croce, 8
tel: (055) 85 32 97
Open daily except Wed 9h30–12h30;
15h30–19h30
Extensive range of Chianti Classico
Max 50 pers.
Some English spoken.

50026 San Casciano Val di Pesa

Cantinetta del Nonno
Via 4 Novembre, 18
tel: (055) 82 05 70
Vast selection of Chianti Classico, and also
grilled specialities served during
mealtimes only.
Closed Wed

50100 Florence

Cantinone del Gallo Nero
Via S Spirito, 6r
tel: (055) 21 88 98
Selection of Chianti Classico
Closed Mon

Wine Festivals

1st two Suns in May	Iris Festival Flowers, wine, oil, honey, 'gastronomic village', evening dancing. For information telephone (055) 85 51 10	S. Polo in Chianti
May or June	*Firzenze a Tavola* Large and important annual food and wine fair, also displaying fine crystal, china, etc. For information telephone (055) 22 23 50	Fortezza da Basso, Florence
End of May/ Early June	*Sagra del Pinolo* Pinenut festival. For information telephone (0577) 74 60 31	Chiesanuova (Ama)
Early Sep	Wine Festival For further information telephone (0577) 35 90 80	San Gusme
Mid Sep	*Mostra Mercato del Chianti Classico* The most important festival in the region. 'Gastronomic village', and wine for sale. Fireworks display on final Sunday evening. For further information and exact date, telephone Consorzio Chianti Classico in London 01-734-8927 or in Florence (055) 22 93 51/2/3	Greve in Chianti
Last Sun in Oct	Thrush Festival	Montalcino

Regional Gastronomy

Crostini di fegatini Tuscan appetizers consisting of rounds of bread spread with a paste made from chicken liver and anchovies, toasted over an open fire: delicious with Chianti. *Crostini* can be also spread with other toppings, such as tomato sauce or anchovy butter.

Pappardelle con la lepre Wide, flat home-made noodles served with a rich gamy sauce made from left-over hare.

Ribollita Characteristic regional bean and vegetable *minestrone* that is 'reboiled' to further thicken and concentrate its flavours.

Incavolata Cabbage and bean soup.

Salvie fritte Deep-fried sage 'sandwiches', served as part of a platter of *antipasti*.

Polenta fritta Characteristic dense corn mush, deep-fried until crunchy, and served as an *antipasto*.

Finocchiona Type of Tuscan salami flavoured with wild fennel seeds.

Bistecca alla fiorentina Perhaps the most famous dish of the region: an enormous t-bone or rib steak of Chianina beef (it should be *vitellone* – neither beef nor veal) traditionally cooked over the *carbone*, a wood-fired stove.

Pollo alla diavola Chicken marinated in olive oil, lemon juice, and coarsely crushed sage leaves and peppercorns, cooked over a wood fire.

Fritto misto Mixed platter of meats and vegetables, including calves' brains, sweetbreads, chicken breast, zucchini, cauliflower, and artichokes dipped in light batter or egg and breadcrumbs, then deep-fried.

Arrosto girato Chicken, rabbit, beef, lamb, or game birds spit-roasted over a wood fire.

Faraona Guinea fowl.

Fagiano Pheasant.

Stracotto alla fiorentina Beef stewed in Chianti.

Trippa alla fiorentina Tripe simmered with tomatoes, wine, and seasonings.

Maiale con cavolo nero Loin of pork stewed with kale.

Petti di pollo Tender chicken breasts cooked simply in wine and lemon juice.

Fagioli nel fiasco White haricot beans, boiled in a Chianti flask (a method which preserves the flavour of the beans), then seasoned with olive oil, black pepper, and fresh sage.

Fagioli all'uccelletto Beans cooked with tomatoes and sage (so-named because this is also a manner of cooking small game birds).

Funghi porcini Wild *boletus* mushrooms, either used as a flavouring, or else served fresh when in season.

Panzanella Florentine tomato, onion, and bread salad.

Salsicce e fagioli Hearty country dish of home-made sausages and beans.

Cacciucco Mediterranean fish soup available on the Tuscan coast.

Cieche Elvers fried in olive oil and sage, a speciality of Pisa.

Panforte Flat, hard spiced cake from Sienna.

Castagnacci Characteristic desserts made from chestnut flour.

Buccellato Ring-shaped fruit bread from Lucca.

Restaurants

53100 Sienna

Ristorante al Mangia
Piazza del Campo, 42
tel: (0577) 28 11 21
Located in the famous *piazza*, a **Moderate** restaurant serving Siennese specialities such as *trippa alla senese, lombatina di vitella al chianti*.
Closed Mon

Ristorante Tullio ai Tre Cristi
Vicolo Provenzano, 1
tel: (0577) 28 06 08
Siennese specialities and home-produced Chianti.
Open Tue–Sun 12–15h; 19–22h
Inexpensive to **Moderate**

Vagliagli Castelnuovo Berga

La Taverna
tel: (0577) 32 25 32
Home-made pasta such as *tagliatelle al porcini* is a speciality of this **Inexpensive** to **Moderate** restaurant.
Closed Mon.

53013 Gaiole in Chianti

La Pineta
Monteluco T.V.
tel: (0577) 74 94 51

Inexpensive *trattoria* with gardens, specializing in game and traditional *cucina toscana*. Open all year.
The restaurant also has a hotel with 18 rooms.

Badia a Coltibuono
tel: (0577) 74 94 24
Wine produced on the premises of the historic abbey is accompanied by authentic Tuscan dishes such as *stracotto con funghi porcini* and home-made pasta.
Closed first fortnight in September; Mon
Expensive

53011 Castellina in Chianti

Antica Trattoria la Torre
Piazza del Comune
tel: (0577) 74 02 36
Specialities include *stracotto con sformati di verdura, faraona*, and *formaggi del Chianti*.
Closed Sept 1–Sept 10; Fri
Inexpensive to **Moderate**

Conca d'Oro
Il Pestello
Sant'Antonio al Ponte
tel: (0577) 74 02 15
Home-made *pappardelle* and *ribollita* are specialities of this **Inexpensive** restaurant.
Closed Aug 15–Sept 15; Wed

50022 Greve in Chianti

Da Carlino
tel: (055) 85 81 93
Inexpensive *trattoria* serving *ribollita, arrosti misti, pomodori al forno* in the garden in good weather.
Closed Oct 1–March 31; Wed

Cantinetta di Rignana
Fattoria di Rignana
tel: (055) 85 20 65
It is essential to book in advance for this restaurant connected with the wine estate of Fattoria di Rignana. Specialities include *crostini in 16 modi, cannelloni con sugo e ricotta di Rignana* and others. Chianti Classico from the estate.
Closed Nov; Mon
Inexpensive to **Moderate**

Giovanni da Verrazzano
tel: (055) 85 31 89
Restaurant/hotel in the heart of the Chianti region, serving typical *cucina*, including *panzanella, ribollita, trippa*, together with a wide selection of Chianti Classico.
Closed Jan 15–Feb 15; Mon (advisable to book)
Inexpensive to **Moderate**

San Donato in Poggio

Villa Francesca
Località Cortine
tel: (055) 80 72 849
The *trattoria* of the wine estate of the
same name serves specialities such as
pappardelle con la lepre and spit roasts,
together with various vintages of its own
wines.
It is essential to book in advance.
Moderate

Strada in Chianti

Trattoria Bartoli
tel: (055) 85 80 15
Bistecca alla fiorentina, pollo fritto and roast
lamb are some of the dishes served in this
Moderate *trattoria*.
Open Sun only

Mercatale Val di Pesa

L'Antica Trattoria
tel: (055) 82 12 28
Traditional Tuscan grills and home-made
pasta.
Closed Tue eve; Wed
Inexpensive to **Moderate**

50028 Tavarnelle Val di Pesa

Torricelle
tel: (055) 80 81 672
Inexpensive restaurant serving *penne
piccanti, arrosti misti* and home-made
desserts.
Closed Wed

53035 Monterrigioni

Ristorante Il Pozzo
Piazza Roma, 2
tel: (0577) 30 41 27
Regional cooking and local wines.
Closed Sun eve; Mon
Open 12–15h; 20–22h
Moderate

53204 Montalcino

Taverna dei Barbi
Località Podernovi – Fattoria Barbi
tel: (0577) 84 82 77
Own-produced Brunello served with local
foods.
Closed Wed
Inexpensive to **Moderate**

53045 Montepulciano

Ristorante Il Cantuccio
Via delle Cantine, 1–2
tel: (0578) 77 87 0
Pasta made by hand daily; other typical
Tuscan foods include meats spit-roasted
over a wood fire.
Closed Mon
Open 9–16h; 19–24h
Inexpensive

52100 Arezzo

Buca di San Francesco
Via San Francesco, 1
tel: (0575) 23 27 1
Restaurant situated in a *cantina* of a
14th-century *palazzo* decorated with
frescoes.
Closed Mon eve; Tue
Closed 12–14h30; 19–21h30
Moderate

Florence

Enoteca Pinchiorri
Via Ghibellina, 87
tel: (055) 26 36 53
It is essential to book in advance for this
popular, **Very Expensive**
restaurant/*enoteca* offering innovative and
traditional cuisine, and a vast selection of
not only Tuscan, but wines from
throughout the great regions of Italy and
elsewhere.
Closed Sun

Ristorante Il Podere
Via Incontri, 42
tel: (055) 41 31 84
Set in a 14th-century villa in the hills above
Florence, this **Moderate** characteristic
restaurant serves Florentine specialities
and grills.
Closed Wed

Trattoria Antico Fattore
Via Lambertesca, 1/3r
tel: (055) 26 12 15
Typical Florentine *trattoria* serving rustic
specialities such as *ribollita, trippa alla
fiorentina, stracotto*.
Closed July–Sept; Sat; Sun
Inexpensive to **Moderate**

Ristorante La Botteghina Rossa
Via Alfani, 24r
Simple **Inexpensive** restaurant serving
good country specialities with fresh
seasonal ingredients.
Closed Aug; Sun

Calenzano
(outskirts of Florence)

Bar-Trattoria Tre Caci
Via Baldanzese, 98
tel: (055) 88 79 403
Within walking distance of the 'Autosole'
campsite, this *trattoria* serves authentic
Tuscan specialities, such as *bistecca alla
fiorentina* cooked over traditional *carbone*.
Inexpensive to **Moderate**

Hotels

53100 Sienna

Park Hotel (part of CIGA group)
Via di Marciano, 16
tel: (0577) 44 803
15th-century *palazzo* 2 km from city centre.
Each of the 46 rooms have bathrooms, and
there are lovely gardens, swimming pool,
and restaurant. The hotel's own farm
supplies it with fruit, olive oil, fresh
vegetables, poultry, and, of course,
wine.
Open all year
Expensive

Villa Scacciapensieri (north 3 km)
tel: (0577) 41 44 2
Classic Tuscan villa, with views over
Tuscan hills and Sienna.
Hotel has swimming pool and tennis
courts, and an elegant restaurant.
Hotel closed Nov–March
Restaurant closed Wed
Moderate

Pensione Palazzo Ravizza
Pian dei Mantellini, 34
tel: (0577) 28 04 62
Five minutes walk from the city centre,
this peaceful 17th-century *palazzo* has 28
rooms, garden with wonderful views of
the Tuscan hills, and restaurant.
Open all year
Moderate

53017 Radda in Chianti

Albergo Ristorante 'La Villa Miranda'
tel: (0577) 73 80 21
Built in 1842, this hotel has restaurant
serving *chiantigiana* specialities such as
ravioli con nostra ricotta, arrosto girato, and
others.
Open all year
Inexpensive to **Moderate**

53011 Castellina in Chianti

Villa Casalecchi
(1 km south of town)
tel: (0577) 74 02 40
Old Tuscan villa with swimming pool and
restaurant serving classic Tuscan *cucina*.
Hotel closed end of Oct–end of March
Expensive

50020 Panzano in Chianti

Villa Le Barone
tel: (055) 85 22 15
15-room hotel located in the former villa of
the famous Della Robbia family, with
garden, swimming pool, and restaurant
specializing in classic *chiantigiana* cooking.
Half or full board only and minimum stay
of three days.
Open Easter–Oct 1
Moderate

53034 Colle Val d'Elsa

Ristorante 'La Vecchia Cartiera'
Via Oberdan, 5
tel: (0577) 92 11 07
Moderate hotel with restaurant
Hotel closed May
Restaurant closed Mon; Sun eve

53048 Sinalunga

Locanda dell'Amorosa
Località l'Amorosa
tel: (0577) 69 49 7
Built within a 14th-century castle; each
room has panoramic views and bathroom.
The old stables now house the restaurant
which serves classic specialities such as
*ribollita, ravioli di ricotta, bistecca alla
fiorentina*.
Hotel open all year
Restaurant closed Mon eve; Tue
Open 12h30–14h30; 20–21h30
Expensive

53037 San Gimignano

Albergo la Cisterna – Ristorante le Terraze
Piazza della Cisterna
tel: (0577) 94 03 28
Hotel with restaurant serving local and
regional dishes.
Panoramic views from the terraces.
Hotel open all year
Restaurant closed Tue; Wed eve
Open 12–14h30; 19h45–21h30
Moderate

Hotel Bel Soggiorno
Via S Giovanni, 89
tel: (0577) 94 03 75
Quiet hotel with spectacular views. 30
rooms each with bathroom. Restaurant
uses its own products, including
home-produced olive oil.
Hotel open all year
Restaurant closed Mon
Inexpensive to **Moderate**

Hotel Pescille
Località Pescille
tel: (0577) 94 03 75
Quiet, comfortable hotel converted from
an old Tuscan farmhouse.
Open all year.
Inexpensive to **Moderate**

53045 Montepulciano

Residence S Albino
Via delle Terme, 36
S Albino
tel: (0578) 79 013
Mini-apartments with swimming pool.
Open all year
Moderate

Figline Val d'Arno
Norcenni Girasole Club
Via Norcenni, 7, tel: (055) 95 96 66
Cavríglia
Piano Orlando
Località Piano Orlando, tel: (055) 96 74 22
Tavarnuzze
Internazionale Firenze
at Boltai, Via S Cristoforo, tel: (055) 20 20
445
Chíusi
Degli Ulivi
at Macciano, tel: (0578) 27 03 2

Bibliography

The Wines of Italy by Cyril Ray, Penguin
1971
Vino by Burton Anderson, Atlantic,
Little, Brown 1980

Villas and Farmhouses

An enjoyable way to explore the Chianti
country is to take a self-catering farmhouse
or villa in the heart of the wine country.
Private villas are often advertised at
favourable prices, while tour operators
offer inclusive packages.

Camping

Sienna
Colleverde
Str Scacciapensieri, 37
tel: (0577) 28 00 44
Castellina in Chianti
Luxor Quies
Località Trasqua, tel: (0577) 74 03 47
San Gimignano
Boschetto
at Santa Lucía, tel: (0577) 94 03 52
Florence
Autosole
at Calenzano, exit autostrada
Prato-Calenzano, tel: (055) 88 79 641
Villa di Camerata
Viale Righi 2, tel: (055) 61 03 00

Where to Get Additional Information

Italian Government Tourist Office
(E.N.I.T.)
630 5th Ave
NY NY 10111
tel: (212) 245–4822

Ente Provinciale per il Turismo di Siena
Via di Città, 5
53100 Siena
tel: (0577) 47 051

Ente Provinciale per il Turismo di Firenze
Via A Manzoni, 16
50121 Firenze
tel: (055) 67 88 431

Consorzio Vino Chianti Classico
Via de'Serragli, 146
50124 Firenze
tel: (055) 22 93 51

Consorzio Chianti Putto
Lungarno Corsini, 4
50123 Firenze
tel: (055) 21 23 33

VENETO

The vineyards of Veneto, like those found throughout Italy, blend into the surrounding countryside, in perfect harmony with a gentle land. On hills above Verona, near walled medieval towns such as Soave, and above lovely lakeside villages like Lazise and Bardolino, vines thrive on grassy slopes and terraces. Trained into pergolas, they spread wide, dappled 'ceilings' of foliage, creating grassy shaded corridors in which to stretch out after a long midday meal, or one glass of wine too many.

The countryside is quiet; the squared-off towers that rise above the smallest, most modest village, the remains of solid fortified town ramparts, all attest to a grander, more violent age than ours – an age when the mighty Venetian Republic ruled over not only most of north-east Italy, but also parts of present-day Yugoslavia and the eastern Mediterranean. If today its capital city (from which the region gains its name) is no longer a force to be reckoned with, the magical spell of Venice remains evident throughout the region, in the architecture of municipal buildings and villas dotted across the country, and in styles of cooking. Above all, from the vineyards of Verona across the flat plain of the Po Valley to the gentle slopes below the Austrian and Italian Alps where vines ripen near towns like Treviso and Conegliano, one senses a feeling of well-fed contentment, of satisfaction and utter peace.

Veneto is one of Italy's most important wine-producing regions, the home of both well-known DOC wines exported throughout the world (Soave, Bardolino, and Valpolicella), as well as vast quantities of humbler everyday table wines known only by the grape used to produce them, Merlot del Veneto, Tocai del Veneto and Riesling Italico, for example. Many small farmers continue to make and vinify their own wine, even if only for their own consumption. The most important wine-growing areas of this prolific region centre on the hills that rise above Lake Garda north of Verona and, further east and north of Venice, the distinguished vineyards in the province of Treviso.

A tour of the wine regions of Veneto, therefore, can be combined with a holiday based in either Venice or Verona. On the other hand, one might choose to stay in hotels or campsites on Lake Garda (making frequent forays into the wine country above the lake), or to hide out in delightful inland towns such as Bassano del Grappa and Asolo. In addition to touring the vineyards of Verona and Treviso, we also provide an appetizer for a most interesting wine region which lies beyond our present scope but within the larger regional area known as the Tre Veneti (Three Venezias), that of Friuli-Venezia Giulia.

Though the wines of Friuli are not well-known abroad, knowledgeable Italians count them as among the finest in Italy. There is not (as yet) a sign-posted wine road through this region's lovely wine country, but we include a little background information on the area and its wines, as well as some additional addresses of wine producers that welcome visitors.

The Wines of Veneto and Friuli-Venezia Giulia

Bardolino Terraced vineyards rise from the shores of Lake Garda above the tiny resort villages of Bardolino, Lazise, Garda and others to produce a light, bright, popular red wine meant to be drunk young. Wine from the central Classico zone is generally considered the best; the adjective *'superiore'* applies to wine with a minimum alcohol content of 11.5%, and which has aged for a minimum of one year.

Bianco di Custoza Light, dry white wine produced from vineyards west of Verona and south of Lake Garda. DOC zone overlaps with zone for Bardolino.

Cabernet The classic grape of Bordeaux has been planted in Veneto to great success, particularly in the Piave vineyards around Treviso. Sometimes blended with Merlot, it produces a mellow 'claret'-style wine that is an ideal accompaniment to

How to Get There

By Car
The vineyards of Verona are flanked by a major *autostrada*, the A4, making this delightful region within easy driving distance of Venice, Milan, or Turin. The vineyards of Treviso are but a short and lovely drive north of Venice (N13 or A27). The wine regions of Friuli are just beyond Conegliano (continue to Pordenone and Udine). The A4 east from Venice leads, eventually, to Trieste.

By Plane
There are direct, non-stop flights from the US to Milan. Alitalia have flights from Rome and other major cities to Milan and Venice. Connecting flights from the US to Venice are available on various airlines.

By Train
Verona is located along a major rail route, thus connecting it with Turin and Milan to the west, and Venice and Trieste to the east. Trains from Rome and Florence lead to Verona via Bologna, while Treviso and Conegliano are but a short train ride from Venice. There are direct trains to Verona from Paris. Romantics (and millionaires) can take the Venice Simplon-Orient Express from London or Paris to Venice.

Local Public Transport
Lake Garda, Verona, and Vicenza are all on the main rail line from Milan to Venice. There is also a local rail line on Lake Garda, with stops at Garda and Sirmione. Conegliano and Trieste are on the main rail route between Venice and Vienna. Local bus services are good, but as in most regions it is advisable to have the use of a car to explore vineyards and wine villages.

Car Rental Information
Verona
  Avis: Villa Franca Airport
      tel: (045) 26 63 6
      Stazione Porta Nuova
      tel: (045) 26 63 6
  Hertz: Villa Franca Airport
      tel: (045) 25 83 2
      Stazione FF SS
      tel: (045) 25 83 2
Venice
  Avis: Marco Polo Airport
      tel: (041) 96 40 30
      Piazzale Roma, 496-H
      tel: (041) 25 82 5
  Hertz: Marco Polo Airport
      tel: (041) 96 40 60
      Piazzale Roma, 496-E
      tel: (041) 23 00 0

Maps Touring Club Italiano no. 4 (Venice and NE Italy)

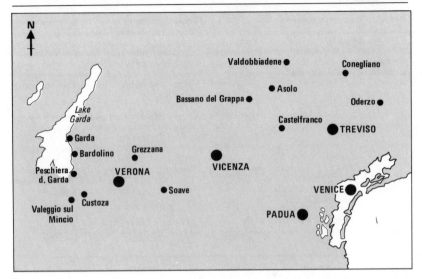

roast meats, and small game birds served with *polenta*. In Friuli, good weighty examples come from the district of Collio.

Chiaretto Classico Produced in the delimited region of Bardolino: an extremely pale red wine which is fresh, slightly *frizzante*, and with a firm, flinty dryness. Excellent with grilled prawns and shellfish.

Garganega di Gambellara Dry white wine from near the town of Vicenza. Lacks the class and finesse of Soave, though useful as an everyday table wine.

Grappa Local 'firewater' produced by distilling the skins and pips left over after the pressing (as in French *marc*).

Merlot del Veneto French grape variety which produces full red table wine with a characteristic soft roundness. Good with *pastae fagioli*, sausages and *polenta*, *spezzatino*, and other hearty Venetian dishes.

Piave The general name for the wine district centred around Treviso, north of Venice.

Piccolit Rare, distinguished sweet wine from Friuli – expensive and elusive.

Pinot Bianco Dry white wine produced in the Piave region, and also in Friuli.

Pinot Grigio Dry white wine produced throughout Veneto and Friuli. Excellent examples – fruity and full-bodied – come from Grave del Friuli district.

Prosecco One of the great wines of Veneto, though surprisingly, not widely exported. Produced around the towns of Conegliano and Valdobbiadene, it is extremely versatile, for both dry and sweet versions are produced, as well as still and sparkling wines. The still, dry Prosecco is excellent with shellfish and asparagus, while sparkling Prosecco is the preferred wine of the north-east for celebrations – and still inexpensive enough to celebrate with daily.

Raboso Native grape variety producing robust red wine in the Piave region.

Recioto Various types of wine produced by gathering the 'ears' of grapes (that is, the tops of the bunches, which have had more sun and are thus riper), then semi-drying them in racks to further concentrate their sugar content. Recioto can be either red or white, a full if rather soft sweet wine. Recioto Amarone, on the other hand, is a distinguished powerful red wine that is dry and full-bodied and has a characteristic bitter flavour.

Refosco Full red wine from Friuli.

Riesling Italico Italian or Welsch Riesling (as opposed to the German or Rhine Riesling) grown throughout the region to produce plentiful everyday white wine.

Sauvignon Classic grape variety producing full-bodied aromatic dry white wines from throughout the region.

Soave Firm, fresh dry white wine produced in the hills west of Verona principally from the Garganega grape. Straw-yellow, full-bodied, it is excellent with freshwater fish from Lake Garda, and with other seafood and *risotti*. The central Classico zone produces the finest wines. Though much comes from large-scale cooperatives, individual estates produce and bottle fine wines.

Tocai Vasts amounts of Tocai del Veneto are produced; often sold in 2-litre screw-topped bottles, it is a useful everyday white wine. Finer individual examples come from the Piave and Friuli.

Valpantena Light red wine produced near Valpolicella.

Valpolicella Popular well-known red wine produced from a variety of grapes grown on the hills east of the Adige River, and north of Verona. Though it can be drunk very young, the best examples (from the Classico zone) develop, after two or three years, into a bright, garnet-coloured wine with a hint of sweetness yet a slightly bitter aftertaste.

Verduzzo Native grape producing dry white wines in the Piave and Friuli regions.

The Vineyards of Verona

Verona, one of the most beautiful cities in Italy, is the obvious centre for touring the wine regions which virtually surround it. A moody mixture of ancient, medieval Gothic, and Renaissance, its cobbled streets lead past the impenetrable facades of still-noble *palazzi* (indeed, one such thirteenth-century mansion claims to be the house where Juliet Capulet lived) to fine old squares like the Piazza delle Erbe – the former Roman forum, today a lively everyday market spread out with typical canopied stalls selling fruit and vegetables – and the Piazza Bra, dominated by its famous Roman Arena, best preserved of all Roman amphitheatres, and a magnificent summer setting for an annual open-air opera season. There is much to see and do in Verona, and there is no

shortage of both excellent and elegant restaurants (the most famous is 12 Apostoli), as well as humble *trattorie* and *osterie* serving not only good, simple foods but also the excellent wines of the region.

The fertile hills to the north, north-east, north-west and south-west have probably changed little over the centuries. Terraced vineyards are broken by lines of attentive cypress which loom atop hills like watchful sentries, while elsewhere the protruding turret of an ochre villa and the corduroy pattern of weathered, brick roof tiles punctuate the pastoral vista. This is not a single wine region but several, producing a variety of plentiful and fine white, rosé, light and heavy red wines; each region, all of them compact and in close proximity, can be visited in turn.

Strada del Vino di Bardolino *and* Strada del Vino di Bianco di Custoza

To the west of Verona on slopes descending to the olive-lined Garda Riviera lie the vineyards of Bardolino, producing not only that light, delicately scented, and well-known red wine, but also the even paler Chiaretto, an elegant and distinguished pink wine. Another DOC wine comes from within the

demarcated Bardolino region, the white Bianco di Custoza. Two sign-posted wine roads extend through the wine country, the *Strada del Vino di Bardolino* and the *Strada del Vino di Bianco di Custoza*; both utilize the same distinctive logo, a winding road leading up to a bunch of grapes, red for Bardolino, yellow for Bianco di

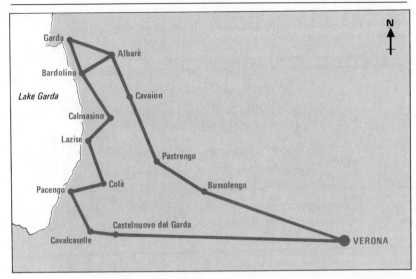

Custoza. Along each there are numerous *punti di vendita* – producers where wines can be sampled and purchased. Both wine regions can be reached from Verona by taking the N11 in the direction of Peschiera del Garda, which lies at the base of this largest of the Italian lakes.

The *Strada del Vino di Bardolino* begins before Peschiera is reached. Turn right at Cavalcaselle to climb into the hills of Bardolino briefly, before descending to the lake at Pacengo, one of a number of holiday and fishing towns spread out in a line along the shores of the lake. Such resorts are crowded in season, their little harbours full of pleasure craft as well as working boats, the numerous lakeside campsites packed, the stout Romanesque parish churches a social gathering point for Italian holidaymakers and villagers alike. The so called Olive Riviera follows the lake north, but the wine road ascends into the moraine hills once more, through the little community of Colá, before returning to the water and the walled town of Lazise, once an important port of the Venetian Republic. The thirteenth-century Scala castle is worth a visit, and there is a small *enoteca* where the wines of Bardolino can be purchased (via Porta del Lion). Directly opposite the town, the wine road heads sharply into the vineyards again, thus making a roundabout, if picturesque, detour via Calmasino back to the lake and

to the precious town of Bardolino itself. En route, no fewer than five *punti di vendita* are encountered. The best place for sampling (and purchasing) both Bardolino Classico and Chiaretto Classico, however, is at the *Enoteca Permanente del Bardolino* located along the town waterfront. During the autumn (end of September) there is a lively four-day wine festival with folk music, traditional games, much wine drinking, arranged visits to cellars along the wine road, sports and other competitions, and as a grand finale, a fireworks display along the lake.

From Bardolino, either follow the lake road (N249) to Garda, an ancient Roman village at the head of the bulging bay which has given the lake its name, then continue around to Marciaga, Castion Veronese (the Villa Pellegrini of Castion is a fine example of an eighteenth-century country mansion, beautifully in harmony with the surrounding countryside), and so to Albarè; or else, if time is short, cut across directly from Bardolino to Albarè, pausing at least to take in the panorama from the monastic complex of the ancient Convent of S. Colombano. At Albarè, the wine road continues to Affi and Cavaion, before crossing under the autostrada, and continuing to Pastrengo and Bussolengo (those with children may wish to visit the zoo-park), and so back to Verona.

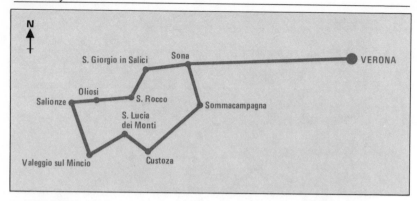

The *Strada del Vino di Bianco di Custoza* is reached from Verona by turning left on the main N11 road westwards to the village of Sona. Along this brief but lovely wine road, whose heart is bisected by the little meandering Tione River, there are 25 *punti di vendita* – places of production where this sound white wine may be purchased – in addition to more than twenty *punti di ristoro* – literally, places of refreshment –

restaurants, *trattorie* and the like which serve local specialities as well as the wines of the region. The white wine road runs from Sona to Sommacampagna, then on to little Custoza itself. Throughout the region there are numerous impressive and ancient villas crowning the rolling hills; and many are still privately owned and lived in today. The Villa Pignatti Morano on the hills above Custoza stands in an impressive position overlooking the plains of Villafranca and Valeggio. This region was the scene of much fierce fighting during the battles for Italian independence. From Custoza, make a detour to S Lucia dei Monti to see a beautiful natural amphitheatre formed by the sinuous Tione River. The next wine town is Valeggio sul Mincio where a fine fourteenth-century bridge spans the Mincio Valley. Continue north to Salionze, then across to Oliosi and San Rocco (visit the fourteenth-century church of San Rocco), before returning to Sona and Verona.

The Valpolicella and Valpantena

North of Verona, between Bardolino to the west and Soave to the east, the high, undulating plateau of the Lessinia Mountains is furrowed by two rich and fertile valleys, the Valpolicella and the Valpantena, regions well known for the production of their distinguished red wines. The origins of this light, brilliant ruby-red wine go back before Roman times. An indigenous population, the Retica, inhabited these hills, and produced wine that was later praised by Virgil,

Suetonius, Martial, and Pliny the Elder. It was a favourite wine of St Zeno, Bishop of Verona during the fourth century, and it is his image that is depicted on the Consortium labels for the approved DOC wines of Verona. The image of this smiling patron saint, who left detailed descriptions of how to cultivate grapes and make wine, can be taken as a guarantee of quality. In addition to Valpolicella and Valpantena (both similar smooth wines with a slight but characteristic bitter aftertaste), the

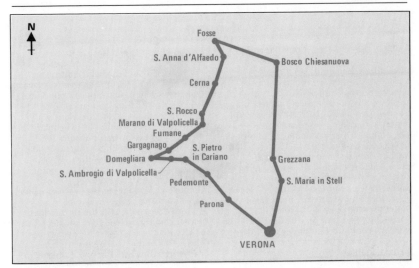

region is also the centre for the production of Recioto della Valpolicella and Recioto della Valpolicella Amarone. 'Recce' in Venetian dialect means 'ear' (*orecchio* in Italian); thus, the grapes used to produce these rare and distinguished wines are harvested from the 'ear of the bunch' (the top, which has received more sun and is thus riper) and are then dried on trellises to concentrate their flavour and sugar. The former is a fine, deep sweet wine; Amarone, on the other hand, is an austere, full-flavoured red wine suitable for serving with game, roast meat, and strong cheese.

While the Bardolino region has its own sign-posted *Strada del Vino*, the regions of Valpolicella and Valpantena are somewhat disjointed, for they are made up of a series of lovely valleys, vine-covered slopes, and hill towns spread across a zone 45 km long and about 5 to 8 km wide. Nevertheless, the region is easily explored from Verona. To reach the zone of Valpolicella Classico – the heart of the region and the area producing the finest wines – leave Verona on the N12 (which continues, eventually, north to the Brenner pass through the Alps). Branch off right at Parona, and continue to Pedemonte, S Pietro in Cariano, and S Ambrogio di Valpolicella (which, with nearby Domegliara, is the centre of an important marble industry). Follow the road back around via Gargagnago to little Fumane, a typical one-street village, and to Marano. This is the most ancient zone and villages stand

proud and isolated, with their noble villas, and Romanesque churches, and their cluster of little shops. Continue north up the valley into the mountain zone for a pleasant excursion through S Rocco, Cerna, and Sta Anna d'Alfaedo to Fosse, and around, via Ronconi, Selvavécchia, and Masselli to Boscochiesanuova (a popular summer and winter sports resort). Descend through the Valpantena via Grezzana, Santa Maria in Stelle, and Quinto, and so return to Verona. There are numerous small wine producers throughout this central zone, some of them producing distinguished and individual wines. Write or telephone in advance to arrange visits.

Soave

Soave is one of the most popular and exported white wines of Italy, known throughout the world, yet the sleepy, walled medieval town is marvellously unselfconscious, unspoiled. During autumn, horsedrawn carts and belching tractors carry plastic tubs and trailers full of grapes to the local *cantina cooperativa*. The Scaligero castle, originally founded on the site of an old Roman fort, overlooks the town, a fine, restored example of a medieval bastion, and the scene, in the past, of numerous bloody battles. Today the castle is surrounded by the prize vineyards that produce a wine more famous than the castle or even the town itself.

The Soave zone of production extends in a broad arc of hills east of Verona. There is no sign-posted wine road, but from Verona an interesting tour can be made through vineyards and wine villages to reach Soave itself. From Verona, take the N11 eastwards to S Martino Buon Albergo, a typical wine commune. Turn left into the vine-covered hills, and then continue right to S Pietro di Lavagno, and on to Colognola ai Colli. The *Cantina Sociale di Colognola*, located outside the village, is typical of the large installations found throughout the region. In late September it is a thrilling sight to see the tractor-loads of grapes weighed, then dumped into vast, churning below-ground-level vats. The

Garganega and Trebbiano grapes are automatically destemmed and crushed, then pressed, and the heady autumnal scent of fresh juice running freely into vast concrete fermentation tanks is wonderful. While such wines are produced in bulk by modern methods, a rare, precious wine, Recioto di Soave, continues to be made in limited quantity by traditional methods, the selected grapes dried until raisin-like then fermented slowly in the new year to produce a heavy, fragrant dessert wine. Visit small wine producers between October and December to see the grapes spread out and drying in racks.

From Colognola, take the road to Illasi then turn right up the winding, steep lane to Montecchia di Crosara, with its castle ruins. Follow the road up the Alpone Valley to S Giovanni Ilarione. Either continue northwards to explore further small villages, or else return down the valley road. Turn off right to Castello and Castelcerino. The latter is set on a remarkably steep and terraced hill with superb views of the plain of Verona. From here take the minor road to Brognoligo and through the valley to Monteforte d'Alpone and Soave, centres of the Classico zone. Reward yourself with a glass of Soave in the comfortable *Enoteca del Soave* (Via Roma 25), along with tasty little *tartine*, and other snacks.

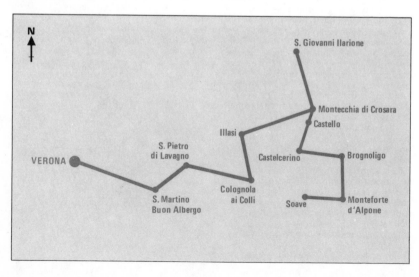

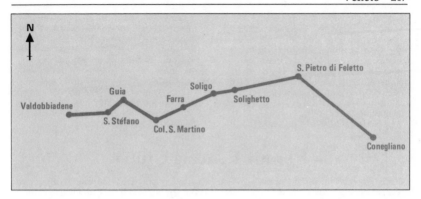

Treviso

While wines are produced throughout the Veneto (Breganze, Colli Euganei, Vicenza, and elsewhere), the region north of Venice, centring around Treviso and Conegliano, is probably the most important after the vineyards of Verona. It is easily reached from Venice; there are brief sign-posted wine roads, and fascinating tours can be made through the wine regions, encompassing towns such as Asolo, Bassano del Grappa, and Castelfranco Veneto.

The wines of Treviso are known broadly as the wines of the Piave, for this important river that has its source high in the Alps cuts through the region, watering its rich and fertile valleys. A variety of fine wines are produced on hills surrounding Treviso and extending from Conegliano across to Valdobbiádene. Typical of the region are Tocai del Piave, Cabernet, Merlot, Pinot Grigio, Pinot Bianco, Verduzzo, Raboso, and Prosecco Conegliano-Valdobbiádene. While the finer wines are sold in 75cl corked bottles, the region is also the source of vast amounts of everyday table wines sold in 2-litre screw-topped bottles (and in larger containers, too).

Treviso, located some twenty miles north of Venice, is a most interesting and picturesque town, surrounded by its old fortified ramparts, and with numerous canals recalling its former allegiance to La Serenissima. The old section of the town – *città antica* – is particularly atmospheric on warm summer evenings when anybody who is anybody makes a *passeggiata* to the Piazza dei Signori, being seen and watching the world go by. From Treviso

the *Strada del Vino Rosso* run across the Piave Valley, crossing the river at Ponte di Piave and continuing on to Oderzo. Oderzo is the centre of the *Consorzio Cantine Sociali della Marca Trevigiana*, an organization which both ensures the quality of its members' wines, and bottles, ages, markets, and promotes them. The symbol of such wines is a square seal showing two 'thumb's up' hands, one holding a glass of wine, the other a bunch of grapes. (Consorzio Cantine Sociali della Marca Trevigiana, Società Cooperativa a.r.l., Via Verdi, 94, 31046 Oderzo, Treviso, Italy – tel. (0422) 713400). From Oderzo the red wine road continues to Conegliano.

Conegliano, a small and pleasant wine town surrounded by vine-covered hills and fragrant fruit orchards, is also the home of a well-known institute specializing in oenology, the Viticultural Research Institute of Conegliano. Prosecco di Conegliano-Valdobbiádene is an important and distinguished wine, one of the best from the Veneto, though it is much less well-known abroad than the wines from Verona, probably because the crafty Venetians drink all that they can get hold of. A versatile wine, Prosecco can be either still or sparkling, bone dry, or slightly sweet. The dry, still version is an excellent partner to seafood from the Adriatic; sparkling Prosecco is the preferred wine for celebrations in north-east Italy.

Another brief wine road, the *Strada del Vino Bianco*, extends from Conegliano across to Valdobbiádene, through picturesque villages such as S Pietro di

Feletto, Solighetto, Col S Martino, S Stéfano, and others. There are numerous small farmhouses along the way, and lots of little bars and restaurants in which to sample this fine wine, together with home-made sausages and hams. Also along the *Strada del Vino Bianco* are rustic dairies producing *formaggio casareccio* – hand-made local cheese: delicious with the local wines.

Beyond Valdobbiádene, a rare (if not necessarily wine-related) treat awaits, three of the loveliest villages in northern Italy: Asolo (Browning's favourite town), Bassano del Grappa (located in the shadow of Monte Grappa, and the home of some of the finest *grappa* produced in the region), and Castelfranco Veneto (don't miss the Giorgione Madonna – the painter was born in this picturesque medieval village). From Castelfranco, either return to Venice, Treviso, Padua, or Vicenza.

Friuli-Venezia Giulia

Friuli-Venezia Giulia is a small region located between the Veneto and the Yugoslav border. In the nineteenth century it gave the Austro–Hungarian Empire access to the sea. Trieste is its capital city and this former Austrian port reflects the entire region's heterogeneous character. The people themselves actually look Slavic, not Mediterranean, and the influence of Austria, Hungary, and Slovenia are evident in the lively cuisine of the region, which includes such specialities as Friulian goulash, *cotoletta alla viennese* (no more than a variation of the famous Wiener Schnitzel), and German-style sausages, along with unique fare such as *prosciutto di S Daniele*, game from the alpine regions, smoked salamis, hearty bean and vegetable soups (such as the favourite *jota* of Trieste), and a wealth of fish specialities.

The wines of Friuli-Venezia Giulia are excellent and can be sampled throughout the region. There are actually five distinct areas of production within the region: Aquileia (a small stretch of coastal vineyards between Venice and Trieste), Collio (a region of low, rolling, green hills whose centre is Gorizia), Grave del Friuli (a large area including the principal towns of Pordenone and Udine), Latisana (bordering the picturesque lagoon of Marano), Colli Orientali del Friuli and Isonzo (extending north along the Yugoslav border from Trieste to Gorizia, and famous for its distinguished Cabernet). A wine tour of the region might stop in Pordenone, S Daniele (where wines can be sampled together with the delicate, sweet mountain ham), Udine, Cividale, Cormòns, Gorizia, and Trieste; then return to Venice along the coastal road via Monfalcone, Aquileia, and Latisana.

————— *Wine Producers and* —————
Enoteche

The Vineyards of Verona

37017 Lazise

Enoteca di Lazise
Via Porta del Lion

37011 Bardolino

Enoteca Permanente del Bardolino
Piazza Pr Amedeo
tel: (045) 62 38 99
Permanent display of Bardolino and Chiaretto Classico for tasting and for purchase. Appointments to visit producers located along the *Strada del Vino* can usually be arranged here.
Charge for *degustazione.*

Azienda Agricola Guerrieri Rizzardi
Via Verdi, 3
tel: (045) 72 10 028
Bardolino Classico Superiore, Chiaretto Classico, Valpolicella, Recioto Amarone della Valpolicella
Open Sat 9–12h
Other times by appointment only.
Min 5, max 50 pers.
English spoken.
Charge for *degustazione.*

37010 Affi

Cooperativa Agricola del Moscal – F.lli Poggi
tel: (045) 72 35 044
Bardolino Classico, Chiaretto Classico,
Bianco Valdadige
Open Mon–Fri
Appointment necessary for large groups.
Max 150 pers.
English spoken.
Charge for *degustazione*.

37010 Calmasino di Bardolino

Azienda Agricola Colle dei Cipressi
tel: (045) 62 90 78
Bardolino Classico Superiore, Chiaretto
Classico, Merlot, *vino bianco*
Mon–Fri 8h30–12h; 14h30–17h
Appointment necessary.
English spoken.

37010 Pastrengo

Lamberti SpA
tel: (045) 71 70 055
Bardolino Classico, Chiaretto Classico,
Valpolicella, Soave, Lugana, Recioto
Amarone della Valpolicella
Open Mon–Fri 9–12h; 14–17h
Appointment preferable.
Max 40 pers.
English spoken.

Castelnuovo del Garda

Cantina Sociale Veronese del Garda
Via Cantina Sociale, 3
tel: (045) 64 40 76
Bianco di Custoza, Bardolino, Chiaretto
Classico
Open daily 9–18h
Appointment preferable.
Max 40 pers.
English spoken.

Staffalo di Custoza

Cantina Sociale di Custoza
tel: (045) 51 60 17
Bianco di Custoza

37067 Valeggio sul Mincio

Azienda Agricola Piccoli Gianni
Località Gardoni
tel: (045) 63 53 82
Bianco di Custoza, Bardolino, Chiaretto
Classico
Mon–Sat
Appointment necessary.

San Pietro in Cariano

Azienda Agricola Nicolis Angelo e Figli
Via Villa Girardi, 29
tel: (045) 77 01 261
Valpolicella Classico Superiore, Recioto
della Valpolicella, Recioto Amarone della
Valpolicella
Open daily
Appointment necessary.
English spoken.
('The most interesting time to visit is from
late October to late January when the
grapes used to make Recioto can be seen
drying.')

37020 Gargagnago di San Ambrogio

Masi Agricola SpA
tel: (045) 77 01 696
Reciota Amarone della Valpolicella,
Recioto della Valpolicella *riserva*,
Valpolicella Classico, Bardolino Classico,
Soave Classico
Open Mon–Fri 8h20–12h; 15–18h
English spoken.

Azienda Agricola Ferrari Aleardo
Via Giare, 15
tel: (045) 77 01 379
Valpolicella Classico Superiore, Recioto
della Valpolicella, Recioto Amarone
Open daily by appointment.
Max 60 pers.
English spoken.

37022 Fumane di Valpolicella

Agricola Allegrini
Corte Giara
tel: (045) 77 01 138
Valpolicella Classico Superiore, Recioto
della Valpolicella, Recioto Amarone della
Valpolicella
Open Mon–Sat 8–12h; 15–19h
Telephone in advance.
Max 60 pers.
Wine can be purchased, but not tasted.

37024 Negrar

Cantina Sociale Valpolicella – Società
Cooperativa a.r.l.
tel: (045) 75 00 070
Valpolicella Classico, Recioto della
Valpolicella, Recioto Amarone, Bardolino,
Soave, Bianco di Custoza, Chiaretto
Classico
Daily except Sat & Mon
Appointment necessary.
Max 50 pers.

37030 Mezzane di Sotto

Azienda Agricola Fioi
Via Capovilla
tel: (045) 89 028
Valpolicella Superiore, Recioto della
Valpolicella, Recioto Amarone, *vino
spumante*
Open Sat by appointment.
Max 20 pers.
English spoken.

37031 Illasi

Cantina Sociale di Illasi, Società
Cooperativa a.r.l.
Via Restel Rosso 1
tel: (045) 78 34 001
Soave DOC, Valpolicella DOC
Open daily except Sat 15–18h
Appointment necessary.
English spoken.

37030 Cazzano di Tramigna

Cantina Sociale Valtramigna
Via Molini, 1
tel: (045) 78 20 524
Soave DOC, Valpolicella DOC
Open Mon–Fri by appointment.

37038 Soave

Enoteca del Soave
Via Roma, 19
tel: (045) 76 80 093
Soave Classico, Recioto di Soave, Soave
spumante, Valpolicella, Recioto della
Valpolicella, Bardolino, Chiaretto.
Taste and purchase the local wines in
this comfortable *enoteca* in the centre of
the medieval village. Small snacks
available.
Closed Jan 25–Feb 5; Thur
Open 10–13h; 16–24h
Appointment necessary for large
groups.
Appointments to visit the *cantina sociale*
can be arranged here.

Azienda Agricola Bisson di Battocchia Lino
Via Bisson
tel: (045) 76 80 775
Soave Classico Superiore, Soave DOC,
Recioto di Soave, Soave *spumante*
Open daily 8–18h
Appointment necessary.
Max 60 pers.
English spoken.

Treviso and Friuli

31046 Oderzo

Consorzio Cantine Sociali della Marca
Trevigiana
Società Cooperativa a.r.l.
Via Verdi, 94
tel: (0422) 71 34 00
Write in advance to visit this
super-modern 'wine factory'. Modern
bottling-lines and vast stainless steel
storage tanks complement traditional
Slavonian oak casks for the stocking and
ageing of wines from the region's various
local *cantine cooperative*. The Cooperative
Stores Association is thus able to market its
wines direct. In addition to this central
store, smaller *cantine sociali* are located in
Campodipietra, Musile di Piave, Zerman
di Mogliano, Villorba, Vittorio Veneto,
Orsago, and elsewhere. Though such
establishments are not generally prepared
to accept visitors, it has been our
experience that the interested visitor, if he
does not come at an extremely busy
moment, will usually be shown around.
Alternatively, arrange appointments
through the *Consorzio*.

31049 Valdobbiádene

Nino Franco di Franco Giovanni
Via Garibaldi, 167
tel: (0423) 72 05 1
Prosecco *spumante*, Merlot, Cabernet,
Pinot Grigio, Tocai, Raboso *rosato*
Open Mon–Fri 8–18h
Appointment necessary.
Max 20 pers.
English spoken.

39080 San Quirino Pordenone

Azienda Agricola Villa Sospisio
Via Villa Sospisio N23
tel: (0434) 91 01 5
Pinot Grigio, Cabernet, Merlot, Refosco,
Prosecco di Valdobbiadene, *grappa*
Appointment necessary.
Max 20 pers.
English spoken.
Home-made salami and *prosciutto* can be
sampled and purchased.

Capriva del Friuli

Azienda Agricola Instituto 'A Cerruti' Villa
Russiz
Russiz Inferiore, 5
Open Mon–Fri 8–18h
Appointment necessary.
Max 50 pers.

34070 Lucinico

Azienda Agricola Conti Attems di Attems
S Douglas
Via G Cesare, 46
tel: (0481) 39 02 06
Collio Pinot Grigio, Collio Sauvignon,
Collio Tocai Friulano, Collio Riesling
Italico, Collio Merlot, Collio Cabernet,
Isonzo Pinot Bianco, Isonzo Cabernet
Open Mon–Fri 8–12h; 13–17h
Appointment necessary.
Max 40 pers.
English spoken.

34071 Cormòns

Cantina Produttori Vini del Collio e
dell'Isonzo
Società Cooperativa a.r.l.
Via Mariano, 31

tel: (0481) 60 57 9
Vini del Collio e dell'Isonzo
Open all year.
Appointment necessary.
Min 15 pers; max 50 pers.
English spoken.

34072 Gradisca d'Isonzo

Enoteca Permanente della Regione
Friuli-Venezia Giulia
"La Serenissima"
Via C. Battisti
tel: (0481) 99217
A vast selection of wines, *spumanti* and
grappe from Friuli-Venezia Giulia available
for tasting and purchase.
Open daily 10–12h30; 16–24h
Appointment necessary only for large
groups.

Wine Festivals

April (generally)	Vinitaly – major exhibition of Italian wines, primarily for the trade. Further details from Ente Autonoma Fiere (see below)	Verona
1st Sun in May	Festival of Soave Classico	Soave
Mid Sept	Festival of the wines of the Adige Valley	Rivoli Veronese
Mid Sept	Festa dell'Uva	Monteforte d'Alpone
End Sept	Fiera dell'Uva	Soave
End Sept	Festa dell'Uva	Bardolino
Early Oct	Wine Festival	Fumane
Oct	Wine Festival	Rivoli Veronese

For exact dates of festivals, write to:

Ente Autonoma Fiere di Verona
Casella Postale 525
371500 Verona

Regional Gastronomy

Polenta Characteristic corn mush which is a staple accompaniment to meat or fish. Sometimes baked with sauce or sausages, or deep-fried until crunchy.

Risi e bisi Rice and pea *risotto* eaten as a first course.

Prosciutto di S Daniele Sweet, fragrant air-dried mountain ham, served razor thin.

Pasta e fagioli Heavy, robust macaroni and bean soup.

Zuppa di trippa Tripe soup.

Zuppa di pesce Fish soup.

Jota Thick bean and vegetable soup.

Baccalà alla vicentina Dried salt-cod stewed very slowly in onions and milk until it becomes a thick paste.

Insalata di mare Seafood salad of squid, shrimps, mussels, crayfish, and whatever else is available, dressed with oil and lemon juice.

Risotto More popular in Veneto than pasta – medium-grain Italian *arborio* rice cooked slowly in stock, with the addition of any variety of ingredients – *pesce* (fish), *funghi* (mushrooms), *asparagi* (asparagus), *scampi*, for example. Authentic *risotto* must be prepared fresh, so do not order in a restaurant unless prepared to wait at least 20 minutes.

Carpaccio Venetian speciality of slices of thin, top-quality raw fillet steak served with sauces.

Seppia alla veneziana Squid stewed in its own ink, and served with *polenta*.

Trota Trout.

Triglia Red mullet.

Tonno Tuna fish (often served fresh, cut into thick steaks).

Sogliola Sole.

Coda di rospo Monkfish tail, usually grilled in abundant butter.

Spezzatino di vitello Veal goulash.

Scampi alla griglia Scampi grilled over an open fire.

Fegato alla veneziana Thin strips of calves' liver fried with onions.

Radicchio Bitter red lettuce from Treviso.

Soppresa Pork and beef sausage, served hot with fruit mustard.

Musetto con brovada Boiled pork sausage served with sour turnips – a speciality of Friuli.

Tiramesù Rich chocolate cake with a filling of *zabaione* – in Venetian dialect means 'pick me up'.

Restaurants

37100 Verona

Ristorante 12 Apostoli
Vicolo Corticella San Marco, 3
tel: (045) 24 68 0
Famous, traditional Venetian restaurant with medieval atmosphere, serving regional dishes and good selection of the finest *vini veronese*.
Open 12h30–15; 19h30–22h
Expensive

Ristorante Marconi
Vicolo Crocioni, 6
tel: (045) 27 47 2
Unusual dishes, and good selections of wines from Soave and Valpolicella.
Closed Tue eve; Sun; two weeks in August
Moderate

Ristorante Arche
Via Arche Scaligere, 6
tel: (045) 21 41 5
Originally a *taverna* in the 15th century, today a restaurant serving traditional Venetian dishes, including fish transported daily from the market at Chioggia.
Closed Sun eve; Mon
Expensive

Ristorante Due Mori
Vicoletto Due Mori, 5
tel: (045) 30 03 0
Cucina casalinga (home cooking), including *risotto all'amarone*, and *filetto al pepe*.
Closed Wed
Moderate

Ristorante Accademia
Via Scala, 10
tel: (045) 26 072
Regional dishes such as *pasta e fagioli, gnocchi alla veneta, baccalà alla vicentina*.
Closed Wed; Sun eve
Open 12–15h; 19h30–22h
Moderate to **Expensive**

Borghetto di Valeggio sul Mincio

Antica Locanda Mincio
Via Michelangelo, 12
tel: (045) 63 50 59
Medieval house serving Venetian specialities in the old dining room with its large fireplace or, in fine weather, on the garden terrace beside the Mincio River. Bianco di Custoza, Bardolino, and other local wines.
Closed Thur
Open 12–14h30; 19–22h
Moderate

25019 Sirmione

(located on peninsula at southern end of Lake Garda)

Trattoria Vecchia Lugana
Strada Statale, 43
tel: (030) 91 90 12
Atmospheric, elegant restaurant with wide selection of fish fresh from the lake.

Specialities include *fritto misto, trota al Lugano, anguilla alla gardesana.*
Closed Mon eve; Tue
Expensive

Ristorante Grifone – da Luciano
Via Bisse, 5
tel: (030) 91 60 97
Located right on the edge of Lake Garda with veranda and gardens.
Open March 10–Oct 10
12–14h30; 19–22h30
Inexpensive to **Moderate**

37038 Soave

Ristorante El Grìo – da Gianni
Via Costeggiola, 6
tel: (045) 76 80 596
Local dishes and regional wines.
Closed Mon eve; Tue
Open 9–23h
Moderate

31100 Treviso

Ristorante Alfredo El Toula
Via Collalto, 26
tel: (0422) 40 275
Elegant restaurant serving classic *cucina veneta,* including *risotto con le seppie,* (squid risotto), home-made pasta, and a good selection of wines.
Expensive

31015 Conegliano

Tre Panoce
Via Vecchia Trevigiana, 50
tel: (0438) 60 07 1 .
2 km from town centre, situated on the top of a hill – Venetian cuisine, utilizing unique local specialities such as *radicchio, funghi porcini.*
Closed Mon
Moderate

Ristorante Al Salisà
Via 20 Settembre, 2
tel: (0438) 24 28 8
Local wines and personal cooking.
English spoken
Closed Mon
Moderate

Hotels

37100 Verona

Hotel Due Torri
Piazza Sant'Anastasia, 4
tel: (045) 59 50 44

Modern luxury hotel in centre of city. 100 rooms all with bathrooms and decorated in 18th- and 19th-century style.
Restaurant serves local and international dishes.
Hotel and restaurant open all year
Very Expensive

Hotel Arena
Stradone Porta Palio, 2
tel: (045) 32 440
Small, **Moderate** hotel without restaurant.

De'Capuleti
Via del Pontiere, 26
tel: (045) 32 970
36-room hotel without restaurant.
Moderate

37016 Garda

Hotel Regina Adelaide Palace
Via XX Settembre
tel: (045) 72 55 013
Hotel with gardens, terrace, and restaurant serving home-made dishes with a good selection of local wines.
Hotel open all year
Restaurant open March 8–Oct 15; Dec 20–Jan 15; 12h30–14h; 19h30–21h15
Moderate

Locanda S Vigilio
Small, quiet, picturesque, 18th-century hotel directly on the lake with good restaurant.
Open summer only

37011 Bardolino

Hotel Kriss Internazionale
tel: (045) 72 10 242
Holiday hotel with garden, solarium, and restaurant.
Hotel open all year
Restaurant open March–Oct daily
Moderate

31100 Treviso

Hotel-Ristorante Al Foghèr
Viale della Repubblica, 10
tel: (0422) 20 68 6
Hotel with ample parking, each room with bath. Restaurant serves traditional and regional cuisine with good local wines.
Hotel open all year
Restaurant closed Fri
Moderate

31049 Valdobbidene

Hotel Diana
Via Roma, 49
tel: (0423) 72 23 7
Inexpensive hotel without restaurant.
Closed Jan

31015 Conegliano

Hotel-Ristorante Canon d'Oro
Via 20 Settembre, 129
tel: (0438) 22 17 1
Situated in a quiet spot with gardens, and
restaurant serving regional dishes.
Hotel open all year
Restaurant closed Sat
Open 12–14h30; 19h30–21h45
Inexpensive to **Moderate**

Camping

The Garda resorts are particularly
well-equipped for camping; additionally,
campsites are found in most of the main
towns of northern Italy. The following is a
brief selection only.

37100 Verona
Romeo e Giulietta
tel: (045) 56 49 12
37011 Bardolino
Communale
tel: (045) 72 10 051
Continental
tel: (045) 72 10 192
Europa
tel: (045) 72 10 073
37016 Garda
Beato
tel: (045) 62 42 73
Parco del Garda
tel: (045) 62 43 86
37017 Lazise
Belvedere
tel: (045) 64 52 28
Euro Camping
tel: (045) 64 50 12
La Quercia

Where to Get Additional Information

Italian Government Tourist Office
(E.N.I.T.)
630 5th Ave
NY NY 10111
tel: (212) 245–4822

Ente Provinciale per il Turismo
Via C. Montari, 14
37100 Verona
tel: (045) 25 065

Associazione Vini Veronese DOC
Corso Porta Nuova, 96
37100 Verona
tel: (045) 59 10 77

Consorzio Tutela Vino Bardolino e Vino
Bianco di Custoza
Via Verdi, 8
37011 Bardolino
tel: (045) 62 38 20

Consorzio Cantine Sociali della Marca
Trevigiana
Società Cooperativa a.r.l.
Via Verdi, 94
31046 Oderzo
Treviso
tel: (0422) 71 34 00

tel: (045) 64 30 51
Municipale
tel: (045) 64 30 20
31100 Vollorba (near Treviso)
Belvedere
tel: (0422) 92 07 0

Bibliography

The Wines of Italy by Cyril Ray, Penguin
1971

Vino by Burton Anderson, Atlantic,
Little, Brown 1980

——COLLI ALBANI——

Overlooking vast, sprawling Rome and, on a clear day, ancient Ostia and the sea, lies a compact, congenial wine region: the Colli Albani. This series of gentle rolling hills has for two millennia served as a retreat for Romans, to escape the cares of their busy city and of the world: Cicero, for example, had a villa at ancient Tuscolo near Frascati, where he retired to compose his famous treatises; and the Pope himself continues to find peace and solace at the Villa del Papa in Castel Gandolfo. Less famous citizens of the Eternal City and visitors from further afield come to this region to relax in a bucolic landscape which, despite its proximity to Rome, remains surprisingly unspoiled. Here they explore meandering ancient villages, sniff out rustic *osterie*, and sit for

How to Get There

By Car
From Central Rome, take the N215 (Via Tuscolana) to Frascati, and begin the wine tour from there. The N215 can be reached, if by-passing central Rome, by way of the circular ring road. The N7 (Via Appia Nuova) leads to Albano.

By Plane
Alitalia, Pan Am, and TWA offer direct, non-stop flights from the US to Rome. Alitalia, furthermore, have an extensive network of internal flights connecting Rome with most other major cities in Italy, including Milan, Venice, Pisa and Turin. There are direct flights to Rome from most major European capitals.

By Train
The 'Palatino Express' runs daily from Paris to Rome. In Italy, all roads, and indeed, all rail lines, lead to Rome, thus connecting the capital by direct service to most, if not all, major cities.

Local Transport
There are guided coach tours from Rome to the Colli Albani. They run three days a week, departing from the Piazza della Repubblica in the afternoon, and include stops at the main towns with wine tastings. The use of a car, however, is advisable, as the smaller villages are not connected by train or bus.

Car Rental Information
Rome
  Avis: Piazza Esquilino, I/C
     tel: (06) 4701
     Via Sardegna, 38/A
     tel: (06) 4701
     Fiumicino Intl Airport
     tel: (06) 601579
  Hertz: Via Sallustiana, 28
     tel: (06) 065171
     Via del Gelsomino, 42
     tel: (06) 632832
     Fiumicino Intl Airport
     tel: (06) 601448

Map Touring Club Italiano no 9

hours on outdoor terraces or in cool, underground *cantine*, drinking the wines for which the region is so justly famous.

The hills themselves are extinct volcanoes, their craters filled in now to create beautiful, sheltered lakes such as Lake Albano and the smaller Lake Nemi. The grapes that produce the wines of the Colli Albani thrive in this black, mineral-rich soil; trained on traditional pergolas, they spread out on the slopes overlooking Rome, and extend up to and even over the top, spilling into the craters themselves. Frascati, Marino, Albano, and Velletri are the towns whose vineyards produce both the best-known, and probably the best wines: fragrant, forceful, dry whites which are both clean and strong, and thus excellent with the food of the region. Much wine, made in *cantine cooperative* or by small individual growers, is sold simply as Castelli Romani and may never even reach the bottle, for it is drunk on the spot, in wine taverns, *osterie*, and Roman *ristoranti*, or else is taken home, in plastic jugs, huge wicker-wrapped demi-johns, earthenware containers – anything at all!

The Colli Albani, compared to a wine region such as Piedmont or Burgundy, is tiny. There is no sign-posted wine road through the vineyards; few established producers with either the time or resources to give guided tours of their premises, explain processes and methods, offer free tastings; no wine museums, courses, or seminars. And yet it is extremely pleasant and rewarding to visit, perhaps because it is so easy-going, so haphazard, so relaxed. One doesn't come here to analyse wine, or pontificate about it; one simply comes to drink it.

When in Rome's vineyards, do as the Romans do: purchase a slab of succulent *porchetta* – suckling pig stuffed with fresh rosemary, copious amounts of garlic and *pancetta*, then roasted in a wood-fired oven – and a large round of *pane casareccia* (home-baked bread). Take this paper-wrapped, moveable feast to any of the numerous, unpretentious *cantine*, underground taverns where local families and friends gather, where cool, golden wine is drawn into litre carafes straight from the barrel, where it is not frowned on to eat with your hands or to laugh too loudly, where people are welcoming and where, if you make just a little effort, you are rewarded with acceptance, and can join wholeheartedly in an everyday celebration of life.

As well as its hospitable *cantine*, the region is renowned for the quality of its food. *Buongustai* inevitably bypass the larger, well-lit establishments in favour of small family-run *osterie*, for it is in such places that one finds the best home-made *fettucine*, *saltimbocca*, or trout, fresh that day from river or lake and grilled to perfection over a fire of pruned vine-shoots.

It is possible to tour the Colli Albani in a single-day excursion from Rome. But it would be a pity not to spend more time here. Do keep in mind that during summer months all of Rome (so it seems) has the same idea.

The Wines of the Colli Albani

Castelli Romani The legal *denominazione d'origine controllata* (DOC) for the general wine region south of Rome centres around 13 towns and villages (themselves known as the Castelli Romani) on the volcanic slopes of the Colli Albani. The best wines are white, such as Frascati, Marino, and others (see below) and qualify for their own *denominazione*, though there is a certain amount of red wine produced here which is not widely exported. Wine sold under this general name is generally straightforward, firm white wine that goes well with the robust, direct flavours of the *cucina romana*.

Cesanese Local red wine produced from a grape of the same name. Neither as distinctive nor as well known as the white wines of the region, it is nonetheless an honest *vino di pasto*, which, served from open carafes in the region, is well-suited to accompany those Roman meat, game, and pasta dishes that require red wine.

Colli Albani This more limited *denominazione* refers to Castelli wines that come from hillside vineyards around Albano, Castel Gandolfo, Arricia, and those which encircle the smaller volcanic Lake Nemi. Such dry, fairly full-bodied wines go well with freshwater fish straight from these deep, cool lakes, either fried in abundant oil, or seasoned with fragrant herbs and baked in a traditional wood-fired oven.

Frascati Possibly the best known Italian white wine, dry, straw-yellow in colour, firm and ripe-tasting. Medium-sweet *(abboccato)* Frascati is available locally, and ought to be tried.

Marino The town of Marino, farther up the slopes from Frascati, overlooks Lake Albano; its vineyards spread up to the crater and actually spill over it to produce slightly deeper, heavier white wines.

Merlot di Aprilia This grape from Bordeaux, which has been grown with great success in northern Italy, here in vineyards south of the Colli Albani produces soft red wine with the pronounced fruity aroma of the grape.

Sangiovese di Aprilia The Sangiovese is the great grape of Tuscany, used primarily in the production of Chianti and distinguished, heavy red wines such as Brunello di Montalcino. Here, however, it produces surprisingly light reds and delicate rosés.

Trebbiano di Aprilia Another varietal from this southern DOC area that was cultivated after the reclamation of marshland. Trebbiano is a useful everyday white, but it is not as fine as the other quality wines from the Castelli Romani.

Velletri Delicate, almost clear white wine from this south-eastern town in the Colli Albani. Some good red wines are also produced here.

Wine Tour of the Colli Albani

The Colli Albani is a small but important wine region, its wines well-loved locally and abroad. Yet the region remains unselfconscious, her people not exactly unaware of its worth so much as matter of fact in their acceptance of the importance of good wine and food in everyday life. For centuries, Romans have come to these vine-covered hills to sit under trellises on terracotta terraces, to eat simple foods, and to drink fresh, young wines drawn from the barrel on long, sultry summer evenings. While the region can be included in brief one- or two-day excursions from Rome (some tour operators give whirlwind half-day tours), it is antipathetic to the relaxed spirit of the Colli Albani not to approach it in a more leisurely frame of mind. From Rome, leave the city on the Via Tuscolana (N215) to reach, some 21 km later, the town of Frascati. If approaching Rome from the south on the A2 motorway, exit at Monte Porzio.

Frascati has always been one of the most popular and fashionable resorts of the

Castelli Romani, as evidenced by the numerous and elegant villas that overlook its winding streets. Indeed, visit the Piazza Marconi on a summer Saturday night, and it seems as if virtually all the youths of Rome itself have gathered to insouciantly rev their minuscule yet thunderous motorbikes, or their tiny, screeching Fiats; then you may well ask where is this tranquillity, this relaxed spirit which is the essence of the Colli Albani? Yet Frascati, like the Roman god Janus, has two faces; it is at once virtually a suburb of Rome and a quaint, cobbled medieval wine town, unchanged for centuries. Park your car (and lock it, for if Frascati is not Rome, it is *quasi Roma* – almost Rome – and snatch and grab thefts are not uncommon), and wander through the town's winding streets until you find the timeless wine *cantine* where locals gather. Take your paper-wrapped *porchetta*, oozing of garlic and fresh rosemary, and a loaf of crusty country bread, order a carafe or two of golden wine, and enjoy this simple feast, either while sitting at outdoor tables (in summer), or underground on benches where men in hats, their shirt-sleeves rolled up, play interminable card games.

Frascati, sadly, was bombed severely in the last war, though many of her churches, public buildings, and famous villas have been restored. Some of the villas can be visited (details from the local *Azienda Autonoma di Soggiorno e Turismo*). The finest is Villa Aldobrandini. An interesting excursion can be made from Frascati to ancient Tuscolo, birthplace of Cato the Censor, and once also surrounded by wealthy villas, including that of the great orator Cicero.

From Frascati, continue to Grottaferrata, another little wine town located amidst the region's vineyards, and with its own collection of rustic *cantine*. Above their dark arched stone portals are hand-scrawled signs: *'Vino propria produzione – Per portare via! Lira 500 litro'* – 'Own-produced wine to take away, 500 lira a litre.' Inside, great oak barrels are lined along the cool walls, incongruous beside small modern presses, and shiny apparatus for filtering the wine. And along benches, or sitting at card tables, as always, the men gather to drink wine and while away the hours. Grottaferrata is famous for its eleventh-century Greek Orthodox monastery which can be visited. The view from its terrace over the slopes of the Colli Albani to the Roman Campagna is splendid.

The N216 from Grottaferrata leads next to Marino, whose wines are probably the region's best known after Frascati. A lively annual wine festival, the *Sagra dell'Uva* takes place on the first Sunday in October, and during this time the town's fountain spouts wine. Marino perches virtually on the edge of a long extinct volcanic crater, which has filled now to form Lake Albano. Follow a small road from Marino down into the crater and continue around the shore of the lake. In summer, there are *porchetta* stands here, selling the fragrant meat by the *etto* (100 g – about ¼ lb) or in *panini*, that is, stuffed in rolls. Continue round, then up again to Castel Gandolfo, a pretty village located, like Marino, on the edge of the crater. Its position makes it a favourite resort town, and it is also, of course, the site of the vast Villa del Papa, where the Pope traditionally spends summer.

The lake road continues along the edge of the crater then branches left to Albano Laziale, bombed severely during the last war, though today a popular (and noisy) tourist centre. The town is actually located along both the Via Appia Antica, and the modern Via Appia Nuova (N7), so access to and from Rome has always been easy. Albano is one of the oldest of the Castelli Romani, its name derived from ancient Alba Longa, founded, according to legend, in 1150 BC. The town probably increased in importance in the second century AD as a staging post along the Appian Way. The Villa Communale, at the entrance to Albano, overlooks the Roman Campagna and was once owned by Pompey. The *Cisternone*, which dates from the second century AD, is a massive reservoir hewn out of solid rock with a capacity of over 80,000 gallons of water for the former use of the town's inhabitants and thirsty Roman legions.

Charming little Ariccia is next reached on the N7, another ancient village once surrounded by villas, now by vineyards and chestnut groves. From Ariccia, continue on the N7 to Genzano, located on the lip of another volcanic crater, which again has filled to form the smaller Lake Nemi. Genzano is famous for its annual flower festival, the *Infiorata*, during which time the main street is carpeted with flowers.

Small, deep, circular Lake Nemi was known in ancient times as the Mirror of Diana because a sacred grove and temple used to stand on its north-east side, reflected in the still dark waters. Today it

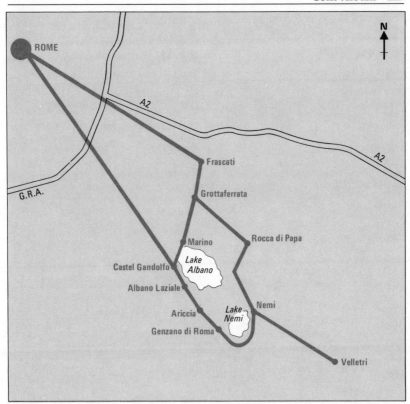

remains remote, peaceful, and almost mysterious: on a stormy autumn-into-winter afternoon, when its waters churn black, and angry clouds spill over the wooded lip of the crater, one feels an overwhelming sense of the sinister power of nature and of pagan rites which took place here to pacify it. Follow the lake around to Nemi itself, a little village overlooking the water, well-preserved and with an intact castle which dominates the scene. Despite its small size, Nemi is an excellent place to rest. There are some good traditional *osterie* here. The village is also famous for its exquisite wild strawberries, celebrated in a *Sagra delle Fragole* held annually in June.

Velletri is located some five miles south of Nemi on the N217 road, which is an extension of the Via dei Laghi from Marino. Velletri is not one of the thirteen Castelli Romani towns, but it is an important wine commune that produces both white and, rare for this region, a certain amount of red wine. From Velletri return along the Via dei Laghi and, a few miles past the turn-off to Nemi, find the N218 road right to Rocca di Papa, highest village of the Castelli Romani; higher still, the summit of Monte Cavo can be reached either by following a small private road, or on foot via the ancient Roman Via Sacra. The view from here at sunset is particularly breathtaking.

From Rocca di Papa, continue back to Grottaferrata, and either return to Rome on the N511 or, from Frascati, on the Via Tuscolana. While the tour is relatively brief, it ideally should be spread out over a period of days, with overnight stops in Frascati or Grottaferrata, and at Castel Gandolfo or Nemi. The region, surprisingly, has few campsites.

Wine Producers

00044 Frascati

Vini di Fontana Candida SpA
Via Vanvitelli, 20
tel: (06) 9420066
Frascati DOC, Frascati Superiore DOC
Mon–Fri, mornings only. Telephone in
advance.
Max 30 pers.
English spoken.

Colli di Tuscolo
Via de Passolombardo, 137
tel: (06) 61 30 161
Frascati DOC, Frascati Superiore DOC
Open Wed and Thurs 9–12h; 15–17h by
appointment.
Max 50 pers.
English spoken.

00040 Monteporzio Catone

Cantine San Marco
Via di Frascati 60
tel: (06) 94 22 689
Frascati DOC, Frascati Superiore DOC,
Castelli Romani
Open Sat and Sun 8h30–12h30; 14h30–17h
by appointment.
Max 30 pers.

Rome

Cantine Conte Zandotti
Via Colle Mattia, 8
tel: (06) 61 60 355
Frascati DOC, Frascati DOC Superiore
Open office hours. Telephone for
appointment.
English spoken.

Wine Festivals

June	Sagra delle Fragole	Nemi
June	Exhibition of wines	Velletri
July	Sagra delle Pesche	Castel Gandolfo
Sept	*Porchetta* Festival	Ariccia
End of Sept	Festa dell'Uva	Velletri
1st Sun in Oct	Sagra dell'Uva	Marino

Regional Gastronomy

Porchetta Roast suckling pig, stuffed with
rosemary, garlic, and *pancetta* and cooked
in a wood-fired oven.

Bucatini all'Amatriciana Elbow macaroni
served with a fiery tomato and hot pepper
sauce, and freshly grated Pecorino cheese.

Spaghetti alla carbonara Spaghetti tossed
with *pancetta* and raw eggs, which cook
from the steam of the hot pasta.

Gnocchi alla romana Semolina dumplings
baked with cheese and lots of butter.

Fettuccine al burro Thin home-made egg
noodles, served simply with abundant
butter and freshly grated cheese.

Suppli al telefono Little balls of *risotto* stuffed
with Mozzarella cheese, coated in

breadcrumbs and deep-fried. When
bitten, strings of melted cheese stretch out
into 'wires', hence the name 'telephone
wires'.

Saltimbocca Thin slices of veal rolled up
with sage leaves and *prosciutto*, then fried
in butter and olive oil.

Polpettone Meat balls.

Abbacchio alla cacciatora Lamb stewed in
rosemary, anchovies, oil, vinegar, and
wine.

Coda alla vaccinara Rich, flavourful oxtail
stew.

Trippa alla romana Tripe braised in a tomato
and cheese sauce.

Fritto misto Mixed platter of meat and
vegetables, dipped in batter, egg, or
breadcrumbs and deep-fried.

Carciofi alla giudia Baby artichokes, flattened out and deep-fried, a dish that originated in the ancient Jewish quarter of Rome.

Agrodolce Sweet and sour sauce in which vegetables like onions or peas are cooked.

Budino di Ricotta Ricotta cheesecake.

Cheese:
Pecorino Dry, hard, cheese made from sheep's milk curdled with lamb's rennet.
Ricotta Fresh, moist curd cheese, used for both sweet and savoury dishes.
Gorgonzola Creamy, rich, blue-veined cheese.
Mozzarella The real thing is authentic buffalo milk cheese.
Caciotta Romana Semi-hard, sweet sheep's cheese.

Restaurants

00044 Frascati

Ristorante Spartaco
Viale Letizia Bonaparte, 1
tel: (06) 94 20431
Regional and family specialities such as *cannelloni alla Spartacus, lombate all'arancio, crostate delle nonno*, served on the terrace in good weather.
Open daily except Tue 12–15h30; 19h30–24h
Inexpensive

Cantina Vigna Verde Aiomone
Via Michaelangelo Gaitani, No 8
Typical wine *cantina* – a place to take parcels of paper-wrapped *porchetta*, to settle in for a few hours, spinning out carafes of strong, golden Frascati. Sliced meats, cheeses, and sandwiches available.
Very Inexpensive

Ristorante al Due Ceppi di Mancinelli
Via Prataporci, 32
tel: (06) 94 22 106
Home-cooked regional specialities and own-produced Frascati.
Closed Tue
Open 12–24h
Moderate

00046 Grottaferrata

Ristorante al Fico
Via Anagnina, 86
tel: (06) 94 52 90
Regional foods and a large selection of local wines.
Closed Wed
Moderate

Ristorante Il Castagneto
Via Tuscolana Km27,700
tel: (06) 94 68 289
Moderate restaurant serving home-cooked regional foods.
Open daily 9–24h

00047 Marino

Ristorante 'Antonio al Vigneto'
Via dei Laghi
tel: (06) 93 87 034
Roman specialities and fish from the lake.
Closed Wed
Moderate

00040 Nemi

Ristorante da Tiberio
Piazza Umberto, 1
tel: (06) 93 78096
Typical rustic *osteria* – family atmosphere and home-cooked specialities including fresh pasta such as *pappardelle alla lepre, fettucine coi funghi.*
Open 11–15h; 19–22h
Inexpensive

Restaurant Specchio di Diana
Corso Vittorio Emanuele, 13
tel: (06) 93 78016
Restaurant with roof garden overlooking Lake Nemi serving Roman specialities and Castelli Romani wines.
Closed Wed
Inexpensive

Monte Compatri

Ristorante d'Artagnan di Sandro Fiorito
Via Tuscolana
tel: (06) 94 68291
Imaginative and regional cooking such as *lombata in agrodolce, funghi fioriti*
Open Tue–Sun 12–15h30; 19–24h
Moderate to **Expensive**

00040 Monte Porzio Catone

Hostaria Fontana Candida
Via di Fontana Candida, 19
tel: (06) 94 49 614
Typical Roman *osteria* owned by this well-known wine firm. Fontana Candida wines and Roman foods served on veranda in summer.
Closed Tue
Open 12–15h; 19–22h
Moderate

Hotels

00044 Frascati

Eden Tuscolano
Via Tuscolana 0
tel: (06) 94 24001
Comfortable **Moderate** to **Expensive** hotel
with restaurant, garden, and parking.

Where to Get
Additional Information

Italian Government Tourist Office
(E.N.I.T.)
630 5th Ave
NY NY 10111
tel: (212) 245–4822

Ente Provinciale per il Turismo di Roma
Via Parigi, 11
00185 Roma
tel: (06) 46 18 51

Azienda Autonoma Soggiorno e Turismo
Piazza Marconi, 1
Frascati
tel: (06) 94 0331

Consorzio Tutela Denominazione Frascati
Via Matteotti, 12/a
Frascati
tel: (06) 94 00 22

Commune di Roma
Assessorato per il Turismo
Via Milano, 68
Roma

Rome Automobile Club
Via Cristoforo Colombo, 261
Roma

00046 Grottaferrata

Villa Fiorio
Viale Dusmet, 25
tel: (06) 94 5276
Pleasant, elegant hotel with swimming
pool, garden, and restaurant.
Expensive

Castel Gandolfo

Hotel Pagnanelli
tel: (06) 93 60 004
Small hotel overlooking the lake, with
good restaurant serving fish specialities
cooked over a wood fire.
Inexpensive

00041 Albano

Miralago
Via dei Cappuccini
tel: (06) 93 22253
Modern, with good facilities.
Moderate

00040 Nemi

Al Bosco
tel: (06) 93 78085
Inexpensive hotel with good views,
garden, and restaurant.

00040 Rocca di Papa

Angeletto
Via del Tufo, 32
tel: (06) 94 9020
Moderate hotel with garden and
restaurant.

Bibliography

The Wines of Italy by Cyril Ray, Penguin
1971
Vino by Burton Anderson, Atlantic,
Little, Brown 1980

─AUSTRIA─

——AUSTRIA'S—— WINE GARDENS

Austria is not well-known as a wine-producing country, but in the past the vineyards of the Austro–Hungarian Empire were vast, including those of present-day Hungary, the Ljutomer and Maribor vineyards of Slovenia in northern Yugoslavia and those of the Alto Adige region of northern Italy (an area which even today continues to produce wines closer in style to Austrian than Italian and which still exports much of what is produced across the border). Today, though her wine area is naturally much smaller, Austria remains an important wine-producing country with distinct wine regions whose diversity, both in styles of wines produced and in atmosphere and ambience, reflects the former contrasts of the Empire. Its wine regions are fascinating and delightful to visit.

The vineyards of the Burgenland, for example, extend around the steamy, exotic Neusiedlersee and are adjacent to the border with Hungary. Much of this region, in fact, once formed part of Hungary, though the residents voted after World War I to become part of Austria. Not surprisingly, Hungarian influence is apparent not only in styles of wine produced, but in the atmosphere found in typical wine villages such as Rust and Podersdorf, where lively gypsy *csárdás* (both the name of the tavern and the folk dances performed there) serve vivid, exciting paprika-flavoured foods accompanied by rich, spicy wines. The vineyards of Styria once continued across the present-day border into Slovenia; indeed, the famed Ljutomer vineyards are only some fifty miles away and similar fruity, pleasant, and sometimes pungent wines are produced in both.

Lower Austria is the largest wine-producing province in Austria, both in terms of quantity of wine produced and in area. The province is extremely varied, and includes the vineyards of Retz which extend to the Czechoslovak border (the town itself is famous for its atmospheric cellars burrowed into hills, and under undulating streets), the craggy stretch of vineyards that rises above the Danube known as the Wachau, the famous vineyards of Voslau and Baden (wine from little Gumpoldskirchen is among the best-known from Austria), and others, all with a unique atmosphere and character that is reflected in the wines themselves. The country's capital also remains an important wine region. The vineyards of Vienna are unique, for though the great city is ever-encroaching on wine suburbs such as Grinzing, Heiligenstadt and Nussdorf, the young wines produced in these towns continue to be important, providing the *Heurige* (this year's wine) so loved by the Viennese (composers such as Beethoven, Mozart, and Schubert, for example, came to these wine towns to drink *Heurige* and to work – two activities, it seems, that were inseparable). No visit to Vienna – no matter how brief – is complete without taking the Hohenstrasse through the Wienerwald to these happy wine suburbs.

Austria's wine regions, like her wines, are not well-known outside their own country, but they are delightful in character and atmosphere and deserve to be visited by all who not only love drinking good wine, but who also enjoy good living.

How to Get There

By Car
The vineyards and happy wine gardens of Austria are all easily reached from Vienna itself. It is but a brief drive to the wine suburbs which are found to the north and south of the capital (for directions, see tour below). The vineyards of the Wachau are located just off the main A1 which connects Vienna with Salzburg. The Burgenland lies to the south of Vienna, and is reached by either Highway 16 which leads to the elegant provincial town of Eisenstadt, or Highway 10 to reach the beginning of the sign-posted *Neusiedlersee Weinstrasse*.

By Plane
From the US there are direct, non-stop flights to Vienna. Salzburg is also a popular destination, and there are numerous connecting flights from many major European cities.

By Train
There are frequent direct trains via Paris to Vienna. The Paris–Warsaw Express runs a number of trains daily, and takes about 15 hours to reach Vienna, with stops in Austria at Salzburg and Linz.

Local Public Transport
There is a main railway between Salzburg, Linz, Melk (Wachau) and Vienna, with frequent trains daily. There is also a good local service between Vienna, Neustadt, and Sopron (Hungary). Local coaches offer tours from Vienna to the 'wine suburbs' of Grinzing, Heiligenstadt, Nussdorf, and others. This is a wise alternative to driving, for inevitably in a Viennese *Heurige* it is all too easy to drink more than one plans to!

Boat trips up or down the Danube are also available. The Soviet Danube Line and the Danube Steamship Co run from Passau (Germany) to Vienna, with stops at Melk, Dürnstein, and Krems. It is also possible to travel by hovercraft along the Danube from Vienna to Budapest. For further information, contact the Austrian National Tourist Office, or the local tourist office in Vienna (addresses below).

Car Rental Information
Salzburg
Avis: Ferdinand Porscherstrasse 7
    tel: (06 222) 77 278
    Salzburg Airport
    tel: (06 222) 77 278
Hertz: Ferdinand Porscherstrasse 7
    tel: (06 222) 76 674
    Salzburg Airport
    tel: (06 222) 27 138

Linz
Avis: Tourotel, Untere Donaulande 9
    tel: (0732) 74 853
Hertz: Hotel Schillerpark, Rainerstrasse 2
    tel: (0732) 64 211

Vienna
Avis: Opernring 1
    tel: (0222) 57 35 95
    Schwechat Airport
    tel: (0222) 77 70 27 00
Hertz: Kaerntner Ring 17
    tel: (0222) 52 86 77
    Schwechat Airport
    tel: (0222) 77 70 26 61

Michelin Map No 426

Austrian Wine

Austria produces a remarkable range and variety of wines including plentiful light, medium-dry white table wines, distinctive estate-bottled white wines from single *rieds* (vineyards); rich, raisiny dessert wines produced from overripe grapes affected by *botrytis cinerea*; and notable, soft, full-bodied red wines. Labels of Austrian wines generally indicate the region or commune of production, as well as the grape variety or varieties. Quality levels (*Kabinett, Spätlese*, etc.) are also indicated where relevant. There are four principal wine regions in Austria:

Lower Austria Both the largest in area and in production (accounting for nearly ⅔ of the country's entire output), this broad and diverse province is divided into eight distinct wine zones. The Wachau is probably the best known of these, producing both plentiful dry to medium-dry white wines, as well as distinctive wines from historic individual *rieds* (vineyards) located in communes such as Dürnstein, Loiben, Joching, and Spitz to name but a few. Other important zones of production in Lower Austria include Falkenstein and Retz (extending north of Vienna to the Czech border), Klosterneuburg (centring around the famous abbey of the same name), Krems (an important and fascinating old town on the Danube bordering the Wachau) and, south of Vienna, the distinguished vineyards of Gumpoldskirchen and Voslau. The most widely-planted and successful vine is the distinctive and unique Austrian variety known as Grüner Veltliner, which produces both sprightly *Heurige* as well as distinguished, elegant

table wines. Other important grape varieties include Rhine Riesling, Welsch Riesling, and Weisser Burgunder. Sweet speciality wines come from Gumpoldskirchen, while the vineyards of Voslau and Baden produce primarily red wines.

Burgenland South of Vienna, bordering Hungary, and enclosing the flat, elongated Neusiedlersee, a hot Pannonian climate combined with a high level of evaporation from this strange steppe lake, results in the large-scale production of extremely ripe, rich dessert wines that rival their German counterparts. The climate and hothouse atmosphere allows *botrytis cinerea* to set in with remarkable regularity, and a full range of exceptional dessert wines are produced, categorized by increasingly higher levels of ripeness (*Kabinett, Spätlese, Auslese, Beerenauslese*, and *Trockenbeerenauslese*). The qualification for these accolades, based on minimum must weights, is even higher than in Germany (a different scale of measurement is used

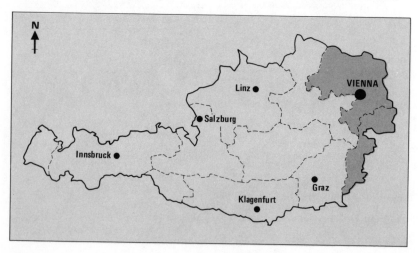

here, known as KNW). *Ausbruch* is a speciality dessert wine from Rust and other wine communes in Burgenland. The most important vineyards of this region centre around the Neusiedlersee, and grapes such as Weisser Burgunder, Welsch Riesling, Müller-Thurgau, and others are widely cultivated. In addition to its sweet dessert wines, pithy, dry white wines are produced from Grüner Veltliner (such wines have a completely different character to those produced from the same grape in Lower Austria), as well as from Traminer, and Muskat-Ottonel, while notable red wines are produced from the Blaufränkisch and the Portugieser grapes.

Vienna Austria's capital today remains an important wine-producing region, not so much in terms of quantity, as in its contribution of lively, sprightly *Heurigen* wines produced from vineyards around suburbs such as Grinzing, Sievering, Nussdorf, and Heiligenstadt. Such wines, mainly produced from the Grüner Veltliner, Weisser Burgunder, and Rhine Riesling, are generally never even bottled, for they are consumed on the spot in the numerous and delightful taverns.

Styria The vineyards of Styria, in the south-east of the country, are virtual extensions of the well-known vineyards of Slovenia, across the border in Yugoslavia. Though it is a small region, notable wines are produced here, including pungent, spicy Traminer and Gewürztraminer wines, as well as Welsch Riesling (which corresponds to Yugoslavian Laski Riesling), Müller-Thurgau, and aromatic Muskat-Ottonel.

Weingutsiegel A guarantee of quality, this neck seal is only awarded to quality wines that have undergone strict tests, reach minimum must weights, and are typical of the region where they are produced.

—Austrian Wine Tours—
The Vineyards of Vienna

There is no 'wine road' that leads from central Vienna to the wine-producing and -drinking suburbs to the north. Nor is there need of one, for the lilt of the Schrammel music and the scent of yeasty, youthful wine drawn from the barrels of village wine producers is enough to draw Viennese and visitors alike to the numerous *Heurigen* found in Nussdorf, Heiligenstadt, Grinzing, Sievering, Neustift, and elsewhere. (Indeed, those who plan on drinking more than a couple of mugs of wine – and it is a difficult feat to drink less – would be well advised to consider taking a coach tour, or else to stay in one of the Gasthofen or private homes in these villages which rent out rooms.) A brief and pleasant tour can be made from Vienna through the Wienerwald to the wine suburbs first, and then on to the vineyards and abbey of Klosterneuburg.

From central Vienna, follow the Mariahilfer Strasse south-west to the Schonbrunn Palace (a grandiose Imperial residence set within a magnificent park and one of the important historical monuments of the Austro–Hungarian Empire), then continue on briefly to Hütteldorf where the road to the right leads into the Wienerwald. As the road climbs into the wooded hills and carries on through Neuwaldegg and Neustift, splendid views are glimpsed of Vienna and the Danube below. Carry on along the winding Höhenstrasse, pausing to take in the view at Hauserl am Roan and at Cobenzl, before reaching the famous Kahlenberg which overlooks the vineyards of Grinzing. Descend to the wine villages of Nussdorf and Heiligenstadt (a favourite abode of Beethoven's), to Grinzing and to Sievering, pausing wherever fancy strikes to sit in the shade of a linden tree, drinking fresh wine and eating simple Viennese foods such as *backhendl* (Viennese fried chicken), smooth-textured, hot *leberkäse*, roast hocks of pork, juicy blood sausages and piquant *Wursten*, Liptauer and other cheeses, pickled vegetables, raw onions, long mild radishes, and much else. The tally of what you have eaten and drunk (such places are never expensive) is kept on a slip of paper in a mug on the table.

The Grüner Veltliner, Weisser Burgunder, or Rhine Riesling served in the numerous *Heurigen* – grand as well as small – which proliferate in these wine

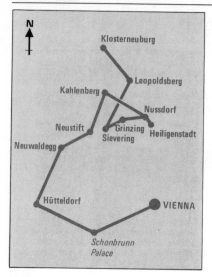

Before returning to Vienna (the next morning, preferably, if you have spent the night in an inn here, having sung and drunk the night away) make a tour by way of Leopoldsberg to nearby Klosterneuburg. Klosterneuburg is another important wine town, famous for its thirteenth-century Augustinian abbey, Stift Klosterneuburg, known popularly as 'the abbey of the flowing tap'. For indeed, the vineyards of the abbey still produce some of the finest and most famous wines of this region; moreover, since 1860 the abbey has also been the home of the most important viticultural institute in the country. The abbey can be visited (there is a wine museum), and there are numerous *Heurigen* in Klosterneuburg. Each year, too, wine festivities take place on St Leopold's Day (November); one unique event calls for everyone to slide down an enormous 'thousand jug' cask which stands in the extensive and fine wine cellars of the abbey.

In addition to the wine villages and *Heurigen* to the north of Vienna, there are also numerous vineyards, wine villages, and wine gardens to the south which can also be visited, perhaps en route to Burgenland. In particular, the spa towns of Baden and Bad Voslau are worth visiting (the rich red wines produced on these sheltered southern slopes are popular), as well as the village of Gumpoldskirchen famous for its Rotgipfler and Zierfändler wines – rich, distinguished specialities that are among Austria's best and most famous. There are, of course, both numerous *Heurigen* and private guest houses which serve good, simple home-cooking, along with plenty of local wine.

villages is, or should be, actually produced by the proprietor himself. This peculiar Austrian institution legally came into being in the eighteenth century when an Austrian Emperor declared that wine producers could sell both wine and food on their premises provided that it was produced by themselves. '*Heurig*' means 'this year's', and the new wine, traditionally, is drunk as early as the November after the vintage. The bunches of fir branches and the straw wheels which hang over the door of the premises to signify that they are open stay up only for as long as 'this year's' wine lasts.

The Wachau

Between the grandiose, yellow Baroque abbey of Melk and the equally ornate abbey known as Stift Gottweig, the Danube carves its way through a steep and craggy gorge: hot, rocky, tortuous land that is virtually opposite in character to the expected Austrian scene of grassy alpine meadows covered in wild flowers. This is the Wachau, a region which, despite its inhospitable appearance, produces not only much fine wine but also an abundance of superb fruits and vegetables. It is a small region, easily reached from Vienna, or else en route to the capital from Salzburg. Wine villages such as Spitz,

Dürnstein, and Stein are both historically interesting and welcoming, and there are campsites along the Danube as well as numerous inexpensive inns and *Heurigen*. The Wachau, compared to wine regions in France or Germany, is virtually unvisited; yet a sign-posted wine road, an excellent wine museum in Krems, and numerous opportunities to taste the local products make a tour of this vineyard particularly satisfying.

If en route from Salzburg to Vienna, exit the A1 autoroute at Melk and either visit or admire the conspicuous and grand abbey from the road, before crossing the Danube and continuing downriver on the left bank. The steeply-terraced vineyards of the Wachau soon come into sight, and the sign-posted wine road leads through small and picturesque wine villages nestled beneath them. Villages such as Spitz, Joching, and St Michael must be explored on foot; climb up the steep streets to the vineyards, poke your head into flowered courtyards, settle into vine-shaded *Heurigen*, or spend the night in one of the small guest houses that are found throughout the region. Though much local wine is produced in large cooperatives (in Dürnstein, Loiben, Krems and elsewhere), individual wines from single vineyards – the name of the *reid* is sometimes indicated on labels – can be enjoyed in small wine taverns.

Spitz is one of the larger communities of the Wachau, though it is still just a small wine village clustered around a vine-covered hill known as the 'thousand pail hill' because of the amount of wine produced from it. Climb up the terraced slopes to the Jauerling ridge for a spectacular panorama of the vineyards and

river gorge, and refresh yourself afterwards with a bracing tot of the famous apricot *schnapps* known as 'Marillenlikor', also a product of this fertile region. Weissenkirchen is another popular wine village, noted for its charming and colourful houses. The Wachau Museum, located in the nineteenth-century Teisenhofer-Hof, is worth visiting for it traces the history and folklore of the region. After Weissenkirchen the wine road and river turn briefly but sharply south, diverted by a steep and rocky spur. Perched on this stark outcrop, looking down on the village of Dürnstein, are the ruins of a medieval castle where, legend has it, Richard the Lionheart was imprisoned on his return from the Holy Land. He was not released until his faithful Blondel, searching for his master, sang a song that Richard heard and recognized. Dürnstein is the most charming wine village in the Wachau, huddled under the castle, beside the Danube, its old streets lined with *Heurigen* and inns, as well as two excellent hotels. The historic *Winzergenossenschaft 'Wachau'*

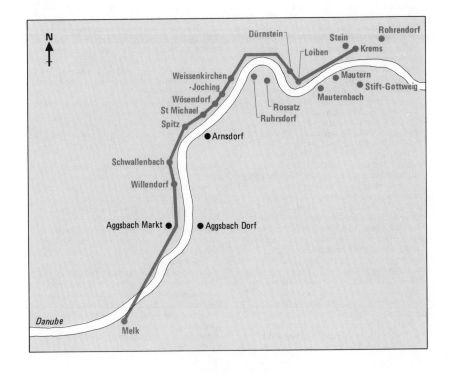

(wine cooperative) of Dürnstein can be visited by appointment.

Beyond Dürnstein, the land near the river flattens somewhat, while the steep terraced hills rise above this brief plain.

Ober- and Unter-Loiben are the next wine villages reached, no more than small clusters of houses separated by stretches of flat vineyards. The vineyards which thrive on these richer, lower fields are cultivated by the so-called 'high culture' system pioneered by the great Austrian viticulturist Dr Lenz Moser. The high-culture system, whereby vines are planted and trained in such a manner as to allow greater use of machinery (a tractor, for example, can easily pass between the rows of vines), results in higher yield per vine and more efficient and cost-effective production, though it is not a method that necessarily produces the finest wines. Indeed, the most individual and distinguished wines of Loiben, and other communes of the Wachau, are undoubtedly produced from the steep, terraced vineyards in the hills beyond, vineyards that are labour-intensive due to their position, and which still must be worked by man. Drive out from Loiben (after visiting the modern cooperative *Winzergenossenschaft Dinstlgut Loiben*) through the flatter fields, then up into the hills to gain an idea of this essential contrast. The individual sites – *rieds* – such as Sussenberg, Schutt, Burgstall and hundreds of others have been producing unique wines since the Middle Ages. From the top of the hills, one looks across the Danube to Stift Gottweig.

The most distinctive grape variety of Austria is the Grüner Veltliner, which in the Wachau ripens to produce a piquant and fresh wine that is ideal drunk as *Heurige* (wines from the finest *rieds*, however, gain in character from bottle-ageing). The Rhine Riesling (the true Riesling of Germany and Alsace, as opposed to the Welsch or Laski Riesling) also develops well on the rocky terraces of the Loiben Berg, for in steepness and degree of difficulty of cultivation, the Wachau rivals even the Mosel, though its hotter continental climate and different soils result in wines of entirely different character to those from that great German vineyard. Another popular and useful grape variety planted throughout the Wachau is the Neuburger (legend says that it was first cultivated in vineyards around Spitz, after a bundle of vines was washed up from the river – indeed, some of the best examples of this rather full and soft wine still come from that village). The Müller-Thurgau is also planted here, while the St Laurent, a black grape, produces perfumed and aromatic red wine.

Krems, a busy market town, stands at the eastern end of the Wachau. Make sure to visit the Weinbaumuseum (located in the Dominikanerplatz) before strolling to the adjacent village of Stein to admire its Baroque residences found along quaint and quiet cobbled streets. Painted in subtle shades of peach, mauve, pale green and Wedgwood blue, they are decorated with wreaths and columns and bear witness to the prosperity of this established centre of trade and culture. Wander along to the old church and climb a steep set of steps for a view of the river; continue through a cobbled residential area to reach the vineyards once more, before descending the steep hill to the cool shelter of a *Heurige*, or else refreshing yourself with a goblet of Marillen Schaumwein – sparkling apricot wine produced from the luscious fruit that grows on the plains of the valley. In spring, the scented apricot blossoms lay a fragrant veil over the moist, fertile loess terraces.

From Krems, a brief detour must be made to nearby Rohrendorf, home of the Lenz Moser Company, one of the most important and well known of Austrian wine producers, before crossing the 500-year-old bridge at Krems and exploring villages such as Mautern and Rossatz, and the monastery of Stift Gottweig.

Burgenland

Burgenland is a strange and exotic Central European wine region. This eastern-most of Austria's nine autonomous provinces borders Hungary and actually belonged to that nation for several hundred years (the massive Esterhazy Palace in Eisenstadt, where Haydn was the court composer, is a reminder of the noble Hungarians who settled here). The residents of the region, primarily German speaking, voted after World War I to join the newly formed Austrian Republic; after World War II, however, when Austria was ruled by the four Allied powers, Burgenland came under the Soviet sphere of influence. The region today remains an intersection of West and East; tourists in the resorts along the Neusiedlersee likely as not come from Hungary, Czechoslovakia, and Poland, rather than countries to the west.

The region is geographically exotic. The Neusiedlersee, the third largest lake in Europe, is a steppe lake, never more than six feet deep, its banks covered in a wide thicket of reeds in which an amazing variety of wildfowl make their home (Viennese families, too, have curious holiday homes which stand on stilts amidst the reeds). A steamy, Pannonian continental climate, combined with a high level of evaporation from the lake (it has even been known to dry up completely) provide the unique conditions necessary for the production of fine and richly-flavoured wines. Numerous grape varieties are cultivated: Welsch Riesling, Grüner Veltliner, Müller-Thurgau, Neuburger, Muskat-Ottonel, Traminer, and Rhine Riesling all ripen to produce notable dry wines, as well as naturally-sweet dessert wines bearing quality designations of *Beerenauslese*, *Ausbruch* (a unique Austrian speciality) and *Trockenbeerenauslese*. Distinguished,

and surprisingly full-bodied red wines are produced in Burgenland, too; indeed, Bismarck's favourite wine was Blaufränkisch from Pottelsdorf, while the Emperor Franz Josef preferred the red wines of Mattersburg.

There are four sign-posted wine roads in Burgenland, but the most accessible wine region, as well as the most important zone of production in terms of both quality and quantity, centres around the area known as Rust-Neusiedlersee. The easiest way to reach this region from Vienna is by way of either Highway 10 or 16. If coming via the former, turn right at the intersection with Highway 304, and continue to Jois where the sign-posted *Neusiedlersee Weinstrasse* begins. Follow the wine road through Winden am See (where the oldest wine press in Burgenland, dating from 100 AD, was discovered in a Roman courtyard) and Breitenbrunn, both popular resorts as well as wine towns, though the lake is a considerable distance from the town centres due to the wide zone of reeds and marsh. The vineyards extend over the gentle, rich slopes that rise above the lake, and local wines can be sampled throughout in numerous *Heurigen* found in every village, indeed, around every corner. Whereas elsewhere in Austria, wine drunk in *Heurigen* is often fresh, crisp, sprightly stuff meant to be quaffed in quantity with food, wines offered in Burgenland's *Heurigen* are often rich (and elsewhere extremely rare), marvellously luscious dessert wines of *Auslese*, *Beerenauslese* and *Ausbruch* standard. Purbach am See, the next wine village encountered, recalls the Turkish invasions and occupation of this historic, age-old land; for one of its houses (and many of its wine labels) depicts the curious story of the so-called Purbach Turk who, when the

Burgenland *Neusiedlersee* Weinstraße

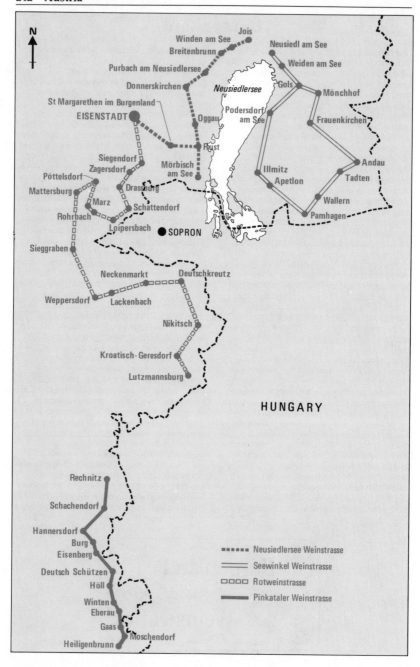

Turks were finally expelled, had drunk so much wine that he fell asleep, only to awake and realize that his friends had fled. He climbed up a chimney to hide, but was later discovered; the Turk stopped in Purbach, became a convert to Christianity and, presumably, a firm advocate of wine drinking.

From Purbach continue to Donnerskirchen. This small wine village and resort offers, in summer, a wide range of specialized wine and food courses (for further information, write to: *Winzergenossenschaft 'St Martinus'* – address below). Cherry trees blossom in spring, and the rows of smug *Winzerhofen*, wine farmers' houses, attest to the region's comfortable prosperity. The *Heurige im Martinsschlossl* has a particularly fine reputation for serving the specialities of Burgenland.

After Donnerskirchen, take the left fork which leads to Oggau, renowned for its rich wines, particularly its red Oggauer Blaufränkisch. The next village, Rust, is the most famous of the wine communes on the Neusiedlersee. It was named a free-town in 1681, on the condition that it delivered 500 jugs of wine annually to the royal table, so its wines have been undoubtedly highly regarded for centuries. Rust is a good holiday centre; its old houses topped by heavy storks' nests (curiously reminiscent of Alsace), its holiday chalets on stilts down by the lake, its *csárdás* and *Heurigen* alike, its remarkably varied wildlife (there are over 200 species of birds found here), and of course, its world famous wines, makes Rust a particularly pleasant centre to stay in.

From Rust, continue along the lake-side wine road to Mörbisch, a strange, moody little village with old balconied houses located (almost) on the impassable frontier with Hungary (there is a romantic 'sea stage' here where concerts and operettas are produced in season). Return to Rust, and take the wine road which leads eventually to Eisenstadt. Just out of Rust, however, two notable 'monuments' should be visited: the famous Roman quarry at St Margarethen, and the

enormous cooperative of Burgenland, *Zentralkellerei Burgenlandischer Winzerverband Rust* which can be visited.

Eisenstadt is an elegant provincial capital; as well as tasting wines and regional foods, the visitor may wish to visit the Esterhazy Palace, Haydn's house (Haydngasse 21) and the composer's tomb. There is a wine museum in the Landesmuseum of Eisenstadt. The old village of Kleinhoflein (part of Eisenstadt) is most interesting to visit for its old wine cellars and caves, and, of course, its *Heurigen*.

In addition to the *Neusiedlersee Weinstrasse*, there are three other wine roads through the vineyards of Burgenland. The *Seewinkel Weinstrasse* runs across the hot, gravelly Parndorf plateau through wine villages on the east side of the lake. The dryness of the climate, the deep sandy soil, and an intense summer heat result in large quantitites of rich, mild wines that are extremely ripe in flavour and scent. The *Rotweinstrasse* extends below Eisenstadt, through hills and wine villages bordering Hungary. It is not surprising, in fact, that the vineyards around the Hungarian town of Sopron produce red wines similar in character to those from these Austrian wine communes; though a border now separates them, for centuries the small communities on either side were neighbours. Blaufränkisch from Austria, Kékfrankos from Hungary (both names mean 'Blue French'), these red wines match the character of the lively paprika-flavoured foods served in both places. The final wine road of Burgenland is the *Pinkataler Weinstrasse*, so named because the vineyards are located in the picturesque Pinka Valley. Wines are only produced in small quantities around villages such as Rechnitz (which lies at the foot of the Geschriebensteine, highest mountain in Burgenland), Hannersdorf, and Burg to the north, and Höll, Winten, Eberau, Moschendorf, and Heiligenbrunn to the south. The ancient wine cellars in Heiligenbrunn are particularly noteworthy. Both red and white wines are produced in this tiny wine region.

Wine Producers

A-3495 Rohrendorf (near Krems)

Weinkellerei Lenz Moser
Lenz Moser Strasse 4–6
tel: (027 32) 55 41
Open daily 9–15h
Appointment preferable but not essential.
Max 60 pers.
English spoken.

A-3500 Krems

Winzergenossenschaft Krems
Sandgrube 13
tel: (027 32) 55 11
Mon–Thur 7–12h; 13–16h45; Fri 7–12h
Appointment necessary.
Max 60 pers.
English spoken.
A variety of wines can be tasted for a small charge.

A-3601 Unter-Loiben

Winzergenossenschaft Dinstlgut Loiben
und Umgebung
tel: (027 32) 55 16
Mon–Thur 7–12h; 13–17h; Fri 7–12h
Appointment necessary.
Max 100 pers.
English spoken.
Weinproben of 8 different wines for a small charge.

A-3601 Dürnstein

Winzergenossenschaft 'Wachau'
tel: (027 11) 217
April–Oct Tue & Thur 14h30–17h
Appointment necessary.
Max 50 pers.
English spoken.
Weinproben of 6 or 12 wines for a small charge.

A-2352 Gumpoldskirchen

Gumpoldskirchner Winzergenossenschaft
Jubiläumsstrasse 43
tel: (022 52) 62 129
Mon–Thur 8–16h
Appointment necessary.
Max 40 pers.

A-7071 Rust am See

Burgenländischer Winzerverband
Zentralkellerei am Rusterberg
tel: (026 85) 544
Mon–Thur 8–17h
Appointment necessary.
Max 50 pers.
English spoken.
Wines can be tasted without appointment for a small charge.

Wine Festivals

End of May/ early June	Österreichische Weinmesse (Austrian Wine Fair with wines from all the different Austrian wine regions on show)	Krems
Late summer	Burgenland Wine Week	Eisenstadt
Aug 13–15	Rieslingfest in der Wachau	Weissenkirchen

Additional there are numerous small festivals that take place in most wine villages. In particular, there are opportunities for tastings of full ranges of different vintages and quality levels at festivals known as *'Weinkosten'* which take place locally over the summer. Write to tourist offices for exact dates and further information (addresses below).

Wine Museums

Krems

The museum is in the former Dominikanerkirche (Dominican Church). Open Easter to end of Oct only Tue–Sat 9–12h; 14–17h Sun and holidays 9–12h

Eisenstadt

The Wine Museum is part of the important Landesmuseum. Open all year, Tue–Sun 9–12h; 13–17h

Additionally there are small local wine museums in numerous villages throughout the wine regions, including Weissenkirchen, Lagenlois, Retz, and others, and in the abbey of Klosterneuburg.

Wine Courses

Wine and food courses are run in summer months in Donnerskirchen (Burgenland). Further details from:

Winzergenossenschaft 'St Martinus' A-7082 Donnerskirchen Austria

Courses, lectures, tutored tastings, visits to vineyards, growers, and cooperatives, as well as boat trips on the Danube, and visits to *Heurigen* are organized in the Wachau. For further information write to:

Fremdenverkehrsverband Wachau A-3500 Krems Austria

Regional Gastronomy

Liptauer Käse Pungent paprika-flavoured cheese-spread often served with wine at the *Heurigen*.

Speck Home-cured and -smoked bacon, served in chunks, along with cheese, other smoked meats and sausages, and bread at the *Heurigen*.

Leberkäse Extremely finely-minced liver, bread, and spices, baked in a loaf: delicious served warm from the oven. Also served cold.

Wiener Schnitzel Veal dipped in egg, coated in breadcrumbs, and quickly fried in smoking lard.

Backhendl Viennese fried chicken.

Tafelspitz Boiled beef served with dumplings and horse-radish.

Bauernschmaus Smoked pork and sausages served with sauerkraut and dumplings.

Rind gulasch A milder thicker version of the Hungarian's favourite paprika-flavoured stew, there known as *gulyás*.

Kalbshaxen Braised knuckle of veal.

Schweinsbraten Roast pork.

Röstbraten Braised steak and onions.

Blau forelle Fresh trout poached in wine or vinegar *court bouillon*.

Rindsuppe Clear beef broth, often garnished with one of the following: *leberknödeln* (liver dumplings), *speckknödeln* (bacon dumplings), *fritatten* (strips of pancake), or simply *'mit Ei'* (with poached egg).

Semmelknödeln Bread dumplings.

Serviettenknödeln Dumplings steamed in napkins.

Desserts: The Austrians are famous for their desserts, pastries, and cakes. Many are best sampled in coffee houses, institutions as important in the lives of the Austrians as their beloved *Heurigen*. The following is a brief selection only of some of our favourites.

Marillenknödeln Sweet steamed dumplings filled with fresh apricots.

Sachertorte Famous chocolate cake layered with apricot jam, then covered with a rich, smooth chocolate icing.

Kaiserschmarrn 'Emperor's pancake' cooked with raisins soaked in Kirsch, torn into small pieces, and dusted with sugar.

Linzertorte Almond-flavoured tart filled with raspberry jam and decorated with a lattice of pastry.

Salzburger Nockerl Sweet omelette soufflé.

Palatschinken Dessert pancake.

Apfelstrudel Extremely thin, elastic dough stuffed with a mixture of apples, cinnamon, sugar, and raisins.

Heurigen and Restaurants

The wine lover in Austria will probably spend a lot of time in *Heurigen*, for these unique taverns provide excellent (and numerous) opportunities to taste a full range of wines made by the proprietors themselves, as well as to gain an impression of Austrian country life. Most *Heurigen* serve a variety of simple foods to accompany the wines, including cheese, sausage, and cold meats, pickled vegetables, and bread and pretzels, as well (sometimes) as hot typical foods such as *Kalbshaxen, Wiener Schnitzel, Backhendl* and others. Traditionally, *Heurigen* display a bunch of fir branches or a straw wheel to indicate that they are open for the season. The *Heurigen* of Vienna's wine suburbs are naturally larger, well-suited to cope with the coachloads of visitors who ascend to these happy noisy spots nightly; they are an experience not to be missed. The rural *Heurigen*, set up in the country wine-producer's back garden, or even just his driveway, where the wines and foods are served to regular friends and customers by family members are, to our way of thinking, even more enjoyable. The following list of *Heurigen* is by no means complete. In addition to the restaurants below, check the Hotel section for other listings.

Heurigen near Vienna

A-1190 Sievering

Elfi Köller
Sieveringer Strasse 112
tel: (0222) 32 11 09
Hot and cold buffet.
Open Mon–Sat 16–24h
Inexpensive

Johann Detter
Agnesgasse 5
tel: (0222) 44 17 123
Inexpensive

Gustav Schreiber
Sieveringer Strasse 58
tel: (0222) 32 17 662
Inexpensive

There are many other *Heurigen* in Sievering, most located on Sieveringer Strasse.

A-1190 Grinzing

Weingut Bach-Hengl
Sandgasse 79
tel: (0222) 32 30 84
700-year old family establishment with Schrammelmusik and Viennese food.
Open daily 16–24h
Inexpensive

Heuriger Am Cobenzl
Am Cobenzl 96
tel: (0222) 32 14 88
Viennese cooking, grills, and barbeques, as well as home-made typical Austrian dumplings and noodles.
Tue–Sun 11–24h
Inexpensive

Heuriger Karl Hengl
Himmelstrasse 7
tel: (0222) 32 25 02
Traditional, family-run *Heurige* with hot and cold buffet.
Inexpensive

A-1190 Heiligenstadt

Brunner-Diem Buschenschank
Eroicagasse 21
tel: (0222) 37 35 60
Local homecooking and variety of wines.
16–24h
Inexpensive

A-1190 Nussdorf

Mayer Am Pfarrplatz
Beethovenhaus
Pfarrplatz 2
tel: (0222) 37 33 61
Located in the actual house that Beethoven lived in and worked in 1817, today one of the most popular and well-known Viennese *Heurigen*, serving wines from family vineyards, and a vast cold and hot buffet.
Daily 16–24h
Inexpensive

Brunner-Diem Weingut
Kahlenberger Strasse 1
tel: (0222) 37 33 82

Local homecooking and wines.
Daily 16–24h
Inexpensive

A-1190 Neustift am Walde

Fuhrgassl-Huber
Neustift am Walde 68
tel: (0222) 44 14 05
Inexpensive

Franz Bachmann
Rathstrasse 4
tel: (0222) 44 27 20
Inexpensive

A-3400 Klosterneuburg

Café-Restaurant Veit
Niedermarkt 13–15
Inexpensive restaurant serving
home-cooked Viennese dishes and local
wines.
Closed Oct; Wed
Open 11–24h

Heurigen and Restaurants in the Wachau and Lower Austria

A-3620 Spitz

Terrassen-Restaurant 'Strandcafe Spitz'
Ulrike Grünberger
tel: (02 713) 320
Inexpensive to Moderate restaurant with
terrace overlooking the Danube.
Specialities include fresh fish, *Weinsuppe*,
local wines and apricot brandy.
Open mid March–end of Oct 10–21h
Closed Wed

Heuriger Johann Donabaum
Laaben 15
tel: (02 713) 488
Inexpensive

Heuriger Frieda Stierschneider
Am Zornberg 6
tel: (02 713) 201
Inexpensive

A-3610 Wosendorf

Restaurant Florianihof
tel: (02 715) 2212
Regional cooking and local wines.
From March to Nov closed Thur
From Dec to Feb closed Wed; Thur
Moderate

A-3610 Weissenkirchen

Restaurant-Weingut Prandtauerhof
Weissenkirchen-Joching 36
tel: (02 715) 2310
Family-run *Weingut* and restaurant built in
1695. Atmospheric dining room and
attractive sheltered courtyard.
Closed Tue afternoon; Wed
Inexpensive to Moderate

Heuriger Rudolf Denk
Weissenkirchen 76
tel: (02 715) 257
Inexpensive

Anton F. Noibinger
Weissenkirchen 35
tel: (02 715) 288
Inexpensive

A-3601 Dürnstein

(see hotels)

A-3601 Loiben (Unter- and Ober-)

Restaurant Loibnerhof
Unter-Loiben 7
tel: (02 732) 2890
Large Inexpensive to Moderate restaurant.
Closed Tue

Heuriger Johann Edlinger
Unter-Loiben 6
tel: (02 732) 69 353
Inexpensive

Heuriger Justine Riesenhuber
Ober-Loiben 41
tel: (02 732) 5368
Inexpensive

A-3500 Krems-Stein

Gasthof-Weinkellerei Jell
Hoher Markt 8–9
tel: (02 732) 2345
Inexpensive *Weinkeller*
Closed Tue

Heuriger 'Am Rebentor'
Kellergasse 40
tel: (02 732) 2636
Inexpensive

Weinstube Kremsmünster
Kellergasse 29a
tel: (02 732) 4568
Inexpensive

A-3495 Rohrendorf

Heuriger Ettenauer
Untere Hauptstrasse 28
tel: (02 732) 60 305
Inexpensive

Heuriger Lethmayer
Obere Wienerstrasse 68
tel: (02 732) 3702
Inexpensive

A-3621 Rossatz

(opposite side of the Danube; good
camping by the river)

Heuriger Alfred Steinmetz
Rossatz 53
tel: (02 714) 307
Inexpensive

Heuriger Anton Fischer
Rossatzbach 15
tel: (02 714) 295
Inexpensive

Heurigen and Restaurants in Burgenland

A-7000 Eisenstadt

Weinbaumeister Franz Lehner
Kirchengasse 47
tel: (02 682) 30 222
Rustic food such as home-made sausages
and *sauerbraten*, accompanied by local
wines.
Open March, May, July, August, Nov
Daily 9–24h
Inexpensive to Moderate

Heuriger Helmut Gruber
St Rochusstrasse 44
tel: (02 682) 2285
Inexpensive

Heuriger Anton Wagner
Schubertzplatz 3
tel: (02 682) 4343
Inexpensive

Josef Eiweck
Bergstrasse 8
tel: (02 682) 3151
Inexpensive

A-7071 Rust

Buschenschank Peter Schandl
Josef Haydngasse 3
tel: (02 685) 265
This business has been run by the Schandl
family since 1742.
Typical *Heurigen* specialities, and 20
different wines served by the glass or
bottle. Music from May to Nov.
Open March–Nov 10–24h
Inexpensive

Paul Huber
Hauptstrasse 12
tel: (02 685) 6269
Open March–Oct
Inexpensive

A-7100 Neusiedl am See

Heuriger Ludwig und Monika Vollath
Kirchengasse 2
tel: (02 167) 283
Cold meat platters, and Hungarian *gulasch*.
Inexpensive

Heuriger Emmerich und Christine
Rittsteuer
Feldgasse 1
tel: (02 167) 449
Open May–Sept
Inexpensive

A-7083 Purbach

Weingut Ing Michael Sandhofer
Kellergasse 6
tel: (02 683) 5502
Open May–Sept
Inexpensive

A-7082 Donnerskirchen

Heuriger im Martinsschlössl
Im Martinsschlössl
tel: (02 683) 8512
Hot and cold specialities of Burgenland,
and gypsy *csárdás*.
Inexpensive to Moderate

Spezialitatenrestaurant Gasthof Engel
Hauptstrasse 59
tel: (02 683) 8502
Burgenland specialities in a comfortable
dining room.
Moderate

Hotels

Near Vienna

A-1190 Grinzing

Müllner-Gasthof
XIX Grinzinger Allee 30
tel: (0222) 32 23 17
Inexpensive *gasthof* conveniently located
in Vienna's 'wine suburbs' for exploring
Heurigen.

A-3400 Klosterneuberg

Frühstückspension 'Alte Mühle'
Mühlengasse 36
tel: (02 243) 7788
Guest house in this historic wine town just
north of Vienna, serving full buffet
breakfast.
Open all year.
Inexpensive to **Moderate**

A-2540 Bad Voslau

Hotel Stefanie
Badplatz 1
tel: (02 252) 7236
Bad Voslau is a small spa resort and the
centre for a red-wine producing zone
south of Vienna. This family hotel is close
to the thermal baths, and the Vienna
Woods.
Moderate

Wachau

A-3620 Spitz

Hotel Restaurant 'Wachauerhof'
Hauptstrasse 15
tel: (02 713) 303
Inexpensive family-run hotel with
restaurant serving homecooked Viennese
specialities and wines from the Wachau.
Hotel closed Nov–March
Restaurant open all day.

Frühstückspension 'Haus Burkhardt'
Kremserstrasse 19
tel: (02 713) 356
Bed and full Austrian buffet breakfast in
this 16th-century Baroque house which
has been in the same family for 200 years.
Set within orchards and adjoining family
vineyards. No restaurant.
Closed Nov–March
Inexpensive

A-3601 Dürnstein

Hotel Schloss Dürnstein
tel: (02 711) 212
In a magnificent position overlooking the
Danube, this elegant first class hotel is
located in an early Baroque palace,
occupied for centuries by the Starhemberg
Princes. Each room is beautifully and
individually furnished, with private
facilities.
Swimming pool, restaurant with terrace
overlooking the Danube, and well-stocked
wine cellar.
Closed end Nov–mid March
Expensive

Hotel-Restaurant 'Richard Löwenherz'
tel: (02 711) 222
Elegant 100-bed hotel in traditional
Wachau house. Swimming pool, and
restaurant.
Moderate to **Expensive**

Gasthof 'Sänger Blondel'
tel: (02 711) 253
Attractive family-run *gasthof* with own
vineyards and cellars.
There is a large chestnut garden where
meals are served in fine weather.
Hotel closed Dec; Jan
Restaurant closed Mon
Inexpensive

A-3504 Krems

Hotel-Restaurant 'Am Förthof'
Förthofer Donaulande 8
tel: (02 732) 3345
Family-run hotel with swimming pool,
terrace, gardens, and restaurant serving
fresh fish, game and a good selection of
Wachau wines.
Hotel closed Jan–Feb
Restaurant closed Wed
Moderate

A-3512 Mautern

Hotel-Spezialitätenrestaurant Bacher
Südtirolerplatz 208
tel: (02 732) 2937
Hotel with restaurant specializing in new
style of lighter cooking. Wine and food
seminars, as well as seasonal speciality
weekends (asparagus, game) run
throughout the year.
Closed Jan
Inexpensive to **Moderate**

Burgenland

A-7000 Eisenstadt

Hotel Burgenland
Schubertplatz 1
tel: (02 682) 5521
Comfortable hotel with swimming pool,
sauna, restaurant, and *Weinstube* with over
65 different wines on offer by the glass or
bottle.
Hotel open all year.
Restaurant open daily 8–23h
Moderate

Hotel Mayr
Kalvarienbergplatz 1
tel: (02 682) 2751
Inexpensive hotel with homecooking.
Restaurant open evenings only 19–24h

A-7071 Rust

Hotel Sifkovits (Tomschitz')
Am Seekandl 8
tel: (02 685) 276
Luxury hotel with swimming pool, sauna,
squash court, and restaurant serving local
and international cuisine.
Open all year
Expensive

Seehotel
tel: (02 685) 313
First-class hotel with indoor swimming
pool, squash courts, sauna, and
restaurant.
Open all year.
Expensive

Pension Magdalenenhof
Feldgasse 40
tel: (02 685) 373
Inexpensive, without restaurant.
Closed Dec–Feb

A-7100 Neusiedl am See

Hotel Wende
Seestrasse 40–42
tel: (02 167) 8111
Hotel with indoor pool, sauna, and
restaurant serving local Burgenland
specialities, including home-smoked trout.
Good selection of Burgenland wines.
Hotel closed Jan–Feb
Restaurant open daily 11h30–22h
Moderate

Camping

Vienna

Vienna
Campingplatz der Stadt Wien, Wien-West I
Hüttelbergstrasse 40, tel: (0222) 94 14 49
Campingplatz der Stadt Wien, Wien-West II
Hüttelbergstrasse 80, tel: (0222) 94 23 14
Campingplatz der Stadt Wien, Wien-Süd
Breitenfurter Strasse 269
tel: (0222) 86 92 18

Wachau

Krems
Donaucamping, tel: (02 732) 4455
Rossatz
Campingplatz Rossatzbach
tel: (02 714) 217

Aggsbach Markt
Campingplatz, tel: (02 712) 266

Burgenland

Rust
Campingplatz, tel: (02 683) 390
Donnerskirchen
Campingplatz, tel: (02 683) 8241
Purbach am See
Campingplatz, tel: (02 683) 5120

For more detailed information write to
Austrian National Tourist Office (address
below) for brochure *Camping-Caravaning*.

Bibliography

The Wines and Wine Gardens of Austria by
F & F Hallgarten, International
Publications Service 1979

Where to Get Additional Information

Austrian National Tourist Office
545 5th Ave
NY NY 10017
tel: (212) 287–8742

Local Tourist Offices:

Vienna
Fremdenverkehrsverband für Wien
Kinderspitalgasse 5
A-1095 Vienna
tel: (0222) 43 16 08

Lower Austria
Niederösterreichische
Fremdenverkehrswerbung
Paulanergasse 11
A-1041 Vienna
tel: (0222) 57 67 18

Burgenland
Landesfremdenverkehrsverband für das
Burgenland
Schloss Esterhazy
A-7000 Eisenstadt
tel: (02 682) 3384

——— SPAIN ———

RIOJA

Rioja is Spain's finest wine region, yet it is not, unlike most of Europe's wine country, an obvious area to visit. This brief inland region, in its sheltered, verdant valley that lies below the rugged Sierra de Cantabria remains separate and self-contained, both in atmosphere and climate at odds with a stereotyped image of holiday Spain. Located mainly in historic Old Castile (in the provinces of Logrôno, Alava, and Navarre), it does not cater overtly for the visitor. Yet its wine industry which, more than that of many other great wine regions, combines modern technology with centuries-old tradition, coupled with its essentially relaxed yet thoroughly modern attitude to living, makes Rioja an intriguing region to visit.

The region is divided into three districts: Rioja Alta, the Upper Rioja, extending from the mountains through the principal wine town of Haro across to the region's capital, Logroño; Rioja Alavesa, which lies on the north side of the Ebro in the Basque province; and finally, Rioja Baja, the lower part of the region, extending from Logroño through ancient Calahorra to Alfaro. Though the land is generous, yielding not only the valuable and numerous varieties of grapes used to produce the wines but also an abundance of prime vegetables such as the favourite *pimientos* (peppers), artichokes, asparagus and much else, for visitors it has tended to be a region that one passes through, not stops in. It has probably always been so. In medieval days Logroño was best known as a halting place along one of Europe's main religious and cultural arteries, the road to Santiago de Compostela. Thus, pilgrims from throughout Europe passed through and took refuge here, and at Santo Domingo de la Calzada, where an ascetic hermit had settled on the banks of the tiny Rio Oja (which gives its name to the region), and there installed a hospice for the weary. Discerning pilgrims, no doubt, sampled the fine wines of the region en route, for Rioja wine has been popular for hundreds of years, and was being exported as long ago as the twelfth century. Wine pilgrims today can stop at Santo Domingo de la Calzada in the three-star Spanish National Parador which is actually located in the old hospice.

If in the past, pilgrims pushed on to St James's shrine on the Galician coast, the wine lover – even if en route to the sunny resorts of the south – will want to stop for long enough to explore this sometimes strange, even remote, northern region, and to sample the great wines of Rioja at the source.

How to Get There

By Car

The Rioja region is not on the main routes usually traversed by the motoring tourist in Spain; however, it is an easy detour to reach it either from Santander, off the main Madrid road, or across from Barcelona. If entering Spain at Irún, or if landing at Santander, the quickest route is to continue around the coast to Bilbao then to take the toll motorway (A68) south through Miranda de Ebro to Haro. This excellent motorway connects Logroño, the region's capital, with Zaragoza and Barcelona.

From Madrid take the main N1 highway north through Burgos to Miranda de Ebro, and so down to Haro to commence the wine tour.

By Plane

For touring the Rioja, the nearest international airports for visitors from the US are Madrid and Barcelona. Internal and European flights are available to Bilbao which is but a short drive to the wine region.

By Train

Logroño is a main stop for trains running between Bilbao and Zaragoza. They leave from Bilbao daily, and take about three and a half hours. From Paris, take direct train through Orléans, Tours, Bordeaux, crossing the border at Irún. Change at Irún for local train to Bilbao.

Local Public Transport

There is a main railway running through the heart of the region, from Miranda del Ebro in the west, to Calahorra in the east, with numerous local stops along the way. Buses travel from Bilbao to Zaragoza daily, except Sundays.

Car Rental Information

Santander
Avis: Nicolas Salmeron 3
tel: (942) 22 70 25
Hertz: Alcazar de Toledo 6
tel: (942) 37 02 25

Bilbao
Avis: Doctor Areilza 34
tel: (94) 444 22 16
Bilbao Airport
tel: (94) 453 12 09
Hertz: Nicolas Achucarro 10
tel: (94) 415 36 77
Bilbao Airport
tel: (94) 453 05 52

Vitoria
Avis: Avda Gasteiz 27
tel: (945) 24 46 12/6
Hertz: Vitoria Airport
tel: (945) 27 98 48

Firestone Hispania Map C2; **Michelin Map** 990, 42

The Wines of Rioja

The wine region of Rioja extends from west of Haro through descending levels of the Ebro Valley to Alfaro. Different climate and soil result in wines with markedly different characters. There are three distinct zones of production: Rioja Alta, Rioja Alavesa and Rioja Baja. The two former regions are influenced by the Atlantic, while the hotter, flatter Baja has a Mediterranean climate. The Rioja region is known primarily for its mellow, oak-aged red wines, though good white and pink wines are also produced here. Some fifty large producers, many located around the principal wine towns of Haro and Logroño, produce the majority of quality wines that are exported. Though some may own their own vineyards, most must generally purchase grapes and wine from small growers or growers' cooperatives. The red wines of Rioja, like red Bordeaux or Chianti, are produced from a blend of different grapes, primarily the Tempranillo, with the addition of Graciano, Mazuelo, and Garnacho. Sometimes wines from the three different zones are blended to produce a more balanced end-product. After the tumultuous and malolactic fermentations, the wines are transferred into new oak casks where they age for a minimum of one year, racking taking place two or three times during this period.

Consejo Regulador de la Denominacion de Origen 'Rioja' This official organization maintains quality by making regular checks in both vineyards and *bodegas* to ensure that the regulations laid down for the production of Rioja wine are carried out (including rules governing types of vines, yield per hectare, methods of cultivation and vinification, and minimum ageing periods). Their official stamp, which appears on approved bottles of wine, is a guarantee of quality and authenticity.

Rioja Alta The westernmost vineyard region, nestled in a basin under the Sierra mountain range producing sturdy,   . long-lived, medium-strength wines that are among the finest in Spain. The majority of the region's important *bodegas* are located in the Rioja Alta, in wine towns like Haro, Cenicero, Fuenmayor, and Logroño itself.

Rioja Alavesa So named because this sub-region lies within the Basque province of Alava. The finest wines from the Alavesa are equal to the finest from the Rioja Alta, though generally, they are perhaps somewhat more delicate: very pretty wines that are vibrant and exciting, but which may not last as long as the greatest from the Rioja Alta. There are, of course, exceptions to this generalization. Laguardia and Elciego are its important centres of production.

Rioja Baja The eastern zone of the region is both hotter and has less rainfall, and in spring, warm *solanos* from the east scorch both the ground and the vines. The wines produced in the Baja, as a consequence, tend to be somewhat coarser and higher in alcohol. The region, however, does produce good wines in its own right, as well as large quantities that, when blended judiciously, add body and backbone to wines from the other zones.

Vino de crianza Like the *négociant-éleveur* in Burgundy, the large firms in Rioja are concerned with 'elevating' wines through blending and then ageing. *'Crianza'* means raising, or rearing; the term *vino de crianza* indicates that the wine has been aged for a

minimum of one year in the characteristic oak *barricas* that give them their unique mellowness and flavour, then aged for some months in bottle; such wine may not be sold until its third year.

Reserva Wine from an excellent harvest, aged for a minimum of two years in oak, and one year in bottle. This time requirement is a minimum only, and many firms traditionally age their *reservas* in oak for considerably longer periods.

Gran reserva The greatest wines are aged for a minimum of three years in oak, and two in bottle, or vice versa. Such wines must age for a total of seven years before leaving the *bodega*. Often the bottles of these special aristocrats are distinguished by being enmeshed in metal, a traditional guarantee of quality. This mesh was originally applied to prevent pilfering in the *bodegas* as the cork could not be disturbed without removing the wire.

Rioja 'tinto' Various styles of red wine are produced in the region. *Tinto* indicates a darker, deeper, full-bodied wine (sometimes a sloping-shouldered Burgundy-type bottle is used for such wines).

Rioja 'clarete' Lighter red wine, often found in a straight 'claret' type bottle.

Rioja blanco Dry, medium-dry, and a few sweet white wines are also produced in the region. In the past, the white wines, like the red, were aged for considerable periods in oak, but fresher, younger styles, produced primarily from the Viura grape, are gaining favour.

Rioja rosado Dry and medium-sweet rosé wines that are also aged in oak for a short period, or produced by the chilled fermentation method.

───── *Wine Tour of the Rioja* ─────

Although there is no sign-posted wine road through the region, there is a suggested *Ruta del Vino de Rioja* which leads to the principal wine towns, and the most important *bodegas* in each. Begin a tour in the region's capital, Logroño, a busy manufacturing centre, as well as an important hub of the wine trade. The Ebro passes languidly along the northern edge

of the town, spanned by stone and iron bridges that lead to the civic centre. The *espolon* is a pleasant shaded central square (the local office of information and tourism is found on its south side); wide avenues to the south, such as the Gran Via, and the Avenida de la Republica Argentina are lined with sleek, modern banks and fashionable shops selling clothing and expensive furniture, indicating the modern prosperity of the city; head to the north, however, to explore older parts of Logroño within the old fortified walls. The Imperial Church of Santa María de Palacio, for example, with its remarkable 146-foot high pyramidal tower was founded in the eleventh century. The highly decorated cathedral of Santa María de la Redonda is also worth a visit. Wander through the old streets, and visit Logroño's unique 4-storey indoor market where a variety of meats, fish, sausages, vegetables, and fruits are displayed under sallow, dangling, bare-bulbed lights. Afterwards, emerge into daylight once more, and head around the corner to the nearby Calle Laurel where numerous crowded bars and restaurants offer the simple yet flavourful specialities of the region. Though on first sight the area may seem a little run down, at lunchtime it is swarming with bankers, businessmen, wine merchants, and workers, all talking loudly, gesticulating, and swilling back goblets of red Rioja over great platters of roast meats, fried fish, and hearty stews.

From Logroño, one has the choice of either first exploring the Rioja Alta and Alavesa, or the Rioja Baja. If time is limited then the former is suggested, for though the towns of Calahorra, Alfaro, and Arnedo are all worth visiting, the Rioja Alta and Rioja Alavesa undoubtedly produce the region's finest wines. Since many of the region's finest vineyards, as well as numerous *bodegas*, lie between Logroño and Haro, a circular tour of the region on either side of the Ebro can be made between these two centres. Logroño itself is the home of several well-known firms, including Marqués de Murrieta, Campo Viejo de Savin, S.A., Olarra, S.A., and Franco-Españolas, S.A.

Cross the Ebro on the stone bridge, and take the Pamplona road (N111) briefly before branching off left to the little wine village of Oyón. The Ebro separates the provinces of Logroño and Alava, and thus wine communes encountered on this northern side form part of the Rioja Alavesa. The wines of the Alavesa are the most delicate of all Riojas – *muy bonito* – with a brilliant colour, and a fine, elegant balance of fruit and oak. Oyón is the home of the Bodegas Faustino Martínez, and of Martínez Bujanda, S.A.; (there is also a popular regional restaurant here, Méson 'La Cueva'). Return towards Logroño, then branch off right on the N232 road that follows (at first) the Ebro before continuing

on to Laguardia. Laguardia is the principal town of the Rioja Alavesa, still strangely medieval in character, perched on a high ridge, its fortified ramparts guarding its old narrow streets and houses, and its numerous *bodegas*, large and small. Larger concerns located in or near Laguardia include Bodegas Alavesas, S.A.; Bodegas Palacios, S.A.R.A.; and Vinicola Vizcaina Rojas y Cia., S.R.C.

Turn off the main road at Laguardia to the little village of Elciego, located in the very heart of the Alavesa. Two well-known firms have their *bodegas* here: Marqués de Riscal, S.A. and Sociedad General de Viñas, which is owned by the sherry firm of Pedro Domecq. From Elciego, either continue to Cenicero, or else return in the direction of Laguardia, and take the left fork that leads back to the N232. Further along, before Samaniego, branch off right to climb up to the so-called *'Balcón de la Rioja'* – 'balcony of the Rioja' – which provides a particularly striking view of the Ebro Valley, and of the vineyards sprouting on the scruffy, orange-brown hills down to the river and beyond. Return to the N232, and continue on to Haro, passing through the wine villages of Samaniego and Labastida along the way.

Haro, some 43 km west of Logroño, is the true centre of the wine trade, nestled under the mountains in the heart of the Rioja Alta. Eleven major wine producers have their main *bodegas* in or around this bustling provincial town, and restaurants such as the Terete or the Beethoven are always full at lunchtime with members of the wine trade, at extended meals that sometimes continue well into the early evening (indeed, four o'clock is not

considered an abnormal time to begin lunch!). Haro was inhabitated in Roman times, and its central position in the rich alluvial valley of the Ebro, crisscrossed by other tributaries such as the Tirón, the Glera, and the little Oja, which has given its name to the region, combined with the abundant vegetation and pastureland, has made the town an important market centre (indeed, Haro used to be the principal market for the distribution of fish to central Spain; thus, though landlocked, the region has a great tradition of fish dishes). Its position has brought prosperity, as evidenced by the many fine manorial houses dating from the sixteenth, seventeenth, and eighteenth centuries, and there seems a rather gothic, aristocratic air to its narrow streets and squares in old quarters such as the Plaza de San Martín and the Plaza de la Paz. Haro is not an openly warm and inviting town on first impression; yet persevere, for faded or inviting fronts open onto lively bars or restaurants with clean white tablecloths, and earnest proprietors who take their job of serving good regional specialities seriously.

Notable monuments in Haro include the Parish Church of St Thomas, with its interior of soaring columns and interlaced vaulting, the *Ayuntamiento* (Town Hall), and the Palace of the Counts of Haro. If in the region during late July, don't miss the *Romería*, a lively folk festival dedicated to the hermitage of San Felices de Bilibio. This takes place annually on July 29, and part of the festivities includes a curious *Batalla del Vino*, an event that has been declared of national touristic interest. Naturally, the wines of the Rioja Alta, combined with gastronomic delicacies such as *pimientos rellenos* (stuffed peppers), *lechazo* (roast baby lamb) and much else also add to the festivities. The major *bodegas* in Haro inciude Bilbainas, S.A.; Carlos Serrés, S.A.; Muga, S.A.; Ramón Bilbao, S.A.; Rioja Santiago, S.A.; Compania Vinícola del Norte de España (CVNE); Federico Paternina, S.A.; La Rioja Alta, S.A.; Martínez Lacuesta Hnos, Ltda; R López de Heredia, Viña Tondonia, S.A.; and Gómez Cruzado, S.A. Some of these large firms are vast, modern wineries with the latest technologies; others still retain traditional methods and procedures – this essential contrast between the ultra-modern and traditional craftsmanship makes the Rioja a particularly interesting wine region to

visit. For even in modern computerized factories one observes traditional and classic cellar techniques: the ageing of the wine in new oak *barricas*, the continuous racking (transferring the wine to older barrels), the fining with egg white to clarify the wine, even the repair work on the barrels themselves, continue to be activities that must be done manually by skilled craftsmen.

From Haro either travel south to Santo Domingo de la Calzada, or else return to Logroño along the south bank of the Ebro, thus encountering more important but unassuming wine towns of the Rioja Alta. Santo Domingo de la Calzada is an historic pilgrim town certainly worth a visit, even for those who choose not to stay at the superb Spanish National Parador that was converted from the actual hospice itself, founded by Santo Domingo in the eleventh century. *Calzada* means 'causeway', for the eponymous saint erected a bridge here over the little Oja for pilgrims to cross on their way to Santiago. He later founded a hospice for the weary which was subsequently enlarged, and it thus became one of the principal halts on the well-travelled road to Compostela. As well as the hospice, the important Romanesque-Byzantine Cathedral should be visited; wander down old roads such as the Calle Mayor, and the arched Calle del Cristo, and view the remains of the former town fortifications. The patronal festivities in honour of Santo Domingo take place annually from 10th to 15th May. Because of their striking originality and colour, they have been declared of interest to tourists. From Santo Domingo de la Calzada, either return to Haro to continue the tour of the wine region, or else make your way to Logroño via Nájera and Naverrete (Nájera was the former residence of the Kings of Castile, as well as the ancient court of the Kings of Navarre).

From Haro, the wine tour to Logroño continues through the towns of Ollauri, Cenicero, and Fuenmayor, all three of which are the homes of principal wine producers. The modern château-like *bodega* of Bodegas Beronia, S.A. is found in Ollauri, situated in the midst of its esteemed vineyards. Cenicero (the name means 'ash dump') is the home of Bodegas Berberana, S.A., Bodegas Riojanas, S.A., and Bodegas Marques de Caceres, all three familiar names to Rioja *aficionados*. From Cenicero, make a detour to Elciego (if this has not already been done from Laguardia

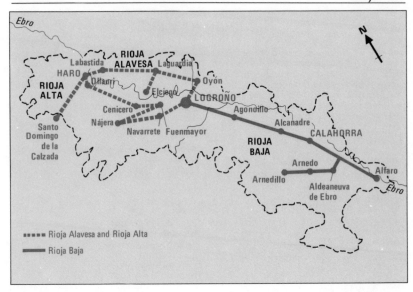

===== Rioja Alavesa and Rioja Alta
━━━━ Rioja Baja

on the first part of the tour), or else continue to Fuenmayor, where several more wine producers are located, including AGE-Bodegas Unidas, S.A., Lagunilla, S.A., Bodegas Lan, S.A., and López Agos y Compañia, S.A. From Fuenmayor visit Navarette and Nájera before returning to Logroño.

A tour of the Rioja Baja begins in Logroño. Leave the city on the N232 in the direction of Zaragoza to arrive, some 48 kilometres from the capital, at Calahorra, second largest town in the province. This important and ancient episcopal seat was already an important township 200 years before Christ, and it was the birthplace of the Romans Marcus Flavius Quintilianus, and Aurelius Prudentius Clemente. The massive town walls that still remain are evidence of its importance in the Middle Ages. The vineyards of the Rioja Baja follow the Ebro Valley; wine villages en route to Calahorra include Agoncillo and Alcanadre. Past Calahorra, however, vineyards share the extensive plain, the *vega* of Calahorra, with other luscious fruits and market vegetables, in particular the bright red *pimientos* that grow here, and which are such a favourite ingredient in the food of the Rioja. Indeed, on a cold autumn day, one can often see workers in

blue overalls hunched over an outdoor brazier, warming their hands while roasting peppers on long forks. There is a 4-star Spanish National Parador in Calahorra, the 'Parador Nacional Marco Fabio'.

From Calahorra, follow the valley to Alfaro, principal wine town of the Baja, and, like Haro, a prosperous and historic medieval town, as its notable seignorial mansions testify. Wine producers in Alfaro include the Cooperativa del Campo San Antonio; José Palacios Remondo; and De la Torre y Lapuerta, S.A. While it is popular to pass off the Rioja Baja as 'the ugly sister of the Rioja', it should be pointed out that good, plentiful – if somewhat powerful – wines are produced in this region which are eminently drinkable on their own, and are often blended with other wines by firms in the Rioja Alta or Alavesa to add backbone and strength, something which the producers in those élite and privileged zones do not always readily tell the visitor. From Alfaro either continue east to Zaragoza and the Catalonian coast, or else return to Logroño via Rincón de Soto, from there making a brief detour into the rich Cidacos Valley, and through Aldenueva de Ebro to Arnedo (famous for its shoe industry), and Arnedillo, a quiet spa town.

Bodegas to Visit

The *bodegas* of Rioja are some of the most fascinating wine cellars in Europe, and though the region is not yet widely visited, the producers here are noted for their warm welcome and generous hospitality. It is essential, however, that arrangements for visits be made in advance, by writing (or telephoning) direct to the firm concerned. Wine merchants in the US may be able to help customers procure a letter of introduction from a principal's US agent; or else, when in the area, make arrangements through your hotel, or through the local tourist office in Logroño.

The Rioja Alta

Logroño

Bodegas Campo Viejo de Savin SA
Gustavo Adolfo Becquer, s/n
tel: (941) 23 81 00
Open daily 10–12h; 15h30–17h30
Appointment necessary.
Max 25 pers.
English spoken.

Bodegas Franco-Españolas S A
Cabo Noval, 2
tel: (941) 21 13 00
Open daily 10–12h
Appointment necessary.
Max 40 pers.
English spoken.

Cenicero

Bodegas Riojanas S A
Estación 1, 21
tel: (941) 45 40 50
Open Mon–Fri
Appointment necessary.
Max 30 pers.

Bodegas Marqués de Cáceres
Unión Viti-Vinícola S A
Carretera de Logroño s/n
tel: (941) 45 40 00
Open daily 9–13h; 16–18h
Appointment necessary.
Max 20 pers.
English spoken.

Fuenmayor

Bodegas Lagunilla S A
Apartado 6
Carretera de Vitoria Km 182/183
tel: (941) 45 01 00
Open daily 9–14h
Appointment necessary.
English spoken.

Haro

Bodegas Bilbainas SA
Estación 7

tel: (94) 416 57 18
Open Mon–Fri 9–13h; 16–19h
Max 12 pers.
English spoken.

Gomez Cruzado SA
Avda Vizcaya 6
tel: (941) 24 15 98
Open daily 9–13h; 16–19h
Appointment necessary.
English spoken.

Bodegas Muga SA
Barrio de la Estación, s/n
tel: (3104 98) 31 18 25
Open daily 9–12h; 16–19h
Appointment necessary for groups.
Max 15 pers.
English spoken.

Bodegas Ramón Bilbao SA
Carretera Casalareina, s/n
tel: (941) 31 02 95
Open after 16h by appointment only.
Max 6 pers.
English spoken.

Compañia Vinicola del Norte de España
(CVNE)
Avda Costa del Vino, 21
tel: (941) 31 06 50
Open daily 10–13h
Appointment necessary only for
groups larger than 5.
English spoken.

Federico Paternina SA
Carretera Santo Domingo, s/n
tel: (941) 31 05 50
Open daily 10–13h
Appointment preferable.
Max 40 pers.
English spoken.

Martinez Lacuesta Hnos Ltda
Calle la Ventilla, 71
tel: (941) 31 00 50
Open Mon–Fri
Max 10 pers.
English spoken.

The Rioja Alavesa

Laguardia

Bodegas Alavesas SA
Carretera de Elciego, s/n
tel: (91) 457 35 16
Open Mon–Fri 8–18h
Appointment necessary.
Max 40 pers.
English spoken.

Elciego

Sociedad General de Viñas (Bodegas
Domecq Rioja)
Carretera de Valbuena, s/n

tel: (941) 10 60 01
Appointment necessary. Visits only for
customers and members of the wine trade.
Max 50 pers.
English spoken.

The Rioja Baja

San Adrián

Bodegas Gurpegui
Apartado 3
tel: (948) 67 00 50
Open daily 9–13h; 15–18h
Appointment necessary.
Max 5 pers.

Wine Festivals

May 10–15	Fiesta de Santo Domingo de la Calzada	Santo Domingo de la Calzada
29th July	*'Batalla del Vino'*	Haro
2nd week in Sept	Wine Harvest Festival (Festivities are accompanied by bullfights, parades, and local folklore activities)	Logroño

Regional Gastronomy

Banderillas Northern name for bar-top finger snacks (both hot and cold) – see *tapas*, p. 268.

Pimientos a la riojana Red peppers roasted over an open fire, skinned, then stewed in garlic and olive oil.

Alubias pochas con chorizo White beans cooked with *chorizo*, paprika, and water, resulting in a pale-orange bean and sausage soup.

Menestra riojana Mixed vegetable stew of peas, beans, potatoes, celery, and *acelgas* (coarse lettuce-like green), all cooked separately, then simmered together in a saffron-scented sauce of onions, garlic, tomatoes, bacon, and ham.

Patatas riojanas A supremely simply yet delicious dish of potatoes cooked with *chorizo* (spicy sausage), garlic, and red peppers.

Sopa de ajo Garlic soup.

Cordero asado Milk-fed baby lamb *(lechazo)* baked in an oak-fired oven.

Cabrito asado Kid cooked in the same manner.

Cochinillo Roast suckling pig.

Chuletas de cordero Baby lamb chops grilled over an open fire of vine-shoots.

Angulas Basque speciality of tiny elvers fried quickly in garlic and olive oil.

Cangrejos Freshwater crayfish.

Bacalao a la riojana Dried salt cod stewed with red peppers, onion, olive oil, and tomato.

Callos a la riojana Tripe cooked for several hours, then chopped, and stewed with red peppers, onion, fried ham, and tomatoes.

Trucha Freshwater trout.

Delgadilla Small local blood sausage.

Riojanitos Marzipan coated with bitter chocolate.

Cuajada Type of junket of curdled milk served in a wooden bowl called a *kaiku*.

Restaurants

Logroño

El Cachetero
Calle Laurel, 3
tel: (941) 21 21 24
Typical busy eating house on this popular
street, serving only regional specialities
and Rioja wines.
Moderate

Los Gabrieles
Calle del Peso, 4
tel: (941) 220043
Large selection of *banderillas*, as well as
regional dishes and good selection of
wines.
Inexpensive to **Moderate**

Casa Matute
Calle Laurel, 6
Unpretentious restaurant serving local
dishes and wines.
Inexpensive

Haro

Casa Terete
Lucrecia Arana No 17
tel: (941) 31 00 23
Extremely popular **Inexpensive** restaurant
serving Rioja specialities such as *cordero
asado* (cooked on the ground floor in a
wood-fired baker's oven), *alubias pochas*,
menestra de verduras, and others.
Closed Sun eve; Mon
Open 13h15–16; 20–23h

Restaurante Beethoven II
Santo Tomas 3–5
tel: (941) 31 11 81
Extensive fish and shellfish specialities,
and other regional dishes, including
*corderos asados, menestra de verduras, patatas
riojanas*, together with a large selection of
wines from the *bodegas* of Haro.
Closed Mon
Open 13h30–16; 21–24h
Inexpensive to **Moderate**

Oyón (near Logroño)

Mesón 'La Cueva'
Calle Concepcion 15
tel: (941) 11 00 22
Popular **Inexpensive** restaurant 4 km from
Logroño in small wine village, serving
regional specialities, and a good selection
of Rioja wines.

Hotels

Logroño

Carlton Rioja
Gran Vía del Rey Juán Carlos 1,5
tel: (941) 24 21 00
Open all year
Restaurant open 13–15h; 21–23h
Moderate

El Cortijo Hotel
Ctra. El Cortijo Km 2
tel: (941) 22 50 54
Located outside Logroño, a comfortable and friendly small hotel with
restaurant.
Inexpensive

Hotel Murrieta
Avda Marques de Murrieta 1
tel: (941) 22 41 50
Situated in centre of Logroño. 113 rooms
each with private facilities. Restaurant
serves local specialities and wines.
Open all year.
Restaurant open 13h30–15h; 20h30–23h
Inexpensive to **Moderate**

Where to Get
Additional Information

Spanish National Tourist Office
665 5th Ave
NY NY 10022
tel: (21) 759–8822
Offices also in San Francisco, Chicago,
Houston, and St Augustine

Tourist Information Office
Miguel Villanueva, 10 (off Espolon)
Logroño
tel: (941) 21 54 97

Rioja Wine Information Bureau
220 E 42nd St
NY NY 10017
tel: (212) 907–9385

Grupo Exportadores de Vinos Rioja
Gran Via, 14–3
Logroño
tel: (941) 22 28 37
(for complete lists of the principal *bodegas*
and other useful information – this office
may be able to help arrange visits when in
the region)

Haro

Hotel Iturrimurri
N232
tel: (941) 31 12 13
Conveniently situated on the main road
outside Haro, a comfortable 'motel' with
bar and restaurant. Proprietor will help
visitors arrange visits to *bodegas* as well as
suggest tourist routes.
Restaurant 'Costa del Vino' open daily
13–15h30; 20h30–23h
Inexpensive

Calahorra

Parador Nacional 'Marco Fabio
Quintiliano'
Avda Generalísimo
tel: (941) 13 03 58
Part of Spain's excellent chain of national
inns, this Parador is run as a first-class
hotel with restaurant.
Moderate to **Expensive**

Arnedo

Hotel Victoria
General Franco 103
tel: (941) 38 01 00

Hotel with swimming pool, tennis court,
and restaurant serving local dishes.
Hotel open all year
Restaurant open daily 13–15h30; 21–23h30
Inexpensive

Santo Domingo de la Calzada

Parador Nacional Santo Domingo de la
Calzada
Plaza del Santo, 3
tel: (941) 34 03 00
Located in the former pilgrims' hospice,
this Spanish National Parador is a
welcome resting place for today's wine
pilgrim.
Restaurant serves both regional and
international cooking, and has an
extensive selection of the finest Riojas.
Hotel and restaurant open all year
Restaurant open daily 13–17h; 20h30–23h
Moderate

Bibliography

*Monarch Guide to the Wines of Spain and
Portugal* by Jan Read, Monarch Press 1978

JEREZ

Settled by the Phoenicians more than three thousand years ago, a Greek and then a Roman colony, plundered by the barbarians and by marauding pirates, Jerez de la Frontera – frontier between Christian and Moor – is, and has been for centuries, famous for the wine to which it has given its name: sherry. The sherry region is small and compact, forming a triangle over the dusty, sometimes chalk-white hills that range between Jerez and the other two principal towns, Puerto de Santa María, and Sanlúcar de Barrameda. Devoted almost entirely, as are all great wine regions, to viticulture, it is an essential element in a vibrant Andalusian landscape: the drama of the bullfight, of the brilliant, frenetic clack of castenets, the *flamenco* and the *fandango*, and of fresh wine drawn from age-old oak casks with a slender whalebone instrument – the

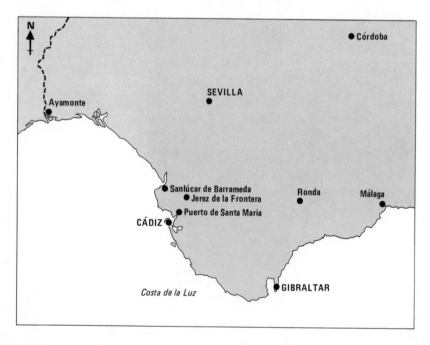

venencia – then dashed with a graceful flick-of-the-wrist flourish from on high into a waiting handful of tulip *copitas*.

The wine region itself stands midway along the Costa de la Luz – the Coast of Light – on the Atlantic fringe of Andalusia. Glistening beaches, historic towns with whitewashed walls and buildings evocative of their Moorish past, a lively Andalusian cuisine that makes full use of the range of fish and shellfish that the sea yields, and famous wine shippers who generously open up their splendid cathedral-like *bodegas* to the public, make the sherry region particularly popular with the wine-loving tourist. Moreover, not only is Jerez de la Frontera within easy reach of the beaches of the Costa de la Luz, it is also just a stone's throw away from the popular Costa del Sol, near historic and beautiful centres such as Seville and Granada, and also an easy drive from the Portuguese Algarve; thus one is able to combine a visit to this great wine region with a relaxing holiday at some of Europe's most popular resorts.

How to Get There

By Car
From Madrid, take the NIV to Jerez de la Frontera via Valdepeñas, Córdoba, and Seville. For tourists who have flown to one of the many nearby holiday resorts, it is easiest to rent a car, then drive on to Jerez. From the Portuguese Algarve, take the N431 east, crossing into Spain on a small car ferry (which can involve a lengthy wait in high season), then continue on N431 through Huelva to Seville. From Seville, take the A4 motorway to Jerez de la Frontera. From the Costa del Sol, reach Jerez either via the mountain road to Ronda (one of the most picturesque towns in Spain), and Arcos de la Frontera, or by following the coast road through Algeciras and Cadiz, and so on to Puerto de Santa María.

By Plane
It is possible to book flights direct from the US to Jerez de la Frontera via either Madrid or Barcelona. Málaga is a popular holiday destination, and those who fly to the Costa del Sol will enjoy a most pleasant drive to Jerez from Málaga via the mountain road through Ronda. Both Iberian Airlines and Aviaco offer internal flights to Jerez de la Frontera from various Spanish cities.

By Train
Daily trains via Paris to Madrid. Change in Madrid for regular service to Seville and Jerez de la Frontera.

Car Rental Information
Jerez de la Frontera
Avis: Sevilla 25
    tel: (956) 344311
Hertz: Ruiz de Alda 29
    tel: (956) 335520
Seville
Avis: Avda de la Constitucion 15B
    tel: (954) 216549
    Seville Airport
    tel: (954) 514315
Hertz: Avda Republica Argentina 3
    tel: (954) 270798
    Seville Airport
    tel: (954) 514720
Cadiz
Avis: Avda Cayetano del Toro 16
    tel: (956) 271100
Hertz: Condes Bermeja 5
    tel: (956) 271895
Málaga
Avis: Málaga Airport
    tel: (952) 313943
Hertz: Málaga Airport
    tel: (952) 318740

Firestone Hispania Maps T-30, C-9;
Michelin Map 990

Sherry

The Solera System The unique process of dynamic ageing that visitors witness in the great *bodegas*. Whereas vintage wines, that is wines from a single year, are aged statically in barrel or bottle, sherry gains its character by an intricate and involved process whereby small amounts of younger wines are constantly mixed with quantities of older wines, the rationale being that the character of the older wines will gradually be absorbed by the younger. Thus, wines of varying ages but of essentially similar character (*finos, olorosos,* etc.) are categorized into varying scales, from the oldest, the *solera* itself, to the youngest. As small quantities of wine are drawn from the *solera* to be blended with other wines, then bottled and sold, those barrels are topped up with wine from the next oldest scale; they in turn are blended with a small quantity of wine from the next scale of wine above them and so on, right through the chain. Each firms' various *soleras* all maintain a unique character, thus enabling the skilled blender to produce consistent house brands year after year. Some *soleras* were started well over a hundred years ago; thus, in theory at least, a minute quantity of that oldest wine still remains in the final blend, contributing its age-old character. As well as sherry, many of the large firms produce Spanish brandy by the *solera* system.

Types of sherry: There are two essential 'families' of wines which produce most of the different styles of sherry. For as the wines are fermented in contact with air some, at an early age, demonstrate an unpredictable propensity to grow a white fungus known as *flor* on their surface. This fungus is highly desirable, for as it dissolves it gives inimitable bouquet and flavour, and produces the lightest and most elegant wines. These wines that grow *flor* form the family of *fino* sherries and result in *fino, manzanilla* and *amontillado* wines. Others (often fortified with brandy to ensure that no fungus can grow on their surface) form the broad and important group of *olorosos* which produce the rich, fat cream and brown sherries so loved by the British. Wines from both the *fino* and *oloroso* families are fully fermented, and are thus initially bone dry in their natural state before blending.

Manzanilla *Fino* sherry from vineyards around the seafront town of Sanlúcar de Barrameda. The salt air, and the élite *albariza* chalk hills upon which the Palomino grapes ripen are said to give *manzanilla* a unique salty tang and character.

Fino Bone-dry, light, and elegant, possibly the best aperitif in the world, especially when drunk fresh, chilled, and on the spot, in a bar laden with an assortment of *tapas*.

Amontillado *Finos* that are aged for long periods lose their freshness and elegance, but take on a rounder, fuller, darker character. Natural *amontillados* are of course dry, but favourite commercial blends range from dry to medium-sweet.

Palo Cortado A rare wine: an *oloroso* with *fino* characteristics.

Oloroso The basis for the great sweet blends that are known as cream and brown sherries. Dry, natural *oloroso*, though rare, is also a fine wine of considerable distinction.

Tour of the Sherry Region

There is no sign-posted wine road through the vineyards of Jerez, though the élite *albariza pagos* on which the finest Palomino grapes ripen can be explored en route from Jerez de la Frontera to Sanlúcar de Barrameda and to Puerto de Santa María. Indeed, it is a dramatic experience to strike out into the bare hills of Macharnudo, Carrascal or Miraflores (to name but three of the finest *pagos*) to see the low, white buildings with their tiled roofs overseeing the golden grapes baking in the sun. Not all vines, however, grow in this blazing white chalk soil; lesser vineyards bearing primarily Moscatel and Pedro Ximénez grapes (generally used to sweeten blends) are also cultivated, but on *barros* (heavy, darker clay) and *arenas pagos* (primarily sand). After the *vendimia* – the harvest – the Palomino, as well as the Pedro Ximénez and Moscatel grapes, are spread out on grass *esparto* mats to further dry and concentrate their sugar and scent, fanned by the stuffy Levant wind, and by the sun which shines in Jerez nearly 300 days out of the year.

After driving through the sunbaked vineyards above Jerez, or Puerto de Santa María, or Sanlúcar de Barrameda, it is all the more pleasant to enter a cool, quiet *bodega* in any of these three towns, to see and learn about the wines patiently maturing in row after row of casks, and to sip a chilled *copita* of *fino*, without doubt the best wine in the world to drink on a blistering Spanish afternoon. A visit to one or several *bodegas* will certainly be the highlight of any wine lover's tour of the sherry country. Some of the well-known shippers welcome casual visitors without prior appointments, though it is always worthwhile for those who wish to visit a particular property either to write to the firm directly in advance, or to procure a letter of introduction from its British agents. The *bodegas* of each establishment are unique, many with long and colourful histories, and reminders of famous people who visited and tasted wine from the cask. Through visiting such firms one is best able to learn both about the different types of sherry produced (and about each firm's individual brands), as well as about the unique *solera* system. For it is this remarkable system of dynamic ageing that both gives sherry its inimitable character and which also allows favourite brand wines to be produced consistently year after year, perhaps one key to the commercial success of this marvellous wine. First-time visitors to Jerez often expect to see *soleras* arranged as in a diagram, that is with the scales of younger wines physically located upon rows of barrels of older wine. In practice, however, the *solera* system is not an isolated activity that one views, but rather an integral process that is taking place constantly throughout the *bodega*; in fact, the different scales of wine may not even be in close proximity.

While tours of sherry *bodegas* are of course the wine lover's primary reason for visiting the region – and there are some fifty in Jerez alone – the sherry towns themselves are worthy of exploration. Jerez, as its modest archaeological museum demonstrates, is an ancient and historic town, inhabited at times by Phoenicians, Greeks, Romans, Barbars, Visigoths, and Moors. As well as its pride in wine, Jerez is also famous for its Carthusian horses – indeed, many sherry firms have collections of prize steeds, and the members of their aristocratic families compete in riding competitions. The town's second most important festival – after the *Fiesta de la Vendimia* (vintage festival), of course – is the *Fiesta del Caballo*, or horse fair that takes place annually in the spring. In addition to raising these sleek and graceful beasts, the Jerezanos also place great pride on their fierce fighting bulls that are raised in the oak-studded mountains and the open plains – the bullfight is a product of Andalusia and still an important and central occasion in the people's lives.

The *Fiesta de la Vendimia* is a joyous affair, dedicated each year to a different foreign country (indicating the continued importance of the export trade to sherry producers), and marked by a procession through the narrow streets of the town. There is much pageantry, flamenco dancing, bull fighting and, of course, eating and drinking. It takes place annually during early September; it should be noted, however, that many firms close while the festivities take place. This time of year, at any rate, is not necessarily the best to visit *bodegas*, for wine producers are inevitably at their busiest while the grapes are being harvested. The proclamation of

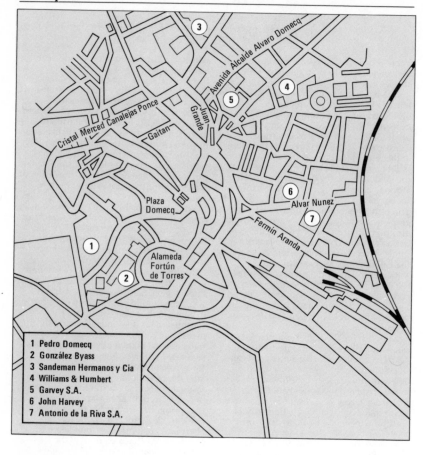

1 Pedro Domecq
2 González Byass
3 Sandeman Hermanos y Cia
4 Williams & Humbert
5 Garvey S.A.
6 John Harvey
7 Antonio de la Riva S.A.

the grape harvest takes place in one of the town's outstanding monuments, the sixteenth to seventeenth-century Collegiate Church. The remains of the Alcázar, dating from the eleventh century, are also worth viewing. The walls of this old Moorish fortress are surrounded by lovely gardens. The Moorish baths; the Gothic Santo Domingo Convent; the numerous and prosperous civil manor houses and palaces dating from the sixteenth, seventeenth, and eighteenth centuries; and, a few miles from the town, the Cartuja, with its splendid Gothic cloisters all reflect the importance of Jerez de la Frontera over the centuries. The Cartuja, or Carthusian monastery, was once a stable for breeding horses giving its name to the beautiful Carthusian horses of the region.

Puerto de Santa María, located some nine or ten miles from Jerez, is both a fishing harbour and an important wine shipping centre, and many well-known firms (such as Duff Gordon & Co., and Osborne) have their headquarters here. An important centre in the development of the wine trade, Puerto de Santa María is a pleasant, quiet town, with a shaded promenade that leads up to the thirteenth-century San Marcos castle. From Puerto de Santa María boat trips can be arranged to the nearby busy and important port of Cadiz, located on the tip of a narrow isthmus. Visit the old districts of Cadiz, such as El Populo or Santa María, with their narrow streets, whitewashed buildings and old stones; make a seafront promenade, and eat in a *freiduria* where packets of sizzling *boquerones* (fresh anchovies), sardines, baby sole and inkfish, *gambas* and other shellfish are all fried to perfection.

Sanlúcar de Barrameda, the third principal sherry town, is the home of a unique wine, *manzanilla*, an extremely dry, pale *fino* with a pungent, salty tang which is gained not only from the chalk soil above this harbour, but also from the proximity and humidity of the sea air. Visit the Santiago castle, located on the highest part of the town (this provides splendid views over the mouth of the Quadalquivir to the Doñana National Park). Many *bodegas* are located in the old quarter of the town below the castle; however, there is less opportunity for casual visits in Sanlúcar because many smaller firms do not have the facilities to cater to casual visitors, or to provide multi-lingual guides. One of the great experiences of any trip to the sherry region, however, must be to sit on the seafront of Sanlúcar de Barrameda, at any of numerous fish and shellfish restaurants, munching on grilled prawns or fried fish, while sipping a cool glass or two of pungent, sea-fresh *manzanilla*.

Sherry Producers

It is possible for the casual tourist to visit wine establishments in the region, but the serious wine lover will, to avoid disappointment, arrange visits by favourite *bodegas* in advance, either directly or through that firm's US agent. Write in advance, preferably including your destination in Jerez (name of hotel) so that the firm can contact you if necessary. Alternatively, have your hotel make arrangements when in the region. The following are only a handful of the numerous establishments in the area.

Jerez de la Frontera

Gonzalez Byass SA
Manuel Maria Gonzalez 12
tel: (956) 34 00 00
Daily 11–14h
Appointment necessary.
English spoken.

Sandeman Hermanos y Cia
Pizarro 10
tel: (956) 33 11 00
Daily 9–14h
English spoken.

Pedro Domecq SA
tel: (956) 33 18 00
Customers and interested wine lovers can visit this well-known establishment by making an appointment through their UK agent. Write to Luis Gordon & Sons, Ltd., 18 Dartmouth Street, London SW1H 9BL.

Williams and Humbert Ltd
Nuño de Cañas, 1
tel: (956) 33 13 00
Open Jan–Aug Mon–Fri 10h30–13h30
Sept–Dec Mon–Sat 10h30–13h30
Appointment necessary for groups only.
English spoken.

Garvey SA
Bodegas de San Patricio
Guadalete 14
tel: (956) 33 05 00
Mon–Fri by appointment.
Max 40 pers.
English spoken.

Croft Jerez SA
Carretera Circunvalación
tel: (956) 34 66 00
Daily 9–14h
Appointment necessary at least two days in advance.
English spoken.

John Harvey & Sons (España) Ltd
Alvar Núñez 53
tel: (956) 34 60 00
Mon–Fri 8h30–13h30
Appointment preferable.
English spoken.

Puerto de Santa María

Duff Gordon & Co SA
Fernan Caballero 6
tel: (956) 85 51 11
Daily 11–14h
Appointment necessary.
Max 10 pers.
English spoken.

Wine Festivals

| Mid May | *Fiesta del Caballo*
(Horse Festival) | Jerez de la Frontera |
| Weekend closest to
September 8th | *Fiesta de la Vendimia*
This weekend of
celebration heralds the
start of the harvest with
a grand procession,
bullfights, flamenco
dancing, and fireworks. | Jerez de la Frontera |

Regional Gastronomy

Tapas An impressive variety of bar-top finger foods that are enjoyed throughout the day, invariably accompanied by a *copita* of sherry. Some favourite *tapas* include *tortillas* (Spanish omelette), *chiperones* (fried ink-fish), marinated vegetables, grilled prawns, *chorizo*, cod's roe in mayonnaise, *jamón serrano* (air-dried mountain ham), and much else. Select these snacks one at a time while standing at the bar.

Gazpacho Iced summer soup made with finely chopped tomatoes, peppers, cucumbers, onion, and garlic, mixed with ice water, vinegar and bread.

Sopa de almendras Cold almond and grape soup.

Sopa de pescado Fisherman's soup made with the daily catch.

Sopa al cuarto de hora 'Quarter of an hour soup' of clams, eggs, and vegetables, simmered in water and sherry.

Mejillones a Jerez Mussels steamed in sherry.

Gambas a la plancha Giant prawns cooked in olive oil on an extremely hot, flat griddle (other fish and meats *a la plancha* are prepared in this manner).

Huevos a la flamenca Characteristic dish of eggs baked with a tomato and pepper sauce flavoured with spicy *chorizo* and *jamón serrano*.

Riñones al Jerez Kidneys cooked in sherry.

Perdices a la torera Partridge 'bullfighter's style' – stuffed with bacon and anchovies, then stewed in white wine.

Espada Swordfish.

Besugo Sea bream.

Pulpo Octopus.

Pescados fritos Variety of small fish such as sardines, anchovies, squid, baby sole, deep-fried in boiling oil. Best sampled from *freidurias* in Cadiz.

Pollo al Jerez Chicken stewed in sherry.

Esparragos Asparagus.

Tocinillo almendra Almond sweetmeat.

Bizcocho de almendras Almond sponge cake.

Restaurants

Jerez de la Frontera

Restaurante Gaitan
Gaitan 3
tel: (956) 34 58 59
Extensive selection of *tapas* and other regional foods in this sherry producers' favourite restaurant. Intimate and friendly atmosphere.
Closed Sun eve; Mon
Open 13–16h30; 20h30–23h30
Inexpensive to **Moderate**

Tendido 6
Circo 10
tel: (956) 34 48 35
Regional foods and wines in another highly-recommended restaurant.
Inexpensive to **Moderate**

Venta Los Naranjos
Carretera Jerez-Sanlúcar (C440)
On the road to Sanlúcar de Barrameda, many say that this modest restaurant serves the best fish and seafood in the area.
Inexpensive to **Moderate**

Hotels

Jerez de la Frontera

Hotel Jerez
av Alcalde Alvaro Domecq 41
tel: (956) 33 06 00
The best in town: an **Expensive**
comfortable hotel with bedrooms
overlooking the attractive gardens.
Moderate restaurant.
Hotel open all year.
Restaurant open 13h30–16h30; 21–23h30

Hotel Capele
General Franco 58
tel: (956) 34 64 00
Moderate hotel with 30 rooms. No
restaurant.

Hotel Mica
Higueras 7
tel: (956) 34 07 00
Small **Inexpensive** hotel without
restaurant.

Puerto de Santa María

Hotel Melía Caballo Blanco
NIV
tel: (956) 86 37 45
Attractive with bungalows in garden.
Swimming pool and restaurant.
Expensive

Arcos de la Frontera

Parador Nacional Casa del Corregidor
Plaza de Espana
tel: (956) 70 05 00
Located 32 km to the east of Jerez on the
dramatic high road to Ronda. This
parador, like most others, is extremely
popular, so it is essential to book in
advance.
Moderate

Sanlúcar de Barrameda

Hotel Guadalquivir
Calzada del Ejército
tel: (956) 36 07 42
Inexpensive

Hotel Andalucia
González Montoro
tel: (956) 36 01 40
Inexpensive

Where to Get Additional Information

Spanish National Tourist Office
655 5th Ave
NY NY 10022
tel: (212) 759–8822
Offices also in San Francisco, Chicago,
Houston, and St Augustine

The Sherry Institute of Spain
220 E 42nd St
NY NY 10017
tel: (212) 907–9381

Exporters Group of Jerez
Apartado No 411
Jerez de la Frontera

Office of Tourist Information
Calderón de la Barca, 1 dupl
Cadiz
tel: (956) 21 13 13

Local office of tourism:

Alameda Cristina
Jerez de la Frontera
tel: (956) 34 20 37

Camping

Puerto de Santa María
Guadalete
tel: (956) 86 17 49
Puerto Real
Pinar
tel: (956) 83 08 97

Bibliography

Sherry by Julian Jeffs, Faber & Faber,
paperback edition 1982

*Monarch Guide to the Wines of Spain and
Portugal* by Jan Read, Monarch Press 1978

—PORTUGAL—

NORTHERN PORTUGAL

Northern Portugal remains remote, unspoiled, and far-off, distant not so much in terms of mileage (in this age of package holidays) as in differences in temperament and lifestyle, and in the strange contrasts of this gentle, devout, untouched rural landscape with most other parts of Western Europe. Small villages huddle on the banks of indolent, shallow rivers, while great broad oxen, joined together with carved wooden yokes, lumber through verdant fields, or along ancient roads that seemingly have yet to acknowledge the existence of the automobile. In the Minho, gnarled vines wrap themselves along trees and up other living supports, freeing the land below for more essential crops; in the stark Upper Douro, the vineyards lie upon tortuous, sunbaked terraces.

Oporto, Portugal's second largest city, and capital of the north, itself appears remote, far-off, even inhospitable. It is neither particularly prosperous, nor very pretty, perched in isolation high above the steep Douro gorge, with its moody, brooding carless alleys, its hectic riverside market of Ribeira, and its sombre, unyielding churches which reflect the deeply religious, simple Catholic faith of the country. Yet in the midst of it all, in this city which seems so far from home, a most British welcome awaits the visitor who crosses over the two-tiered iron bridge that spans the Douro and leads to Vila Nova de Gaia. Not all the port producers in Vila Nova de Gaia today are British by any means; nevertheless, it was the British taste which, in the eighteenth century, transformed the rather harsh, dry table wines of the Douro into the rich, sweet, fortified wine that is today loved throughout the world. The great port lodges located in Vila Nova de Gaia offer tours to casual visitors without appointment. Visitors are shown the cellars, and the processes of blending and maturing the different styles of port are explained. Afterwards, free samples of wine are offered in the tasting rooms, and purchases can be made directly.

Some port firms will make arrangements for the interested visitor to see their *quintas* high in the Upper Douro Valley. The vineyards that produce the grapes for this magnificent wine lie far upriver in a land even less visited, more remote; it is a fascinating region to tour. Northern Portugal's most distinctive table wine is Vinho Verde, and an equally satisfying, equally interesting wine tour leads through the verdant Minho province, home of this much-loved wine. The rich, fertile intensively cultivated land is virtually opposite in character to the harsh Upper Douro – as great a contrast, in fact, as between fresh, sharp, mouth-puckering Vinho Verde and rich, warming port. Tours of both the Upper Douro, and the Minho regions can be undertaken from Oporto.

How to Get There

By Car
Portugal is a most rewarding country for motorists. The drive from Lisbon to Oporto is fascinating, but though the distance is only some 300 km, it is a road to take your time on, as are most roads in Portugal (there are few motorways).

From Madrid, or the north of Spain, head for Salamanca and Ciudad Rodrigo, then follow the N16 across to Aveiro. From Aveiro drive north to Oporto. An alternative, if slower route travels north at Viseu (centre of the Dão wine region) to Lamego, where a tour of the Upper Douro can commence, before continuing downriver to Oporto.

An alternative route if coming from northern Spain is via the beautiful and unspoiled north and west coasts. Continue across to La Coruña, then down through Santiago de Compostela, crossing the border at Valença do Minho. At Valença, begin a tour of the Vinho Verde country en route to Oporto.

By Plane
TWA and TAP fly direct, non-stop from the US to Lisbon. There are frequent flights from Lisbon to Oporto. Connecting flights are also available from the US to Oporto.

By Train
Take the Paris/Lisbon train to Salamanca. Change there for direct train to Oporto. The train journey from here is most dramatic, for it follows the Douro Valley from the Spanish border, through the terraced port vineyards (stopping at Régua), down to Oporto.

Local Public Transport
There are daily trains from Oporto up the Douro Valley to Régua. The journey takes a little over two hours. Thus if time is limited, a visit to the Upper Douro can be made in a day, by taking the early morning train, and returning in the evening. Additionally, there are frequent trains to Viana do Castelo, and Braga, as well as express trains that connect Oporto with Lisbon and the south.

Car Rental Information
Oporto
  Avis: Rua Guedes de Azevedo 125
    tel: (02) 31 59 47
    Pedras Rubras Airport
    tel: (02) 94 81 525
  Hertz: Rua de Sta Catarina 899
    tel: (02) 31 23 87
    Pedras Rubras Airport
    tel: (02) 94 81 400
Viana do Castelo
  Avis: Hotel Afonso III
    tel: (0028) 24 123
Braga
  Avis: Rua Gabriel, Pereira Castro 28
    tel: (0023) 26 460
Barcelos
  Avis: Largo da Calcada No 30
    tel: (0023) 82 265

Michelin Map 37

The Wines of Northern Portugal

Vinho Verde Portugal's distinctive 'green wine', so named not because of its colour (which is both white and red), or because of the mistaken impression that the grapes used to produce it are underripe, but because it is wine that is meant to be consumed while extremely fresh and young, as opposed to mature wines, *vinhos maduros*. The demarcated region extends roughly between the Douro and Minho Rivers, and there are six sub-regions that all produce wines with individual characteristics: Monção (considered to be the best), Lima, Braga, Penafiel, Amarante, and Basto (in practice, in fact, wines from these various regions are often blended together). Vinhos Verdes are fresh and young; the grapes used to produce them are relatively low in sugar and high in acid. A secondary malo-lactic fermentation that takes place in the bottle gives the wines a slight characteristic 'prickle' which, combined with their refreshing acidity, makes them ideal light summer wines. Red Vinho Verde, hardly exported at all, is frothy and astringent, rich in acid and tannin. Perhaps an acquired taste, it should be well chilled before serving. It is good with the rich and spicy foods of the region.

Vinho Maduro Mature, as opposed to 'green' wine (most restaurants divide their wine lists along these lines). Many of the country's best mature table wines – both reds *(tintos)* and whites *(brancos)* – come from central Portugal in the large region known as Dão (not covered in this book). Such wines are available throughout Portugal, and visitors will want to gain a familiarity with them. Red Dão is robust and full-bodied; white Dão is generally dry to medium-dry, with a full firm flavour and bouquet. The Douro region also produces robust, deep-red and strong white table wines, particularly around centres such as Vila Real, Mesao Frio, Favaios, Murca, and Armamar; such wines are available throughout the region. Other *vinhos maduros* available in the north come from undemarcated zones, though this is not necessarily a reflection of their quality; the terms *reserva* and *garrafeira* are general indications of quality.

Vinho espumante Lamego, just south of Régua, is the centre for excellent (and inexpensive) sparkling wines produced by the *méthode champenoise*. Sparkling wine establishments (such as Raposeira) can be visited, and the wines are available throughout the country. They are particularly good in accompaniment to rich and oily foods, such as the popular *leitão assado* (roast suckling pig). Much good sparkling wine is also produced in the Bairrada region between Coimbra and Aveiro, centred around Mealhada.

Rosado Vast quantities of Portuguese rosé are produced and exported throughout the world. In the Douro one firm in particular dominates: SOGRAPE, which gives the world literally millions of litres of wine sold in its familiar squat bottle under the label Mateus. Vila Real is the home of Mateus. Many other brands of Portuguese rosé are produced, ranging in colour from various shades of pale pink and coral to light orange. The colour is drawn from the skins of black grapes which remain in contact with the wine during fermentation for only a brief time. Portuguese rosé ranges from dry to medium-sweet, and it is sometimes semi-sparkling.

Port One of the great fortified wines of the world, produced by arresting the natural fermentation with the addition of brandy, thus allowing the wine to retain a natural residual sweetness. The grapes come from the Upper Douro Valley, but once they have been pressed, fermented into wine, and fortified, they are transported downriver to Vila Nova de Gaia where the great port shippers blend and mature them into the various styles and brands known throughout the world. The following are the principal styles of port:

White port Made exclusively from white grapes, and ranging in style from dry to medium-dry. Though not widely exported, it is often drunk chilled, and is excellent as an aperitif.

Ruby port A blended port aged in oak and consumed while relatively fresh and young. As the name suggests, it is usually a brilliant bright colour, full-bodied, and sweet.

Tawny port Like ruby, a blend of various wines, but matured for considerably longer periods. As a consequence, the wine tends to shed its youthful hue and fades to a pale shade of amber. It is a lighter and more delicate wine with a characteristic nutty flavour. Fine old tawny is the highest quality of 'wood' port (as opposed to vintage port), produced from selected reserves and matured for long periods in cask.

Vintage port Made from wines of a single (and exceptional) year only. Unlike other styles of port, vintage is aged in wood for a maximum only of three years, before being bottled then laid down for the ten and often twenty and more years that such wines need to develop and reach their peak. As the wine ages it throws a heavy crust, or sediment, and so must be carefully handled, and always decanted before drinking.

Late-bottled vintage port Wines from one excellent year aged (unlike vintage) for upwards of five years in oak casks. The wine is lighter, cheaper, and much easier to handle than vintage (since it does not throw a crust).

Crusted port Non-vintage wines that are bottled early and laid down for long periods of ageing. The wine, as the name suggests, throws a crust, and must therefore be decanted carefully (like vintage) before drinking.

Wine Tours in Northern Portugal
Vila Nova de Gaia and the Upper Douro

There are about 80 port lodges in Vila Nova de Gaia, and no visit to northern Portugal would be complete without visiting at least a few of them. As in Champagne, many of the large and well-known establishments keep 'open house' to visitors, and no advance arrangements need to be made. During the summer season, too, English-speaking guides are generally available. Anyone with specific requirements, however, should either write to the particular firm direct, or else arrange an appointment through that firm's US agent. Visits to *quintas* in the Upper Douro can also be arranged though this too must be done in advance.

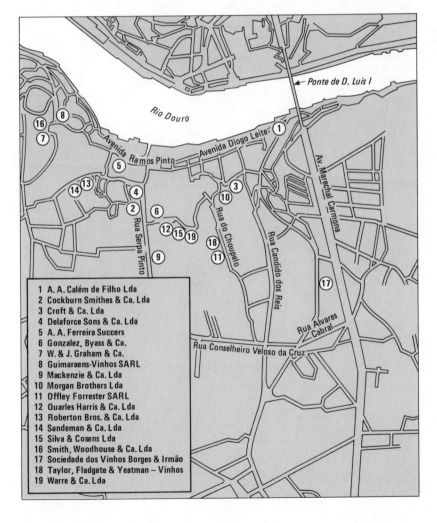

1 A. A. Calém de Filho Lda
2 Cockburn Smithes & Ca. Lda
3 Croft & Ca. Lda
4 Delaforce Sons & Ca. Lda
5 A. A. Ferreira Succers
6 Gonzalez, Byass & Ca.
7 W. & J. Graham & Ca.
8 Guimaraens-Vinhos SARL
9 Mackenzie & Ca. Lda
10 Morgan Brothers Lda
11 Offley Forrester SARL
12 Quarles Harris & Ca. Lda
13 Roberton Bros. & Ca. Lda
14 Sandeman & Ca. Lda
15 Silva & Cosens Lda
16 Smith, Woodhouse & Ca. Lda
17 Sociedade dos Vinhos Borges & Irmão
18 Taylor, Fladgate & Yeatman — Vinhos
19 Warre & Ca. Lda

A most interesting tour of the Upper Douro can be made from Oporto. Obviously there is much more flexibility and mobility for those with a car; however, a dramatic train journey from Oporto to Régua takes about two hours. On our suggested motoring tour, we reach the Upper Douro via Penafiel, Amarante, and Vila Real, thus allowing visits to be made to Vinho Verde establishments and the Mateus estate before entering the port country.

From Oporto, take the N15 highway east to Penafiel. (Before reaching Penafiel, make a brief detour off the main road some four miles south of Paredes, to Paço de Sousa, a small village whose well-restored church and Benedictine monastery are fine examples of Portuguese Romanesque architecture, rugged, solid edifices built when a young warlike nation was involved in endless fighting and skirmishes.) Penafiel stands on a hill above the quiet waters of the Sousa and the Cavalum Rivers, an old town which reflects its colourful past not only in its mixed architecture (Romanesque, Gothic, Manueline), but also through its lively traditional festivals and folk dancing. The Quinta da Aveleda is a few miles outside the town, a country house set in a beautiful estate, and the home of two well-known and popular Vinhos Verdes: Casal Garcia and Aveleda. Both the *quinta* and the modern winery can be visited, but an appointment in advance is necessary.

Continue along the N15 through this varied agricultural landscape to Amarante, another picturesque town located along the wooded banks of the lovely Tamega River. Like Penafiel, it is the centre of one of six sub-regions producing lively, tart Vinhos Verdes. Amarante is also known for its exuberant annual celebration of its patron saint, São Gonçalo, and also for its imaginatively-shaped sweets such as *pão de lo, doces de ovos, foguetes, galhofas, papos de anjo*, and many others. Try them.

Amarante is the 'door to the mountains' and upon leaving the town on the N15 the road begins a steep ascent up to the Alto do Espinho pass which leads to the Serra do Marão, a mountainous range of granite and shale. Stop overnight here at one of Portugal's national *pousadas*, the Pousada de São Gonçalo, which enjoys spectacular views over the valley. *Pousadas* are state-run inns, usually located either in historic settings or buildings, or in spots of great natural beauty; they are reasonably priced, and offer good regional foods and wines. Not surprisingly, they are extremely popular and it is necessary always to book well in advance.

The road continues through the mountains, then descends to Vila Real, a town best known for the Mateus Palace, located two miles outside the town. Indeed, its elegant facade is familiar to millions from the label of this pretty, fizzy pink wine that is exported throughout the world. The Palace can be visited (it is a national monument, either because it is yet another fine example of the gaudy Portuguese Baroque, or because it is a symbol of one of the country's commercial success stories). While a certain amount of production takes place here, the great bulk of wines are produced and bottled in an ultra-modern 'wine factory' located in Avintes outside Oporto. (Write to SOGRAPE for an appointment – see address below.)

From Vila Real, continue along the N322 to Sabrosa, then turn south on the N323 to reach, finally, the port vineyards of the Upper Douro. Some of the best centre around the unimposing yet dramatically sited village of Pinhão, just a cluster of streets and houses nestled beneath the contoured terraced gorge of the Douro. About a dozen varieties of vines grow on these rocky, schistous slopes; the climate here in summer is uncomfortably hot, but winters are wet and cold. The vineyard area was demarcated as long ago as the mid-eighteenth century, and there are numerous strict regulations that must be adhered to at every stage in the production of this unique wine. The Port Wine Institute, an official organization that supervises and regulates the port wine trade, tastes and examines each lot of wine destined for export, and only gives a Certificate of Origin and Quality to those that are approved.

After the grapes are harvested, they are taken to any of numerous whitewashed *quintas* where they are pressed (either traditionally by human treading or, more likely these days, by mechanical presses). The dark, rich purple must is then fermented into wine, but before all the natural grape sugars are transformed into alcohol, it is given an addition of brandy. This arrests the process of fermentation, fortifies the wine, and thus allows it to retain a natural residual sweetness. The raw young port generally stays in the Upper Douro over the winter. It used to be shipped downriver the following spring in graceful *barcos rabelos*, narrow ships with large square sails; today, however, the wine reaches the port lodges at Vila Nova de Gaia by way of lorry or train: less picturesque, certainly, but quicker and safer. There, in the lodges of the famous firms, it is blended (except for rare single *quinta* vintage wines), matured in oak casks that are known as 'pipes' (each holds about 530 litres) or in bottles (in the case of vintage port), for the length of time necessary to develop the character of each particular type of wine, before it is finally put on the market.

From Pinhão, explore the Upper Douro. Travel further up the valley to Alijo, a grape growing centre (Pousada Barão de Forrester, named after the legendary *entrepreneur* who tragically drowned in the Duoro when his *barco rabelo* overturned in the rapids), or return downriver to Régua, a small, busy river port, like Pinhão, nestled in the midst of prized vineyards, and surrounded by the well-known *quintas* of numerous firms, located in nearby hills. Being the westernmost edge of the demarcated region, Régua is the centre from which wines are often shipped down to Vila Nova de Gaia. The Casa do Douro of the Port Wine Institute is located in Régua.

From Régua, head south briefly, crossing the river again on the N2 that leads to Lamego, an old historic town rich in Baroque architecture, and famous now as the centre for the production of both excellent hams, and also excellent *vinhos espumantes* – sparkling wines produced by the traditional *méthode champenoise*. The largest firm in the area is Raposeira; they warmly welcome visitors who view the fascinating process in their deep natural caves. The museum in Lamego is also we'l worth a visit, while the Nossa Senhora dos Remédios, a place of pilgrimage, overlooks the town, and provides a dramatic vista of the surrounding countryside. Lamego is a good overnight stopping place.

Return to Oporto via the N222 along the south bank of the Douro. The *Miradouro da*

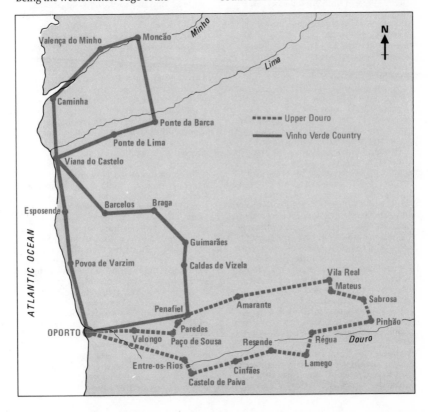

Boa Vista provides a last tremendous view of the vineyards of this remote outpost, looking across to Régua, before leaving the ravine and re-entering the gentler Vinho Verde countryside. Pass through Resende (with its Romanesque church of São Salvador), Cinfães (which has a Roman bridge spanning the Bestanca), and finally through the lower valley to Castelo de Paiva. Recross the river once more to Entre-os-Rios, and return on the N108 to Oporto, or else head north to Penafiel, for further exploration of the delightful countryside of the Minho.

'Entre-Douro e Minho' – The Vinho Verde Country

The north-west corner of Portugal, between the country's northern border with Spain (formed by the Minho River) and the Douro River (thus the name 'Entre-Douro e Minho'), is a region of singular beauty and history, for indeed, its numerous old towns and villages played important roles in the development of the Portuguese nation. It is a densely populated region, and there are many remains from the Roman occupation and from medieval times. Throughout, there is a keen sense of time having stood still, for the picturesque markets and the lively fairs and processions that are encountered in every village can hardly have changed over the centuries. It is a land of lively regional cooking, and of never-empty clay jugs of crisp, tart, local wines. Winding through it all, over hedges and man-made supports and up into high trees, interlaced from branch to branch, are the gnarled vines that have been cultivated in this unique fashion probably for almost 2000 years, vines that produce Portugal's most distinctive table wine, Vinho Verde.

This land known as Entre-Douro e Minho is an ideal tourist region, for its Atlantic coast is flanked by long sandy beaches, while inland there are the rugged and beautiful mountains of the Gerês National Park. For the wine lover, though there are few properties or wine estates to visit, the charm lies in simply exploring this unique landscape, driving through idyllic and unspoiled countryside where even trees seem to bear grapes, coming upon weekly markets selling traditional craftware, then stopping in any of the many historic towns and villages, to eat regional foods and drink local wines. There are few wine lands in all of Europe that are less spoiled. While a circular tour of the region can be made from Oporto, our suggested route leads through the Vinho Verde country en route to Spanish Galicia (useful for those who are returning to – or coming from – the Plymouth/ Santander ferry).

Leave Oporto on the N15 road east to Penafiel. The vineyard area around this old town is one of six sub-regions within the demarcated zone for the production of Vinho Verde. The other sub-regions are Monção, Amarante, Lima, Braga, and Basto. At Penafiel, visit the Quinta da Aveleda, a country estate that produces two well-known Vinhos Verdes (see address below). From Penafiel, take the small N106 road north to Caldas de Vizela (the region is rich in natural mineral springs, and this is one of its spa towns, popular since Roman times, as evidenced by the Roman bridge and pavements). Continue north to Guimarães, the so-called 'cradle of the nation', for it was the birthplace of Afonso Henriques, first King of Portugal, in the eleventh century. The old quarter, overlooked by its austere, granite castle, is evocative of those days when this medieval town was the most important in the country. Today it is an industrious centre for the production, among other things, of local handicrafts, including coarse hand-woven linen, fine embroidery, cutlery, and wood carvings.

From Guimarães, follow the N101 to Braga, passing through, en route, another Roman spa town, Caldas das Taipas (camping along the river). Braga, like Guimarães, is one of the most interesting and historic towns in northern Portugal. It was founded by the Romans in 296 BC, and its cathedral is the oldest in the country, testimony to its ecclesiastical eminence (the Bishops of Braga were once said to have greater power than the Kings of Portugal). Lively religious and folk processions take place during the *Festas de São Joao* (end of June) and the Solemnities of Holy Week (March or April). Like many other towns in the region, Braga continues to produce much traditional craftware: beautiful and functional items that are used in everyday life (the weekly market is held Tuesdays in the Largo da Feira).

Barcelos, downriver from Braga, is a

charming and peaceful town, set beside the slow waters of the Cávado River. Its central location makes it a good base for exploration of the region. Barcelos, is famous for a legend that has virtually become the tourists' symbol of Portugal, the gaily-painted cock of Barcelos. This, and far more interesting local handicraft, can be found in the best weekly market in the country, held every Thursday in the Campo da Republica.

Continue on the N103 to Viana do Castelo, a busy town located both along an enviable stretch of coastline, and also along the banks of the lazy Lima River. Viana was once the centre of a prosperous British community who traded first in dried salt cod (the *bacalhau* so loved by the Portuguese, who have at least 365 different methods of preparing it), and then in the wines of the Minho. A British Factory was established here in 1700, but with the growth of the port wine trade it eventually moved to Oporto. There is a superb view of the pine-forested coast, and the gentle hills of the Minho which flank the broad Lima from Monte Santa Luzia, which overlooks the town to the north. The best place to stay is the Hotel de Santa Luzia, which tops the mountain and is part of the chain of Portuguese National *pousadas*.

From Viana, follow the N202 along the north bank of the Lima to Ponte de Lima. The country is very beautiful and peaceful, and perhaps for this reason the Romans thought the Lima to be the Lethe, river of forgetfulness, causing all who crossed it to forget their homeland and family. The market at Ponte de Lima, along the banks of the river, is the oldest in Portugal, founded in 1125 by charter. It still takes place every Monday. Continue further up the valley on the N203 to Ponte da Barca, then head north on the N101 to Monção.

The Alvarinho Vinho Verde produced around Monção is generally considered to be the region's finest. It is produced solely from the local grape of the same name, and

has both deeper scent and flavour and, unlike most other Vinhos Verdes, improves with some bottle ageing. Alvarinho was one of the first Portuguese wines to be exported, way back in the fifteenth century, but the wines from the sub-region were popular well before that date. Indeed, they were documented as long ago as the tenth century and were praised by the Romans. Monção itself is a small fortified town, overlooking the Minho, and across the river, Spanish Galicia. It is known, also, for its superb river lampreys which should be sampled (they are a delicacy akin to the *bordelaise* speciality), and also for a powerful, local firewater known as *bagaceira* (a type of spirit distilled from the grape residue left after the pressing).

Visit nearby Barbeita where an historic meeting took place in 1386 between King Dom João I and John of Gaunt, Duke of Lancaster, which resulted in an important alliance cemented through the marriage of the former to the Duke's daughter Philippa. Their son, Prince Henry, earned the sobriquet 'Navigator' for the voyages of discovery that he launched which resulted, after his death, with Vasco da Gama's discovery of a sea route to India.

Follow the Minho downriver to Valença do Minho. Another good stopping place is found here, the Pousada de São Teotonio, which overlooks Spanish Tuy. It is, like all *pousadas*, renowned for its hospitality, and the quality of its regional cooking. It is also a good place to sample the wines of Monção. Valença itself, however, cannot avoid that hectic, frenzied feel of a border town, although the older quarter, behind its fortified ramparts is well-preserved. From Valença, either continue north into Spain, or else return to the coast, passing through picturesque Caminha, en route back to Viana do Castelo. The coastline south of Viana is worth exploring; return to Oporto via Esposende and Póvoa de Varzim.

Wine Producers

Port Lodges

The famous port lodges in Vila Nova de Gaia are extremely welcoming and hospitable, and the casual visitor can visit establishments without arranging prior appointments. During summer months, many have multi-lingual guides on hand.

Those with particular requirements, however, are advised to write in advance. Some are happy to arrange visits to *quintas* in the Upper Douro for interested parties. The following is a list of some of the better-known firms who welcome visitors.

4400 Vila Nova de Gaia

Warre & Ca Lda
Travessa do Barão de Forrester, 10
Apartado No 26
tel: (029) 39 60 63
July 1–Sept 15 Mon–Sat; Sun morning
9h30–12h30; 14–17h
Sept 16–June 30 weekdays only (hours as above)
Appointment necessary for groups.
Max 100 pers.
English spoken.

Sandeman & Ca Lda
Largo Miguel Bombarda, 3
tel: (029) 30 40 81
Mon–Fri 9h30–12h30; 14–17h
Appointment necessary for groups.
Max 50 pers.
English spoken.

A A Ferreira Succrs
rua da Carvalhosa, 19
tel: (029) 30 08 66
Mon–Fri 9–17h30; Sat 9–12h
Motorboat trips on the Douro River from
May–Oct.
English spoken.

A A Cálem e Filho Lda
rua da Reboleira, 7
tel: (029) 24 86 7
Daily 9–17h
50 pers max.
English spoken.
Visits to *quintas* in Pinhão with
English-speaking guide can be arranged by
prior appointment.

Sociedade dos Vinhos Borges & Irmão
SARL
avenida da Republica, 796
tel: (029) 30 50 02
Mon–Fri 9–12h; 14–18h
English spoken.

Cockburn Smithes & Cia Lda
rua D Leonor de Freitas
tel: (029) 39 40 31
Mon–Fri 9h30–11h; 14–16h
Appointment preferable.
Max 50 pers.
English spoken.
The tour includes a visit to the cooperage
(one of only two remaining in Vila Nova de
Gaia) where the characteristic barrels
known as 'pipes' are made and repaired.
Visits can also be arranged to Quinta de
Santa Maria, 1 mile from Régua, where
there is the largest collection of wooden
vats in Europe.

Quinta da Noval-Vinhos SARL
rua Cândido dos Reis, 575
tel: (029) 30 20 20
Daily 9–13h; 14–19h
Appointment necessary.
Max 100 pers.
English spoken.
(note: the cellars, bottling line, and
reception facilities will soon be transferred
to the Upper Douro, 5 km north of Pinhão;
visitors will be welcome there.)

Delaforce Sons & Ca Vinhos Lda
rua das Coradas
tel: (029) 30 22 12
Mon–Fri by appointment for trade visitors
only.
English spoken.

Taylor, Fladgate & Yeatman-Vinhos
P Ó Box 24
Mon–Fri by appointment.
English spoken.

Table Wines

4560 Penafiel

Sociedade Agricola e Comercial da Quinta
da Aveleda
Quinta da Aveleda
tel: (0025) 22 041
Daily 9–17h
Appointment necessary.
The Quinta da Aveleda estate is one of the
most beautiful in the Vinho Verde region,
and visitors can stroll through the lush
wooded gardens and around the mansion
before touring the Old Wine Lodge, the
Fig Tree Lodges, and the modern bottling
and packing plants. Samples of wine are
offered on a pleasant balcony overlooking
the rose garden.
For appointments write to the following
address:
Quinta da Aveleda
P O Box No 121
4002 Oporto
Max 40 pers.
English spoken.
Charge for tasting.

Vila Real

Mateus Palace
Mateus (two miles outside Vila Real,
direction of Sabrosa)
Open daily to the public 9–13h; 14–16h
Guided tours of the palace are given
regularly; however, to visit the nearby

winery, it is necessary to obtain permission from SOGRAPE. The vast main factory for the production of this fabulously popular rosé and other table wines is at Avintes, just outside Oporto. Write to the following address for appointments to this plant and to the winery in Mateus:
SOGRAPE-Vinhos de Portugal, SARL
rua Sá da Bandeira, 819-2-Dto.
4000 Oporto
tel: (029) 20 761

5100 Lamego

Caves da Raposeira Lda
tel: (0095) 62 003/4
Mon–Sat

Guided tours of the sparkling wine caves are given on the hour from 10–16h. English spoken.

3050 Mealhada (north of Coimbra)

Sociedade Agricola e Comercial dos Vinhos Messias, SARL
tel: Mealhada 22 027/8
Mon–Fri 9–12h; 14–17h
Appointment only necessary for groups. This firm is not located on our wine tour, but if travelling south from Oporto, it is well worth stopping here to see the cellars where both still and sparkling table wines are produced. Mealhada is also a good place to sample the characteristic *leitão assado* (roast suckling pig), delicious with chilled *vinho espumante*.

Wine Festivals

Surprisingly, there are few harvest- or wine-related festivals in northern Portugal. Perhaps this is because there are so many other religious and folk festivals that take place in villages and towns throughout the year. In these colourful events solemn processions are followed by popular rejoicing which manifests itself in lively folk music and traditional dancing, and of course, much eating and much drinking (for indeed, the wines of this land are not products to be celebrated in isolation, but rather form an integral part of everyday life). Such festivals known as *Romarias* are too numerous to list here; write to the various tourist offices (addresses below) for exact places and dates. The following are some of the principal festivals.

March or April (depending on the liturgical calender)	Solemnities of Holy Week	Braga
Early June	Grand Pilgrimage of 'São Gonçalo'	Amarante
End of June	Festival of 'São Pedro'	Póvoa de Varzim
Mid Aug	Festival of 'Senhora do Socorro'	Régua
Third week in Aug	Pilgrimage of 'Nossa Senhora da Agonia'	Viana do Castelo
Around Sept 8th	Festival of 'Senhora dos Remedios'	Lamego

Regional Gastronomy

Caldo verde Simple, hearty soup made from finely shredded kale and potatoes.

Canja de galinha Chicken soup (soups are often eaten after, not before the main meal).

Açordas Simple bread-based soups.

Presunto Air-dried ham (particularly good hams come from Lamego; they are superb with the sparkling wines produced in the same area).

Bacalhau Dried salt cod, prepared in any number of fashions (the Portuguese claim to have at least one different recipe for each day of the year). It is a speciality that should be tried.

Arroz de frango Chicken and rice.

Caldeirada Fish stew prepared with the day's fresh catch.

Dobrada à moda do Porto The most famous dish of Oporto: tripe, chick peas, sausages and chicken stewed together for several hours.

Frango no espeto Spit-roasted chicken.

Cozido portuguesa Hearty winter stew of beef, tongue, chicken, and sausages, cooked together with vegetables and served with rice.

Leitão assado Roast suckling pig.

Feijoada Bean and sausage stew.

Lampreias Lampreys (speciality of Monção).

Rojões do porco à moda do Minho Pork marinated in white wine and stewed.

Sardinhas assadas Sardines grilled over an open brazier – delicious on the beach.

Lagosta Lobster.

Truta Trout.

Sweets: Every village in the north of Portugal has its own collection of local and whimsically named sweets and cakes, often made with eggs, rice, and lots of sugar. Try different varieties as you drive through little villages: *papos d'anjo, lerias* (Amarante), *crista de galo* (Vila Real), *touchinho do céu* (Guimarães), *pão de lo* (different varieties of this rich sponge cake from each village), and many others.

Pousadas

Pousadas are government-run inns located in historic buildings or places of great natural beauty. Accommodation is first-class (generally the equivalent of a three- or four-star hotel) but at moderate prices. Their dining rooms have the well-earned reputation of serving authentic regional foods and wines, and they, too, are excellent value. The tradition of these national inns goes back to the 12th century when a Portuguese queen decided to offer pilgrims and travellers 'a roof, a bed, and a candle'. This simple tradition of goodwill upon which they were founded remains today, and they are well worth a detour. Not surprisingly, they are extremely popular, so it is essential to book

in advance. The dining rooms are open to non-residents. The following *pousadas* are on or near our suggested routes.

3800 Aveiro

Pousada da Ria
Murtosa
tel: (0034) 46 132
South of Oporto, situated directly on this atmospheric lagoon.
Moderate

4600 Amarante

Pousada de São Gonçalo
tel: (0025) 46 123
Superb location high in the dramatic Serra range. This *pousada* is well-situated en route to the Upper Douro.
Moderate

Alijo

Pousada Barão de Forrester
tel: Alijo 62 215
Located 34 km east of Vila Real, in the heart of the port wine country. Visit the Cooperative of Alijo for wine-tasting.
Moderate

4900 Viana do Castelo

Hotel de Sta Luzia
tel: (0028) 22 192/3
Views over Viana do Castelo, the Atlantic coastline, and the wide, placid Lima River valley. Excellent restaurant with good selection of Vinhos Verdes, and *vinhos maduros*. Good base for exploring Vinho Verde country.
Moderate

Caniçada

Pousada de São Bento
tel: (0023) 57 190
Situated in the Gerês National Park. Quiet, comfortable, with restaurant.
Moderate

4800 Guimarães

Pousada de Nossa Senhora de Oliveira
Largo de Oliveira
tel: (0023) 41 21 57
Centrally situated in the medieval quarter of this ancient town, with restaurant serving regional specialities and local wines.
Moderate

4930 Valença do Minho

Pousada de São Teotonio
tel: (0021) 22 252
Overlooking Minho, and across the river
to Spain. All 16 bedrooms have private
facilities.
Moderate

Restaurants

4000 Oporto

Restaurante Portucale
rua da Alegria 598
tel: (02) 57 07 17
Panoramic views of the Douro River and
international as well as regional
specialities.
Daily 12h30–14h30; 19h30–22h
Reservations recommended.
Moderate

Restaurante Abadia
rua Ateneu Comercial do Porto 22
tel: (02) 28 757
Regional dishes such as *dobrada à moda do
Porto* and *bacalhau*, and good local Vinhos
Verdes.
Open 12–15h; 19h30–22h
Inexpensive

Restaurante Palmeira
rua Ateneu Comercial do Porto 36
tel: (02) 31 56 01
Inexpensive restaurant serving regional
specialities such as *bacalhau* and *rojões à
moda do Minho*.
Open 12–15h; 19–22h

Restaurante & 'Snack-Bar' Orfeu
rua de Júlio Dinis 928
tel: (02) 64 322
Regional and international dishes in this
Inexpensive to Moderate restaurant.
Open daily 10–24h

5050 Peso da Régua

Restaurante Arco – Iris Godim
tel: (095) 23 524
Good service and comprehensive wine list.
Moderate

4575 Entre-os-Rios

Pensão Miradouro
tel: (0025) 62 422
Restaurant with good view and a few
rooms.
Moderate

4700 Braga

Pensão Inácio
Camp das Hortas 4
tel: (0023) 22 335
Inexpensive

Viana do Castelo

Alambique
rua Manuel Espregueira 86
tel: (0028) 23 894
Rustic atmosphere, regional foods and
wines.
Moderate

Os 3 Potes
Beco dos Fornos 7
tel: (0028) 23 432
Atmospheric little restaurant serving local
foods and wines.
Booking advisable.
Moderate

Hotels

4000 Oporto

Hotel Infante de Sagres
Praça D Filipa de Lencastre 62
tel: (02) 28 101
Centrally situated, a modern luxury hotel
with restaurant serving international and
regional foods and wines.
Hotel open all year.
Restaurant open daily 12h30–14h30;
19h45–22h
Very Expensive

Hotel Porto Atlantico
rua Alfonso Lopes Vieira 66
tel: (02) 69 49 41
Situated between the city centre and the
airport, a modern hotel with complex
comprising swimming pool, gymnasium,
sauna, shops, bars, and restaurant. 58
rooms, each with bathroom.
Expensive

Hotel do Império
Praça da Batalha 130
tel: (02) 26 861
Hotel with 100 rooms, each with
bathroom. Restaurant serves both
international and regional foods.
Restaurant open daily 12–14h30;
19h30–21h30
Moderate

Albergaria Miradouro
rua da Alegria 598
tel: (02) 57 07 17

Comfortable hotel with panoramic views over the Douro. No restaurant. Open all year.
Inexpensive to **Moderate**

4600 Amarante

Pousada de São Gonçalo
(see *pousadas* above)

5100 Lamego

Hotel Parque
Parque de Nossa Senhora dos Remédios
tel: (0095) 62 105
Hotel with restaurant in this historic town. Restaurant serves regional foods accompanied by sparkling and other local wines.
Hotel open all year.
Restaurant open daily.
Inexpensive

5050 Régua

Residencial Columbano
avenida Sacadura Cabral
tel: (095) 23 704
Inexpensive hotel with swimming pool, and 56 rooms, each with private facilities, located in the heart of the port wine country. Restaurant serves regional foods and wines.
Hotel open all year
Restaurant open 12–14h30; 19–21h30

Alijo

Pousada Barão de Forrester
(see *pousadas* above)

4800 Guimarães

Pousada de Nossa Senhora de Oliveira
(see *pousadas* above)

Hotel Fundador Dom Pedro
avenida D Afonso Henriques 760
tel: (0023) 41 37 81
Inexpensive modern hotel located in the centre of town. No restaurant.
Open all year.

4750 Barcelos

Albergaria Condes de Barcelos
avenida Alcaides de Faria
tel: (0023) 82 061
Comfortable 30-room hotel, each with bath. Good base for exploring Vinho Verde country from this charming village.
Expensive

4900 Viana do Castelo

Hotel de Sta Luzia
(see *pousadas* above)

Hotel Afonso III
avenida Afonso III 494
tel: (0028) 24 123
Luxury hotel with swimming pool and restaurant.
Expensive

Where to Get Additional Information

Portuguese National Tourist Office
548 5th Ave
NY NY 10036
tel: (212) 354–4403
Offices also in Chicago and Los Angeles

Portuguese Trade Commission
548 5th Ave
NY NY 10036
tel: (212) 354–4610

Port Wine Institute
rua de Ferreira Borges
4000 Oporto
Portugal
tel: (02) 26 522/5

Local Tourist Offices:

4000 Oporto
Praça Dom João I
Posto de Turismo
tel: (02) 37 514
Praça Gen Humberto Delgado
tel: (02) 29 871
4750 Barcelos
rua Duques de Bragança
Esplanada do Turismo
tel: (0023) 82 882
4700 Braga
avenida da Liberdade 1
tel: (0023) 22 550
4800 Guimarães
avenida Resistência ao Fascismo 83
tel: (0023) 42 450
4900 Viana do Castelo
avenida Cândido dos Reis
Palácio dos Távoras
tel: (0028) 22 620

Hotel do Parque
Praça da Galizia
tel: (0028) 24 151
Modern comfortable hotel with swimming
pool and solarium.
Restaurant has good view of river, and
serves regional specialities.
Hotel open all year.
Restaurant open daily 12h45–14h30;
19h45–21h30
Moderate

4700 Braga

Hotel Turismo Dom Pedro
Praça João XXI
tel: (0023) 27 091
Modern comfortable hotel with 132 rooms
all with private bath. Swimming pool,
sauna, bars, and restaurant.
Hotel open all year.
Restaurant open daily 13–15h; 20–22h
Moderate

4930 Valença do Minho

Pousada de São Teotonio
(see *pousadas* above)

Camping

4000 Oporto
Parque de Campismo da Prelada
tel: (02) 62 616

Vila Nova de Gaia
Canidelo-Salgueiros
tel: (02) 98 10 500
Amarante
Parque dos Frades
tel: (0025) 42 133
Guimarães
Penha
tel: (0023) 42 936
Penha (near Braga)
Parque de Campismo de Penha
tel: (0023) 42 936
Calda da Rainha (near Leiria)
Orbitur Parque D Leonor
tel: (062) 22 367
Viana do Castelo
Orbitur Cabedelo
tel: (0028) 22 135
Espinho
Camara Municipal
tel: (02) 92 06 98
Lamego
Parque de Campismo de Lamego
tel: (0095) 62 090

Bibliography

Portuguese Wine by Raymond Postgate, J M
Dent, 1969

*Monarch Guide to the Wines of Spain and
Portugal* by Jan Read, Monarch Press 1978

ACKNOWLEDGEMENTS

To gather our information we travelled thousands of kilometres through Europe's wine lands, meeting, talking with, and learning from the people who make up the core of this book: the wine producers themselves, as well as restaurateurs, and hotel owners. We owe an enormous debt to them.

Additionally, we would like to thank the following organizations for practical assistance received: French Government Tourist Office; Comité Interprofessionnel des Vins d'Alsace; Comité Interprofessionnel des Vins de Bourgogne et Mâcon; Union Interprofessionnelle des Vins du Beaujolais; Comité Interprofessionnel de la Côte d'Or et de l'Yonne; Conseil Interprofessionnel du Vin de Bordeaux; Comité Interprofessionnel du Vin de Champagne; Champagne Information Bureau; Comité Interprofessionnel des Vins des Côtes du Rhône; Comité Interprofessionnel des Vins des Côtes de Provence; Comité Interprofessionnel des Vins d'Origine du Pays Nantais; Conseil Interprofessionnel des Vins d'Anjou et de Saumur; Comité Interprofessionnel des Vins de Touraine; Union Viticole Sancerroise; German National Tourist Office; Deutsche Wein-Information; Wines from Germany Information Service; Italian State Tourist Board; Consorzio Chianti Classico; Consorzio Chianti Putto; Camera di Commercio di Asti; Associazione Vini Veronesi DOC; Austrian National Tourist Office; Spanish National Tourist Office; Rioja Wine Information Centre; Federación Provincial de Criadores/Exportadores de Vinos de Cádiz; Portuguese National Tourist Office; Portuguese Government Trade Office; Port Wine Institute; Comissão de Viticultura da Região dos Vinhos Verdes; Charles Spackman of Trips & Company.

We would also like to thank Hilda Stretton; Ingrid Budge; Keel Data Systems Ltd; and our research assistant Michele Millon, who helped with translating foreign correspondence, and in manuscript preparation.

Marc and Kim Millon